'We live in times of super complexity, due to a multitude of understandings in an unknowable world. There has never been so much interest in fashion and sustainability; hardly surprising due to fashion's industrial and social activity being directly and indirectly complicit in climate change, biodiversity loss, social inequality and wellbeing concerns. However, we are very far from having learnt how to thrive as humans in a more than human world. This book takes a much-needed, pragmatic and illustrative approach to fashion as a professional practice that connects a range of disciplines. It informs decision-making and idea-generation for a range of learners that can be applied across and beyond fashion's activities.'

Dilys Williams, *Professor of Fashion, Design and Sustainability, Director of the Centre for Sustainable Fashion, a University of the Arts London research centre based at the London College of Fashion, UK*

Sustainable Fashion Management

This book provides a holistic and accessible approach to sustainable fashion management. It offers an interdisciplinary and practical outlook, combining theory with practical application from a management perspective and underpinned by the Sustainable Development Goals throughout.

The book helps students to gain a better understanding of what sustainable fashion is and how it is implemented across the fashion industry, through business model innovations, innovative designs, new technology and digital approaches, and material innovations. Global case studies are employed throughout each chapter, including fashion companies and events of all sizes, alongside other pedagogical features to aid learning, including key learning points, chapter objectives, and textboxes explaining key terminology.

This is an essential textbook for those investigating sustainable fashion, whether from a design or management perspective, providing the knowledge and tools for a future career. It is designed to serve Fashion Business and Management, Fashion Marketing, Fashion Buying and Merchandising, and Fashion Technology courses, at all levels, and will also be valuable reading for those already working within the fashion industry and studying for professional qualifications. Online resources include chapter-by-chapter PowerPoint slides and a test bank.

Claudia E. Henninger is Senior Lecturer in Fashion Marketing Management at the University of Manchester, UK.

Kirsi Niinimäki is Associate Professor in Design at Aalto University, Finland.

Marta Blazquez is Senior Lecturer in Fashion Marketing at the University of Manchester, UK.

Celina Jones is Lecturer in Fashion Technology at the University of Manchester, UK.

Mastering Fashion Management

The fashion industry is dynamic, constantly evolving and worth billions worldwide: it's no wonder that Fashion Business Management has come to occupy a central position within the Business School globally. This series meets the need for rigorous yet practical and accessible textbooks that cover the full spectrum of the fashion industry and its management.

Collectively, *Mastering Fashion Management* is a valuable resource for advanced undergraduate and postgraduate students of Fashion Management, helping them gain an in-depth understanding of contemporary concepts and the realities of practice across the entire fashion chain – from design development and product sourcing, to buying and merchandising, sustainability, and sales and marketing. Individually, each text provides essential reading for a core topic. A range of consistent pedagogical features are used throughout the texts, including international case studies, highlighting the practical importance of theoretical concepts.

Postgraduate students studying for a Masters in Fashion Management in particular will find each text invaluable reading, providing the knowledge and tools to approach a future career in fashion with confidence.

Fashion Marketing and Communication
Theory and Practice across the Fashion Industry
Olga Mitterfellner

Fashion Buying and Merchandising
The Fashion Buyer in a Digital Society
Rosy Boardman, Rachel Parker-Strak, and Claudia E. Henninger

Sustainable Fashion Management
Claudia E. Henninger, Kirsi Niinimäki, Marta Blazquez and Celina Jones

For more information about the series, please visit https://www.routledge.com/Mastering-Fashion-Management/book-series/FM

Sustainable Fashion Management

Claudia E. Henninger, Kirsi Niinimäki, Marta Blazquez, and Celina Jones

Routledge
Taylor & Francis Group

LONDON AND NEW YORK

First published 2023
by Routledge
4 Park Square, Milton Park, Abingdon, Oxon OX14 4RN

and by Routledge
605 Third Avenue, New York, NY 10158

Routledge is an imprint of the Taylor & Francis Group, an informa business

British Library Cataloguing-in-Publication Data
A catalogue record for this book is available from the British Library

Library of Congress Cataloging-in-Publication Data
A catalog record has been requested for this book

ISBN: 9780367564544 (hbk)
ISBN: 9780367564551 (pbk)
ISBN: 9781003097846 (ebk)

DOI: 10.4324/9781003097846

Typeset in Giovanni
by Deanta Global Publishing Services, Chennai, India

Visit the support materials: www.routledge.com/9780367564551

Contents

List of figures   xi
List of tables   xii
Preface   xiii

Part 1   Management of sustainable fashion   **1**

**Chapter 1.1 – Emergence of sustainability and its management
in the fashion industry**   **3**
  1.1.1   Management – art and science   3
  1.1.2   Sustainability – definitions and meaning   11
  1.1.3   Sustainability in fashion and sustainable fashion   15
  1.1.4   Importance of sustainable fashion in the 21st century   17

Chapter 1.2 – Sustainable fashion: company perspective   **25**
  1.2.1   Sustainability as a strategy   25
  1.2.2   Issues in the fashion industry surrounding
          sustainable fashion   36
  1.2.3   Case study: understanding sustainability and
          value – the example of We Are Knitters   41

Chapter 1.3 – Sustainable fashion: consumer view   **49**
  1.3.1   Sustainable fashion and consumer perceptions   49
  1.3.2   New developments in sustainable fashion   53

Chapter 1.4 – Circular economy   **59**
  1.4.1   Evolution of the circular economy   59
  1.4.2   Case study: thinking outside the box – the
          example of Freitag   64
  1.4.3   Business model innovations   68
  1.4.4   The circular economy – zero waste fashion   70

1.4.4.1 Zero waste fashion – pre-consumer
           approaches   72
1.4.4.2 Zero waste fashion – post-consumer
           approaches   75
1.4.5 Opportunities and barriers to the circular economy   77
1.4.6 Case study: circularity in the fashion industry –
         the example of Hetty Rose   79

Part 2   Managing sustainable fashion through design   87

Chapter 2.1 – New system understanding for design   89
         2.1.1   Redesigning industrial design processes   90

Chapter 2.2 – Design for a circular economy   93
         2.2.1   Intentional design for recycling   94
         2.2.2   Design for alternative business models   97

Chapter 2.3 – Slowing down the fashion system through design   101
         2.3.1   Slow fashion and garment lifetimes   101
         2.3.2   Designing value for secondhand fashion   106

Chapter 2.4 – Designing carbon-neutral fashion   109
         2.4.1   Responsibility, safety, and risk management 113
         2.4.2   Transparency and code of conduct   113
         2.4.3   Clean chemistry and ethical fashion   117
         2.4.4   Control, trust, and crisis management   119

Chapter 2.5 – Fashion design in a new paradigm   123

Part 3   Digital sustainable fashion   131

Chapter 3.1 – Sustainability, fashion, and technology   133
         3.1.1   The current scenario for fashion retail:
                  from multichannel to omnichannel   133
                  3.1.1.1 The role of technology in omnichannel
                           retailing   135
                  3.1.1.2 Consumers' approach to the use
                           of technology   137
                  3.1.1.3 Digital channels   139
         3.1.2   The use of technology to promote sustainable
                  behaviours   139
         3.1.3   The importance of sustainability communication   141

Chapter 3.2 – **Digital sustainability**   **147**
    3.2.1 Introduction   147
    3.2.2 The impact of online shopping: returns   148
    3.2.3 The nature of online shopping: the importance of
           touch and vision   149
    3.2.4 The role of specific technologies   150
           3.2.4.1 Image interactive technology   150
    3.2.5 Sustainability communication and digital channels   154
           3.2.5.1 The importance of narrative strategies in
                  social media communication   155
    3.2.6 Key developments and industry practices   157

Chapter 3.3 – **Digital fashion**   **163**
    3.3.1 What is digital fashion?   163
           3.3.1.1 Digital fashion   164
           3.3.1.2 Non-fungible tokens   165
           3.3.1.3 Digital fashion marketplaces   166
           3.3.1.4 The metaverse   167
           3.3.1.5 Digital fashion shows   168
    3.3.2 Will digital fashion become mainstream?
           The importance of communication   168
    3.3.3 Key developments and industry practices   170
    3.3.4 Case studies   171

Part 4   Material innovations in sustainable fashion   179

Chapter 4.1 – **Fibre selection**   **181**
    4.1.1 20th-century production   181
    4.1.2 Natural fibres   182
           4.1.2.1 Plant fibres   183
           4.1.2.2 Animal fibres   189
           4.1.2.3 Man-made (manufactured) fibres   190
    4.1.3 21st-century developments   193
    4.1.4 Case study task: alternative fibres for textile
           production – Bananatex®   194

Chapter 4.2 – **Fabric creation**   **205**
    4.2.1 Preparation of raw materials   207
    4.2.2 Woven fabrics   209
    4.2.3 Knitted fabrics   212
    4.2.4 Nonwoven fabrics   214

4.2.4.1 Leather 214
*4.2.4.2 Case study task: the knitted jumper
        that used to be a pair of woven jeans –
        innovations in fabric construction by We
        Are Knitters* 216

Chapter 4.3 – Fabric finishes and surface design **225**
4.3.1 Fabric colouration – overview 225
4.3.2 Fabric preparation 226
4.3.3 Application of colourants 227
4.3.4 Innovative approach to colouration 231
4.3.5 Case study: Sustaina-jeans Innovation Capsule 231

Index 239

Figures

1.1.1	Simplified version of a linear supply chain	4
1.1.2	Stakeholders in the fashion industry	8
1.1.3	Snapshot of sustainable fashion timeline	16
1.2.1	Options for implementing sustainability in an organisation	27
1.2.2	Sustainable supply chain management – the 9R model	31
1.2.3	Performance indicators	40
1.2.4	Example of applied performance indicators	40
1.2.5	We Are Knitters – recycled wine-coloured yarn (© We Are Knitters)	43
1.3.1	Supply curve	50
1.3.2	Demand curve	50
1.4.1	Cradle-to-grave	60
1.4.2	Circular design thinking process	65
1.4.3	F12 Dragnet and F14 Dexter	65
1.4.4	Freitag factory bag design tarp	66
1.4.5	FREITAG F-ABRIC clothing	67
1.4.6	FREITAG F-ABRIC biodegraded	67
1.4.7	Simplified illustration of circular thinking	79
1.4.8	Botanical shoes by Hetty Rose©	80
1.4.9	Dahlia shoes by Hetty Rose©	81
1.4.10	Workspace by Hetty Rose©	81
3.3.1	Digital garments	172
3.3.2	HOT:SECOND pop-up draft	173
3.3.3	Karl Lagerfeld NFT	175
3.3.4	Digital garments	175
4.1.1	Bananatex® lifecycle	196
4.1.2	Bananatex® logo	196
4.1.3	Fibres in storage	197
4.1.4	Bananatex® plant	197
4.1.5	Bananatex® stripping process 1	198
4.1.6	Bananatex® stripping Process 2	198
4.2.1	Simplified version of a linear supply chain	206
4.2.2	Percentages of cost for a T-shirt	207
4.2.3	A loom, showing woven structure	210
4.2.4	We Are Knitters© Recycled Yarn Spotted Pink	218
4.2.5	We Are Knitters© The Tape Yarn Beige	218

Tables

1.1.1	Key Managerial Decisions and Their Implications	6
1.1.2	PEST – Factors, Examples, and Impacts	10
1.1.3	Sustainable Development Goals and Implications/ Challenges for the Fashion Industry	13
1.1.4	Terminology of "Sustainable Fashion"	18
1.1.5	Key Figures and Facts about the Fashion Industry	19
1.2.1	Selection of Certifications and Standards Available for the Fashion Industry	29
1.2.2	The 9R Model and the SDGs	35
1.4.1	Opportunities and Drawbacks of Circular and Sharing Economy Principles Linked to SDGs	71
2.2.1	Limitations and Possibilities in Intentional Design for Recycling	96
2.2.2	Business Strategy, Approach for Sustainability, and Design Principles	98
2.2.3	How to Handle Product Obsolescence through Design Approaches	98
2.3.1	Seven Principles of Slow Design	102
2.3.2	Elements Providing Attachments in Textiles and Garments	103
2.4.1	Environmental Impact and CO_2 Analysis per Tier to Help Enhance System-level Thinking in Fashion	112
2.5.1	Design for System-level Transformation	125
4.1.1	United Nations Sustainable Development Goals Relating to Fibre Selection	186
4.2.1	Textile Recycling and SDG 12	209
4.3.1	Summary of Dyes That Can Be Used on Different Fabric Types	227
4.3.2	Textile Finishing and SDG 12	229

Preface

The aim of this book is to provide an insight into sustainable fashion and its management, by focusing on an interdisciplinary approach. Thus, this book is divided into four distinct parts that complement one another by reflecting on the diversity of the fashion industry and showcasing that solutions to problems cannot be viewed in isolation, but rather should be addressed as part of a holistic picture.

To succeed in a highly volatile market environment such as the fashion industry, it is essential for our readers to gain a better understanding of what sustainable fashion is and how it is implemented in the fashion industry, which can be through business model innovations, innovative designs, new technology and digital approaches, or material innovations. This is reflected in this book, in which the four parts are connected by the theme of sustainability and management.

Part 1: Management of Sustainable Fashion is designed to set the scene by introducing key terms and concepts used within the management and marketing remit, thereby allowing you to gain a better understanding of why we focus on management and what the significance is of sustainability within the fashion industry. In doing so, we will not only provide theoretical underpinnings, but also encourage you to actively reflect on current events and their impact on how stakeholders may tackle the issue of sustainability in the fashion industry.

Part 2: Managing Sustainable Fashion through Design further focuses on the circular economy and circular thinking and design approaches. Thus, it extends and further explores aspects discussed in **Part 1**. Designing garments is more than simply developing a pattern and sewing the pieces together. As will be highlighted, the decision-making process underpinning the design phase is complex and includes the initial creation process as well as the end-of-life challenges the fashion industry is facing.

Part 3: Digital Sustainable Fashion centres its attention on new trends in the industry that have been enabled by the development of new technology and technological processes. It highlights how aspects raised in **Part 2** concerning sustainable fashion design can be transformed through a technological revolution by keeping sustainability as the key focus. Leading on from **Part 1**, it demonstrates how the industry is dealing with consumer perceptions and acceptance of digital sustainable fashion.

Lastly, **Part 4: Material Innovations in Sustainable Fashion** connects to all the areas discussed earlier by focusing specifically on the raw material side that plays a crucial role in the fashion industry. Without raw materials, fashion production and consumption are impossible. This slightly more technical part will delve into issues related to sustainability in the early stages of the apparel pipeline and investigate current practices and solutions.

For ease of navigation, each chapter will provide learning outcomes at the beginning before moving on to defining key terms and providing carefully selected examples and case studies. The book is designed to encourage critical thinking and the questioning of current practices, whilst at the same time providing insights into key theoretical concepts.

PART 1
Management of sustainable fashion

Part 1 is dedicated to the marketing and management of sustainable fashion by providing key definitions of terminology that is used throughout the book whilst also providing insights into the emergence of sustainability, especially within the field of fashion, before moving on to an overview of sustainable fashion from the viewpoints of organisations and consumers, and closing with a more recent phenomenon: the circular economy.

DOI: 10.4324/9781003097846-1

1.1 Emergence of sustainability and its management in the fashion industry

Learning outcomes

1. To critically examine key terminology, including management, sustainability, and sustainable fashion.
2. To understand the significance of the fashion industry within a global context.
3. To explore the emergence of sustainability within the fashion industry.
4. To critically investigate the significance of sustainable management in the 21st century.

As indicated in the learning outcomes, this chapter provides an overview of the emergence of sustainability within the fashion industry and its management by clarifying key questions, such as: *What is management? Why is it important to focus on sustainability within the fashion industry? And what makes sustainability so important in the 21st century.* Prior to providing a critical overview of sustainability in fashion, it is vital to clarify how different terms are defined and utilised within this chapter.

1.1.1 Management – art and science

A question you may have asked yourself is: What do we mean by management? In very simple terms, management implies controlling and/or organising a business in its entirety. A business, on the other hand, is comprised of people (e.g., employees, suppliers, buyers), technologies (e.g., machinery, internet, design software), and of course monetary assets (e.g., financial capital, buildings, factories). In looking at a simplified version of the linear supply chain (Figure 1.1.1), managers are involved in decision-making processes that can be complex and impact every aspect of the business. Thus, managers need to understand what is needed across the supply chain and how to ensure that profits can be achieved, in order to be able to keep the business afloat and re-invest any surplus (e.g., profits) back into the company, thereby fostering research and development (R&D), as well as to keep hold of employees and other stakeholders that may form part of its unique capabilities that translate into a unique selling proposition (USP).

It may not be surprising that although managers may have the final say in terms of the decision-making process and what might be delivered as an end-product, they are heavily reliant on different teams who can provide them with key information to make the "right" decision. Here, making a "right" decision implies that managers may have liaised with, for example, the buying department to gain a better understanding

DOI: 10.4324/9781003097846-2

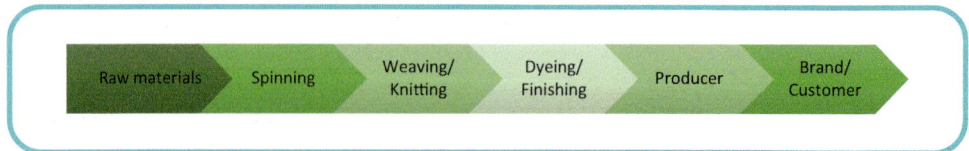

Figure 1.1.1   Simplified version of a linear supply chain

of current trends and what can be sourced. Managers may also work very closely with designers, as they often have the very difficult task of making a vision a reality. You will be able to read more on the role of designers and key challenges they may be facing when it comes to incorporating aspects of sustainability and the circular economy in **Part 2: Managing Sustainable Fashion through Design**.

Example – decision-making process for a pair of jeans

Let us imagine we are the owner of a sustainable jeans company named Sustaina-jeans. What type of decisions might we have to make along the way? Initially, we may need to think ahead and understand what type of jeans we want to produce and what they will look like once the consumer sees them, as well as potentially envision what will happen to them after they have fulfilled their initial useful life. At this stage, we may also liaise with designers to get a better understanding of what is and is not possible.

The decision-making process is usually divided into five key steps (e.g., Drucker, 1967), where Step 1 is recognising a problem. Here, *recognising a problem* refers to the need for Sustaina-jeans products. To explain, there may be a need in the market to produce a pair of jeans that is classified as being sustainable, and thus there is a need for Sustaina-jeans.

Step 2 is classified as the information searching stage. Within the scenario provided, information search can link to finding suppliers, investigating different options for raw materials, and understanding performance properties of the product that is designed (e.g., waterproof finishing, elastic material). (For more details on raw materials and performance properties, please see section 4.1, "Fibre Selection"). Again, as managers we may need to get input from different departments, such as the buying, finance, design, and merchandising departments.

In Step 3, alternatives are evaluated – you may have noticed that companies often refer to bids and tenders, which implies that the best value for money is explored. In this case, we may want to see which supplier can provide us with the best material at an acceptable cost.

Step 4 is when an actual purchase decision is made, in terms of raw materials, fixtures, fittings, and potentially also machinery, that will allow the garment to be created, which is evaluated in Step 5.

To provide a more elaborate example, if we consider the first step of "raw materials", a key question we need to ask ourselves is what raw materials we may want to use to produce our sustainable jeans and how this may complement the overall design idea. **Part 4** will elaborate how different materials, material structures, and finishing processes may impact on the finished product's performance by also alluding to opportunities and challenges of the end-of-life treatment of materials. What becomes apparent here is that selecting raw materials for a pair of jeans is not an easy task, but rather involves various teams throughout the production process, from designers to suppliers to manufacturers to marketers and consumers. This highlights that making a decision, and subsequently *managing* the production of a pair of jeans can be challenging and also time-consuming. The latter aspect is also of key importance to managers, as we are well aware that the fashion industry works at a fast pace, whereby trends can go in and out of style very quickly. Thus, the entire decision-making process, even though it is very complex, cannot take very long, as lead times need to be short to stay competitive. Lead time is defined as the period of time it takes to get a product from the initial idea to the consumer (Boardman et al., 2020).

Once we have selected our raw material, the decision-making process is not fully complete since we need to understand where we may be able to source the raw material. For example, are there any suppliers that produce the material within a local vicinity, or will we need to source the material internationally, or do we actually need to source traditional raw materials since digital fashion is one of the newest trends in the industry (for more, see **Part 3: Digital Sustainable Fashion**). Based on simple business management principles, we may also need to ensure that we, as a business, stay competitive, whilst at the same time offer fair competition, which is why we may contact several suppliers for our raw materials and gain different quotes in order to select the one that is most competitive (e.g., best value for money).

Since we decided to be a sustainable jeans company, some of our decision-making process may also be influenced by how the material is produced: for example, if we decide on cotton, will we only purchase "organic" cotton that is certified, or do we trust suppliers to highlight that they have used less chemicals? We may further want to investigate how workers are treated along the supply chain and whether working conditions are safe and workers are paid a living wage. At the same time, as a business we need to ensure that we are sustainable and can make profits, as without them, our operations may not be financially viable.

If we fast-forward to the dyeing and finishing processes, we again need to think back to the initial step of what we envisioned our pair of jeans to look like: will we have rips and a stone-washed look, or perhaps printed or embroidered elements? Each of these different finishing touches is once again based on a variety of decisions.

Table 1.1.1 provides a broad overview of what decisions may need to be made across a product's life cycle, from the initial design to sourcing to distributing to producing the garment and considering the end-of-life stage. Although these questions and implications highlighted are not exhaustive, they provide an initial starting point for consideration.

> **Decision-making process** – a complex process which is most commonly divided into five consecutive steps (problem recognition, information search, evaluation of alternatives, purchase decision, evaluation of purchase decision), which can be influenced by the external environment (e.g., stakeholders).

Table 1.1.1   Key Managerial Decisions and Their Implications

	Key questions	Potential implications
Design	• Who is the target audience for our jeans (e.g., high street, luxury)? • How will we produce our pair of jeans (e.g., based on circular design thinking – see **Part 2**)? • Will it be a physical or online product (e.g., physical garment versus digital fashion – see **Part 3**)? • What type of raw material and finishing will we use (see **Part 4**)?	• May impact on raw materials being considered for production • Can have an impact on cost (e.g., mass-produced versus made-to-order) • Can have implications for environment (e.g., CO_2 emissions of physical versus virtual garment)
Sourcing	**Raw Material** • What material will be used (e.g., plant- or animal-based, man-made fibre)? • Where to get it from (local, international)? • Virgin material or pre-loved? • Certified or non-certified? **Spinning/Knitting/Weaving** • Are local factories available, or will it need to be transported? **Dyeing/Finishing** • Do different types of dyeing require different skill sets and/or chemicals? • Are different finishings needed, depending on whether garment is designed as work wear or casual going-out jeans?	• The choice of raw materials can impact on aspects of social and environmental sustainability (see Section 1.1.2) • Might have an impact on lead times of producing garment • Different material structures may impact the product's performance properties (e.g., elasticity, water absorbency – see **Part 4**) • Can have environmental implications, as some finishing processes may use harmful toxins whilst some dyeing processes may be water-intensive
Production	• Will it be nationally or internationally produced?	• Can have social implications, for example poor working conditions and lack of living wage pay

(Continued)

Table 1.1.1 Continued

	Key questions	Potential implications
Distribution	• How will the product be distributed, not only between the supplier and the company, but also to the end consumer? • What type of packaging will be used?	• Can have environmental implications, for example excessive use of plastic packaging
End-of-life	• What are the options we see for our pair of jeans (e.g., secondhand market, recycling of raw materials, landfill)? • Will repair services be offered?	• Can have an impact on the business model chosen, for example whether the pair of jeans is leased and we expect the pair of jeans to be returned • Is infrastructure available to make different options easily accessible for our customers?

What becomes apparent here is that whilst managers may make key decisions, the actual decision-making process may also be influenced by a variety of stakeholders. The term "stakeholder" refers to individuals, groups, and/or organisations which have a vested interest in the organisation. To explain: stakeholders – and here, fashion organisations – may have a mutually dependent relationship, in that both parties need each other to fulfil their own goals. Within the fashion industry there are a variety of different stakeholders, ranging from those that are internal (e.g., employees) to those that are external to the company (e.g., suppliers, buyers), some of which are highlighted in Figure 1.1.2 (Fletcher, 2008; Pookulangara and Shepard, 2013).

To further reiterate the mutual dependency between some of the stakeholders identified, it is said that customers can "make or break" a fashion trend and are also partially responsible for enabling the transitioning of the fashion industry to become more sustainable (e.g., Brydges et al., 2020). Without customers, fashion companies are unable to sell their stock, so customers have the power to make an item in a collection a best seller or a slow seller (e.g., Boardman et al., 2020). Similarly, if consumers are increasingly demanding more sustainable fashion items, and thus increase the demand for such clothing, the industry needs to respond if it wants to continue selling items. On the other hand, if companies stop producing garments or only provide a limited-edition collection, customers are unable to purchase products that may either be needed (e.g., winter jackets) or desired (e.g., special editions). A key aspect that can also be highlighted here is that various companies have been criticised in the past for burning unsold stock, which signifies that perhaps some companies produce too much in the first instance, so reducing production could not only overcome the sharp critique of destroying items that are perfectly useable, but also foster Sustainable Development Goal 12 of responsible production (and consumption). This aspect (responsible production) is explored in Section 1.1.2.

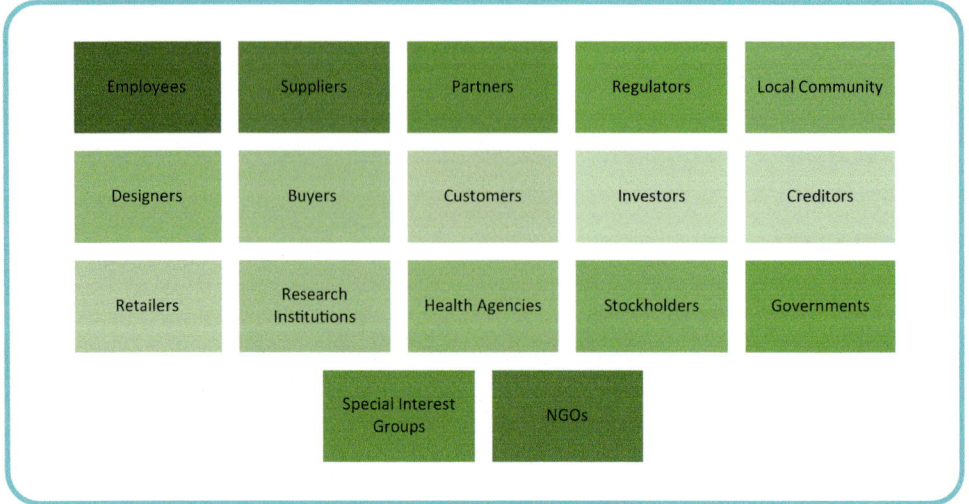

Figure 1.1.2   Stakeholders in the fashion industry

Non-governmental organisations (NGOs) often put pressure onto fashion businesses. For example, in the 1980s we saw *anti-fur* campaigns with NGOs such as People for the Ethical Treatment of Animals (PETA) leading the movement to pressure companies into stopping the use of fur in their collections whilst at the same time campaigning for animal rights (Adegeest, 2020). Whilst some of these campaigns may utilise more radical methods than others, raising awareness of issues in the fashion industry also helps organisations, as some are teaming up with these NGOs in order to (1) be seen to move towards the right direction and actively counteracting criticism they may have received in the past and/or (2) gain advice on what needs to be done, as not all companies may have the necessary expertise in-house.

As a final example, creditors may provide businesses with money in the form of short-term loans that allow these companies to invest in new technologies. Creditors have a vested interest in these organisations, as their business model is contingent on gaining back the money they have loaned with interest, whilst fashion companies have the opportunity to make necessary upgrades (e.g., new technology) in order to further enhance their production processes or product design.

You may have noticed that although the relationship between stakeholders may be mutually dependent, the power dynamics within these relationships may be skewed slightly. It could be argued, for example, that creditors may have more power over their clients (fashion organisations), as they have the finances to support them (or not). On the other hand, suppliers have sometimes been described as having less power, especially if there are a lot of suppliers and only a limited number of fashion organisations that purchase from them. There may also be an equal distribution of power, if, for example companies of perhaps a similar size collaborate. The key message is thus that not all mutually dependent relationships necessarily have the same power dynamics: some may be skewed, whilst others may be balanced.

> **Stakeholder** – an entity that has a vested interest (stake) in an organisation and forms a mutually dependent relationship with this organisation.

Now that we have a better understanding of what managers may do and whom they may be working with, we return to the initial question of how *management* can be defined. According to Shenher and Renier (1996), management can be both an art form and a science. To explain: viewing management as an artform can be illustrated on a more personal level. Each individual has a certain way of dealing with things, developing their own personal style of *management*, which is strongly aligned with their personality, their own personal values, and attitude towards doing things. Thus, management could be described as a subjective way to achieve an overarching goal, which in the case of a business is often linked to economic performance. You may have also noticed that some businesses have a strong affiliation with their founder, whose characteristics and personality traits may be embodied not only in the type of fashion they make, but also in the way the company is led. Examples here could be Dame Vivienne Westwood, a style icon known for her activism and outspokenness about sustainability in fashion, or Stella McCartney, who is an advocate for animal rights and one of the first companies to promote and produce vegan collections (Klokar, 2021; Stella McCartney, 2021).

On the other hand, management is a science, in that knowledge and know-how are needed in order to be successful. Knowledge and know-how can relate not only to the actual organisation an individual is working in, but also the industry at large. Without knowing who one's competitors are and what they are doing, or understanding current trends and changes in the environment, an individual will not be able to make decisions that allow for success to become a reality. Similarly, if we are unaware of how things are run in an organisation and/or the cultural environment, we may not be successful. The importance of know-how can be illustrated when it comes to larger companies acquiring, for example, companies that have a sustainability focus. Examples that can be provided here are The Body Shop, which was at the time acquired by L'Oréal, or Stella McCartney, who signed a deal with LVMH, the conglomerate that owns Louis Vuitton (Conlon, 2019). The reason behind these acquisitions is often strategic, in that both The Body Shop and Stella McCartney are renowned for their sustainable ethos, and thus their experience of making decisions that align with that ethos, which is hoped to be transferred to and/or implemented in the companies that make the acquisition or at least make it part of their portfolio.

What might become apparent here is that management is goal-oriented and at the same time involves complex decision-making processes that are based on observations of the macro and micro environment. As such, it can be described as subjective, due to being based on an individual's style of leadership.

> **Management** – implies leading and controlling a business entity, (which includes people, technology resources, etc.) to achieve overall success based on the goal-oriented tasks set.

Within the business management literature, the macro-level environment is often ana-lysed using the PEST(EL) framework, which looks at the Political, Economic, Socio-cultural, Technological (Environmental and Legislative) aspects which may have an impact on a business (Johnson and Scholes, 2002).

Table 1.1.2 provides an overview of a limited number of factors that can impact fashion businesses. These are not exhaustive, but rather are a starting point for you to develop and contemplate further. Focusing on economic factors, and more specifically exchange rates, these can have key implications for fashion businesses. As a fashion business, we may need to purchase fabric to produce our newest fashion collections, and depending on the currency we use and its strength, we may either get a lot for our money or we may have to invest more than anticipated. Currencies and exchange rates may fluctuate, so it is vital to keep an eye on them, especially when doing business.

Thinking more broadly about the global environment in which the fashion indus-try is operating, both the exchange rate and the inflation rate can have impacts for buyers and suppliers, depending on whether they have agreed upon fixed prices for a certain amount of fabric to be delivered or whether this is subject to change in line with inflation.

As indicated, aside from the macro environment, managers also need to take the micro environment into consideration, which takes into account customers, compet-itors, and market analysis. Thus, we not only need to develop a detailed customer profile, to understand how old our consumers are, what their lifestyle looks like, and how much disposable income they may have, but we also need to consider how we

Table 1.1.2   PEST – Factors, Examples, and Impacts

	Examples	Impacts
Political	• Government stability • Trade regulations	• Unstable government could have an impact on gaining access to raw materials
Economic	• Exchange rates • Inflation • Disposable income	• Lack of disposable income can imply less money being spent on non-essential items, such as luxury fashion products
Socio-cultural	• Lifestyle • Education • Sustainability	• Sustainability and how it is perceived may impact on products being offered in market
Technological	• New developments • R&D • Media influence(s)	• Social media influencers have gained increased importance and have fostered the "selfie phenomenon", which as impacted on the development of digital fashion

set ourselves apart from in competition by, for example, looking at Porter's (1980) five forces. These analyse: (1) how far "buyers" (organisations and end-customers) can influence the price of a product and subsequently the profits an organisation might make (Buyer Power); (2) how much suppliers can bargain – if there is high demand and only a limited number of suppliers available, suppliers have a stronger argument to push prices up; (3) whether there are any alternatives available to consumers (Supplier Power) – for example, consumers could substitute walking shoes with any other type of shoe that allows them to go for a walk (e.g., trainers, hiking boots, loafers) (Threat of Substitute); (4) whether the market is already saturated, so there may be high level of competition (Rivalry among Firms); and (5) how far new firms can enter the market, which may depend on brand loyalty, restricted distribution channels, or patents, among other things (Threat of New Entrants).

Having read this section, you should now be able to clearly define what management entails and why it may be described as either an artform or a science. Although what management entails may often be intuitively understood, it is based on and influenced by a complex decision-making process that further considers the macro and micro level environments of an organisation.

Task

1. Consider why management may be intuitively understood, yet may be hard to describe.
2. For a fashion organisation of your choice, conduct a stakeholder mapping exercise, identifying the reasons why these relationships may be mutually dependent.
3. Using the PEST(EL) framework, consider what current challenges fashion organisations might face, based on their macro environment.

1.1.2 Sustainability – definitions and meaning

One of the most challenging terms to define is perhaps "sustainability", as it "is a concept that everyone purports to understand intuitively, but somehow finds very difficult to operationalize into concrete terms" (Gunder, 2006: 211). Niinimäki (2015: 1) further indicates that it "is (a) fuzzy and wide concept and the discussion what to sustain continues, the resources or lifestyle".

The most frequently cited definition of sustainability, and more specifically sustainable development, is that of the Brundtland Commission, which stated in its report *Our Common Future* that sustainable development involves "meeting the needs of the current generation without compromising the needs of future ones" (WCED, 1987). Although this definition provides a solid starting point for contemplation, it can also be criticised.

If we think about the fashion industry and its evolution, we may notice that prior to the Industrial Revolution, which started in Great Britain in the 18th century, garments were not as readily available as they are today (*Encyclopaedia Britannica*, 2021). Rather than having high street shops and wardrobes full of clothes, garments were handed down from one person to the next until they were no longer useable (Henninger et al., 2020). Prior to the invention of the assembly line, people would not have imagined that garment production could be a quick process that further develops into a throwaway culture based on the take–make–use–dispose phenomenon that is also often referred to as "fast fashion". What is illustrated here is that current generations may not necessarily be able to anticipate what will be possible in the next 10, 15, or 20 years, so they will also not be aware of what a future generation may define as a need.

If we focus on key political events, however, we can see that *Our Common Future* was one of the first milestones that pushed sustainability as a vitally important point on the agenda. The United Nations (UN) Rio de Janeiro Earth Summit in 1992 (UN, n.d.) continued this legacy by emphasising that protecting the natural environment is vital, which led to the creation of Agenda 21. Agenda 21 is seen as "a comprehensive plan of action to be taken globally, nationally and locally of the United Nations System, Governments, and Major Groups in every area in which human impacts on the environment" (UN, 1992). Since then, we have seen various changes, with a further key milestone being the adoption of the 2030 Agenda for Sustainable Development by all members of the UN, which focuses on 17 Sustainable Development Goals (SDGs) that encourage everyone to act in accordance with these goals to tackle our current climate, pollution, and biodiversity crisis (UN, 2021). Table 1.1.3 provides an overview of some of the SDGs and what their implications and/or challenges are for the fashion industry.

Coming back to the initial question of what sustainability is, Elkington (2004, 2008) coined the term *triple bottom line* (TBL), which implies that sustainability is the interplay of focusing on environmental, social, and economic aspects, or in more colloquial terms: planet, people, and profit. The TBL is often displayed as a Venn diagram (of three overlapping circles), with the intersection between all three circles visualising sustainability. In this book, we follow this thought process and see sustainability as a complex issue that looks at economic, environmental, and social goals that may never be reached, but rather form an idealised state.

To explain: with technological advancements – some of which will be outlined in **Part 3: Digital Sustainable Fashion** – we see changes in the macro and micro level environment which can have an impact on what sustainability may mean. In the past, a certain raw material may have been seen as "ideal" due to, for example, being more environmentally friendly than its counterparts (e.g., because it uses less chemicals, water, and land), but this could change in the future. Thus, changes in process (e.g., the way a raw material is cultivated and/or treated), fostered by technological development, could render the initial "ideal" raw material more polluting. Moreover, standards could change: for example, are we considering the use of only toxins and chemicals in the raw material creation process, or also the overall carbon emissions and potential microfibre pollution? The latter has only more recently emerged as a key threat to our environment, and has now been made a top global priority (EEA, 2021). Thus, we see sustainability as a "living and breathing" process that has a meaning that can change over time, based on the (external) environment.

Sustainability – comprised of the interplay between economic, social, and environmental aspects. What is deemed sustainable may change over time, based on changes in the environment.

Table 1.1.3   Sustainable Development Goals and Implications/Challenges for the Fashion Industry

SDG	Title	Description	Implications/Challenges
12	Responsible Consumption and Production	**Responsible Consumption** • Seeks to empower consumers to make informed choices **Responsible Production** • Focuses on how things are being produced by looking at methods that have the least negative impact on the social and natural environment • Has the potential to counteract climate, biodiversity, and pollution crises	• Lack of consumer engagement and continuous hunger for "fast fashion" may hinder responsible consumption patterns • Making changes to production processes IS costly, so companies may opt for the most cost-effective option instead of completely changing all practices
1	No Poverty	Poverty should be made extinct	• Fashion organisations should support local communities and foster sustained growth
3	Good Health and Well-being	Everyone involved has the right to a healthy life, and their well-being should be secured	• Safe working conditions are a vital prerequisite to fulfil this SDG • An example where this was violated is the Rana Plaza Factory disaster (ILO, 2021)
5	Gender Equality	• The focus is on not only promoting, but also achieving equality between genders There is a further emphasis on empowerment of females	• Although the fashion industry is female-dominated, a majority of senior roles are occupied by men • There is also a pay gap between males and females (O'Conner, 2019; Inglesia et al., 2020)

(Continued)

Table 1.1.3 Continued

SDG	Title	Description	Implications/Challenges
6	Clean Water and Sanitation	• Water should be free from toxins and any other harmful substances • Sanitation to be provided for all	• The fashion industry uses a variety of toxins, some of which are released into rivers • Media have previously reported on rivers running red (e.g., Regan, 2020), with countries in the Global South having a greater impact than those in the Global North
8	Decent Work and Economic Growth	• Employment should be available for all in a safe and secure manner • Economic growth should be fostered in a way that can be sustained	• Labour law violations have been repeatedly spotlighted, such as child labour or sweatshops • Accusations of modern slavery, where employees are paid less than minimum wage and lack job security
11	Sustainable Cities and Communities	• Promotes inclusivity, safe environments, resilience, and sustainability within cities and communities	• This can include a focus on providing facilities in manufacturing countries • Focusing on the end-of-life of a garment, waste management is a key component
13	Climate Action	• The world is in a climate crisis, which implies that action needs to be taken to combat and change current practices	• Greenhouse gas (GHG) emissions, which, as the COVID-19 pandemic has shown, can be reduced
14	Life below Water	• Focuses on the protection of marine life and its natural habitat	• Microfibre pollution is currently seen as a key issue that needs further industry attention (Yan et al., 2020)
15	Life on Land	• Focuses on life on land and the use of the natural ecosystem	• Degradation through monocultures, such as cotton, can have devastating impacts, which is showcased in the degradation of the Aral Sea

Source: Adapted from UNECE (2019); Stanton (2020); Cernansky (2020); UN (2021).

We can conclude thus far that sustainability is a top global priority and, as a concept, is rooted within a political agenda (WCED, 1989). Although sustainability may not be defined in a clear-cut manner, it is apparent that it encompasses economic, environmental, and social aspects that need to be carefully considered.

Task

1. Explore the United Nations SDGs and critically evaluate which ones may relate more to the fashion industry than others.
2. Consider what sustainability means to you as an individual and which of the three aspects of the triple bottom line may be most important. Would your choice be different if you were considering sustainability from a company perspective?

1.1.3 Sustainability in fashion and sustainable fashion

Sustainability in fashion is not a new phenomenon, but rather could be described as cyclical, with issues resurfacing over time. Figure 1.1.3 provides an overview of some of the most noticeable events that have led to and magnified issues in the fashion industry. In line with other political events, environmental consciousness emerged in the 1960s. Although sustainability in itself generally has a positive connotation, in the fashion industry this has not always been the case. One explanation could be that in the 1970s it was strongly associated with the "hippie" movement, and thus seen as a political statement not everyone felt comfortable to be associated with (e.g., Henninger et al., 2016). However, this has changed over the years, with "sustainable fashion" often used interchangeably with "eco", "green", "organic", "ethical", or "slow fashion", the latter term coined by Professor Kate Fletcher in 2007 (e.g., Fletcher, 2010; Fletcher and Tham, 2019; Mukendi et al., 2020).

The 1980s saw various forms of activism with the "I'd rather go naked than wear fur!" campaign making headlines, thereby raising awareness of animal rights (e.g., Adegeest, 2020). What is further noteworthy is the emergence of supranational organisations, such as the World Fair Trade Organisation, the World Trade Organisation, or the Alliance for Sustainable Fashion. The latter is part of the UN, where the Alliance for Sustainable Fashion pushes to change "the path of fashion, reducing its negative environmental and social impacts; and turning fashion into a driver of the implementation of the Sustainable Development Goals" (UNFashionAlliance, 2021).

Supranational organisations are those that span across multiple countries, and sometimes even continents, thereby moving sustainability goals onto a global platform and fostering commitment from a global audience. Thus, these supranational organisations transcend national boundaries or interests and instead form common goals and objectives which are voted and decided upon across a wider grouping (UN, 2020).

> **Supranational organisation** – one that transcends national boundaries or interests and forms common goals and objectives which are voted and decided upon across a wider grouping.

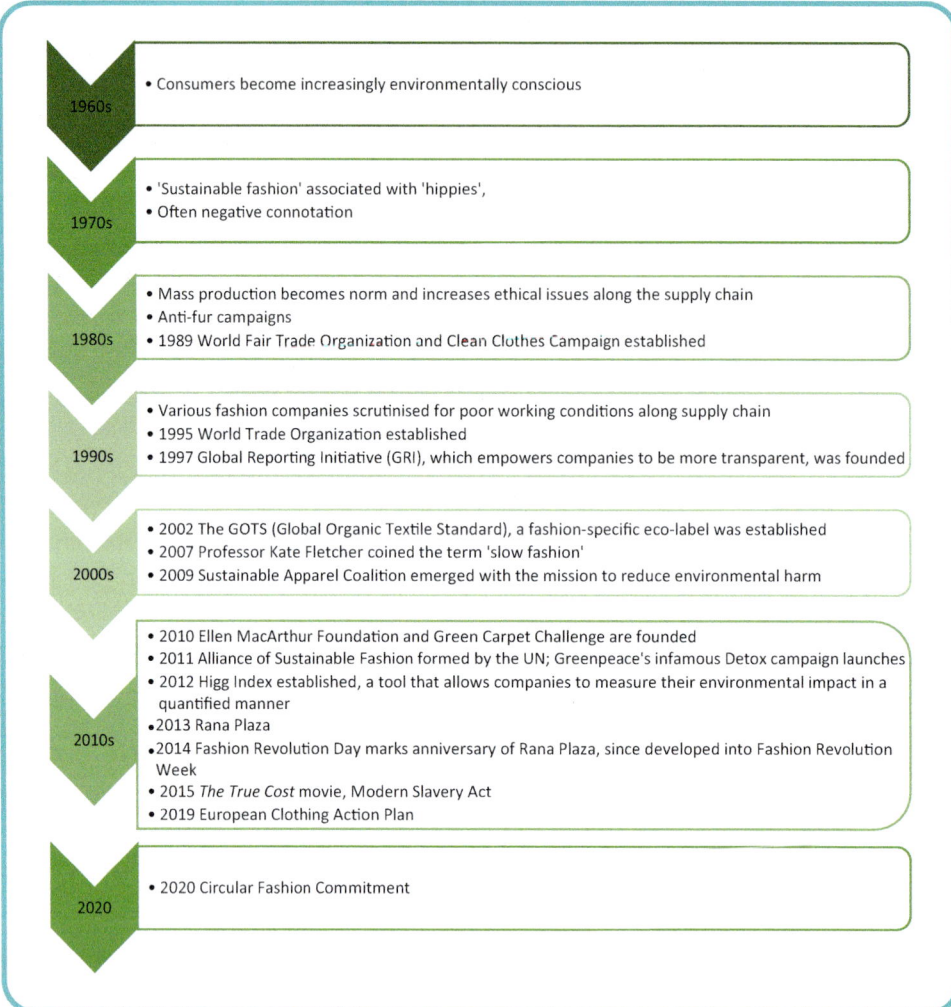

1960s
- Consumers become increasingly environmentally conscious

1970s
- 'Sustainable fashion' associated with 'hippies',
- Often negative connotation

1980s
- Mass production becomes norm and increases ethical issues along the supply chain
- Anti-fur campaigns
- 1989 World Fair Trade Organization and Clean Clothes Campaign established

1990s
- Various fashion companies scrutinised for poor working conditions along supply chain
- 1995 World Trade Organization established
- 1997 Global Reporting Initiative (GRI), which empowers companies to be more transparent, was founded

2000s
- 2002 The GOTS (Global Organic Textile Standard), a fashion-specific eco-label was established
- 2007 Professor Kate Fletcher coined the term 'slow fashion'
- 2009 Sustainable Apparel Coalition emerged with the mission to reduce environmental harm

2010s
- 2010 Ellen MacArthur Foundation and Green Carpet Challenge are founded
- 2011 Alliance of Sustainable Fashion formed by the UN; Greenpeace's infamous Detox campaign launches
- 2012 Higg Index established, a tool that allows companies to measure their environmental impact in a quantified manner
- 2013 Rana Plaza
- 2014 Fashion Revolution Day marks anniversary of Rana Plaza, since developed into Fashion Revolution Week
- 2015 *The True Cost* movie, Modern Slavery Act
- 2019 European Clothing Action Plan

2020
- 2020 Circular Fashion Commitment

Figure 1.1.3   **Snapshot of sustainable fashion timeline (adapted from Gonzalez, 2015; Henninger et al., 2016; Dawson-Elli, 2017; Athwal et al., 2019; Gecseg, 2020)**

You may ask yourself why it is important to highlight the creation of supranational organisations – the answer is quite simple: fashion, and more specifically the fashion industry, concerns everyone. It is a truly global industry, with complex supply chains and highly resource- and labour-intensive (WRAP, 2020). Thus, it may not be a surprise that social and environmental issues have emerged over time. The most devastating example that needs to be highlighted here is the Rana Plaza factory accident, in which thousands lost their lives (e.g., Parveen 2014). To commemorate the event, Fashion Revolution was formed, which started off with Fashion Revolution Day, which challenges consumers to ask questions under the hashtag #WhoMadeMyClothes, and which has since evolved into Fashion Revolution Week and Fashion Revolution Month (FashRev, 2021). Looking at the milestones, what becomes apparent is that sustainability in fashion has been an issue for a long time, and remains one today.

In line with the development of sustainability in the fashion industry, we have also seen the emergence and use of various terms that describe a similar phenomenon: "sustainable fashion". Although it is beyond the scope of this book to provide a clear-cut definition of what sustainable fashion entails, it is vital to understand that different terms, that are often used interchangeably, may have slightly different meanings. Table 1.1.4 provides a summary of key terms used and their meanings within this context.

Providing these different definitions is essential as it may further enable you as a reader to decipher what messages retailers send to their consumers when they classify themselves as, for example, following a circular approach to fashion creation, or producing ethical or sustainable fashion. How and what organisations are communicating will be further explored in Chapter 1.2.

In this section, you will have learned that sustainability in the fashion industry, is not a 21st century phenomenon, but rather has been discussed for a number of decades, with the initial foundations put forward in the 1980s as part of the Brundtland Commission's report (WCED, 1989). Similarly to management, sustainability is intuitively understood, yet can have different meanings, and thus may at times be situation- and context-dependent.

Task

1. Focusing on the timeline provided, are there any other key milestones you would add? Justify why they may be important and how they have influenced the fashion industry.
2. Carefully explore the terminology provided on "sustainable fashion", and research companies that may fall in each of these categories.

1.1.4 Importance of sustainable fashion in the 21st century

As you worked through the previous section, you will have become aware that sustainability in the fashion industry and producing more sustainable fashions are vital aspects. This is further illustrated in Table 1.1.5, which summarises some of the key facts about the fashion industry. Whilst the industry provides employment opportunities for approximately 60.75 million people (FashionUnited, 2021), it can also have detrimental impacts on the environment because raw materials and finishing processes utilise an enormous amount of water, whilst currently a lot of waste is produced, not only in the pre-consumer stage due to waste of materials within the design and production process, but also in the post-consumer stage – once the garment is seen to have reached its end-of-life (e.g., Beall, 2020; BoF, 2021).

Table 1.1.4   Terminology of "Sustainable Fashion"

	Example	Explanation	References
Environmental focus	Eco, bio, organic, and environmentally friendly fashion	• Emphasis on reducing environmental impact of garment production • Raw materials chosen carefully, e.g. organic cotton, recycled materials • Reduced chemical and/ or water use (e.g. dyeing process)	Niinimäki (2010) Carey & Cervellon (2014)
Social focus	Ethical fashion	• Main focus is on safe working conditions • Living things (humans, animals) are at the centre, and environmentally friendly materials and less toxins are used to avoiding harming them	Joergens (2006) Reimers et al. (2016) Blazquez et al. (2020)
Social and environmental focus	Sustainable fashion	• Incorporates aspects of the triple bottom line by focusing on social and environmental aspects	Fletcher (2008)
System thinking approach	Sustainable fashion – Earth Logic	• Earth Logic involves moving away from capitalist thinking and refocusing on flora and fauna • It is an action plan based on six principles: 1. Less: grow out of growth 2. Local: scaling, re-centring 3. Plural: new centres for fashion 4. Learning: new knowledge, skills, mindset for fashion 5. Language: new communication for fashion 6. Governance: new ways of organising fashion	Fletcher & Tham (2019: 15)

(Continued)

Table 1.1.4   Continued

	Example	Explanation	References
System thinking approach	Slow fashion	• Takes a philosophical approach to not only slowing down the creation process, but also fostering a more localised approach • Further details in **Chapter 2.3**	Clark (2008) Pookulangara & Shepard (2013)
System thinking approach	Circular fashion	• Links to a design thinking approach and disruptive business model innovations • Main focus is to design out waste and pollution and keep materials in circulation for as long as possible • Further details in **Part 2**	Niinimäki (2017) Lissaman (2019)

Table 1.1.5   Key Figures and Facts about the Fashion Industry

	Facts and figures	References
Employment	• 60–75 million people globally	FashionUnited (2021)
Global value of fashion industry	• 2020: US$1.5 trillion • 2025: US$2.25 trillion	Shahbandeh (2021)
Gross Domestic Product (GDP)	• 2% of global GDP	BoF (2021)
Environmental issues	• 93 million m³ of water used annually for fashion creation • 2018: 2.1 billion metric tonnes of GHG emissions attributed to fashion industry – equates to 4% of global GHGs ○ 2030: 2.7 billion metric tonnes • 25% of resources (pre-consumer) are wasted, which includes offcuts and fabric and garment leftovers • 92 million tonnes of garments landfilled yearly	Beall (2020)Berg et al. (2020)Ro (2020)
Outlook	• 160 million tonnes of garments estimated to be produced by the year 2050	BoF (2021)

As indicated in the previous section, the term "sustainable fashion" encompasses a number of terms that have previously been used interchangeably, and has the power to eliminate some of this confusion and contribute to SDG 12, Responsible Production and Consumption. You may ask yourself why not every company and/or consumer does their part in making this happen. One explanation could be money, as producing fashion in a more sustainable manner also implies a higher price point because living wages need to be ensured and raw materials sourced and produced in a more environmentally friendly manner. Yet, as you may have noticed in media reports, this is not always the case, and this has fostered many debates within the fashion industry.

Another explanation could be an issue of communication, as consumers may neither understand what is meant by "sustainable fashion" nor trust how it is portrayed. The latter point refers to a phenomenon that is often referred to as "greenwashing", where companies may make claims about their products that are misleading. To provide an example, the colour green is often associated with nature. In the past, products that have been described as being more environmentally friendly have also been referred to as "green" products, so if a company is labelling its products with green writing and/or using symbols such as trees or flowers, consumers may think that these products are more environmentally friendly, and thus sustainable. Yet this may not always be the case. Greenwashing emerged strongly in the 1990s and 2000s – ever since then, consumers have been more suspicious about companies that heavily promote their social and environmental credentials (Belz and Peattie, 2010; Du, 2015)

The 21st century has not only been marked by technological advancements, but also by increased media fragmentation, which has seen a variety of new communication channels emerging, such as Twitter and Facebook, and more recently, TikTok. Consequently, news can now travel instantaneously to a global audience, with consumers and other stakeholders being reachable 24/7. Whilst in the past it may have been possible to "hide" any mistakes, companies can now be scrutinised the very second something is happening along their supply chain (Henninger & Oates, 2018; Blazquez et al., 2020). In a similar manner, various organisations have taken advantage of these social media channels to promote consumer and more general stakeholder engagement and actively communicate their missions and events. These can happen on a societal or individual level or be fostered by the external environment. Let us consider some examples to demonstrate this.

Societal level – Extinction Rebellion

Extinction Rebellion (XR), born in the UK in 2018, is now a global movement which seeks to use "non-violent civil disobedience in an attempt to halt mass extinction and minimise the risk of social collapse" (Extinction Rebellion, 2021). As such, this group seeks to raise awareness of the climate crisis by highlighting that "the time is now" to act and make changes. In September 2020, for example, XR called on the fashion industry to make changes by refocusing its practices from goods that are predominantly trend-led and go in and out of fashion quickly, thus promoting excess consumption, to becoming more mindful (Extinction Rebellion, 2020). At the same time, XR tries to appeal to consumers to hold the fashion industry accountable for its actions.

Individual level – Fashion Detox

In 2021, the Fashion Detox Challenge (FDC) won the SDG Good Practices prize (SDGS, 2021), which focuses strongly on consumer, and thus individual, engagement. The Fashion Detox Challenge encourages "people who usually buy clothing often to stop buying clothes for 10 weeks and to reflect on this process online in a private forum on our website, where they post weekly "Detox Diaries" (FDC, 2021). As such, the FDC can be seen to empower consumers to take responsibility into their own hands by reflecting on their current practices and understanding the implications of their behaviour.

Environmental level – COVID-19

COVID-19 has changed the world as we know it and shaken up daily routines of consumption as well as production practices. The fashion industry overall was hit hard due to restrictions (e.g., lockdown, social distancing) imposed by governments. As a result, profits, which previously had grown year on year, dropped by 93 per cent in 2019–2020 (Berg et al., 2020; BoF, 2021). Although COVID-19 has been devastating, with many lives lost and livelihoods at risk, it has also magnified issues in the fashion industry which are now clamouring to be addressed (e.g., Berg et al, 2020; Brydges et al., 2020; BoF, 2021). Unfortunately, COVID-19 is not an isolated case, and with climate change happening, we will likely face more challenges which may make societal and individual-level initiatives more important than ever.

In summary, the fashion industry is a truly global industry, which not only provides income and economic benefits, but may also face various social and environmental challenges. Increased media fragmentation has made it possible for individuals and stakeholders in general to communicate instantaneously and share information on a global scale. In the 21st century, sustainability has become even more important, which may also be one of the reasons why different calls for action and stakeholder engagement initiatives are emerging that seek to counteract current practices, raising awareness and empowering people to act accordingly.

Task

1. Critically evaluate what may be the challenges and opportunities of societal, individual, and environmental-level initiatives.
2. Looking at current news and media articles, what are the issues relating to sustainability and the fashion industry?

References

Adegeest, D.A. (2020) *Claiming victory, PETA ends 30-year campaign against fur*, FashionUnited (online): https://fashionunited .uk/news/fashion/claiming-victory-peta -ends-30-year-campaign-against-fur /2020020647402, 22/05/2021.

Athwal, N., Wells, V., Carrigan, M., and Henninger, C.E. (2019) Sustainable luxury marketing: a synthesis and research agenda, *International Journal of Management Review*, 21(4), 405–426.

Beall, A. (2020) *Why clothes are so hard to recycle*, BBC (online): https://www.bbc.com/future/article/20200710-why-clothes-are-so-hard-to-recycle, 19/07/2021.

Belz, F.-M., and Peattie, K. (2010) *Sustainability marketing: a global perspective*, John Wiley & Sons Ltd., Chichester, UK.

Berg, A., Granskog, A., Lee, L., and Magnus, K.H. (2020) *Fashion on climate*, McKinsey (online): https://www.mckinsey.com/industries/retail/our-insights/fashion-on-climate, 19/07/2021.

Blazquez Cano, M., Henninger, C.E., Alexander, B., and Franquesa, C. (2020) Consumers' knowledge and intentions towards sustainability: a Spanish fashion perspective, *Fashion Practice*, 12(1), 34–54.

Boardman, R., Parker Strak, R., and Henninger, C.E. (2020) *Fashion buying & merchandising in the 21st century*, Routledge, Abingdon, UK.

BoF (2021) *The state of fashion 2021*, BoF (online): https://www.businessoffashion.com/reports/news-analysis/download-the-report-the-state-of-fashion-2021?int_source=onsite_marketing&int_medium=launch_article&int_campaign=sof21_02122020&int_content=cta_1, 19/07/2021.

Brydges, T., Retamal, M., and Hanlon, M. (2020) Will COVID-19 support the transition to a more sustainable fashion industry?, *Sustainability: Science, Practice and Policy*, 16(1), 298–308.

Carey, L., and Cervellon, M.-C. (2014) Ethical fashion dimensions: pictorial and auditory depictions through three cultural perspectives, *Journal of Fashion Marketing and Management*, 18(4), 483–506.

Cernansky, R. (2020) *The UN set 17 sustainability goals. It needs fashion's help meeting them*, Vogue (online): https://www.voguebusiness.com/sustainability/un-set-17-sustainability-goals-needs-fashions-help-meeting-them, 18/07/2021.

Clark, H. (2008) SLOW plus FASHION-an oxymoron-or a promise for the future…?, *Fashion Theory*, 12(4): 427–446.

Conlon, S. (2019) *Stella McCartney signs deal with French luxury group LVMH*, The Guardian (online): https://www.theguardian.com/fashion/2019/jul/15/stella-mccartney-signs-deal-with-french-luxury-group-lvmh, 03/08/2021.

Dawson-Elli, M. (2017) *The major milestones of sustainability in fashion*, Thr3efold (online): https://www.thr3efold.com/news/the-major-milestones-of-sustainability-in-fashion, 17/07/2021.

Drucker, P.F. (1967) *The effective decision*, Harvard Business Review (online): https://hbr.org/1967/01/the-effective-decision, 03/08/2021.

Du, X. (2015) How the market values greenwashing? Evidence from China, *Journal of Business Ethics*, 128(3), 547–574.

EEA (European Environmental Agency) (2021) *Textiles in Europe's circular economy*, EEA (online): https://www.eea.europa.eu/publications/textiles-in-europes-circular-economy, 19/07/2021.

Extinction Rebellion (2020) *Extinction rebellion call on fashion to transform our culture of consumption and destruction*, Extinction Rebellion (online): https://extinctionrebellion.uk/2020/09/29/extinction-rebellion-call-on-fashion-to-transform-our-culture-of-consumption-and-destruction/, 19/07/2021.

Extinction Rebellion (2021) *About us*, Extinction Rebellion (online): https://extinctionrebellion.uk/the-truth/about-us/, 19/07/2021.

FashionUnited (2021) *Global fashion industry statistics – international apparel*, FashionUnited (online): https://fashionunited.com/global-fashion-industry-statistics/, 19/07/2021.

FashRev (2021) *We are fashion revolution*, FashRev (online): https://www.fashionrevolution.org, 11/09/2021.

FDC (2021) *About*, FDC (online): https://fashiondetoxchallenge.com/about/, 19/07/2021.

Fletcher, K. (2010) Slow fashion: an invitation for systems change, *Fashion Practice*, 2(2), 259–266.

Fletcher, K., and Tham, M. (2019) *Earth logic-fashion action research plan*, Earth Logic (online): https://earthlogic.info/wp-content

/uploads/2021/03/Earth-Logic-E-version.pdf, 18/07/2021.

Elkington, J. (2004) Enter the triple bottom line, Chapter 1, in Henriques, A., and Richardson, J. (eds.), *The triple bottom line, does it all add up?*, Earthscan, London, UK, pp. 1–16.

Elkington, J. (2008) *People, planet, profit*, John Elkington (online]): http://www .johnelkington.com/journal/journal_entry.asp ?id=25, 18/07/2021.

Encyclopaedia Britannica (2021) *Industrial revolution*, Encyclopaedia Britannica (online): https://www.britannica.com/event/Industrial -Revolution, 18/07/2021.

Fletcher, K. (2008) *Sustainable fashion and textiles: design journeys*, Earthscan, London and Sterling, VA.

Gecseg, P. (2020) *Sustainable fashion milestones from the 2010s*, Sustainable Fashion Collective (online): https://www.the -sustainable-fashion-collective.com/2020/01 /13/sustainable-fashion-milestones-from-the -past-decade, 17/07/2021.

Gonzalez, N. (2015) *A brief history of sustainable fashion*, TriplePundit (online): https://www.triplepundit.com/story/2015 /brief-history-sustainable-fashion/58046, 17/07/2021.

Gunder, M. (2006) Sustainability: planning's saving grace or road to perdition?, *Journal of Planning Education and Research*, 26, 208–221.

Henninger, C.E., Alevizou, P.J., and Oates, C.J. (2016) What is sustainable fashion?, *Journal of Fashion Marketing & Management*, 20(4), 400–416.

Henninger, C.E., Blazquez Cano, M., Boardman, R., Jones, C., McCormick, H., and Sahab, S. (2020) Cradle-to-cradle vs consumer preferences, in Choudhury, I., and Hashmi, S. (eds.), *Encyclopedia of renewable and sustainable materials*, Volume 5, Elsevier, Oxford, pp. 353–357.

Henninger, C.E., and Oates, C.J. (2018) The role of social media in communicating CSR within fashion micro-organizations, Chapter 4.3, in Lindgreen, A., Vanhamme, J., Maon, F., and Mardon, R. (eds.), *Communicating corporate social responsibility in the digital era*, Gower Publishing Ltd., Farnham, pp. 232–244.

ILO (International Labour Organization) (2021) *The Rana Plaza accident and its aftermath*, ILO (online): https://www.ilo.org /global/topics/geip/WCMS_614394/lang--en/ index.htm, 18/07/2021.

Inglesia, T., Haverhals, E., and De Wee, T. (2020) *The fashion industry needs to break with its gender and women's rights problems*, Fashion Revolution (online): https://www .fashionrevolution.org/the-fashion-industry -needs-to-break-with-its-gender-and -womens-rights-problems/, 18/07/2021.

Joergens, C. (2006) Ethical fashion: myth or future trend?, *Journal of Fashion Marketing and Management*, 10(3), 360–371.

Johnson, G., and Scholes, K. (2002) *Exploring corporate strategy*, Prentice Hall, New York.

Klokar, E. (2021) *Vivienne Westwood – fashion icon and passionate activist*, Haus von Eden (online): https://www.hausvoneden.com /lifestyle/vivienne-westwood-mode-ikone -und-gelebter-aktivismus/, 03/08/2021.

Lissman, C. (2019) *What is circular fashion?*, Common Objective (online): https://www .commonobjective.co/article/what-is-circular -fashion, 18/07/2021.

Mukendi, A., Davies, I., Glozer, S., and McDonagh, P. (2020) Sustainable fashion: current and future research directions, *European Journal of Marketing*, 54(11), 2873–2909.

Niinimäki, K. (2010) Eco-clothing, consumer identity and ideology, *Sustainable Development*, 18(3): 150–162.

Niinimäki, K. (2015) Ethical foundations in sustainable fashion, *Textiles and Clothing Sustainability*, 1(3): 1–12.

Niinimäki, K. (2017) Fashion in a circular economy, in Henninger, C.E., Alevizou, P.J., Goworek, H., and Ryding, D. (eds.), *Sustainability in fashion: a cradle to upcycle approach*, Springer, Heidelberg, pp. 151–170.

O'Conner, T. (2019) *Fashion's gender pay gap isn't getting any smaller*, BoF (online): https:// www.businessoffashion.com/articles/news -analysis/fashion-gender-pay-gap-2018-2019, 18/07/2021.

Parveen, S. (2014) *Rana Plaza factory collapse survivors struggle one year on*, BBC (online): http://www.bbc.co.uk/news/world-asia -27107860, 11/09/2021.

Pookulangara, S., and Shepard, A. (2013) Slow fashion movement: understanding consumer perceptions – an exploratory study, *Journal of Retailing and Consumer Services*, 20(2): 200–206.

Porter, M.E. (1980) *Competitive strategy: techniques for analysing industries and competitors*, Free Press, New York.

Reimers, V., Magnuson, B., and Chao, F. (2016) The academic conceptualisation of ethical clothing could it account for the attitude behaviour gap?, *Journal of Fashion Marketing and Management*, 20(4), 383–399.

Regan, H. (2020) *Asian rivers are turning black. And our colourful closets are to blame*, CNN (online): https://edition.cnn.com/style/ article/dyeing-pollution-fashion-intl-hnk-dst -sept/index.html, 18/07/2021.

Ro, C. (2020) *Can fashion ever be sustainable?*, BBC (online): https://www.bbc.com/future/ article/20200310-sustainable-fashion-how-to -buy-clothes-good-for-the-climate, 19/07/2021.

SDGS (2021) *Fashion Detox Challenge (FDC) – an experiment in reduced clothing consumption in partnership with Glasgow Caledonian University*, SDGs (online): https:// sdgs.un.org/partnerships/fashion-detox -challenge-fdc-experiment-reduced-clothing -consumption-partnership, 19/07/2021.

Shahbandeh, M. (2021) *Global apparel market – statistics & facts*, Statista (online): https://www.statista.com/topics/5091/apparel -market-worldwide/, 19/07/2021.

Shenhar, A.J., and Renier, J. (1996) How to define management: a modular approach, *Management Development Review*, 9(1), 25–31.

Stanton, A. (2020) *How the United Nations' SDGs relate to the fashion industry*, Remake (online): https://remake.world/stories/news/ how-the-united-nations-sdgs-relate-to-the -fashion-industry/, 18/07/2021.

Stella McCartney (2021) *Sustainability*, Stella McCartney (online): https://www .stellamccartney.com/us/en/sustainability/ sustainability.html, 03/08/2021.

UN (1992) *Agenda 21*, UN (online): https://sustainabledevelopment.un.org/ outcomedocuments/agenda21, 18/07/2021.

UN (2020) *Supranational organisations*, UN (online): https://archive.unescwa.org/ supranational-organizations, 18/07/2021.

UN (2021) *The 17 goals*, UN (online): https:// sdgs.un.org/goals, 18/07/2021.

UN (n.d.) *United Nations Conference on Environment and Development*, Rio de Janeiro, Brazil, 3–14 June 1992, UN (online): https://www.un.org/en/conferences/ environment/rio1992, 18/07/2021.

UNECE (2019) *Fashion and the SDGs: what role for the UN?*, UNECE (online): https://unece.org /DAM/RCM_Website/RFSD_2018_Side_event _sustainable_fashion.pdf, 18/07/2021.

UNFashionAlliance (2021) *What is the UN alliance for sustainable fashion?*, UNFashionAlliance (online): https:// unfashionalliance.org, 19/07/2021.

WCED (1987) *Our common future (The Brundtland report)*, World Commission on Environment and Development, Oxford University Press, Oxford, UK.

WCED (1989) *Our common future (The Brundtland Report)*, World Commission on Environment and Development, Oxford University Press, Oxford.

WRAP (2020) *67 million clothes could be discarded by UK homes post lockdown*, WRAP (online): https://wrap.org.uk/content /67-million-clothes-could-be-discarded-uk -homes-post-lockdown, 27/06/2020.

Yan, S., Jones, C., Henninger, C.E., and McCormick, H. (2020) Textile industry insights towards impact of regenerated cellulosic and synthetic fibres on microfibre pollution, in Muthu, S.S., and Gardetti, M.A. (eds.), *Sustainability in the textile and apparel industry*, Springer, Cham, pp. 157–172.

1.2 Sustainable fashion
Company perspective

Learning outcomes

1. To critically examine how sustainability is incorporated into fashion businesses.
2. To evaluate how the decision-making process may influence supply chain management.
3. To explore key challenges facing the fashion industry within a global context.
4. To understand new developments within sustainable fashion.

The previous chapter provided an overview of key terminologies as well as definitions to what we understand when we talk about *management*, *sustainability*, and *sustainable fashion*. Within this chapter, the first section focuses on the company perspective by illustrating not only how sustainability may be incorporated as a strategy, but also what the implications are of producing sustainable fashion.

1.2.1 Sustainability as a strategy

Sustainability and the facets it entails are no longer optional, but often also enforced through legislation and/or supported by supranational organisations. Nevertheless, organisations may deal with aspects of sustainability differently, depending on – at times – the size of the organisation and its core mission. This further links to whether management is seen as an art or as a science, which may impact on how organisations are dealing with sustainability.

To provide more explicit examples, the European Union Directive 2014/95EU "requires certain large companies to disclose information on the way they operate and manage social and environmental challenges" (Europa, 2021). This is also one of the reasons why you can look at corporate social responsibility (CSR) reports that are included on fashion company websites. Although this aspect of transparency is commendable, Wells et al. (2021: 1) have pointed out that this type of reporting can also fall short, as the focus is more on "symbolic management [which] undermines the legitimacy of sustainability efforts". A key take-away here is that we as consumers also have a responsibility to follow up and reflect on the information we gain, thereby not shying away from demanding more detailed explanations of what organisations are doing, if needed.

In the same vein, some organisations may simply conform with what they must do as almost a bare minimum approach, whilst others may show full commitment and go beyond requirements imposed on them by, for example, investing heavily in

DOI: 10.4324/9781003097846-3

innovative raw materials or ensuring that their carbon footprint is limited by sourcing and producing locally. Again, here you may be able to think of different company examples and their ethos, as well as the size of the company.

Patagonia is described as a sustainable brand, thereby incorporating aspects of sustainability in all its processes, whilst H&M may not necessarily be recognised as *the* sustainable brand, but the introduction of the conscious line and its collaboration with Oxfam on the take back scheme clearly contribute to reducing the brand's impact. On the other hand, we have also seen interesting collaborations emerge that are not only creative in the sense of design, but also creative in the sense of how organisations deal with implementing "sustainable strategies". Examples that come to mind might be *Reclaim To Wear* and *Topshop* with their efforts to reduce textile waste, whereby Orsola de Castro and Filippo Ricci highlight: "with all the environmental challenges we are facing, the fashion industry is looking for design solutions for the future. Sometimes, to be really innovative, you have to take the best from the past and bring it to the future" (cited in Biron, 2016). The collaboration between Reclaim To Wear and Topshop was based on the former utilising pre-consumer textile waste from Topshop to create new fashion lines, which could be seen to be part of "a design solution to an environmental change" (Reclaim To Wear, n.d.). This could be seen as a win–win situation, since Topshop manages to reduce its waste whilst Reclaim To Wear produces a new, unique collection, thereby avoiding materials going into landfill.

From the examples provided, you might notice that it could be beneficial if not all organisations go down the same pathway, since we as consumers also have different ideas of what we want to see organisations do and how we perceive sustainability efforts. Based on our personalities, attitudes, and viewpoints, we may be more drawn towards one company versus another, so having this variety within the market ensures that no one is alienated and we can pick and choose companies that best meet our personal preferences.

Figure 1.2.1 provides a visualisation of how organisations may tackle sustainability, which can be viewed as a continuum that is framed by two extremes, namely those companies that only implement what needs to be done and those that view sustainability as anti-capitalism. It has to be highlighted that these strategies are not exhaustive of what we may find in the industry, but rather they may provide inspiration for how we discuss sustainability strategies.

For example, organisations that focus on sustainability as a means to an end may only implement aspects that are required of them. In other words, companies falling within this category may implement the bare minimum to stay within the legal framework. Thus, companies may adhere to publishing their CSR reports on their websites, and thus align with directives such as 2014/95EU, yet they may not go any further than that to tackle issues associated with sustainability if they do not have to. Whether or not this is a conscious choice, or whether the company may not be able to make any other changes due to, for example, financial constraints, including cash flow and assets, is beyond the scope of this book, but could be a key consideration for future investigations.

Companies that see sustainability as an *add-on strategy* might want to make changes, yet it may not always be possible to implement these quickly. For example, a company that was set up prior to sustainability issues being made centre stage may have already developed long, complex supply chains, and making changes to these can be time-consuming and also very costly. As such, they may develop a different strategy to allow

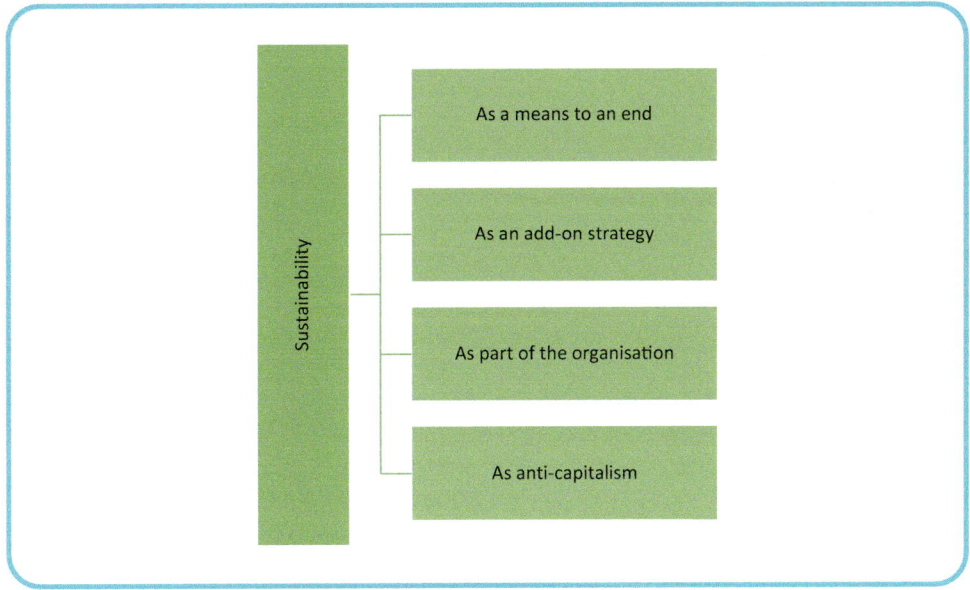

Figure 1.2.1   Options for implementing sustainability in an organisation (adapted from Boardman et al., 2020)

them to incorporate more sustainable approaches. Recently, we have seen a variety of retail brands collaborating with fashion rental companies, as fashion rental (in some instances) is seen to be more environmentally friendly. On the other hand, fast fashion retailers have also changed their material compositions to now sell garments that are made partially from recycled materials or have been certified by eco-labels, such as the Global Organic Textile Standard (GOTS) or Fair Trade. Whilst these fast fashion companies may still be producing more fashion items than are needed, they are moving towards the right direction by ensuring their materials are more sustainable. Moreover, they provide their consumers with a choice, in that they not only sell, for example, fast fashion items, but some lines may be dedicated to incorporating more sustainable practices. What is noteworthy here is that add-on strategies can take any form, including forming a sort of collaboration, or making changes to one line that is being sold. Add-ons, as implied by the name are additions, but may not necessarily transfer to the entirety of the business, but solely parts of it.

You may ask yourself whether this is enough, or whether companies should do more. In this instance, you may want to consider the impact of the following example. Let's say that our Sustaina-jeans brand is successfully making every effort to producing a pair of jeans that is sustainable. All decisions made in the production process are aligned with what is generally considered to be sustainable, from raw materials to working conditions. Yet Sustaina-jeans has a customer base of only 500 people. On the other hand, we have a fast fashion retailer that has an international and/or global presence. It may have only one jeans line that is certified to be more sustainable than other products within the same product category and utilises recycled fibre content. This fast fashion brand has a consumer base of 1 million people. Thus, it could be argued, even though only one jeans line may have been altered to align with the sustainable mission, it may reach more people internationally and/or globally, and thus may raise more awareness than, for example, a smaller brand.

Contemplate whether it is enough to simply have an add-on strategy implemented, or whether companies should do better. Whilst this question would go beyond the scope of the book, what can be pointed out is the fact that any small change can have a big impact, and is thus commendable. Using less virgin materials may have an impact on the overall water usage of the industry, as well as CO_2 emissions, to name but a couple of aspects. Similarly, fast fashion retailers are mainstream, meaning they are found on the high street and accessed by the average consumer. Thus, making more sustainable options accessible to the average consumer can be seen as beneficial. You may also want to look at **Part 4** for further information on materials and alternatives that can be used.

Overall, add-on strategies may not only be a viable option, but also perhaps a preferred option, especially for large retailers with complex supply chains and processes that may be hard to change. Yet be aware that even though companies may offer more sustainable alternatives, it is also up to the consumer to buy into them. If consumers do not perceive these alternatives to be good value for money, producing something that is more sustainable may still be wasteful.

The third strategy that companies may use is having *sustainability fully integrated* as part of the organisation. How does this differ? The answer is rather simple: similar to companies that are "born global", such as Google, there are companies that have been set up with sustainability at the core of their mission and values. Thus, sustainability is quite literally guiding all their decisions, from where products are being sourced to how many items are produced to how their stance is communicated to how social and environmental aspects are addressed. In Chapter 1.1, we outlined that sustainability, and more specifically sustainable fashion, have no clear-cut definitions, but rather there are various terminologies and ways to interpret what "sustainability" means.

An implication here is that there are various examples of companies that can fall within the category of "born sustainable", all of which have a different focus. For example, *People Tree*, which was founded by Safia Minney, produces products that are "made to the highest ethical and environmental standards from start to finish" (People Tree, 2021a). It further highlights that it was the first fashion company to be awarded the World Fair Trade Organisation product label, which outlines that it complies with "the principles of fair trade, covering fair wages, good working conditions, transparency, environmental best practice and gender equality" (People Tree, 2021a). Although People Tree is also GOTS-certified and uses organic raw materials, the brand seems to put a larger emphasis on promoting its social sustainability agenda.

United by Blue emphasises the environmental aspect, outlining that "for every product purchased, United by Blue removes one pound of trash from oceans and waterways" (United by Blue, 2021). Although the company also pays attention to social aspects, evidenced by being BCorp certified, the environmental angle is more prominent on its website.

Although the foci of these two brands are different, it can be argued that they are both born sustainable brands and are producing products in line with their mission statements by actively seeking certifications that emphasise their credentials. Yet, as we have previously outlined, these credentials can also be seen as add-on strategies. What you may notice here is that trying to categorise brands in accordance with their strategies can be rather complex.

As mentioned earlier, companies also have an opportunity to get engaged with standards/certifications, a majority of which are third-party-accredited and confirm that a company is adhering to the criteria imposed by these standards/certifications. Table 1.2.1 shows a limited number of certifications/standards that may be commonly displayed by fashion products and/or companies and may provide you with an understanding of what it means for the companies and their subsequent strategies to invest time and money to apply and adhere to the criteria enforced by these third-party standards.

Table 1.2.1   Selection of Certifications and Standards Available for the Fashion Industry

Certifications	Explanation	Company example	Reference
Certified B Corp	• Implies they balance economic and social considerations • All decisions need to be made with consideration of implications for stakeholders	• Design by Blue, • Patagonia, • Someone Somewhere, • Mud Jeans	BCorp (2021)
Positive Luxury (Butterfly Mark)	• Used within the luxury industry and highlights retailers that have a positive impact on nature and society • Tailored to retailers, as each retailer may have a different set of positive actions	• Christian Dior • Anya Hindmarch • Needle & Thread	Positive Luxury (2021)
Fair Trade	• Described as one of the most recognisable ethical labels • Certifies that companies that have this label support farmers and workers by improving their lives and communities they live in	• People Tree • Little Green Radicals • Bhumi	Fairtrade (n.d.) People Tree (2021a) Rauturier (2020)
GOTS	• Textile processing standard for organic fibres • Has a set of social and ecological criteria, and focuses on entire supply chain	• Veja • Pact • MUD Jeans • ThokkThokk	Rauturier (2020);GOTS (2021)
Oeko-Tex 1000	• Tests for harmful substances	• Loomstate	Rauturier (2020); Oeko-Tex (2021)

To stick with the critical focus of the book, it also needs to be outlined that although these labels may be helpful, in that they can provide assurance to consumers that these companies comply with a certain criterion and/or enable companies to communicate their sustainability efforts, not every company may be able to afford them (e.g., Henninger, 2015). To explain, these certifications often come at a high price, which may not necessarily be affordable for companies of all sizes. A key implication here is that whilst some companies may have these certifications/standards publicly displayed on their products and/or websites, this does not mean that other companies are not aligning with the criteria, but rather that there may be some organisations that adhere to them, but cannot afford to pay for the label. For companies, it is thus important to carefully communicate exactly what they are doing, to avoid any allegations of greenwashing.

> **Greenwashing** – implies that companies may make claims about their products that are misleading.

Lastly, there are also companies that adopt an *"anti-capitalist"* approach, which could perhaps be seen as an extreme opposite to seeing sustainability as a means to an end. Companies that fall within this category not only seek to reduce production of new "virgin" products, but also only utilise raw materials that are already in existence. This can have various implications, not only for the design process of a product, as fashion pieces may be quite unique and innovative, but also for the number of garments that are produced, since raw materials are not infinite, but finite, and at times not reuseable. In terms of the latter aspect, one of the key issues surrounding fast fashion is said to be the quality of the items. If the quality of the raw material is poor, it may not be of any use for the creation of new products.

Choosing one of these strategies can also have implications for supply chain management. As alluded to, supply chain management is the combination of key business processes, "from end-user through original suppliers, that provides products, services, and information that add value for customers and other stakeholders" (Lambert et al., 2006: 2). Thus, the overarching goal is to enhance a company's performance by improving on existing operational processes (Henninger et al., 2015). Sustainable supply chain management implies that rather than solely focusing on efficiency and improving processes, the lens of environmental and social aspects is also employed, which are strategically managed (e.g., Mentzer et al., 2002; Henninger et al., 2015).

> **Supply chain management** – a combination of processes that span from end-consumers to suppliers and provide products/services and information with the end goal of adding value for end-consumers and stakeholders.

The goal of supply chain management is to overhaul and improve existing organisational processes to enhance the company's long-term performance and the overall supply chain. This can be accomplished by implementing strategically managed business processes across the organisation (Mentzer et al., 2002).

One way of thinking about sustainable supply chain management is the *R model*, which was first introduced as the 3R model (reduce, reuse, recycle), and further developed to become 7R (Ho and Choi, 2012), and more recently the 9R model (Henninger et al., 2015). The 3R model will be revisited in **Part 4: Material Innovations in Sustainable Fashion**, when you will have an opportunity to apply it to a case study. The 9R model is the focus here, and is outlined in Figure 1.2.2. It is not important where one starts to think about the 9Rs, so whether you look at re-claim before recycling does not matter: what matters here is that you can actively reflect on what the implications might be of implementing some of the 9Rs in a business environment.

Let's start off with quite an easy aspect of the 9R model that you may be familiar with: *recycling*. This can on the one hand mean recycling the finished end-product, for example by disassembling a pair of jeans into fibres and reusing these fibres for a new product. On the other hand, it could also mean using scrap materials (e.g., -offcuts) and making something else out of them. You can read more on recycling in Chapter 1.4, which focuses on the circular economy. The important take-away here is that recycling implies that materials are diverted from landfill and reused in new products, and thus are no longer in their original state or form. When discussing recycling,

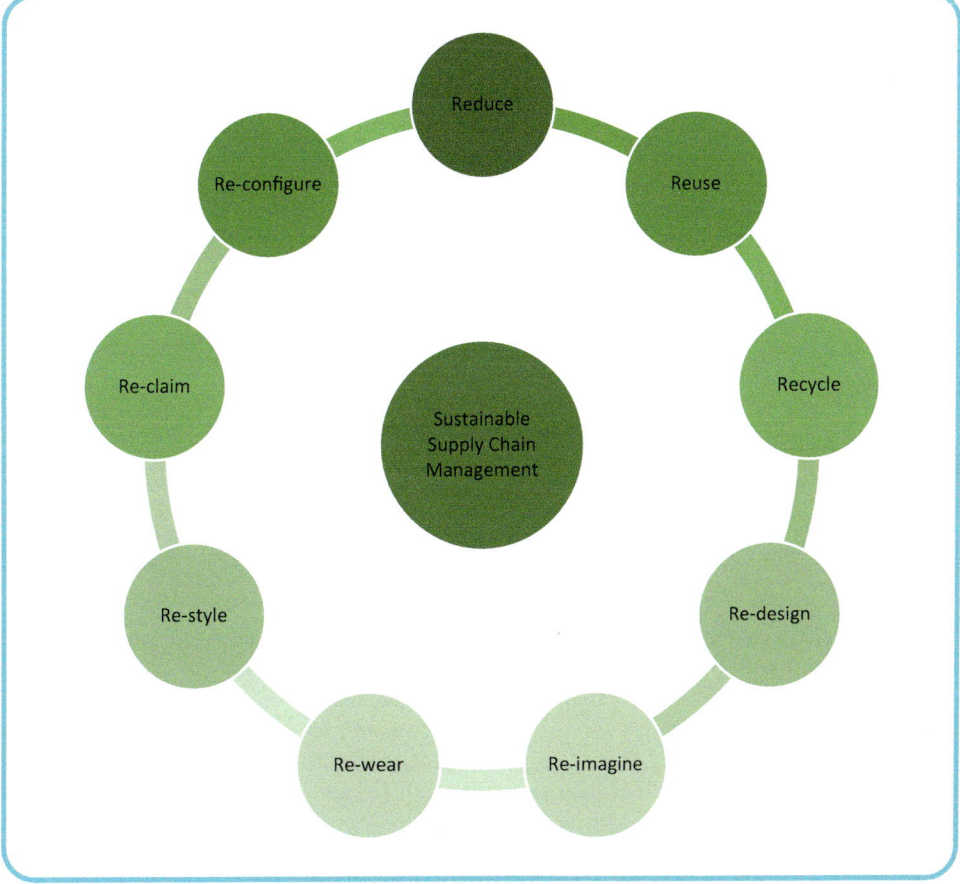

Figure 1.2.2   Sustainable supply chain management – the 9R model

you may also come across the terms up-cycling – which implies making something new out of something you may already have (e.g., a skirt out of a pair of jeans) – or downcycling. Examples of downcycling are shredding garments and using the resulting product either to stuff mattresses or as part of insulation material.

Upcycling leads us nicely into *reuse* as a practice. As indicated, recycling implies that a raw material is used in a new capacity by, for example, making fibres out of fabric before re-spinning them, or reusing waste products (e.g., scraps) and making something new out of them. On the other hand, upcycling is also part of reuse. Upcycling has gained a lot of attention in recent years and is part of the do-it-yourself (DIY) movement. An example of upcycling would be patching up an old T-shirt with embroidery to cover up a hole, or redecorating a garment to look different, whether this may involve cutting off some parts, sewing something else on or even making something new by, for example, designing a backpack out of a pair of jeans. If old garments can no longer be upcycled or recycled we can also repurpose them by creating, say, macrame potholders out of T-shirts or crocheting a bathmat out of old fabric stripes. However, the reuse aspect implies a certain level of skill and imagination, which some sources have claimed are increasingly getting lost within society, yet may be on the rise again through the DIY movement.

The third aspect in the 9R framework is *re-design*, which can be linked to quite creative processes. Re-design implies that companies focus less on trends and more on items being timeless. Some organisations have taken the re-design approach even further by creating items of clothing that can be either reassembled to meet new needs (e.g., Fragments Garments) or used in multiple different ways (e.g., Versalette).

Fragments Garments, for example, designs clothing that can be assembled in a jigsaw-like manner, which implies that items can be easily changed from a long-sleeved jacket to an evening dress (Jayot, 2019). The company highlights that "We conceive [a] garment as an **'open object'** with **reusable spare parts**, just like your car. … All the **products & services** we create are **made to evolve** & we want **you to be part of it**" (Fragments Garments, 2019). Thus, rather than having to purchase a totally new garment, parts of the garment can be used in new pieces without sewing and/or ripping seams open. A possible challenge may be consumer buy-in, in that consumers may not want to take responsibility for re-assembling their own garments and/or may have a different taste, in that the unique forms of the garments – which are a result of the design process – might be seen as too avant-garde.

Similarly, *Versalette by {r}evolution Apparel* provides a different approach to fashion. The Versalette is a piece designed for travellers that can be worn in 30 different ways, either as a T-shirt, scarf, top, blouse, or accessory bag, and thus uses less space (Revapparel, 2012). Yet a key challenge here could be that a "one size fits all" approach may not necessarily work as we all have different body shapes, and what looks fantastic on one person may not suit another.

This latter aspect of possessing less whilst still having more options links also to *reduce*. To explain, a company can reduce the waste it produces by utilising different techniques when cutting patterns, which is also referred to as "nesting". Multiple pattern pieces can be skilfully arranged in a variety of sizes that allow maximisation of fabric use. Returning to an earlier statement, reduce can also imply simply producing less. Media have reported unsold stock being burned (e.g. Dalton, 2018; Siegle, 2018), which is not only ethically questionable, but also reveals that companies may overestimate the amount of garments that are being sold.

A further way of thinking about *reduce* is within the supply chain and across processes. Streamlining processes, and thus cutting out any unnecessary steps, forms the baseline for introducing new systems, such as environmental management systems (EMS) (e.g., ISO14001 series, EMAS, BS8555). EMS are systems that are often implemented to enhance the corporate "greening process", and are voluntary, company-level initiatives that are similar to eco-labels/certifications accredited by third parties (Bansal & Roth, 2000; Boiral et al., 2015). Exploring this further, companies can set themselves targets to reduce certain aspects, such as waste (e.g., raw materials, recycling, CO_2), thereby creating lean operational processes (WRAP, 2015). As such, reduce is not simply associated with the product itself, but could also take a wider angle, in that it can be linked to reducing the company's impact along the supply chain and its operational processes.

Re-imagine provides an opportunity for organisations to build stronger relationships with others through collaborations and ultimately value co-creation. Value co-creation "stands for a notion of modern corporate power that … [is] working with and through the freedom of the consumer" (Zwick et al., 2008: 163). Ultimately, it implies that there is greater stakeholder engagement, and rather than dictating in a top-down approach what may be produced, consumers and other stakeholders are more actively engaged in the dialogue (Prahalad and Ramaswamy, 2000; Ballantyne, 2004; Payne et al., 2008). Examples of re-imagining how the industry is working can be seen in increased collaborations between fashion retailers and rental companies, not only enabling consumers to access items they may otherwise not have been able to afford and/or wanted to invest in, but also making use of idle capacities, and thus reducing waste. Customisations are another example. With consumers being able to change colour palettes or making items more personalised, they will also see more value, and thus gain something from the process (e.g., social status, self-confidence). This again leads to a win–win situation, as consumers may be willing to use these customised items for longer.

In line with re-imagine, *re-wear* encourages us to think about extending the life cycle of a garment by, for example, offering take-back schemes, introducing secondhand lines, and more generally diverting garments from landfill. Thus, the life cycle of a garment focuses on the "acquisition, use, and end-of-life phases" of the product and how these may be extended by keeping garments out of landfill (Vladimirova et al., 2021).

The company Patagonia has created a *Worn Wear* section on its website, emphasising that "the best thing we can do for the planet is cut down on consumption and get more use out of stuff we already own" (Worn Wear, 2021). Similarly, *Filippa K* has previously introduced a secondhand section in its physical stores, which not only allowed the brand to extend the life of its garments, but also ensured quality control – an aspect that is vital for fashion companies (Filippa K, 2021). You may ask yourself why not all companies offer a resale section in-store or online, as this may be one way to clearly demonstrate commitment to sustainability, and more specifically *re-wear*. One explanation as to why this is not happening on a mainstream basis could be logistics, in that secondhand garments would not only need to be cleaned, but also checked to see whether they still comply with quality standards. For a brand, it is vital to uphold its promise to its consumers, so whether they buy first- or secondhand from a brand does not matter, as consumers will expect the same quality. For a company, this would mean a big financial commitment, and depending on its size, this may not be possible. Moreover, if we think about space and location, offering a secondhand range in a physical shop or online will require storing these items somewhere. With rents, especially in city centre locations, being rather high, renting additional space may again not be feasible.

We can further link this to the management decision-making process and also assessing the external environment. In 2020, we had the COVID-19 outbreak, a global pandemic, which has further enhanced concerns about secondhand consumption and hygiene, as the perceived risk and fear of contracting the virus through secondhand garments has been enhanced. Thus, managers need to ask themselves various questions as to whether selling secondhand is: (1) financially viable, (2) possible in terms of logistics, and/or (3) advisable, as any negative press can ruin brand perceptions and reputation.

Re-style is closely linked to re-imagine, in that it focuses on the proverbial "thinking outside the box". Re-style, however goes further, as it also includes services and additional experiences by, for example, including styling workshops, personal recommendations, and/or tips and hints on how to wear certain outfits. During the COVID-19 pandemic, a lot of online platforms that were previously focused on renting and/or swapping clothing have transformed into more community-based sites, providing blogs and comments on how to wear certain outfits. An example here is *ByRotation* (2021), which has initiated Instagram live sessions and increased blog posts, which has benefited it tremendously as its listings have increased by 50 per cent (Banks-Walker & Graddon, 2020).

With increased pressure from stakeholders as well as the implementation of the SDGs, *re-claim* focuses on utilising factory waste, which is often created at the pre-consumer stage in the production process, as well as capitalising on heritage aspects. A company which has been popular on podcasts is *Fabscrap*. Fabscrap is New York city-based and seeks to divert pre-consumer waste away from landfill by offering organisations the facility to drop off their fabric scraps and other materials and/or unwanted prototype collections at Fabscrap's premises, where it carefully sorts through the materials and either resells, downcycles, or recycles the resulting materials (Fabscrap, 2021). It could be said that Fabscrap acts as an intermediary between fashion companies and consumers, as the latter can purchase pieces of fabric for their own use, whilst at the same time Fabscrap is "educating and empowering a diverse COMMUNITY of change-makers" (Fabscrap, 2021).

Re-configure alludes to changes that have happened in more recent years, with fast fashion becoming increasingly a mainstream phenomenon. Whilst previously fashion companies may have had long-term relationships with their suppliers, in the current volatile market environment, value for money has become a key concern, whereby costs are often pushed down and corners cut. Thus, *re-configure* suggests reverting back to key values of building long-term relationships and ensuring that all aspects surrounding sustainability are considered.

What might become apparent here is that the 9R model strongly relates to environmental aspects within the sustainability remit, which could be one of the criticisms that might be levelled at it. Yet it is a useful tool to start thinking about what can be changed and how within an organisation to reduce its overall impact. Since the UN has called for action on its SDGs, it might be useful to also understand how the 9R model may relate to some of the SDGs, which is summarised in Table 1.2.2. It must be highlighted that these are merely suggestions, and not exhaustive. You will be able to come back to these Rs in a slightly different form in **Part 2: Managing Sustainable Fashion through Design**, which encourages you to consider these sustainable strategies within a design thinking process.

Table 1.2.2   The 9R Model and the SDGs

SDG	Title	Description	9R model
12	Responsible Consumption and Production	**Responsible Consumption** • Seeks to empower consumers to make informed choices **Responsible Production** • Focuses on how things are being produced by looking at methods that have the least negative impact on the social and natural environment • Has the potential to counteract climate, biodiversity, and pollution crises	Links to all aspects of the 9R model
1	No Poverty	Poverty should be made extinct	• Links to *re-configure* by focusing on building long-term relationships and ensuring that working conditions are fair
3	Good Health and Well-being	Everyone involved has the right of a healthy life and their well-being should be secured	• *Re-imagine* could be linked here, with the emphasis on fostering a community spirit, which could enhance well-being by providing reassurance to consumers
6	Clean Water and Sanitation	• Water should be free from toxins and any other harmful substances • Sanitation to be provided for all	• Links to the entirety of the 9R model, as the main goal is to utilise resources that are already in existence whilst time reducing waste
13	Climate Action	• The world is in a climate crisis, which implies that action needs to be taken to combat it and change current practices	• With a focus on *reducing* the impact overall, the entirety of the 9R model can have an impact on climate action and foster this
15	Life on Land	• Focuses on life on land and the use of the natural ecosystem	• With less resources being used and resources being used more efficiently, there can be links between all the 9Rs

Task

1. Thinking about various fashion companies you may know, critically evaluate, and justify, what type of strategy they may be using.
2. Looking at the 9R framework, what external and internal factors could impact on each of the individual Rs and thus provide new opportunities or challenges for a fashion company.

1.2.2 Issues in the fashion industry surrounding sustainable fashion

As previously indicated and reflected in the 9R framework (Henninger et al., 2015), environmental sustainability and reducing the overall impact an organisation may have on the natural environment can be challenging, yet these challenges can also act as driving forces, as alluded to in the 9R framework. In Section 1.1.3, we discussed what sustainability means – and as a short reminder, we looked at the triple bottom line (Elkington, 2008), which highlights that environmental factors are not the only challenges a fashion company may face, as there are also social and economic issues.

We can now return to questions asked in previous sections as to why companies may not be acting faster to respond to these sustainability challenges and make the necessary changes. What might seem like an easy task is, however, complex. Think back to how sustainability, and more specifically sustainable fashion, are defined. This is where the challenge starts, as there is no such thing as "sustainable fashion" in the sense of a clearly defined type of garment, but rather it can encompass a variety of different processes, from the choice of raw materials to purchasing second-hand to transferring ownership to simply accessing garments (e.g., Henninger et al., 2021). On top of managers needing to make decisions as to what type of garments and/or sustainability strategy is implemented within an organisation, we need to remember that fashion organisations do not operate in a vacuum. Consumers especially have a lot of power, which can also create a problem. We have reached a proverbial "chicken and egg" question, in that even though consumers may want to be more sustainable and demand more sustainable fashion, they are also accustomed to seeing new items in-store and/or online on a fortnightly basis (BSR, 2012; Pasquinelli, 2012).

Whilst crises such as the 2008 stock market collapse or COVID-19 may have brought about short-term changes as physical stores (perhaps temporarily) ceased operations and supply chains were disrupted, we may soon see consumers returning to their old habits (Bourke, 2021). It could be suggested that organisations are simply reducing their fashion cycles and reverting to pre-fast fashion times, yet this may have business implications that may be felt along the supply chain, especially by the most vulnerable – garment workers.

So what are key issues that have been discussed in the context of the fashion industry? And how can these be addressed? To address these questions, we can use the triple bottom line as a guide.

Social

Social issues are associated with humans and animals and their rights to safe working conditions, fair pay in the case of humans, and humane treatment. We have already heard that supply chains are complex and often span multiple countries and even continents. This has historical reasons, and can be traced back to the Industrial Revolution. With countries becoming increasingly industrialised, not only have people had more employment opportunities, but also the general standard of living has changed, in that skill sets have increased and thus labour costs have risen. This has led to organisations looking for opportunities to produce garments outside their home countries, in locations that still have lower labour costs. You may have heard of offshoring and nearshoring, which are key related terms. To explain: at the peak of the Industrial Revolution, companies started looking to move to either surrounding countries (nearshoring) or further afield (offshoring) (Bock, 2008; Boardman et al., 2020). Nearshoring is a common practice, with companies from Western Europe often having garments produced in Eastern European countries, including Romania, Bulgaria, and Croatia, but also Turkey (ILO, 1996; Barrie, 2014), whilst companies based in the USA often branch out to Mexico, El Salvador, and Honduras (e.g., Shannon, 2017; McKinsey, 2020).

> **Nearshoring** – producing garments/accessories in neighbouring countries that may still have lower wages compared to the home country.
> **Offshoring** – producing garments/accessories in countries that are geographically more distant.

Issues surrounding labour costs are still debated to date, especially living wages, as well as ethical concerns related to working conditions (e.g., Brydges & Hanlon, 2020). It may be a good opportunity here to ask yourself how you, as a manager, would act and what could be seen as "right" or "wrong". Should people along your supply chain be paid the same as they are in the country the company has originated from and/or where it is registered? Should the measures be adhered to in the same manner as in the home country? We have previously heard that supranational organisations may impose certain regulations, in terms of chemicals that can or cannot be used within certain types of garments if they are to be awarded a safety standard. Yet this standard may not exist in the host country that produces our garments. These questions and considerations can be heavily debated and may also act as conversation starters when looking at ethical theories. Whilst beyond the scope of this book, you may want to refer to ethical theories to learn more about these dilemmas that can be faced.

What is clear and within the scope of this book, however, is that managers need to be able to justify their decisions and actively try to counteract these challenges. Within the fashion industry, we see more and more companies implementing corporate social responsibility policies. CSR is defined as "a concept whereby companies integrate social and environmental concerns in their business operations and in their interaction with stakeholders on a voluntary basis" (EC, 2002: p.5). Thus, the aim is not only to be economically viable, but to ensure that social and environmental issues are addressed (Henninger and Oates, 2018). There are some very interesting examples of how companies have implemented these CSR policies. *Toms Shoes* (2016), for example, created the "One For One" campaign, where it promoted that it would provide a free pair of shoes to a child in need for every purchase of a pair of its shoes. This has since shifted slightly, whereby the company interprets the "One for One" campaign in looser terms, and instead of providing shoes, the company donates money to restore sight, provide safe water, promote bullying prevention campaigns, and other causes (Mau, 2019). Similarly, *People Tree* is promoting its CSR message by having created the People Tree Foundation, which "will bring benefits to an even greater number of farmers and artisans through scaling up training, technical support and environmental initiatives as through raising awareness and campaigning for fair and sustainable fashion" (People Tree, 2021b).

> **Corporate social responsibility (CSR)** – is a voluntary strategy whereby companies integrate environmental and social aspects into all aspects of their operations and within interactions with stakeholders.

Although companies have different strategies, the main message of doing good for the community and supporting those in need – whether they are garment workers, their families, or society in general terms – remains the same.

If we look at the root cause of social issues, most of them can probably be linked back to financial considerations and the fact that garments now are classified as cheap. You may think that the obvious solution could and should be to simply increase prices. Yet this can have unfortunate implications: if costs increase and/or fewer garments are produced, garment workers may be affected, who are often heavily reliant on the income, however low it may be. Similarly, not all consumers are able to afford garments that could be seen as higher-priced, with "higher" here being very much a subjective criterion. One of the reasons why fast fashion has taken off and was created in the first place was to make fashion accessible to everyone, no matter their social standing and/or income. From a company perspective, making fashion accessible means having a bigger target market, whilst consumers can show they belong to certain social groups and may not feel alienated (e.g., Boardman et al., 2020). As such, fashion companies are walking a thin line between selling affordable garments while not cutting corners that may have negative implications, especially for those who are already seen as vulnerable (Brydges and Hanlon, 2020).

Environmental

As outlined in Section 1.2.1, through the application of the 9R framework there are various environmental issues that can be overcome by reducing waste, not only within an organisation, but also along the supply chain. More recently, we have seen other issues emerge, such as microfibre or microplastic pollution. As you will see in **Part 4: Material Innovations in Sustainable Fashion**, there are multiple different fibres available to companies – some are natural, others are man-made and/or synthetic. No matter what type of fibre we are using, all of them will inevitably shed fibres, but the ones that have been discussed the most in the news are those from synthetic garments, often made from plastics (e.g., nylon, polyester, elastane, acryl) (RSA, 2021). Each time consumers wear garments and/or wash them, a certain amount of microfibres are released, which often end up in the wastewater system, and ultimately in the oceans (Yan et al., 2020a). Although there are some solutions that can catch these microfibres, such as the Cora Ball, the Guppyfriend Bag, or the Lint LUV-R filter, there are still challenges with how the microfibres that have been caught can be disposed of (Yan et al., 2020b; Kärkkäinen and Sillanpää, 2021). One of the key dilemmas that managers may face here again links back to the decision-making process.

Synthetic fibres currently dominate the market (see **Part 4: Material Innovations in Sustainable Fashion**), and are also often associated with lower costs compared to other fibres and can provide valuable performance advantages (Henry et al., 2019), including aspects such as being fast drying, having anti-crease properties, and being lightweight. Although there are obvious issues with microfibre shedding and use of petroleum raw materials, compared to some natural fibres they overcome other challenges, such as ethical issues (e.g., angora or silk production), as well as other environmental concerns, including the use of pesticides and water consumption (e.g., cotton) (Henninger et al., 2017).

As indicated, the TBL focuses on three aspects, and the economic angle is often not as explicitly discussed, yet links very closely with the environmental angle. Companies need to make profits to be financially viable and able to continue with their operations. Whilst environmental considerations, such as microfibre pollution and ethical concerns of raw materials, will influence some of the decisions that are made, as managers we still need to ensure that our company is profitable. One way of looking at the issue and addressing it is by turning to key performance indicators (Slack et al., 2009): quality, speed, dependability, flexibility, and cost.

Quality is associated with the material and whether it is fit for purpose. A lot of sports and athleisure wear uses plastic fibres, as these dry quickly and are durable (Yan et al., 2020a). Yet these garments could also be produced using merino wool or cool wool, which show similar performance properties but may be more expensive. *Speed* focuses on how quickly finished products can be delivered, whether to the end-consumer or more loosely interpreted as getting the raw materials. *Dependability* relates to the organisational processes, in that it focuses on whether the company can deliver on time. *Flexibility* refers to the ability to change, whilst *cost* focuses on financial aspects, such as price points. Figure 1.2.3 shows a visualisation of the five key performance indicators, which can be compared and contrasted between different companies (Figure 1.2.4).

Returning to the issue of microfibre pollution and/or using less environmentally damaging raw materials, managers can focus on these performance indicators and weigh their options in terms of, for example, quality: which raw materials can be compared with each other? They may also look at costs: how much more would the company have to pay, if it was to switch? As managers, we are of course interested in creating a competitive advantage, so we will be looking at what other organisations are doing, and how ours compares. For example, recently there has been increased awareness raising of brands using ocean plastics in their production processes (e.g., Parley For The Oceans x Adidas, 2021; Waterhaul, 2021; Fair Harbour, 2021).

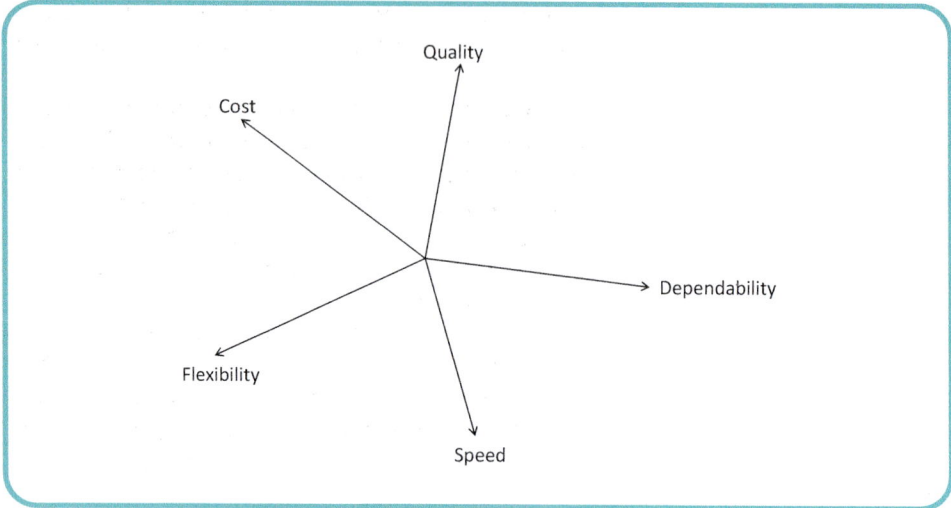

Figure 1.2.3   Performance indicators (adapted from Slack et al., 2009)

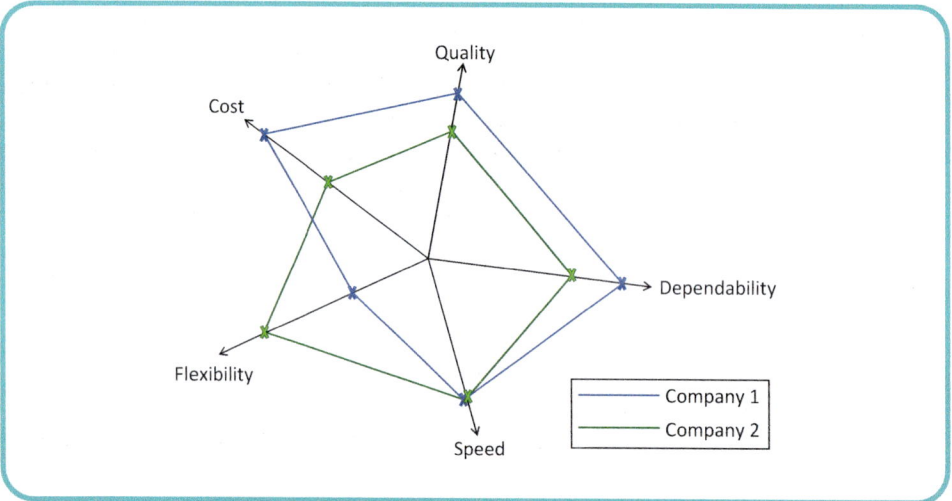

Figure 1.2.4   Example of applied performance indicators (adapted from Slack et al., 2009)

Economic

Economic aspects are associated with monetary gains, and thus being profitable. One of the key issues here can be linked to the fast fashion phenomenon, in that fast fashion items are not only associated with cheap prices, but also often low quality, and thus disposability. Whilst bulk production may have financially attractive qualities – the more that is bought, the less it costs – it can have environmental implications. Fast stock turnaround and producing large quantities of garments implies that items that are slow sellers may have to be discounted to move this surplus stock. Yet recent media reports have indicated that some organisations that were unable to sell their stock have burned excess inventory, which has been – unsurprisingly – heavily criticised (e.g. Dalton, 2018; Siegle, 2018).

Coming back to the aspect of cost, and the fact that T-shirts are sold for prices as low as £2, we may ask ourselves whether this can have social and environmental implications. The deflation of prices can mean cutting corners, to push costs down on the production side, which makes it questionable whether SDG 12 (Responsible Production and Consumption) can be adhered to. Moreover, consumers are educated to expect cheap clothes that are also seen to be easily replaceable. As a result, reports have highlighted that on average garments are worn three to seven times, before being discarded (Pithers, 2015; Šajn, 2019). This leads to one of the other issues faced by the fashion industry: waste. It is estimated that not only does it take more than 200 years for garments to decompose (if at all) (Close The Loop, 2020), but also that the actual worth of these discarded clothes is over US$500 billion annually (EMF, 2017). Some of the key reasons why companies are not capitalising on this waste and reusing it could be (1) lack of infrastructure or (2) lack of technology. The latter aspect refers to challenges of, for example, recycling mixed fibres, or having facilities to sort through garments (e.g., WRAP, 2020).

To summarise this section, what becomes apparent that it may not always be easy to clearly divide social, environmental, and economic issues as, in line with the TBL, these are very much interlinked. Some of the challenges faced by the fashion industry could be classified as being "homemade", in that the ever-increasing urge to produce more garments at cheaper prices comes at a cost. Because the fashion industry is a volatile market environment, staying competitive is vital, so not all companies may feel they are able to make drastic changes, as this could lead to consumers switching to their competitors, and in a worst-case scenario, they may have to cease operations.

Task

1. Focusing on current media and/or industry reports, what are key issues in the fashion industry, and how can they be addressed?
2. Why may it be challenging to implement changes in the fashion industry to address sustainable issues?

1.2.3 Case study: understanding sustainability and value – the example of We Are Knitters

Intended learning outcomes

After working through the case study, students will be able to:

*   Critically reflect on the social aspects of sustainability.
*   Explore the role of the consumer through the lens of a buyer.
*   Examine whether "do-it-yourself" can be a driver for sustainable consumption.

Introduction

As highlighted, sustainability is commonly defined as meeting current generations' needs, whilst at the same time ensuring that future ones have the possibility to also meet theirs (WCED, 1987). Sustainability is often divided into three areas, commonly defined as environmental, social, and economic, or alternatively, *People*, *Planet*, and *Profit* (Elkington, 1994).

The social aspect has received a lot of attention over the past decade, fuelled by negative media reporting of factory accidents such as Rana Plaza, among the most dramatic in history (Safi and Rushe, 2018), labour law violations, including modern slavery allegations (de Ferrer, 2020), and health and safety shortcomings. The latter have been magnified during the global COVID-19 pandemic (Fashion Revolution, 2020). Whilst companies are actively trying to counteract negative media coverage by reinforcing their corporate social responsibility commitments, they are also facing challenges due to supply chains often being complex and spanning across the globe.

More recently, we have seen the emergence of companies that enable consumers to get a better understanding of social responsibility by providing customers with an opportunity to make their own garments.

We Are Knitters

We Are Knitters (WAK) seeks to "change the world one stitch at a time" (WAK, 2021a) by providing individuals with an opportunity to knit or crochet their very own garments. The kits offered on the WAK website cater for all abilities, whether complete beginners or advanced knitters, with dedicated tutorial support, a WAK Friends community, and Instagram knitalong takeovers. The company is committed to sustainability by actively seeking to promote the slow fashion movement. WAK's promise is that "you can be sure everything on your needle is of the best quality" (WAK, 2021a) (Figure 1.2.5).

Following DIY principles, WAK is posing key questions by inspiring a younger generation to (re-)learn valuable handicraft skills (e.g., knitting, crocheting). To expand on this, WAK seeks to encourage its WAK Friends to think:

> if knitting your own sweater takes you more than a week and costs more than $90, how can other brands produce them in less than one day for under $20? We encourage everyone to think about the labour, costs, and production processes that we're supporting. By doing this, we have an opportunity to reduce pollution and our impact on the environment.
>
> (WAK, 2021b)

WAK's ethos is not only reflected through the DIY principles, but also further fostered by having committed to be part of various eco-labelling schemes. Eco-labels are third-party certifications that verify that products are, for example, made from recycled materials (e.g. the Recycled Claim Standard) or have been produced in accordance with Fairtrade (e.g. Peru Fairtrade). Consumers have an opportunity here to take on the role of a buyer by sourcing their own materials, reading up on their performance

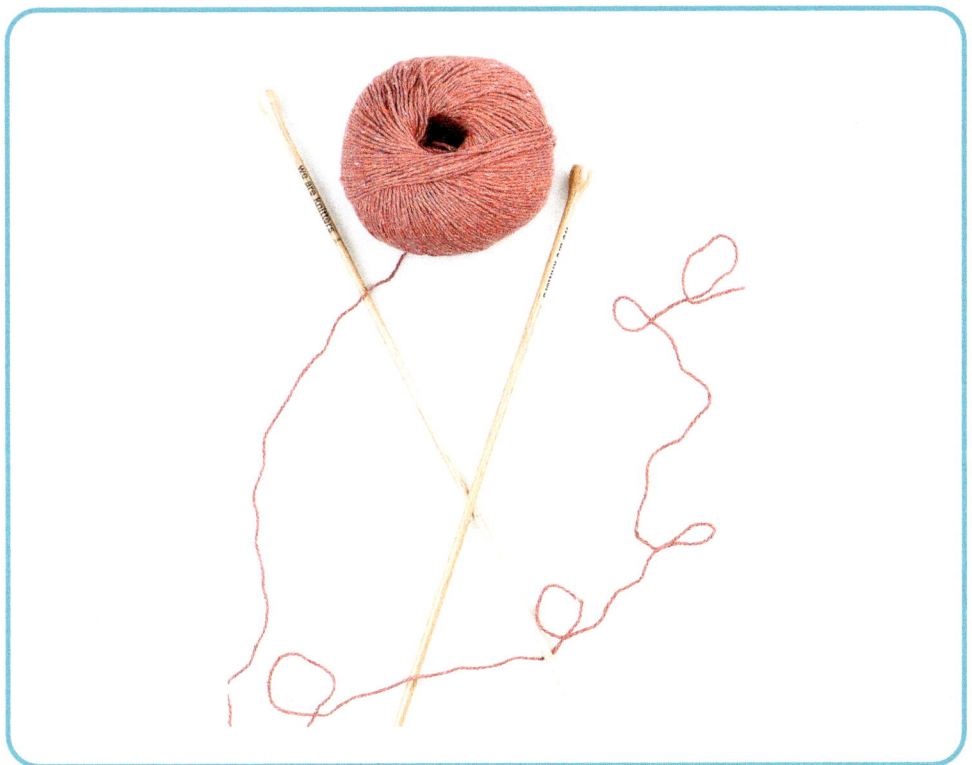

Figure 1.2.5   We Are Knitters – recycled wine-coloured yarn (© We Are Knitters)

properties and environmental benefits, and making their own decisions on what is best for them. WAK offers a variety of yarns that are all made from natural materials, with some giving a second life to materials, such as the Recycled Yarn or The Tape (WAK, 2021b) (Figure 1.2.5).

Questions

1. The social aspect, or *People* part, of sustainability focuses on issues surrounding health and safety concerns, human welfare, and fair wages. Why may participants think differently about social sustainability once they have engaged in crafting their own garments?
2. Examine current practices WAK is engaging in that fall within the wider remit of sustainability. What other opportunities could WAK engage in?
3. Explore the decision-making process of consumers when deciding to create their own garments. How does this process differ (or not) from decisions that may need to be made in an organisation?
4. Thinking about the materials and packaging provided by WAK, how could this drive consumers towards more sustainable consumption practices?

Case study references

De Ferrer, M. (2020) *Inside the Leicester sweatshops accused of modern slavery*, Euro News (online): https://www.euronews.com/green/2020/07/09/inside-the-leicester-sweatshops-accused-of-modern-slavery, 10/06/2021.

Elkington, J. (1994) Towards the sustainability corporation: win-win-win business strategies for sustainable development, *California Management Review*, Winter, pp. 90–100.

Fashion Revolution (2020) *The impact of COVID-19 on the people who make our clothes*, Fashion Revolution (online): https://www.fashionrevolution.org/the-impact-of-covid-19-on-the-people-who-make-our-clothes/, 10/06/2021.

Safi, M., and Rushe, D. (2018) *Rana Plaza, five years on*, The Guardian (online): https://www.theguardian.com/global-development/2018/apr/24/bangladeshi-police-target-garment-workers-union-rana-plaza-five-years-on, 10/06/2021.

WAK (We Are Knitters) (2021a) *We're all about knitting*, WAK (online): https://www.weareknitters.co.uk/about-us, 10/06/2021.

WAK (We Are Knitters) (2021b) *Slow fashion*, WAK (online): https://www.weareknitters.co.uk/sustainability, 10/06/2021.

WCED (1987) *Our common future (The Brundtland report)*, World Commission on Environment and Development, Oxford University Press, Oxford, UK.

References

Adidas (2021) *Run for the oceans*, Adidas (online): https://www.adidas.com/us/runfortheoceans, 14/09/2021.

Ballantyne, D. (2004) Dialogue and its role in the development of relationship specific knowledge, *Journal of Business and Industrial Marketing*, 19(2), 114–123.

Banks-Walker, H., and Graddon, F. (2020, December 31) *2021's biggest trend is set to be renting your wardrobe*, Grazia Daily. https://graziadaily.co.uk/fashion/how-to/sustainability-clothes-rental-services/, 14/09/2021.

Bansal, P., and Roth, K. (2000) Why companies go green: a model of ecological responsiveness, *Academy of Management Journal*, 43(4), 717–736.

Barrie, L. (2014) *Eastern Europe a 'cheap labour sewing backyard'*, Just-Style (online): https://www.just-style.com/analysis/eastern-europe-a-cheap-labour-sewing-backyard_id122003.aspx, 05/06/2020.

BCorp (2021) *Certified B Corporation*, BCorp (online): https://bcorporation.net, 06/08/2021.

Biron, B. (2016) *What's old is green: TopShop offers latest recycled fashion line*, Glossy (online): https://www.glossy.co/sincerity-sustainability/whats-old-is-green-topshop-offers-latest-recycled-fashion-line/, 03/08/2021.

Boardman, R., Parker Strak, R., and Henninger, C.E. (2020) *Fashion buying & merchandising in the 21st century*, Routledge, Abington, UK.

Bock, S. (2008) Supporting offshoring and nearshoring decisions for mass customization manufacturing processes, *European Journal of Operational Research*, 184, 490–508.

Boiral, O., Talbot, D., and Paillé, P. (2015) Leading by example: a model of organizational citizenship behaviour for the environment, *Business Strategy and the Environment*, 24, 532–550.

Bourke, J. (2021) *The Primarni army: huge queues at Primark as unlocked UK hits the high street*, Standard (online): https://www.standard.co.uk/business/leisure-retail/london-lockdown-stores-reopening-april-12-primark-non-essential-b929263.html, 14/09/2021.

Brydges, T., and Hanlon, M. (2020) Garment worker rights and the fashion industry's response to COVID-19, *Dialogues in Human Geography*, 10(2), 195–198.

BSR (Business of a Better World) (2012) *Sustainable fashion design: oxymoron no more?*, BSR (online): http://www.bsr.org/reports/BSR_Sustainable_Fashion_Design.pdf, 05/07/2020.

ByRotation (2021) *Lend, rent, rotate*, ByRotation (online): https://www.byrotation.com.

Close the Loop (2020) *Introduction*, Close the Loop (online): https://www.close-the-loop.be/en/phase/3/end-of-life, 14/09/2021.

Dalton, M. (2018) *Why luxury brands burn their own goods*, The Wall Street Journal (online): https://www.wsj.com/articles/burning-luxury-goods-goes-out-of-style-at-burberry-1536238351, 31/07/2019.

EC (European Commission) (2002) *Corporate social responsibility: a business contribution to sustainable development*, COM (2002) 347 final, Brussels: Commission of the European Communities, Europa (online): http://eur-lex.europa.eu/LexUriServ/LexUriServ.do?uri=COM:2002:0347:FIN:en:PDF.

Elkington, J. (2008) *People, planet, profit*, John Elkington (online): http://www.johnelkington.com/journal/journal_entry.asp?id=25.

EMF (Ellen MacArthur Foundation) (2017) *A new textiles economy: redesigning fashion's future*, EMF (online): https://www.ellenmacarthurfoundation.org/assets/downloads/publications/A-New-Textiles-Economy_Full-Report_Updated_1-12-17.pdf, 14/09/2021.

Europa (2021) *Corporate sustainability reporting*, Europa (online): https://ec.europa.eu/info/business-economy-euro/company-reporting-and-auditing/company-reporting/corporate-sustainability-reporting_en, 19/07/2021.

Fabscrap (2021) *About us*, Fabscrap (online): https://fabscrap.org, 03/09/2021.

Fair Harbor (2021) *Science made simple how plastic is turned into polyester*, Fair Harbor (online): https://www.fairharborclothing.com/blogs/news/science-made-simple-how-plastic-is-turned-into-polyester, 14/09/2021.

FairTrade (n.d.) *The Fairtrade mark*, FairTrade (online): https://www.fairtrade.net/about/fairtrade-marks, 06/08/2021.

Filippa K (2021) *Filippa K second hand*, Filippa K (online): https://www.filippaksecondhand.se/english, 03/09/2021.

Fragments Garments (2019) *Fashion digital crafts*, Fragments Garments (online): https://www.fragmentsgarments.com/, 21/01/2021.

GOTS (2021) *The standard*, GOTS (online): https://global-standard.org/the-standard, 06/08/2021.

Henninger, C.E. (2015) Traceability the new eco-label in the slow-fashion industry? – Consumer perceptions and micro-organisations responses, *Sustainability*, 7, 6011–6032.

Henninger, C. E., and Oates, C. J. (2018) The role of social media in communicating CSR within fashion micro-organizations, in Lindgreen, A., Vanhamme, J., Maon, F., and Mardon, R. (eds) *Communicating corporate social responsibility in the digital era*. Farnham, Gower, Chapter 4.3, pp. 232–244.

Henninger, C.E., Alevizou, P. J., Oates, C.J., and Cheng, R. (2015) Slow-fashion organisations – Communicating sustainable consumption, in Genus, A. (ed.), *Sustainable consumption: design, innovation and practice*. Springer, Heidelberg, Chapter 7, pp. 129–154.

Henninger, C.E., Alevizou, P.J., Goworek, H., and Ryding, D. (eds.) (2017) *Sustainability in fashion: a cradle to upcycle approach*, Springer, Heidelberg.

Henry, B., Laitala, K., and Klepp, I.G. (2019) Microfibres from apparel and home textiles: prospects for including microplastics in environmental sustainability assessment, *Science of the Total Environment*, 652, 483–494.

Ho, H.P.-Y., and Choi, T.-M. (2012) A Five-R analysis for sustainable fashion supply chain management in Hong Kong: a case analysis, *Journal of Fashion Marketing*, 16(2), 161–175.

ILO (International Labour Organization) (1996) *Globalization changes the face of the textile, clothing and footwear industries*, ILO (online): https://www.ilo.org/global/about-the-ilo/newsroom/news/WCMS_008075/lang--en/index.htm, 05/06/20.

Jayot, E. (2019) A designer contribution to the use of CNC machines within the supply chain in order to extend clothing life span, in Vignali, G., Reid, L., Ryding, D., and Henninger, C.E. (eds.), *Technology-driven sustainability: innovation in the fashion supply chain*, Palgrave, London, pp. 27–55.

Kärkkäinen, N., and Sillanpää, M. (2021) Quantification of different microplastic fibers discharged from textiles in machine was and tumble drying, *Environmental Science & Pollution Research*, 28, 16253–16263.

Lambert, D.M., Croxton, K.L., Garc ćıa-Dastugue, S.J., Knemeyer, M., and Rogers, D.S. (2006) *Supply chain management processes, partnerships, performance* (2nd edn.), Hartley Press Inc., Jacksonville, FL.

Mau, D. (2019) *Toms shifts away from one for one, the giving model it originated*, Fashionista (online): https://fashionista.com /2019/11/toms-evolves-one-for-one-model, 14/09/2021.

McKinsey (2020) *The state of fashion 2020 – coronavirus update*, McKinsey (online): https://www.mckinsey.com/~/media/mckinsey /industries/retail/our%20insights/its%20time %20to%20rewire%20the%20fashion %20system%20state%20of%20fashion %20coronavirus%20update/the-state-of -fashion-2020-coronavirus-update-vf.ashx, 05/06/20.

Mentzer, J.T., DeWitt, W., Keebler, J.S., Min, S., Nix, N.W., Smith, C.D., and Zacharia, Z.G. (2002) Defining supply chain management, *Journal of Business Logistics*, 22(2), 1–25.

Oeko-Tex (2021) *Standard 100 by Oeko-tex*, Oeko-tex (online): https://www.oeko-tex.com /en/our-standards/standard-100-by-oeko-tex, 06/08/2021.

Pasquinelli, I. (2012) *Could small be the new big for the fashion industry?*, The Guardian (online): http://www.theguardian.com/ sustainable-business/blog/fashion-industry -trends-innovation-small-business, 25/01/21.

Payne, A.F., Storbacka, K., and Frow, P. (2008) Managing the co-creation of value, *Journal of the Academy of Marketing Science*, 36, 83–96.

People Tree (2021a) *Our story*, People Tree (online): https://www.peopletree.co.uk/about -us, 06/08/2021.

People Tree (2021b) *What is the People Tree Foundation?*, People Tree (online): https://

www.peopletree.co.uk/about-us/people-tree -foundation-, 14/09/2021.

Pithers, E. (2015) *Are you guilty of wearing things just once?*, Telegraph (online): https:// www.telegraph.co.uk/fashion/style/are-you -guilty-of-wearing-things-once/, 03/09/2018.

Positive Luxury (2021) *What is the butterfly mark?*, Positive Luxury (online): https:// www.positiveluxury.com/butterfly-mark/, 06/08/2021.

Prahalad, C.K., and Ramaswamy, V. (2000) Co-opting customer competence, *Harvard Business Review*, 78(1), 79–90.

Rauturier, S. (2020) *The ultimate guide to fair trade clothing brands*, Good On You (online): https://goodonyou.eco/best-fair-trade -brands/, 06/08/2021.

Revapparel (2012) *The Versalette by {r} evolution*, YouTube (online): https://www .youtube.com/watch?v=tGu8lOogDgl, 02/09/2021.

RSA (2021) *Fast fashion's plastic problem*, RSA (online): https://www.thersa.org/globalassets /reports/2021/fast-fashions-plastic-problem .pdf, 14/09/2021.

Šajn, N. (2019) *Environmental impact of the textile and clothing industry*, European Parliament (online): http://www.europarl .europa.eu/RegData/etudes/BRIE/2019/633143 /EPRS_BRI(2019)633143_EN.pdf, 18/07/2019.

Shannon, S. (2017) *Is 'nearshoring' the new offshoring?*, BoF (online): https://www .businessoffashion.com/articles/global -currents/is-nearshoring-the-new-offshoring, 05/06/20.

Siegle, L. (2018) *Destroying unsold clothes is fashion's dirty secret. And we're complicit*, Huffington Post (online): https://www .huffingtonpost.co.uk/entry/burberry-burn -clothes-fashion-industry-waste_n_5bad1ef 2e4b09d41eb9f7bb0?guccounter=1&guce_ referrer=aHR0cHM6Ly9jb25zZW50Lnlhac6G 9vLmNvbS9jb2xsZWN0Q29uc2VudD9zZXNza W9uSWQ9M19jYY1zZXNzaW9uXzc4NmU 4ZTgzLTIxZGEtNGGlwOC04ODE0LWQwMDE5ZD l3M2NlNCZsYW5nPWVuLXVzJmlubGGluZT1mY WxzZQ&guce_referrer_sig=AQAAAKR3rQqR lBUcGZ2E1K0afewGkx__njGShznzy2hk6lz q2a8oQW4RMzC2_j-l8DRwfNCq0je8p7AqE1 Pd4KABNJ4HeQpQdwg2A7PKewLii40DSDQ3n xYsgXDgkSQjqiuEaNAUywN6DZ9K6JOEbegM dAuEl06wnMMV48iJ7azi-nuQ, 31/07/2019.

Slack, N., Chambers, S., Johnston, R., and Betts A. (2009) *Operations and process management*, Prentice Hall, London.

Toms (2016) *One of one*, Toms (online): http://www.toms.co.uk, 14/09/2021.

United by Blue (2021) *Our story*, United by Blue (online): https://unitedbyblue.com/pages/our-story, 06/08/2021.

Vladimirova, K., Iran, S., Barber, J., Blazquez, M., Burcikova, M., Henninger, C.E., Johnson, E., Joyner Martinez, C., Laitala, K., Maldini, I., McNeil, L., Niinimaki, K., Onthank, K., Plonka, M., Sauerwein, M., and Wallaschkowski, S. (2021) *Conceptual framework for sustainable fashion consumption within the circular fashion system*, International Research Network on International Fashion Consumption (online): https://sustainablefashionconsumption.org/key-facts/, 01/09/2021.

Waterhaul (2021) *Our ocean plastic sunglasses*, Waterhaul (online): https://waterhaul.co, 14/09/2021.

Wells, V., Athwal, N., Nervino, E., and Carrigan, M. (2021) How legitimate are the environmental sustainability claims of luxury conglomerates?, *Journal of Fashion Marketing and Management*, 25(4), 697–722.

Worn Wear (2021) *Trade it in, get credit*, Worn Wear (online): https://wornwear.patagonia.com, 03/09/2021.

WRAP (2015) *Your guide to environmental management systems*, WRAP (online): http://www.wrap.org.uk/sites/files/wrap/WRAP%20EMS%20guide%20Mar2015.pdf, 21/05/2017.

WRAP (2020) *Changing our clothes: why the clothing sector should adopt new business models*, WRAP (online): https://www.wrap.org.uk/content/changing-our-clothes-why-clothing-sector-should-adopt-new-business-models?_ga=2.182743332.30533189.1593259255-1614214988.1593259255, 27/06/2020.

Yan, S., Jones, C., Henninger, C.E., and McCormick, H. (2020a) Textile industry insights towards impact of regenerated cellulosic and synthetic fibres on microfibre pollution, in Muthu, S.S., and Gardetti, M.A. (eds.), *Sustainability in the textile and apparel industry*, Springer, Cham, pp. 157–172.

Yan, S., Henninger, C.E., Jones, C., and McCormick, H. (2020b) Sustainable knowledge from consumer perspective addressing microfibre pollution, *Journal of Fashion Marketing & Management*, 24(3), 437–454.

Zwick, D., Bonsu, S.K., and Darmody, A. (2008) Putting consumers to work: 'co-creation' and new marketing governmentality, *Journal of Consumer Culture*, 8(2), 163–196.

Sustainable fashion
Consumer view

Learning outcomes

1. To evaluate what key considerations may be for consumers to engage with sustainable fashion.
2. To critically examine the attitude–behaviour gap.
3. To examine what new trends have emerged to foster sustainable fashion consumption.

By now, it will be apparent that sustainability in fashion is a vital concept for fashion brands and retailers, as they are trying to react to ever-increasing pressures not only from governmental and non-governmental organisations, suppliers, and employers, but also from consumers. This chapter focuses on consumers and their perceptions and attitudes towards sustainable fashion.

1.3.1 Sustainable fashion and consumer perceptions

As previously alluded to, fashion companies are not operating in isolation, but rather need to ensure that the supply and demand of products are ideally in equilibrium. Here you may find it beneficial to think about the supply–demand curve, as shown in Figure 1.3.1.

Figure 1.3.1 shows various scenarios in terms of a shift in supply. The green line labelled S is our baseline of supply, S2 highlights an increase in supply, whilst S1 portrays a decrease in supply. Think back to Section 1.1.1, which explored reasons why there may be changes in the supply side, by exploring the impact of the external environment, through conducting a PEST(EL) analysis.

The intersection between Q1 and P1 visualises the so-called price equilibrium. At this intersection, the company has met all the demand with the amount of product – here, garments – they have supplied. Shifts in the supply curve can mean that the price needs to change by either increasing it if the supply shifts upwards, or decreasing it if the supply line shows a downward shift. Why is this the case? If you have fewer products that you can supply to a market, you have an opportunity to increase the price, thus you may also reduce the demand for this product (Q2/P2). On the other hand, if you have a surplus of products, and thus a lot more supply than originally anticipated, you may need to lower the price to get more people to buy them.

Similar observations can also be made if the demand curve shifts upwards, which means that there may be a greater need to supply more products, which can be sold at

DOI: 10.4324/9781003097846-4

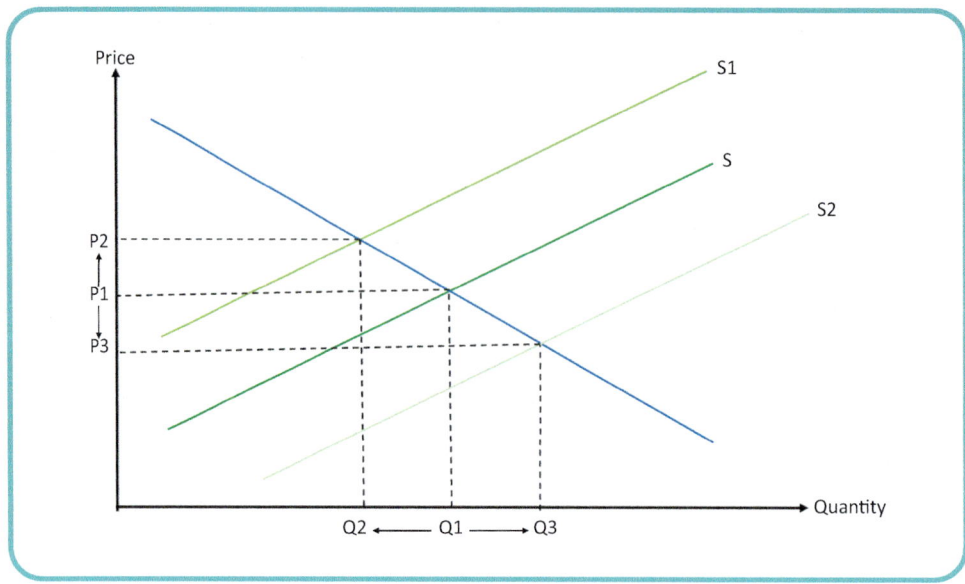

Figure 1.3.1   Supply curve (adapted from Britannica, 2021)

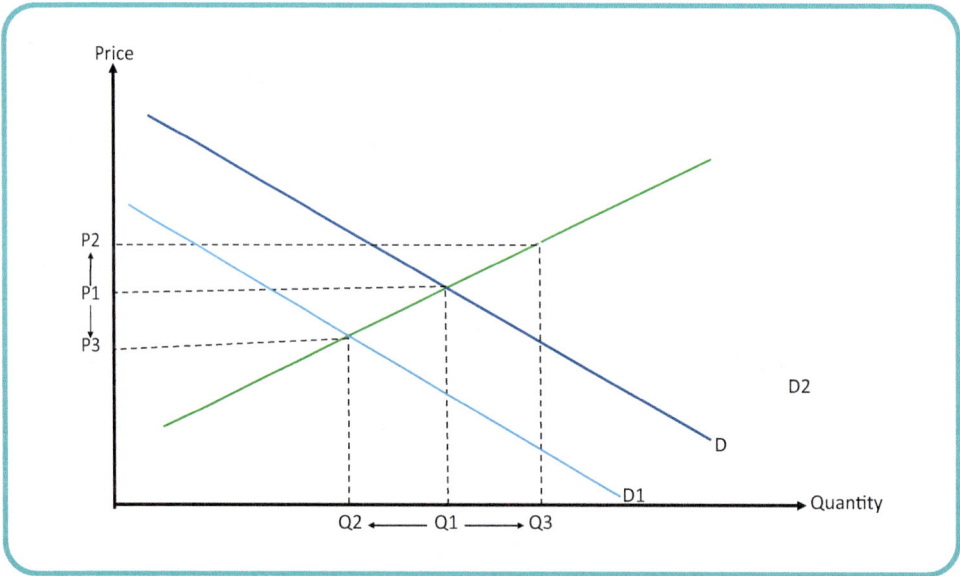

Figure 1.3.2   Demand curve (adapted from Britannica, 2021)

a higher price, whilst if the demand curve shifts downwards, there is a lack of demand for supplied products, so the price may need to be decreased (Figure 1.3.2).

You may ask yourself why the supply and demand curves are important when discussing consumer perceptions towards sustainable fashion. The answer is relatively simple: organisations need to anticipate how many products they may sell at a certain price, to understand how many of these products they need to produce (Boardman et al., 2020). Here it is useful to consider customer preferences, which can be used to predict whether products may be taken up by the market, and thus, whether companies may make a profit.

Consumer preference focuses on how likely it is that an individual purchases, in this case, a sustainable fashion product rather than a competing alternative one that is also available in the market. What must be pointed out here is that consumers' preferences may be rather subjective and can depend on their personal taste, their educational background, and their peer groups. In the past, sustainable fashion may have been negatively perceived (e.g., Henninger et al., 2016). For example, in the 1970s the politically oriented "hippie" movement was often associated with "green" or sustainable fashion, which alienated some consumer groups with different viewpoints. Thus, the demand for these types of garments may have been low.

> **Consumer preference** – provides an indication as to how likely consumers are to buy a product. This may be rather subjective, as it can depend on personal taste, education, peer groups, and preference.

Today the situation has changed, with consumers being increasingly aware of the social impacts of the fashion industry and the adverse effects it may have on the natural environment. In a recent survey of UK and German consumers, 88 per cent of those surveyed indicated that they believed the fashion industry should pay more attention to reducing its impact (Granskog et al., 2020). Pressure from consumers and other stakeholders have already led to various changes in the fashion industry. Whilst perhaps a decade ago it may have been rare to see recycled materials, organic labels, or upcycled clothing ranges in shops, this is increasingly more commonplace across the different fashion segments. For example, Primark sells various items that have recycled content, and has further launched a take-back scheme, "as part of our ongoing commitment to a more sustainable future" (Spragg, 2021). H&M has developed its "Conscious Collection", and Zara has created the "Join Life" project, which is "taking a holistic approach, integrating social and environmental sustainability and the health and safety of our products" (Zara, n.d.) into account. Section 1.4.4.1, "Zero Waste Fashion" will provide you with further examples of organisations that have created a more sustainable and or circular approach to fashion production.

Although we have seen an increase in offerings of sustainable fashion products, the attitude–behaviour gap remains a key challenge. The attitude–behaviour gap is a well-researched area (Reimers et al., 2016; Jacobs et al., 2018; Park and Lin, 2020). When we talk about the attitude–behaviour gap, we discuss the fact that although people may claim they want to buy sustainable fashion, in reality they do not. There are various reasons why this may be the case. First, it could link to the perception that sustainable fashion comes at a higher price. Even if this may not be the case, the fact that consumers think prices for sustainable fashion are higher may already act as a barrier to actively engaging with making a purchase decision. Second, even though "sustainable fashion" is available in the market, as we have outlined in the previous sections of this book, sustainable fashion, like to sustainability and sustainable development, can mean different things to different people. Although there may be garments available that have an eco-label or are produced from recycled materials, if consumers do not see this as being part of the "sustainable fashion" remit, they may feel that there are no offerings, and thus they cannot buy into the concept. In a similar manner, consumers may also be sceptical about different claims that are being made, which is an after-effect of various greenwashing attempts that have been made in the past by companies operating in a variety of contexts.

> **Attitude–behaviour gap** – even though people may have the intention to engage with here sustainable fashion, they may not act upon it, and there may be a variety of explanations for this (e.g., financial, access).

Third, the fashion industry is dominated by the fast fashion paradigm, which has educated consumers to look out for new collections arriving in-store on a bi-monthly, if not weekly, basis. Thus, it may not be surprising that there is an appetite for fashion. Moreover, fashion, by its very definition, implies that it goes *in* and *out* of season, and thus is often trend-led. With increasing trends, fashion companies have started to create a new competitive advantage by no longer producing simply fast fashion, but hyper-fast fashion: examples here include Boohoo.com and Prettylittlething.com, which have continued to record high year-on-year sales (Goeghegan, 2018). We see a vicious circle emerging here, in that fashion companies often seek to respond to increasing demand by producing more products at lower prices, with consumers taking up the offers and often consuming more than they need. Whether or not products are sustainably produced is a secondary point, as overconsumption of any type of product implies waste creation, as we, as consumers, may not be able to wear all of our garments, thus making them idle capacities that may not reach a full use time. Fourth, even though trend-led companies have included sustainable fashion collections, there still seems to be a persistent belief that these types of garments are not as fashionable (Rutter et al., 2017; Blazquez et al., 2020), which makes them less desirable.

The aspects listed here are of course not exhaustive and there may be many more barriers as to why consumers to do not act on making sustainable fashion purchases. What becomes apparent here however, which is also vital for managers to understand is the fact that consumers will only act upon making these purchases, and thus decreasing the attitude-behaviour gap, if the cost-value-benefit ratio is in their favour. If consumers to not believe that there are any increased costs involved when purchasing sustainable fashion, and they gain the same value from these garments and accessories as they would from potential alternatives, they may make a purchase, as they may also feel better about themselves, which links to additional benefits. Thus, whilst consumers are increasingly concerned with the impact the fashion industry has on the natural environment, they only act upon this, if they see personal benefits from doing so (e.g., money saving, personal self image, well-being).

As fashion organisations, we need to provide a careful balance between consumer expectations, perceptions, and actual engagement. As outlined in this book, sustainable fashion may come at a higher price, as corners cannot be cut, so fashion items may be more expensive, yet in order to ensure consumer buy-in, these garments cannot be much more than different alternatives offered, as consumers can easily switch between brands.

Task

1. Thinking about current events in the environment, what might be aspects that can influence our supply curve to be shifted either up or down?
2. Explore potential barriers that may hinder consumers engaging with sustainable fashion.

1.3.2 New developments in sustainable fashion

We have already discussed why companies may engage with sustainable fashion and why they may be implementing a variety of different approaches. We have also highlighted that there may be challenges in terms of consumer perceptions that may act as a barrier for uptake.

What we have not discussed yet is consumer reactions to the external environment. What is meant by this? The fashion industry has been criticised on numerous occasions for its unsustainable practices. We have seen an almost cyclical movement of issues reoccurring over time. Environmental issues emerged in the 1970s, with consumers increasingly becoming more conscious of the impact the fashion industry was having on the natural environment. More recently we have seen slogans such as "Clean laundry, dirty ocean" (Ocean Clean Wash, 2021), a campaign which highlights the issue of microfibres being released from our garments and polluting the oceans. Similarly, scandals surrounding working conditions have been discussed for decades, and have more recently remerged with headlines such as "Why can't fashion wash out the dark stain of modern slavery?" (Sutherland, 2020). Moreover, factory accidents, such as the one at Rana Plaza in 2013, in which thousands lost their lives, have focused attention on the issues of workers' rights, working conditions, and fair wages, which continue to be heavily debated (Brydges and Hanlon, 2020; ILO, 2021).

Although there is outrage in society and consumers, often in the short term only, sometimes make changes to their consumption habits, for example by boycotting brands, overall the situation has not changed much. This can be evidenced by the fact that in today's world, consumption plays a key role and garment sales continue to increase on a global scale. One of the reasons why this may be the case is the "fear of missing out" (FoMO) phenomenon. FoMO can be defined as "a pervasive apprehension that others might be having rewarding experiences from which one is absent, FoMO is characterized by the desire to stay continually connected with what others are doing" (Przybylski et al., 2013). In this context, it implies that if consumers are engaging with fast fashion and thus continue to purchase trend-led items, their peers may feel the need to do the same to be part of the "in-group", and thus not appear to be an outsider.

From a company perspective, this has various implications, as a firm may not want to be seen as an entity that is fostering this phenomenon, as this can have an impact on individuals' well-being. FoMO can create anxiety, with people feeling pressure to continuously keep up with new trends, thereby getting more and more stressed and often spending an increasing amount of money on new items (e.g., Hodkinson, 2019). Thus, it may not be surprising that we have seen marketing campaigns that counteract FoMO by posing questions about whether consumers really need to buy certain items, or offering them solutions to address this problem through, for example, do-it-yourself and/or upcycling tips and hints.

As this chapter is focused on the consumer perspective, we will now turn our attention to what trends have (re-)emerged within the field of fashion to overcome challenges surrounding FoMO, and in more general terms, address issues of non-engagement with sustainable fashion.

Earlier, we alluded to the fact that sustainable fashion may have had – and sometimes even still has – negative connotations which may act as a barrier, as it can be associated with secondhand consumption. Issues surrounding hygiene are most often mentioned when it comes to secondhand consumption (Hu et al., 2018; Henninger et al., 2019; Lo et al., 2019). Yet there are other ways to engage with a more sustainable lifestyle, as we will now explore.

Minimalism

Minimalism can be described as the opposite end of a spectrum to fast fashion, in that minimalism, as the name suggests, seeks to move away from consumerism and go back to "basics". This implies that rather than purchasing a lot of garments, minimalism focuses on fewer items and stripping away those that may be seen as unnecessary (Pater, 2021). Key benefits associated with engaging in voluntary simplicity practices, such as minimalism (e.g., Vladimirova, 2021), are having more time to spend on other activities, as less time is used searching for garments online and/or offline; also, having only limited choices to wear may free up time in the dressing routine (Pater, 2021). Moreover, shopping less will increase financial wealth and also decrease stress, not only in terms of having more money to spend and/or save, but also being removed from FoMO.

One of the questions that often emerges is how many items should there be in a minimalist wardrobe. The answer is not clear-cut, as there is no fixed number of items that defines a minimalist wardrobe. What can be said, however, is that minimalists have usually created their own personal style and may add to their wardrobe without it being excessive (Pater, 2021; Vladimirova, 2021).

Various fashion companies have also caught on to this "trend" of minimalism, by providing consumers with fashion collections that can best be described as "timeless", "sophisticated", and "chic", and thus are less trend-led. In a recent article, Fass (2021) outlined "10 steps to the essential minimalist wardrobe" by showcasing staple pieces that can be dressed up or down depending on the occasion, and can therefore form the baseline wardrobe.

No matter what fashion segment we look at, they all have items that could fall within this category. High street retailers often have "basic lines" that are usually simple T-shirts, leggings, and other products in neutral colours, whilst high-end and luxury fashion retailers often have their "staple" garment or accessory. For example, Mulberry (n.d.) classifies its Bayswater bag as "a timeless and classic shoulder bag, it unites the very best of Mulberry's craft heritage and effortless style". On the other hand, Burberry (2021) has dedicated a website to the Burberry Trench Coat, "the quintessential British coat … created by Burberry founder Thomas Burberry over 100 years ago".

Capsule wardrobe

The capsule wardrobe is very similar to the concept of minimalism, in that garments and accessories are restricted to "essentials". However, there is a key difference, in that whilst minimalism does not have an exact number of garments that can be owned, and thus can be seen as flexible, capsule wardrobes often consist only of eight to ten items that have been carefully selected to be mixed and matched and create different looks with minimal items (Sutton, 2020).

There are different opinions in terms of timings between capsule wardrobes and minimalism. Minimalism is not bound to a time period, whilst the capsule wardrobes are often designed to last for a season. However, this aspect may change, with consumers starting to combine and merge minimalism with capsule wardrobes to be worn all year round, and ideally for a "lifetime" (Almassi, 2021).

The ideas surrounding capsule wardrobes are not new, with TV shows such as *Gok's Fashion Fix* discussing aspects of fashion and showcasing how less can be more. Within the fashion industry, we have also seen companies emerging such as Vetta (2021), which actively promotes its mini-capsule wardrobes. According to Anderson (2016), Vetta provides "just five powerhouse pieces that mix and match to create 30 outfits".

Fashion rental

Renting has been suggested as a further opportunity to engage with a more sustainable lifestyle, although it must be pointed out that opinions on whether renting is sustainable vary quite dramatically (Cline, 2019; Chan, 2021; Elan, 2021). It is not the purpose of this section to go into a lot of detail about this argument, but we want to point out that renting is part of the circular economy, as discussed elsewhere in this book, and is one way of re-evaluating the way we deal with clothing. What we mean by re-evaluating is the fact that if we no longer own our garments, we may have a different relationship with them and also need to care, use, and "dispose" of them in a very different manner (e.g., Mylan, 2015; Mukendi and Henninger, 2020).

A key benefit of renting is that we have less in our wardrobes yet can still enjoy a variety of garments and gain access to often unattainable pieces. Not everyone may have the opportunity to purchase luxury clothing and/or accessories, yet they may be able to rent an item for a short time and thus enjoy access to this luxury piece (e.g., Henninger et al., 2020).

We can see a new market opportunity emerging here, in that rather than purchasing garments new from a store, so-called "idle" or under-utilised garments can be rented out either through online platforms or physical stores. Within the online remit, we can distinguish between business-to-peer platforms and peer-to-peer platforms. Thus, it is either an organisation that is owning the garments and renting them out for a set fee and for an agreed-upon time, or it is a private individual renting out their garments and/or accessories that they may currently not use. In either instance, it has economic potential, in that companies and private individuals can earn money from their garments/accessories (ibid.).

Over the past decade, we have seen an emergence of rental platforms, with companies, such as Rent The Runway, Girl Meets Dress, My Wardrobe HQ, and YCloset being some of the more prominent examples. Although there has been an uptick in rentals, YCloset had to cease its operations in 2021, not because of a lack of interest, but due to numerous other problems (e.g., changes in agreements, poor reviews) (Yang, 2021). Even though some of these companies have been successful, overall the rental phenomenon remains rather niche, and is most popular within the occasion wear and luxury sector.

For consumers, a key benefit of rental is the fact that they can try out new styles without the risk of spending a lot of money on items they may not like, as well as being able to "fit in" by showing a sense of belonging through wearing certain items, which can also have an impact on their well-being (McNeil & Venter, 2019; Alevizou et al., 2021). It is also often seen as a more cost-effective alternative, in that renting, for example, a tuxedo or a ball gown, can be cheaper than purchasing it and only wearing it once (Hu et al., 2018). However, whether or not renting an item provides the same entertainment as the proverbial "retail therapy" remains to be seen (Johnson et al., 2016; Lang and Armstrong, 2018).

Yet, as indicated, renting only implies accessing an item, rather than owning it. Whilst some people may take greater care of items if they do not owned them, this may not always be the case. Receiving damaged items back, even though they must be paid for, can have implications for a business, as it may need to find a replacement for the garment. Moreover, continuous (dry) cleaning of these garments can also have an impact on the fabric. Although garments may be used more by different users, they may also wear out quicker.

Do-it-yourself

The DIY phenomenon is not new *per se*, as its origins can be traced back at least to the 1960s and 1970s, where it acted as a political statement (Miller, 2017). DIY can encompass a variety of different things, from upcycling and reconstructing garments (Maguire, 2020) to protest knits (Iqbal, 2019) to learning knitting and sewing skills in general (Hess, 2020).

There are a variety of reasons why people have taken up DIY practices, whether this as a form of political protest or as part of a boycott, or simply to overcome boredom, and especially during the COVID-19 pandemic, DIY has been increasingly gaining momentum. There are a variety of companies that support the DIY approach: not only traditional fabric and yarn stores, but also companies such as We Are Knitters, Wool and the Gang, or Stitch & Story, to name but a few, have created a business out of providing ready-to-make kits for anyone from total beginners to those with advanced knitting or crocheting skills.

In summary, consumers now have more options than ever to engage in sustainable fashion consumption. Lifestyle choices, such as minimalism and capsule wardrobes can also foster well-being and reduce stress, whilst the DIY movement can not only act as political statement, but also increase skill sets people may have been lacking.

Task

1. What other movements and/or developments are you aware of that could fit within the sustainable fashion remit?
2. What may be barriers to taking up minimalism or adopting DIY practices?

References

Anderson, K. (2016) *The 6 best affordable brands to boost your office dressing game*, Vogue (online): https://www.vogue.com/article/office-clothes-fashionable-workwear-brands, 27/10/2021.

Alevizou, P.J., Henninger, C.E., Stokoe, J., and Cheng, R. (2021) The hoarder, the oniomaniac and the fashionista in me, *Journal of Consumer Behaviour*, 20(4), 913–922.

Almassi, H. (2021) *How to build a capsule wardrobe that will last a lifetime*,

WhoWhatWear (online): https://www
.whowhatwear.co.uk/how-to-capsule
-wardrobe, 27/10/2021.

Blazquez Cano, M., Henninger, C.E.,
Alexander, B., and Franquesa, C.
(2020) Consumers' knowledge and
intentions towards sustainability: a
Spanish fashion perspective, *Fashion
Practice*, 12(1), 34–54.

Boardman, R., Parker Strak, R., and
Henninger, C.E. (2020) *Fashion buying &
merchandising in the 21st century*, Routledge,
Abington, UK.

Britannica (2021) *Supply and demand*,
Britannica (online): https://www.britannica
.com/topic/supply-and-demand, 24/10/2021.

Brydges, T., and Hanlon, M. (2020) Garment
worker rights and the fashion industry's
response to COVID-19, *Dialogues in Human
Geography*, 10(2), 97–106.

Burberry (2021) *Discover all trench fits*,
Burberry (online): https://uk.burberry
.com/c/the-trench-coat/#discover-all-fits,
27/10/2021.

Chan, E. (2021) *Is renting your clothes really
more sustainable?*, Vogue (online): https://
www.vogue.co.uk/fashion/article/is-renting
-your-clothes-really-more-sustainable,
27/10/2021.

Cline, E. (2019) *How sustainable is renting
your clothes, really?*, Elle (online): https://
www.elle.com/fashion/a29536207/rental
-fashion-sustainability/, 27/10/2021.

Elan, P. (2021) *Renting clothes is 'less green
than throwing them away'*, The Guardian
(online): https://www.theguardian.com
/fashion/2021/jul/06/renting-clothes-is
-less-green-than-throwing-them-away,
27/10/2021.

Fass, M. (2021) *10 steps to the essential
minimalist wardrobe*, Vogue (online): https://
www.vogue.com/article/minimalist-wardrobe
-guide-how-to, 27/10/2021.

Geoghegan, J., (2018) *Boohoo sales continue
to soar*, Drapers (online): https://www
.drapersonline.com/news/boohoo-sales
-continue-to-soar/7030763.article, 02/12/2020.

Granskog, A., Lee, L., Magnus, K.H., and
Sawers, C. (2020) *Survey: consumer sentiment
on sustainability in fashion*, McKinsey (online):
https://www.mckinsey.com/industries/retail/
our-insights/survey-consumer-sentiment-on
-sustainability-in-fashion, 23/10/2021.

Henninger, C.E., Alevizou, P.J., and Oates, C.J.
(2016) What is sustainable fashion?, *Journal
of Fashion Marketing & Management*, 20(4),
400–416.

Henninger, C.E., Blazquez Cano, M.,
Boardman, R., Jones, C., McCormick, H.,
Sahab, S. (2020) Cradle-to-cradle vs consumer
preferences, in Choudhury, I., and Hashmi,
S. (eds.), *Encyclopedia of renewable and
sustainable materials*, Volume 5, Elsevier,
Oxford, pp. 353–357.

Henninger, C.E., Bürklin, N., and Niinimäki, K.
(2019) The clothes swapping phenomenon,
Journal of Fashion Marketing & Management,
23(3), 327–344.

Hess, L. (2020) *The DIY lockdown fashion
trend that's taking over Instagram*, Vogue
(online): https://www.vogue.com/article
/skipdin-diy-home-couture-lockdown
-instagram, 30/10/2021.

Hodkinson, C. (2019) 'Fear of Missing Out'
(FOMO) marketing appeals, *Journal of
Marketing Communications*, 25(1), 65–88.

Hu, S., Henninger, C.E., Boardman, R.,
and Ryding, D. (2018) Challenging current
business models, Chapter 3, in Gardetti,
M.A., and Muthu, S.S. (eds.), *Sustainable
luxury: cases on circular economy and
entrepreneurship*, Springer Publishing,
Singapore, pp. 39–54.

ILO (2021) *The Rana Plaza accident and its
aftermath*, ILO (online): https://www.ilo.org
/global/topics/geip/WCMS_614394/lang--en/
index.htm, 27/10/2021.

Iqbal, N. (2019) *A stitch in time: how
craftivists found their radical voice*, The
Guardian (online): https://www.theguardian
.com/world/2019/jul/28/craftivism-protest
-women-march-donald-trump, 30/10/2021.

Jacobs, K., Petersen, L., Hörisch, J., and
Battenfeld, D. (2018) Green thinking but
thoughtless buying?, *Journal of Cleaner
Production*, 203, 1155–1169.

Johnson, K.K.P., Mun, J.M., and Chae,
Y. (2016) Antecedents to internet use to
collaboratively consume apparel, *Journal of*

Fashion Marketing & Management, 20(4), 370–382.

Lang, C., and Armstrong, C.M. (2018) Collaborative consumption: the influence of fashion leadership, need for uniqueness, and materialism on female consumers' adoption of clothing renting and swapping, *Sustainable Production and Consumption*, 13, 37–47.

Lo, C.J., Tsarenko, Y., and Tojib, D. (2019) To tell or not to tell?, *Psychology Marketing*, 36, 287–304.

Maguire, L. (2020) *With Gen Z under lockdown, DIY fashion takes off*, Vogue (online): https://www.voguebusiness.com /fashion/with-gen-z-under-lockdown-diy -fashion-takes-off, 30/10/2021.

McNeill, L., and Venter, B. (2019) Identity, self-concept and young women's engagement with collaborative, sustainable fashion consumption models, *International Journal of Consumer Studies*, 43, 368–378.

Miller, M. (2017) *The radical roots of DIY fashion have never been more relevant*, FastCompany (online): https://www .fastcompany.com/3068706/the-radical -roots-of-diy-fashion-have-never-been-more -relevant, 30/10/2021.

Mukendi, A., and Henninger C.E. (2020) Exploring the spectrum of fashion rental, *Journal of Fashion Marketing & Management*, 24(3), 455–469.

Mulberry (n.d.) *Bayswater*, Mulberry (online): https://www.mulberry.com/gb/shop/women /classics/bayswater-black-small-classic-grain, 27/10/2021.

Mylan, J. (2015) Understanding the diffusion of Sustainable Product-Service Systems: insights from the sociology of consumption and practice theory, *Journal of Cleaner Production*, 97, 13–20.

Ocean Clean Wash (2021) *Clean laundry, dirty ocean!*, Ocean Clean Wash (online): https:// www.oceancleanwash.org, 27/10/2021.

Park, H.J., and Lin, L.M. (2020) Exploring attitude-behaviour gap in sustainable consumption, *Journal of Business Research*, 117, 623–628.

Pater, R. (2021) *What is minimalist fashion? And is it the key to a happier and more sustainable lifestyle?*, Good on You (online): https://goodonyou.eco/minimalist-fashion/, 27/10/2021.

Przybylski, A.K., Murayama, K., DeHaan, C.R., and Gladwell, V. (2013) Motivational, emotional and behavioural correlates of fear of missing out, *Computers in Human Behaviour*, 29(4), 1841–1848.

Reimers, V., Magnuson, B., and Chao, F. (2016) The academic conceptualisation of ethical clothing: could it account for the attitude behaviour gap?, *Journal of Fashion Marketing & Management*, 20(4), 383–399.

Rutter, C., Armstrong, K., and Blazquez, M. (2017) The epiphanic sustainable fast fashion epoch: a new fashion ethical mandate, Chapter 2, in Henninger, C.E., Alevizou, P.J., Goworek, H., and Ryding, D. (eds.), *Sustainable fashion a cradle to upcycle approach*, Springer, Heidelberg, pp. 11–30.

Spragg (2021) *Let your ore-loved be re-loved*, Primark (online): https://www.primark.com /en/the-edit/women/let-your-pre-loved -be-re-loved/a/6c970eb7-a925-4a0f-a104 -66bf490e7bf4, 24/10/2021.

Sutherland, E. (2020) *Why can't fashion wash out the dark stain of modern slavery?*, Drapers (online): https://www.drapersonline .com/insight/analysis/analysis-why-cant -fashion-wash-out-the-dark-stain-of-modern -slavery, 27/10/2021.

Sutton, S. (2020) *What is a capsule wardrobe? 10 tips to help you de-clutter your closet*, InStyle (online): https://www.instyle.com/ fashion/clothing/what-is-a-capsule-wardrobe, 27/10/2021.

Vetta (2021) *The mode capsule*, Vetta (online): https://www.vettacapsule.com, 27/10/2021.

Vladimirova, K. (2021) Consumption corridors in fashion: deliberations on upper consumption limits in minimalist fashion challenges, *Sustainability: Science, Practice and Policy*, 17(1), 103–117.

Yang, Q. (2021) *Chinese fashion rental pioneer YCloset to close?*, BoF (online): https://www.businessoffashion.com/news/ china/chinese-fashion-rental-pioneer-ycloset -to-close, 20/10/2021.

Zara (n.d.) *About join life*, Zara (online): https://www.zara.com/uk/en/z-join-life -mkt1399.html, 24/10/2021.

phenomenon to gain momentum. With fashion not only being produced at ever-increasing speed, but also in higher quantities (WRAP, 2020), it may not be surprising that consumers have started to value garments less. Within as little as 15 years (2000–2015), we have seen the number of garments produced doubling. In line with increased production, the actual wear time of these garments has declined by approximately 36 per cent over the same period (EMF, 2017). One of the reasons that can help to explain this is the fact that fashionable items are often "cheap and cheerful" and easily replaceable. Thus, it could be suggested that this dominant model of creating fashion is not in line with SDG 12 (Responsible Consumption and Production), which seeks to "ensure sustainable consumption and production patterns" (UN, n.d.), thereby reducing waste in form of CO_2 emissions, materials, and energy, to name but a few aspects.

According to a recent Forbes report (Fields, 2021), "less than 1% of materials used to make clothing is currently recycled to make new clothing". To put this in economic terms, the worth of waste is estimated to be US$ 500 billion, and as such could be seen as a highly attractive market segment that remains untapped. Moreover, the Ellen MacArthur Foundation (EMF, 2017) has highlighted that 70 per cent of our clothing either ends up in landfill or is incinerated, with relatively fewer garments being donated and thus entering a different type of "waste stream".

> **Linear economy** – often used synonymously with cradle-to-grave approach, throw-away, or fast fashion. It implies that a product is used for one consumption cycle only before it is discarded.

To counteract the currently dominant production paradigm of the linear economy, circular economy principles have been introduced, which can also be referred to as a *cradle-to-cradle approach*. As you may have noticed from the previous section, the end-of-life stage may not necessarily have to mean the actual end of the garment. It should also be pointed out that not all fast or hyper-fast fashion items are of poor quality, as some can be reused and thus go through at least one further cycle. With consumers becoming increasingly aware of the impact their clothing has on the natural and social environment, reuse has become increasingly more popular. The secondhand market has gained momentum, and has seen a dramatic increase. It is predicted that the secondhand resale market will grow 11 times faster than the firsthand (new) garment market by 2025 (Forbes, 2021).

Now that we have had a bit of a taste of what the circular economy is, it is necessary to define it more widely. Key to the circular economy is to reduce waste by keeping materials and products in use for as long as possible (Circular Fashion, 2021). Thus, waste gains a new meaning here, in that it is not seen as something one discards, but rather is seen as a new resource that can be utilised for other processes. For example, we have seen the emergence of T-shirts made from polyethylene terephthalate (PET) bottles. Oceanness (2021) is one brand that collects plastic bottles to recycle; producing each of its T-shirts, use six to eight PET bottles. The company highlights that "making clothes from discarded plastic bottles means we can reuse plastic that would otherwise end up in landfills, or worse, the ocean" (Oceanness, 2021). In this way, all resources, whether they be raw materials or the energy required to produce items, are used in a manner that is efficient.

Similar to making use of waste, within a circular economy there is an emphasis on ensuring that the overall impact on the environment remains low or is entirely avoided. Thus, companies implementing a circular economy utilise a system thinking approach that not only focuses on the initial design phase of what a garment or product may look like, but also designs it in a manner that allows for an after-use. Here, after-use implies either the actual reuse of the garment/product, or the possibility of recycling it and making use of the newly won raw material (McDonough and Braungart, 2002).

> **Circular economy** – often used synonymously with cradle-to-cradle approach. It implies that a product is kept in use for as long as possible and raw materials are re-looped.

One of the most well-known depictions of the circular economy has been brought forward by the Ellen MacArthur Foundation (EMF, n.d.), which developed a butter-fly diagram that "illustrates the continuous flow of technical and biological materials through the 'value circle'" (EMF, n.d.). To really emphasise a point made earlier, the circular economy is different from the linear economy as it is "looking beyond the current take-make-waste extractive industrial model … [and] is based on three principles: 1) design out of waste and pollution; 2) keep products and materials in use; 3) regenerate natural systems" (EMF, 2017). Thus, the circular economy fosters a different way of thinking about the creation process, in that waste becomes a resource, and thus regeneration and closed-loop systems are seen as the new norm (Niinimäki, 2017). In other words, the focus is on reshaping how we think about the production process and formulate new strategies that also capitalise on underutilised resources (e.g., waste).

The Ellen MacArthur Foundation's (EMF, n.d.) model is a combination of the biological and technical cycle of material recovery, and thus the cradle-to-cradle approach which was developed by McDonough and Braungart (2002).

The *biological cycle* focuses on biodegradability of raw materials, which implies that raw materials may end up becoming soil again. Now, this does not imply that the biodegrading process may happen in our wardrobes and leave us with piles of soil. Rather, items can biodegrade under certain conditions, which are most often achieved in artificial environments. We will revisit aspects of biodegradability in Section 1.4.2.

Thinking about biodegradability, it could be argued that this may be ideal, in that once we no longer use a garment, it can be composted and used as soil for plants, or some may even be utilised as new raw materials. Yet this would be a very simplistic way of thinking about the process. As we learned earlier, our garments have different performance properties and are used for different purposes. For example, raincoats have a special finishing on the material to ensure that water is repelled, whilst we also wear different-coloured items, often dependent on seasonal trends. Thus, garments may be treated with colourants and chemicals prior to being sold to consumers. If garments are left to biodegrade in nature and have been treated with chemicals or artificial colourants, these toxins may filter into the soil, which can be harmful (Niinimäki, 2013).

You may have noticed that these aspects of biodegradability assume that materials are actually able to biodegrade, so the term often refers to products that are made from natural resources, as opposed to, for example, plastics (for more information, see **Part 4: Material Innovations in Sustainable Fashion**). Yet today a majority of our garments are not only made from man-made fibres, but also contain a blend of them. Not only may it take a lot longer for some fibres to biodegrade (if they do so at all), but we may also find it challenging to reuse them, as separating fibres is not only expensive and time-consuming, but may not always be possible. Thus, it may actually be cheaper for organisations to use virgin materials rather than trying to re-loop these back into the production cycle (Henninger et al., 2020).

This brings us to look at the *technical cycle*, which may overcome some of the issues highlighted in the biological cycle. The idea of the technical cycle is to be able to reuse high-quality materials as the basis for new products. This may provide a special opportunity for the fashion industry since it is fast-paced and trend-led, so garments could (ideally) be dismantled into their raw materials and re-made into something new. Yet you may have already seen a flaw here, in that for the technical cycle to be efficient and effective, it is reliant on high-quality materials as an input. Because the fashion paradigm is dominated by fast and hyper-fast fashion, with garments often being of low quality, they may not be of use within the technical cycle (Rutter et al., 2017).

One of the benefits the technical cycle has over the biological one is the fact that toxins and chemicals will not be released into the natural environment, but rather contained, broken down, and reused without causing contamination (McDonough and Braungart, 2002; Henninger et al., 2020). This brings us to another impasse, in that as managers, we may want to align our business with more circular approaches, but this would require us to produce high-quality garments, as these could then be part of the technical cycle. Higher-quality raw materials are often associated with higher prices, which may need to be passed on to consumers to ensure that the business remains profitable.

Herein lies the problem: the fast fashion phenomenon has programmed consumers' minds to look out for bargains and increased their overall fashion appetite for newness on a weekly basis (Sharma and Hall, 2010). The expectation of "cheap and cheerful" clothing comes at a price, which has also been documented in the movie *The True Cost* (2015) and takes the form of social and environmental consequences. Companies often feel pressured to cut corners to stay ahead of the game, yet this comes at a cost, predominantly to the most vulnerable within the industry (e.g., garment workers) (Brydges and Hanlon, 2020).

In summary, it can be said that the circular economy provides a different way to think about the production process and may require a different set of decision-making, based on incorporating the three key principles of designing out and reducing waste and pollution, re-looping materials as much and for as long as possible, whilst also trying to regenerate the natural system. In **Part 2: Managing Sustainable Fashion through Design**, we will revisit the circular economy decision-making process by further exploring design aspects, as well as its associated opportunities and barriers.

Task

1. Critically discuss the differences between a linear and a circular economy?
2. What challenges are associated with the biological and technical cycle?

1.4.2 Case study: thinking outside the box – the example of Freitag

Intended learning outcomes

After working through the case study, students will be able to:

*   Define sustainability and how it links to circular design thinking.
*   Explain and critically evaluate the opportunities and challenges of circular design thinking.
*   Reflect upon circular design thinking and apply this to the case of Freitag.

Introduction

Sustainability is described as an intuitively understood concept that can have different meanings depending on the person and context, and is most commonly characterised by meeting current needs without compromising future ones (e.g., WCED, 1986). Often displayed as a Venn diagram, sustainability is visualised as the intersection of three pillars: the social, environmental, and economic aspects.

Unlike the linear system of production (take–make–use–dispose) or the recycling economy, in which raw materials, even though recycled and re-looped, will be disposed of eventually, the circular economy seeks to eliminate waste by not only designing out waste within the production processes, but also re-looping raw materials, and making use of idle capacities (e.g., EMF, 2017; Lissaman, 2019), thereby focusing on both pre- and post- consumer waste.

Circular design thinking implies not simply adding on a strategy to reduce the environmental and/or social impacts one may have, but also carefully exploring what is currently available and what users may expect and/or want, identifying what current challenges may be and how these could be addressed, developing ideas to overcome the challenges identified, and starting the creation process of, for example a prototype, and finally bringing the solution to the market. This can further create a competitive advantage measured against performance indicators (e.g. quality, cost, speed, flexibility, dependability) (Slack et al., 2009)

Freitag

The Swiss company Freitag was established by two brothers – Daniel and Markus Freitag – who identified a need for a waterproof bag for bike couriers. Since its creation

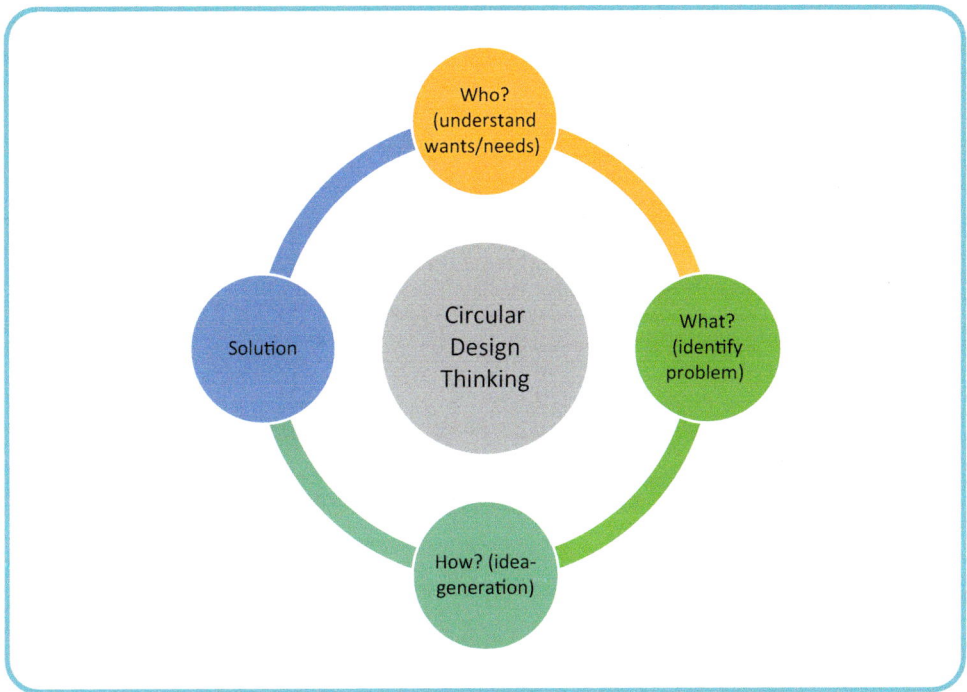

Figure 1.4.2   Circular design thinking process (based on EMF, 2017b)

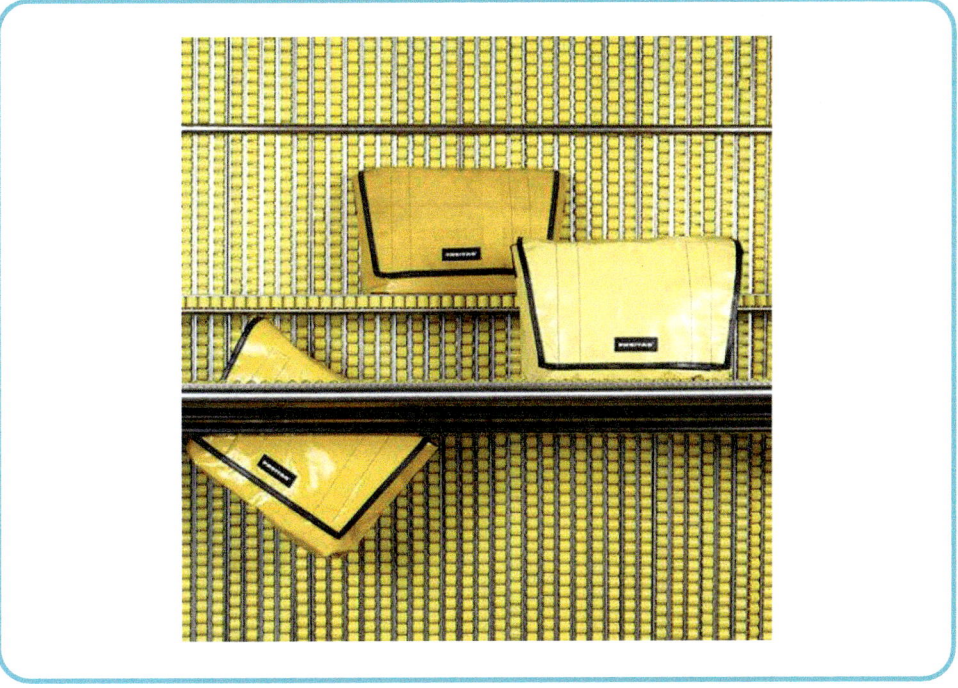

Figure 1.4.3   F12 Dragnet and F14 Dexter (photo credit: Nadja Schmid, Linda Suter)
– Freitag®

Figure 1.4.4   Freitag factory bag design tarp (photo credit: Freitag®)

in the 1990s, Freitag has become renowned for being innovative, creative, and environmentally aware (Freitag, n.d. a). The Freitag bags, which have also featured in the Museum of Modern Art (MoMA) in New York, are one of a kind (Popeson, 2011), not only in terms of their design (actual look), but also in terms of their "out-of-the-box" circular design thinking (Figure 1.4.3).

Having identified a need to create a water-repellent, robust bag that is relatively light in weight, it was not simply about making a new bag, but understanding how this bag could be created to have a relatively low environmental impact. Using waste materials from the transportation industry, each bag has its own unique set of scratches, marks, colour assemblies, and overall unique quirks (Figure 1.4.4), which makes them even more lovable. All the material used, from the handles made of seatbelts to the seams that are made of the insides of bike tyre tubes, are thus given a second lifespan.

Yet environmental awareness and calculations do not stop with the raw materials, but also encompass the production cleaning processes, which utilises rainwater collected from the company's very own rooftops to ensure that the patterns are using as much of the raw material as possible. In order to foster a true circular approach, Freitag has further teamed up with Texyloop®, collecting any scraps that cannot be used in the bag creation process and partnering up with a company that can make further use of them (Vinyl, 2012).

In line with its overall ethos, Freitag has evolved since being created in 1993. Similarly to its bags, its workwear fashion items (Figure 1.4.5) are linked to circular design thinking, with raw materials being sourced (and planted) within a 2,500 km radius of Zurich, and the F-ABRIC textiles being "100% naturally biodegradable – including threads and selvage" (Freitag, n.d. b) (Figure 1.4.6).

Considering the overall approach taken of creating durable products that are designed for longevity, Freitag has demonstrated that sustainability and circular design thinking do not come at the cost of the look of a product, but rather encourage research innovations and out-of-the-box thinking.

Figure 1.4.5   **FREITAG F-ABRIC clothing (photo credit: Nadine Ottawa) – Freitag®**

Figure 1.4.6   **FREITAG F-ABRIC biodegraded – (photo Credit: Oliver Nanzig) – Freitag®**

Questions

1. What are the benefits and drawbacks of circular design thinking?
2. In thinking about performance properties and potential competitors, draw a performance indicator diagram for Freitag.
3. In your opinion, what are key implications of Freitag's approach to circular design thinking?

EMF (Ellen MacArthur Foundation) (2017a) *What is the circular economy?*, EMF (online): https://www.ellenmacarthurfoundation.org/circular-economy/what-is-the-circular-economy.

EMF (Ellen MacArthur Foundation) (2017b) *Circular design*, EMF (online): https://www.ellenmacarthurfoundation.org/explore/circular-design.

Freitag (n.d. a) *History*, Freitag (online): https://www.freitag.ch/en/history.

Freitag (n.d. b) *F-ABRIC apparel*, Freitag (online): https://media.freitag.ch/en/media/fabric.

Lissaman, C. (2019) *What is circular fashion?*, Common Objective (online): https://www.commonobjective.co/article/what-is-circular-fashion.

Popeson (2011) *The Freitag top cat bag*, MoMA (online): https://www.moma.org/explore/inside_out/2011/05/19/the-freitag-top-cat-bag-environmentally-responsible-and-good-looking-too/.

Slack, N., Chambers, S., Johnston, R., and Betts A. (2009) *Operations and process management*, Prentice Hall, London.

Vinyl (2012) *Circular economy: the benefits of closing the PVC loop*, Vinyl (online): https://vinylplus.eu/mediaroom/24/55/Circular-economy-The-benefits-of-closing-the-PVC-loop.

1.4.3 Business model innovations

As indicated, the circular economy fosters a new way to thinking about production and consumption, which very much aligns with SDG 12 (Responsible Consumption and Production), in that the focus is on making efficient use of resources whilst at the same time keeping them in use for as long as possible. From a management perspective, this presents an opportunity to re-think current business practices and develop new strategies that capitalise on currently under-utilised raw materials: waste (WRAP, 2020; Fields, 2021; Forbes, 2021).

It may thus not be surprising that we have seen a variety of "new" business models emerging that take advantage of re-looping products. The RSA Action and Research Centre (2016) identified four potential strategies for enhancing the re-looping process: (1) designing for longevity; (2) leasing or servicing products; (3) reusing raw materials during the manufacturing process; and (4) ensuring material recovery.

Within this section of the book, we focus on business model innovations, which closely align with point 2 about "leasing and servicing products". Business model innovations are often described as disruptive innovations, as they challenge the status quo in the industry and provide an alternative to current market offerings (Christensen 1997; Christensen and Raynor 2003). Although some describe disruptive innovations as inferior in comparison to more established models, key benefits they provide include a more competitive price point and often a convenient location (Henninger et al., 2021a, b). You may ask yourself what we classify as disruptive business model innovations. There are multiple different types, including but not limited to those that are associated with the sharing economy (e.g., renting, swapping) and those that focus more on the product, such as zero waste fashion, upcycling, or take back schemes (Henninger et al., 2017; Park and Armstrong, 2017).

The sharing economy is most often defined as including business models that, quite literally, share resources of some sort. Previous research on the sharing economy has focused on collaborative consumption (Henninger et al., 2019, 2021a), access-based consumption (Mukendi and Henninger, 2020), product service systems (Armstrong et al., 2015), and their respective practices. It is important to note here that currently there is a debate within the literature on whether the sharing economy is a sub-set and/ or linked to the circular economy (Henry et al., 2021). Whilst it is beyond the scope of this book to pursue this debate, an assumption is made here that the sharing economy is part of the circular economy, acknowledging that a key commonality between the concepts is the focus on sustainable development. Yet, as pointed out by Henry et al. (2021), the circular economy is more strongly aligned with the environmental angle of sustainability, whilst the sharing economy is more concerned with the societal aspect.

An example of a company that makes use of both aspects, in that it designs for circularity whilst also ensuring the maximisation of the use of its products, is MUD Jeans. The company highlights that "every pair of MUD Jeans is recycled into a new MUD Jeans, leaving no waste and using 92% less water than average jeans" (MUD Jeans, 2021), whilst it also engages with leasing services. Its slogan is: "Free your mind from owning and experience leasing! You're paying for the performance of your jeans while we make recycling easy for you" (MUD Jeans, 2021). One could argue that the company has developed a truly circular approach, in that it not only keeps its garments in use for as long as possible, but also reuses the raw materials at the end-of-life, thus capitalising on "waste" as a raw material. This of course has implications for managers, since the supply chain can no longer be linear, but needs to be adapted to meet the needs of the company. To explain: the end-of-life stage needs to be re-looped, thus the company needs to ensure that it gets its "raw materials" back from the consumer. The leasing model allows this to happen because ownership is not transferred to consumers, but rather they have a right to use the garments before they need to give them back to the company once they are finished with them. This implies that logistics are essential in the process of ensuring stock gets to but also comes back from the consumer in a way that is not disruptive to the business. Moreover, additional services may be needed, such as cleaning the product if it is to be leased as a secondhand garment, and processes need to be in place if the garment can no longer be used and must be shredded before becoming a new pair of jeans again. Here, it is also essential to understand the supply and demand of the product, as it may not always be clear in what condition garments are given back and whether jeans at the end of the leasing phase can be reused or need to be recycled.

What becomes clear here is that implementing a circular approach adds additional layers of complexity to the decision-making process of a manager, especially within the end-phase of a product. It is apparent that technology is essential here, in that products need to be traced and processes monitored, so it may not be surprising that these business model innovations are often enabled through technology. Taking the example of MUD Jeans, the leasing part of the company needs to be carefully monitored in order to keep track of inventories and cleaning regimes (Botsman and Rogers,

2010; Henninger et al., 2021b). Leasing rather than selling products implies that MUD Jeans is capitalising on idle capacities, thereby ensuring that the use time of its pairs of jeans is maximised. As indicated, leasing is not the only option companies have to maximise on idle capacities. We have seen various high-end and luxury retailers and department stores working together with rental companies to achieve higher use time of their items. Rental platforms can be operated either as business-to-peer or peer-to-peer platforms, and the latter allow individuals to "rent out" their garments that they may currently not need. An added benefit here is the fact that these individuals may also earn some money, whilst at the same time ensuring that their garments have an increased use-time. Similarly, swapping allows for an exchange of garments that is not based on any monetary transactions.

Table 1.4.1 provides insights into how implementing circular and sharing economy principles may enhance the Sustainable Development Goals (UN, 21) whilst further outlining what challenges may be encountered. Again, these aspects listed are not exhaustive, but rather should provide you with food for thought to reflect and think about other aspects that may be fostering positive outcomes and overcoming the challenges outlined.

In summary, it can be said that implementing a circular economy can be challenging, yet rewarding. What becomes clear is that a circular economy cannot happen within a short time, but rather may be a long process that is linked to a complex set of decision-making. As was outlined, there are various challenges associated with the linear economy that a circular approach can overcome; however, this needs to be carefully managed. **Part 2: Managing Sustainable Fashion through Design** will revisit the circular economy decision-making process by further exploring design aspects, as well as its associated opportunities and barriers, which will allow you to further reflect on the complexities.

Task

1. Revisit Table 1.4.1 – can you describe further opportunities and/or challenges that circular and sharing economy approaches may encounter?
2. Critically evaluate why companies may pursue developing a circular approach even though this can add additional complexities?

1.4.4 The circular economy – zero waste fashion

Now that we have a better understanding of what a circular economy is and how it may be defined, it is time to explore different approaches that can enhance circular thinking. As outlined in the previous section, the circular economy not only seeks to keep materials and products in use for as long as possible, but also focuses on waste reduction (Henninger et al., 2018; European Parliament, 2021).

As has been alluded to previously, waste is a key issue in the fashion industry. To provide some more facts and figures, on average a family in the Western hemisphere will discard 30 kg of clothing annually, with half of them throwing their garments straight into landfill (WRAP, 2020a, b; ThreadUp, 2021). This number may have increased, during the COVID-19 pandemic. With people being forced to spend more time at

Table 1.4.1   Opportunities and Drawbacks of Circular and Sharing Economy Principles Linked to SDGs

	Opportunities	Challenges	References
Social	**#3 Good Health and Well-being** • Access to otherwise unattainable garments • Enhanced well-being, as rented garments may allow access to social groupings • Perceived inclusivity • Creation of communities	**#8 Decent Work and Economic Growth** • Labour law issues, e.g., gig economy, lack of pay **#3 Good health and well-being** • Exclusion due to stigma • Perceived health risk (e.g., hygiene)	Schor & Attwood-Charles (2017) Henninger et al. (2019)
Natural	**#14 Life below Water and #15 Life on Land** • Incentivise platforms to increase utilisation of garments and extend service lifetime, which implies producing less and counteracting negative impacts along supply chain that impact life below water and on land • Less raw materials used if products are circulated and used longer	**#6 Clean Water and Sanitation and #13 Climate Action** • Reliance on dry cleaning implies increased use of chemicals • Reduced material longevity due to aftercare • Increased CO_2 emissions due to transportation and laundry	Park & Armstrong (2017) Henninger et al. (2019) Brydges et al. (2020)
Economic	**#1 No Poverty and #8 Decent Work and Economic Growth** • Creation of new jobs • Ability for individuals to earn money on idle capacities	**#1 No Poverty and #9 Industry, Innovation, and Infrastructure** • Tax avoidance by larger companies (researched in tourism and transportation industry) • Loss of jobs along the supply chain	Schor & Attwood-Charles (2017)

Source: Adapted from Henninger et al. (2021).

home, they had an opportunity to actively go through their wardrobes and declutter. Lockdown restrictions and subsequent shop closures meant that people were unable to donate garments to charity shops straight away, which may have increased the amount that was landfilled (e.g., WRAP, 2020b; Granskog et al., 2020). COVID-19 here does not represent a once-in-a-lifetime change, but rather is seen in more general terms as an external change in the environment that can have an impact on how we consume and/ or dispose of garments. This implies that changes in the external environment can have an impact on how we, as consumers, may act – and thus enhances and/or accelerates our behaviour, often only in the short term, as was seen with the Rana Plaza example mentioned earlier.

From an industry perspective, it is estimated that annually the fashion industry creates approximately 92 million tonnes of textile waste (EMF, 2017). This implies that "shockingly, every second, the equivalent of one garbage truck of textiles is land-filled or burned globally" (Dean, 2019). One of the ways to overcome this challenge is through a zero waste fashion approach.

As you may have noticed, "waste" can be created both pre-consumer and post-con-sumer, thus addressing the former focuses more on the fashion industry taking action and designing out waste within its production processes, whilst the post-consumer waste approach puts responsibility on the consumer to counteract the throw-away culture. The following sections introduce various pre- and post-consumer zero waste approaches, before concluding by describing key benefits and drawbacks of the circular economy.

1.4.4.1 Zero waste fashion – pre-consumer approaches

This section will introduce three different approaches to zero waste fashion: pattern cutting, creative design, and 3D printing.

Pattern cutting

Pattern cutting is a vital aspect within the fashion design process, in that an idea is taken, applied onto a fabric, and an actual product is created. The process of creating patterns is complex and an essential skill that needs to be learned by fashion design-ers (Parish, 2020). An interesting aspect that has been reported on in relatively recent media is the fact that fashion houses are "bringing it home" (McGregor, 2019), imply-ing that the pattern cutting process is no longer outsourced, but has been taken back to be an in-house trade. One of the reasons why pattern cutting is moving back is due to consumer satisfaction. As we have explored, the fashion industry is a highly vola-tile market environment in which it is easy for consumers to switch between brands. Having increased satisfaction in terms of fit and sizing, which is part of the pattern cutting process, can enhance consumer satisfaction and thus keep consumers brand-loyal (ibid.).

There are various approaches to pattern cutting, all of which have different benefits and drawbacks. Within this section, we will not focus on different pattern cutting approaches *per se*, but highlight that there are different decisions that need to be made. For example, are we as an organisation creating patterns that are readily assembled and sold, or are we taking a different approach and combining pattern cutting with creativ-ity. The latter aspect links to an example described in Section 1.2.1: *Fragments Garments* (Fragments Garments, 2019a). The company takes pattern cutting to a new level, in that it has created jigsaw-like fashion collections where individual "jigsaw pieces" can be reused in different designs without having to sew them together or rip seams apart.

Pattern cutting and clothing design are interlinked here, with garments being created in a way that allows for easy disassemby and reassembly by having focused carefully on the pattern cutting process. Whilst this process combines the circular fashion design thinking with creative pattern cutting and thus moves closer to creating a circular business approach, there are also some limitations that need to be highlighted. For example, currently the company only offers on-demand, limited-edition products (Fragments Garments, 2019b), which on the one has reduced waste, yet on the other hand may not attract a large consumer base. Fashion is rather tactile, meaning that consumers often want to touch and/or see garments, especially if they are more avant-garde, which is the case with Fragments Garments. The company outlines the fact that its products are **"made to evolve** & we want **you to be part of it"** (Fragments Garments, 2019a). Yet whether consumers are ready to take responsibility for assembling their own clothes is questionable.

Such programs may rely on "nesting" where a computer program is used to "nest" patterns together to maximise the use of fabric and reduce placement errors. Thus, using a nesting technique implies that patterns for multiple sizes can be "creatively" put onto a piece of fabric and cut. However, whether nesting can always be used is a different question, as some fabrics, depending on their texture, can only be used in a certain flow.

Creative design

In **Part 2: Managing Sustainable Fashion through Design**, will have an opportunity to learn more about the role of the designer within the system thinking approach that underpins the circular economy. This section will provide you with an opportunity to reflect on what the implications of creative design might be. Section 1.2.1 introduced a company that falls within the creative design remit: the *Versalette by {r}evolution apparel*. The Versalette is an example of an item that has creativity at the core. In 2013, a Kickstarter campaign was started that looked for backers to create a garment that can be worn in 15 different ways (Kickstarter, 2013). The initial impetus for this creative design was based on saving space when travelling, as the Versalette can be worn as a skirt, a T-shirt, or even be used as a bag (Caroline, 2014). Looking at the Versalette in a more objective manner, it is simply a rectangular item sewn together as a tube which has drawstrings and hidden sleeves attached. Depending on how one pulls on the drawstrings, the rectangular tube can "magically" transform into a short or long skirt, a top, a scarf, a bag, and many other garments. According to a promotional video, the item can be transformed into as many as 30 different outfits, and depending on the how the item is paired, may look like either casual or appropriate eveningwear attire (Revapparel, 2012).

Similar to the example of Fragments Garments, it may be suggested that the Versalette may be seen as too avant-garde and ahead of its time, which could explain why this specific garment is no longer available on the market. Whilst the idea in itself has merits, in that it reduces waste by being more than one "item" (e.g., T-shirt, bag, skirt), the question of what size fits all could be raised. As mentioned in the previous section, various fashion houses have moved the pattern cutting process back in-house in order to be able to provide a better fit (McGregor, 2019). What this acknowledges is the fact that we as consumers, like our garments, come in different shapes and sizes. What might look good on a person who is tall may not necessarily be right for someone who is shorter, and vice versa.

3D printing

Within the past decade, 3D printing has seen increased use within the fashion industry and is often used to produce prototypes of products, and thus falls within the product development stage. Having an actual prototype, as opposed to a computer-animated version of a product, allows testing the new creations in terms of their fit, shape, and form. In more recent years, we have seen fashion collections emerging that rely on this technology, with one of the most iconic collections being "VOLTAGE", designed by Iris van Herpen, which debuted in 2013 at Paris Fashion Week (Materialise, 2013).

In an interview, van Herpen stated:

> I find the process of 3D printing fascinating because I believe it will only be a matter of time before we see the clothing we wear today produced with this technology, and it's because it's such a different way of manufacturing, adding layer-by-layer, it will be a great source of inspiration for new ideas.
>
> (cited in Materialise, 2013)

This statement has various implications. On the one hand, it highlights that producing 3D-printed garments can reduce waste, as they are made-to-order pieces, reducing waste by printing only the garments that are wanted. On the other hand, it provides an opportunity for creativity and uniqueness that may be in stark contrast to the dominant fast fashion paradigm, in which mass production is the norm.

3D printing technologies are becoming increasingly popular, and are no longer only used by Haute Couture houses, but have trickled down to more mainstream fashion production, such as jewellery, bikinis, shoes, and even knitted jackets (aRks, 2016; Heater, 2018; Shapeways, 2018; Sculpteo, 2021). The company Ministry of Supply (2020), for example, has successfully used 3D printing to deliver knitted collections that produce 34 per cent less waste compared to traditional knitting techniques. 3D printing is seen to be a "cost-effective and time-efficient way to produce low-volume, customized products with complicated geometries and advanced material properties and functionality" (Huang et al., 2015: 1). An explanation as to why companies such as Ministry of Supply have managed to reduce waste is the fact that items are made to measure. In traditional garment manufacturing processes, patterns are laid onto a piece of fabric and cut out before they are assembled, thereby leaving unwanted scraps of materials (offcuts) (Berman, 2012; Vanderploeg et al., 2017). These offcuts or surplus material pieces are no longer an issue with 3D-printed knitwear, as the knitted items are created as one piece and in one pass. This means that products that may have previously only been accessible to an elite group (e.g., McCormick et al., 2019) can be sold at price points that are more affordable to the mass market.

Although reducing waste by 34 per cent (e.g., Ministry of Supply, 2020) is a positive step in the right direction, and certainly counteracts one of the key challenges in the fashion industry – waste – there are also challenges with this technique, in that 3D printing machines use a lot of energy, and garments may not necessarily be produced in large quantities, as each one can take a lot of time. For example, in 2016 threeASFOUR created the Pangolin dress; to produce this dress, the company had ten printers work simultaneously for approximately 500 hours, which does not include any of the assembly that still needed to take place (Jacobson, 2017). Clearly, the use of the energy needed to run these machines will have a negative impact on the environment, but the fact that only limited amounts can be produced may be advantageous, in that it supports SDG 12, Responsible Production and Consumption (UN, 2021): reduced supply could also lead to reduced demand and consumers reflecting on whether they actually need any more garments.

1.4.4.2 Zero waste fashion – post-consumer approaches

This section will introduce two different approaches to zero waste fashion: upcycling and recycling.

Upcycling

Upcycling implies that a garment that may have previously been seen as waste is reused and repurposed in such a way as to create a new product of equal or higher quality than it was in its original state. Upcycling is not a new phenomenon, but has been around for more than a decade, when issues surrounding textile waste emerged (Triple Pundit, 2014).

Upcycling is an interesting case, as it can happen during both stages of waste creation: pre- and post-consumer. Within the pre-consumer waste phase, offcuts or any other leftover pieces of fabric can be used to create a new collection. An advantage here is that such fabric is not "contaminated", an issue that has emerged strongly with the COVID pandemic (Gray, 2020). Collections created from post-consumer waste can take apart any type of clothing and create something new. The advantage that comes to mind here is the fact that even garments that may have small faults (e.g., stains, holes) can be used.

Whilst upcycling can be seen as a good way to use textile waste, resources to make these collections may be limited, and designers are very much dependent on the items of clothing, the offcuts, and any other materials they can get at the time. Thus, it may not always be possible to make large collections, multiple pieces, or staple pieces. On the other hand, consumers who want a unique look may be attracted to the fact that all upcycled pieces are one-offs and will not be found anywhere else.

As mentioned earlier, the fast fashion phenomenon has meant that garments may not always be of high quality, which can also impact recycled collections, as low-quality material may not be suitable for use, thus limiting resources even more, or if they can be used, it may not be possible for collections to be worn for an extended period as the quality will deteriorate even further.

There are various examples of companies that use upcycling techniques, for very different reasons. Whilst some could be described as having sustainability at their core (as part of the company – see Section 1.2.1), thus only producing collections made from upcycled garments, in recent years we have seen an increased interest in this approach with media outlets, highlighting "upcycling is the biggest trend in fashion right now" (Chan, 2020) or "the rise of deadstock dressing: designers approach upcycling clothes the chic way" (Harvey, 2021).

One of the reasons why upcycling has increasingly become trendy is the COVID-19 pandemic. With retail stores and fashion brands forced to close their physical stores, and online shopping only gradually filling the gap, the fashion industry in general was faced with more left-over stock, or deadstock. Various luxury companies have taken on the upcycling trend, including Balenciaga and its shoelace fur coat, and Coach and its patchwork outerwear collection.

Miu Miu is a further example that launched "a special collection of vintage dresses reworked by Miu Miu" (Miu Miu, 2019). Miu Miu is interesting in that the company sources its own vintage pieces from the 1930s–1980s, and upcycles them, still keeping true to the original garment. From a company perspective, there are various advantages here: (1) sourcing your own garments implies that the authenticity of the item is guaranteed, and the product is genuine, as opposed to a counterfeit; this not only creates control over what items are being used, but also creates consumer trust, as the new collection is based on "true" vintage items; (2) the company has control over the product and the subsequent quality; because vintage items are relatively old (minimum of 30 years) and may have been worn multiple times, the company can ensure that only garments that still meet the quality criteria are upcycled; and (3) creating a unique upcycled collection that contains limited editions can be a key selling point and draw in consumers who look for uniqueness (e.g. Miu Miu, 2019; Chan, 2020).

Recycling

Recycling implies that textiles and garments (in a broader sense) are "processed" through, for example, the chemical cycle (McDonough and Braungart, 2002) and made into new useful products or materials. As mentioned earlier, recycling implies that ideally high-quality material is used in the process to provide new high-quality resources. However, it must be highlighted that recycled materials may not always have the same strength or performance properties as the original product, due to, for example, reduced twists in the yarn (see also **Part 4: Material Innovations in Sustainable Fashion**).

Textile recycling is an understudied area in the sense that currently only 1 per cent of textiles are recycled (Close the Loop, 2020). Yet within the fashion industry, we have seen an increased effort, with companies starting take-back schemes to encourage consumers to bring back any unwanted garments and divert them from landfill. This is often done by offering incentives in the form of vouchers. Whilst this may be a good strategy for fashion brands and retail stores, as it implies that consumers may enter their shop and seek to spend their newly gained voucher, which is often attached to conditions such as minimum amount that needs to be spent, it could further foster unsustainable behaviour in the form of overconsumption.

We earlier discussed MUD Jeans, which has created a business model around recycling and leasing, not only recycling its own denim products, but also fostering a circular economy approach (MUD Jeans, 2021). A further example of a company that falls within the recycling category is Ecoalf. Ecoalf (2021) has created "recycled PET polyester from the sea (post-consumer waste)" and thus "recycled 4.5 million bottles with our FW21 collection". Within its collection, it also uses other recycled materials, such as wool and cotton, thereby highlighting the benefits of using recycled materials as opposed virgin materials (Ecoalf, 2021).

1.4.5 Opportunities and barriers to the circular economy

From the previous sections, you may have noticed that the circular economy phenomenon has a lot of potential within the fashion industry. As was pointed out, various authors have included the sharing economy within the circular economy design, whilst Henry et al. (2021) see the two concepts as different, in that the circular economy is more strongly aligned with the environmental angle of sustainability, whilst the sharing economy is more concerned with the societal aspect. As previously stated, this book does need to seek to argue one or the other point as this would be beyond its scope, what is seeks to bring closer to you, however, is that designing for a circular economy implies a complex decision-making process and can offer both opportunities and challenges.

With sustainability being the centre of attention within national and supranational governmental organisations and the fashion sector having been declared as the fourth most polluting and GHG-intensive lifestyle domain in Europe (EEA, 2019), it becomes apparent that companies and especially managers need to act.

In the previous section, we referred to a variety of business model innovations, and whether these are classified as disruptive, collaborations, or new ways of operating and setting up supply chains, fashion companies have the opportunity to build customer loyalty or even tap into new markets. If we come back to Miu Miu (2019) as an example of a brand that has created an upcycled collection, its new limited edition collection may not only attract its current clientele, but also those who have an interest in vintage fashion or unique one-off pieces. On the other hand, companies such as Oceanness (2012), United by Blue (2021), or Ecoalf (2021) may not only attract individuals who are interested in their fashion collections due to their design, but also newly emerging conscious consumers (Hackenberg, 2021) as they actively promote the use of waste materials that have been removed from the oceans.

We have also seen the emergence of new business models and collaborations, with luxury fashion retailers in particular more recently starting to build collaborations with external brands to manage the secondhand and resale market. The resale market has emerged as one of the biggest trends in recent years. An example of a resale player is The RealReal (2021), which is "empowering consignors and buyers to extend the life cycle of luxury goods. The future of fashion is circular." Companies such as Burberry, Gucci, Stella McCartney, and Dries Van Noten have all started collaboration projects with The RealReal (McDowell, 2019; Farra, 2020). What does this imply for businesses? The answer is quite simple: companies endorsing The RealReal encourage their current target audience to sell (consign) through the resale in return for being rewarded by either getting store credits or other experiences and special treats form the organisation (e.g., Burberry, Gucci). Although this does not extend their actual target market, it creates an opportunity to extend the use-time of already existing products, whilst at the same time encouraging first-hand shopping. Thus, whilst it could be argued that these resale platforms are moving us into a more circular direction, in terms of promoting the reuse of garments and allowing for an extended wear-time of items, they could also be seen as fostering overconsumption.

Companies such as MUD Jeans (2021) have almost revolutionised their business model, in that they not only lease garments, and thus do not promote a change in ownership, but also recycle their own garments if no longer of use. This approach could be described as truly circular, yet it is questionable whether this can be scaled up and/or implemented within other organisations. Having created this business model not only implies a significant amount of logistics and know-how of reverse supply chains, but also potentially staff and storage capacity. All of these aspects are vital resources that can shape a company's unique capabilities, which makes them hard to imitate.

What you may have noticed is that no matter what approach is taken to becoming more circular, it can be seen as advantageous. Companies that are seen to contribute positively to the SDGs by reducing any impact they may have are also strengthening their (perceived) brand image, in that they are able to portray themselves as "good corporate citizens" that are actively making changes. Being able to further tell a story through, for example, the material they are using (e.g., ocean plastic), they may create connections with their consumer base and foster buy-in. Yet one of the risks with "storytelling" can also be that consumers become increasingly cynical about messages being broadcast. In the past, we have seen the emergence of the greenwashing phenomenon, which needs to be avoided. A further point that needs to be raised here is that we, as managers, need to be aware that our consumer base is not homogenous, which implies that not all our current and potential consumers may feel the same about circularity and sustainability. As such, it is important to carefully weigh messages and ensure that the stories told do not prohibit consumers from buying into the products.

As mentioned earlier, there are not only benefits that can be seen from approaching a more circular business model, but there can also be various challenges. The previous section pointed out that in various approaches to zero waste fashion design – in the case of upcycling and recycling especially, but also with various sharing economy practices (e.g., swapping, renting) and the resale model – stock uncertainties can be a big issue. Without high-quality products in the first-hand market, some of these business models may falter, as they rely heavily not only on the availability of these products, but also on their quality.

If we go back to the idea of the secondhand and resale market, we may also notice that a lot of brands form collaborations with others that have an expertise in this area. This is key, as knowing one's own strengths and weaknesses is essential in staying financially viable. Although models such as renting, leasing, and resale have been around for years, there is still a lack of experience in the market concerning reverse logistics and re-distribution, which is also coupled with the availability of resources. Thus, it may not be surprising that currently, when it comes to circularity in the fashion industry, we still lack examples of best practice and how to tackle issues.

Moreover, businesses do not operate in isolation, but rather are reliant on consumers to buy into different concepts. We have seen the emergence of a more conscious consumer base, which implies that consumers are more clued up on what is achievable and how "sustainable" different brands are, yet this cannot be made into a generalisation of the entirety of the market. To reiterate this point, various market segments and their subsequent consumer base may lack an awareness of a circular economy entails and what it may be. This might not be a surprise because as we can see from this book, there are different approaches on how to tackle the circular economy, and similar to the fact that sustainability is a fuzzy concept that may be intuitively understood, it could be argued the same holds true for the circular economy.

1.4.6 Case study: circularity in the fashion industry – the example of Hetty Rose

Intended learning outcomes

After working through the case study, students will be able to:

- Define and explain zero waste design strategies used in the fashion industry.
- Critically evaluate and distinguish different types of zero waste fashion.
- Reflect upon consumer and business perspectives of zero waste fashion design based on the Hetty Rose case study.
- Examine whether there are other circular design strategies available to Hetty Rose, and use the circular economy model to illustrate their answers.

Introduction

What may be seen as waste in one situation can be a treasure in another, which is a key consideration when thinking about the circular economy and its various strategies to re-loop materials back into the consumption and production stream. The proverbial thinking outside the box is key, thereby capitalising on the value of waste materials, which is especially important for the fashion industry, which has a particular waste problem, with not only garments ending up in landfill, but also fabric scraps in the production process not being utilised and being discarded. The former is part of the post-consumer waste stream, whilst the latter happens pre-consumer, in the production process. Figure 1.4.7 is a simplified illustration of circular thinking, whereby the dominating linear fashion model is changed by re-looping waste back into the system.

Key benefits of circular strategies include capturing the value of secondhand apparel. The annual value of prematurely discarded garments is estimated at US$500 billion (EMF, 2017), and this is anticipated to increase, which is advantageous for businesses that follow circular strategies and thus develop business model innovations to gain a competitive advantage. Examples of these business model innovations are those that have embraced innovative pattern cutting techniques, whereby traditional pattern cutting processes are challenged, in that each pattern has a specific function and is carefully placed in a jigsaw-like manner to maximise fabric use and minimise waste. Creative design is a further example, with garments being created with multiple purposes in mind, so that a single garment can be worn as a snood, T-shirt, or skirt.

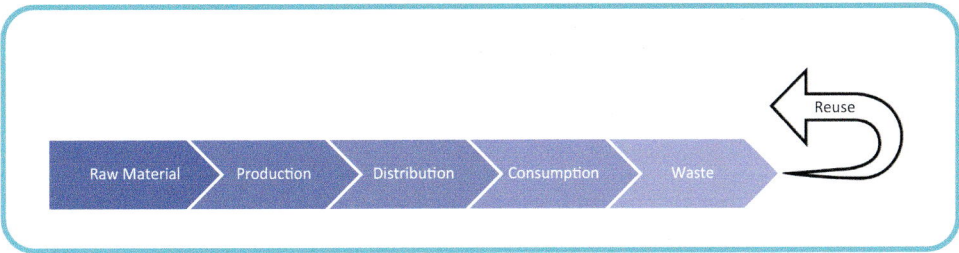

Figure 1.4.7   Simplified illustration of circular thinking

Fashion companies focusing on post-consumer waste capitalise on garments that are already in existence and may no longer be of value to the original owner, yet the material might still be valuable. Key strategies that are associated with this are either recycling, which implies making use of the material by deconstructing it back into fibres, or upcycling, by either changing already existing garments to make them trendier (e.g., adding embroidery) or turning them into something new.

Hetty Rose

Hetty Rose is a shoemaker and designer based in Kent, who specialises in bespoke bridal shoes that can best be described as "one of a kind". Creating one of these unique pairs of shoes can take between eight to twelve weeks. In an interview with the *Telegraph*, Hetty highlighted that "clients really enjoy the experience – I send photos to them along the way so they can see what is happening" (Lambert, 2009). The eponymous brand was established in 2007, and has not only been part of London Fashion Week, but has also gained global attention, having been featured in leading fashion magazines such as *Vogue, Elle, InStyle*, and *Marie Claire* (Hetty Rose, n.d. a).

Hetty describes her brand as "ethical and environmentally considerate" (Hetty Rose, n.d. b) by following a trend that is now commonly referred to as upcycling. Her shoes are made from vintage kimonos personally sourced from Japan (BBC, 2009), which not only showcase beautiful patterns and designs, but are also saturated with different meanings. Depending on how the shoe patterns are placed, different parts of the kimono are featured on the shoe, making them truly unique, but also part of zero waste fashion, as jigsaw placing techniques can be used to minimise fabric waste (Figure 1.4.8).

Hetty tries to adhere to a policy of reusing any of the smaller pieces of fabric or leather left over after the manufacturing process to make other items and accessories. Sometimes the client requests the smaller offcuts of material to use in a creative way within the scheme of their wedding. Hetty has made use of even the smallest pieces of fabric in a creative way: for example, covering the buttons of a groom's shirt in the offcuts of his bride's shoes (Figure 1.4.10).

Figure 1.4.8   Botanical shoes by Hetty Rose©

Figure 1.4.9   Dahlia shoes by Hetty Rose©

Figure 1.4.10   Workspace by Hetty Rose©

Each pair of shoes is made for just one person by upcycling vintage fabrics. Hetty sources her components from local craftspeople and supports small businesses wherever she can.

By making shoes to specification, clients are involved in the process – choosing the fabric, the heel, the shape of shoe, etc. – so they have an emotional connection to the shoes. They are more likely to really cherish and look after the shoes, therefore reducing the need to buy more shoes they just like for a season. By really knowing what your personal style is and what you really love in a pair of shoes (or clothing), you can reduce the number pairs of shoes you buy.

Alongside her bespoke bridal shoe business, consumers can also book a shoemaking course with Hetty Rose, and get hands-on experience of what it is like to create one's own pair of flats or heels. The workshop provides a whistlestop tour of shoemaking essentials by further highlighting the crafts expertise and work needed to create the perfect pair of shoes. Understanding the time and labour that goes into making a shoe is not only a unique experience, but also education. It thus has the potential to stimulate rethinking consumption practices, by gaining first-hand experience of the creation process and value of the product.

Questions

1. The circular economy has become a buzzword of the 21st century. Outline key advantages and drawbacks of creating a circular business models in the fashion industry.
2. What are different modes of achieving zero waste strategies for fashion companies, and which one best describes Hetty Rose?
3. Critically evaluate the zero waste strategy used by Hetty Rose, from a business and consumer perspective.
4. In your opinion, what are the implications of offering bespoke shoemaking workshops?

Chapter references

aRks (2016) *Multidisciplinary creative duo Samuele and Rosanna of aRks studio present 'coral' – their first 3D printed bikini collection*, aRks (online): http://www.arks3d.com/en/press.html, 17/10/2021.

Armstrong, C.M., Niinimäki, K., Kujala, S., Karell, E., and Lang, C. (2015) Sustainable product-service systems for clothing: exploring perceptions of consumption alternatives in Finland, *Journal of Cleaner Production*, 97, 30–39.

BBC (2009) *Shoemaker puts best foot forward*, BBC (online): http://news.bbc.co.uk/local/essex/hi/people_and_places/arts_and_culture/newsid_8310000/8310819.stm.

Berman, B. (2012) 3-D printing: the new industrial revolution, *Business Horizons*, 55, 155–162.

Blazquez Cano, M., Henninger, C.E., Alexander, B., and Franquesa, C. (2020) Consumers' knowledge and intentions towards sustainability: A Spanish fashion perspective, *Fashion Practice*, 12(1), 34–54.

Botsman, R., and Rogers, R. (2010) *What's mine is yours: how collaborative consumption is changing the way we live*, Harper Collins Business, London.

Brydges, T., and Hanlon, M. (2020) Garment worker rights and the fashion industry's response to COVID-19, *Dialogues in Human Geography*, 10(2): 195–198.

Caroline (2014) *Encircled's Chrysalis Cardi: the traveler's scarf, dress and top in one*, HerPackungList (online): https://herpackinglist.com/encircled-chrysalis-cardi-review/, 17/10/2021.

Chan, E. (2020) *Upcycling is the biggest trend in fashion right now*, Vogue (online): https://www.vogue.co.uk/fashion/article/upcycling-trend-ss21, 23/10/2021.

Christensen, C.M. (1997) *The innovator's dilemma: when new technologies cause great firms to fail*, Harvard Business School Press, Boston, MA.

Christensen, C.M., and Raynor, M.E. (2003) *The innovator's solution: creating and sustaining successful growth*, Harvard Business School Press, Boston, MA.

Circular Fashion (2021) *Origin of the concept 'circular fashion'*, Green Strategy (online): https://www.greenstrategy.se/circular-fashion-definition/, 26/09/2021.

Close the Loop (2020) *Introduction*, Close the Loop (online): https://www.close-the-loop.be/en/phase/3/end-of-life, 14/09/2021.

Contreras-Lisperguer, R., Muñoz-Cerón, E., Aguilera J., and de la Casa, J. (2017) Cradle-to-cradle approach in the life cycle of silicon solar photovoltaic panels, *Journal of Cleaner Production*, 168, 51–59.

Dean, C. (2019) *Waste – is it 'really' in fashion?*, Fashion Revolution (online): https://www.fashionrevolution.org/waste-is-it-really-in-fashion/, 17/10/2021.

Diegues, T. (2020) Operationalisation of circular economy: a conceptual model, in Baporikar, N. (ed.), *Handbook of research on entrepreneurship development and opportunities in circular economy*, IGI Global Publishing, Hersey, PA.

Ecoalf (2021) *Recycled materials*, Ecoalf (online): https://ecoalf.com/en/p/materials-80, 23/10/2021.

EEA (European Environmental Agency) (2019) *Textiles in Europe's circular economy*, EEA (online): https://www.eea.europa.eu/themes/waste/resource-efficiency/textiles-in-europe-s-circular-economy, 27/11/2020.

EMF (2017) *A new textiles economy: redesigning fashion's future*, EMF (online):

https://ellenmacarthurfoundation.org/a-new-textiles-economy, 20/09/2021.

EMF (n.d.) *Circular economy diagram*, EMF (online): https://ellenmacarthurfoundation.org/circular-economy-diagram, 26/09/2021.

European Parliament (2021) *Circular economy: definition, importance and benefits*, Europa (online): https://www.europarl.europa.eu/news/en/headlines/economy/20151201STO05603/circular-economy-definition-importance-and-benefits, 17/10/2021.

Farra, E. (2020) *Gucci and The RealReal announcement a game-changing partnership*, Vogue (online): https://www.vogue.co.uk/fashion/article/gucci-realreal-partnership, 23/10/2021.

Faithfull, M. (2021) *Shein: is China's mysterious $15 billion fast fashion retailer ready for stores*, Forbes (online): https://www.forbes.com/sites/markfaithfull/2021/02/10/shein-is-chinas-mysterious-15-billion-fast-fashion-retailer-ready-for-stores/?sh=69228eac6df5, 26/09/2021.

Fields, D. (2021) *Secondhand clothing recyclers growing into IPO digs*, Forbes (online): https://www.forbes.com/sites/mergermarket/2021/09/14/secondhand-clothing-recyclers-growing-into-ipo-digs/?sh=6c7e037c4ff0, 20/09/2021.

Forbes (2021) *Secondhand clothing recyclers growing into IPO digs*, Forbes (online): https://www.forbes.com/sites/mergermarket/2021/09/14/secondhand-clothing-recyclers-growing-into-ipo-digs/?sh=486fc6f44ff0, 26/09/2021.

Fragments Garments (2019) *Fashion digital crafts*, https://www.fragmentsgarments.com/, 21/01/2021.

Fragments Garments (2019b) *We offer*, Fragments Garments (online): https://www.fragmentsgarments.com/we-offer, 17/10/2021.

Granskog, A., Lee, L., Magnus, K.H., and Sawers, C. (2020) *Survey: consumer sentiment on sustainability in fashion*, McKinsey (online): https://www.mckinsey.com/industries/retail/our-insights/survey-consumer-sentiment-on-sustainability-in-fashion, 23/10/2021.

Gray, R. (2020) *Covid-19: how long does the coronavirus last on surfaces*, BBC (online):

https://www.bbc.com/future/article/20200317
-covid-19-how-long-does-the-coronavirus-last
-on-surfaces, 23/10/2021.

Hackenberg, J. (2021) *Brands, you need
to listen to the conscious consumer of the
future*, Forbes (online): https://www.forbes
.com/sites/jonquilhackenberg/2021/04/29/
brands-you-need-to-listen-to-the-conscious
-consumer-of-the-future/?sh=2e89cf451d46,
23/10/2021.

Harvey, J. (2021) *The rise of deadstock
dressing: designers approach upcycling
clothes the chic way*, Elle (online): https://
www.elle.com/uk/fashion/trends/a36282440/
upcycling-clothes/, 23/10/2021.

Heater, B. (2018) *Adidas joins carbon's
board as its 3D printed shoes finally drop*,
Techcrunch (online): https://techcrunch.com
/2018/01/18/adidas-joins-carbons-board
-as-its-3d-printed-shoes-finally-drop/,
17/10/2021.

Henninger, C.E., Alevizou, P.J., Goworek, H.,
and Ryding, D. (eds.) (2017) *Sustainability
in fashion: a cradle to upcycle approach*,
Springer, Heidelberg.

Henninger, C.E., Jones, C., Boardman, R., and
McCormick, H. (2018) The circular economy
phenomenon an overview of its status in the
UK market, Chapter 3, in Niinimäki, K. (ed.),
Sustainable fashion in a circular economy,
Aalto ARTS Books, Helsinki, pp. 62–75.

Henninger, C.E., Bürklin, N., and Niinimäki,
K. (2019) The clothes swapping phenomenon
– when consumers become suppliers, *Journal
of Fashion Marketing & Management*, 23(3),
327–344.

Henninger, C.E., Blazquez Cano, M.,
Boardman, R., Jones, C., McCormick, H., and
Sahab, S. (2020) Cradle-to-cradle vs consumer
preferences, in Choudhury, I., and Hashmi,
S. (eds.), *Encyclopedia of renewable and
sustainable materials*, Volume 5, Elsevier,
Oxford, pp. 353–357.

Henninger, C.E., Brydges, T., Iran, S., and
Vladimirova, K. (2021a) Collaborative fashion
consumption – a synthesis and future research
agenda, *Journal of Cleaner Production*, 319,
128648.

Henninger, C.E., Amasawa, E., Brydges, T.,
and Piontek, F.M. (2021b) My wardrobe in

the cloud – an international comparison of
fashion rental, in Ertz, M. (ed.), *Handbook for
research on the platform economy and the
evolution of e-commerce*, IGI Global, Hershey,
PA, pp. 153–175.

Henry, M., Schraven, D., Bocken, N.,
Frenken, K., Hekkert, M., and Kirchherr,
J. (2021) The battle of the buzzwords: a
comparative review of the circular economy
and the sharing economy concpets,
*Environemntal Innovation and Societal
Transitions*, 38, 1–21.

Hetty Rose (n.d. a) *Press*, Hetty Rose (online):
https://www.hettyrose.co.uk/press.

Hetty Rose (n.d. b) *Creator*, Hetty Rose
(online): https://www.hettyrose.co.uk/about.

Huang, Y., Leu, M.C., Mazumder, J., and
Donmez, A. (2015) Additive manufacturing:
current state, future potential, gaps and
needs, and recommendations, *Journal of
Manufacturing Science and Engineering*,
137(1), 1–10.

Jacobson, R. (2017) *The shattering truth of
3D-printed clothing*, Wired (online): https://
www.wired.com/2017/05/the-shattering-truth
-of-3d-printed-clothing/, 19/05/2021.

Kickstarter (2013) *The Versalette by {r}
evolution apparel*, Kickstarter (online):
https://www.kickstarter.com/projects/
revolutionapparel/the-versalette-by-r
-evolution-apparel, 17/10/2021.

Lambert, V. (2009, May 20) *The very sole of
individuality*, Telegraph (online): http://fashion
.telegraph.co.uk/news-features/TMG5354961/
The-very-sole-of-individuality.html.

Materialise (2013) *Iris van Herpen debuts
wearable 3d printed pieces at Paris Fashion
Week*, Materialise (online): https://www
.materialise.com/en/cases/iris-van-herpen
-debuts-wearable-3d-printed-pieces-at-paris
-fashion-week, 17/10/2021.

McCormick, H., Zhang, R., Boardman,
R., Jones, C., and Henninger, C.E. (2019)
3D-printing in the fashion industry: a fad or
future?, in Vignali, G., Reid, L., Ryding, D.,
and Henninger, C.E. (eds.), *Technology-driven
sustainability: innovation in the fashion
supply chain*, Palgrave, London, Chapter 8,
pp. 137–154.

McDonough, W., and Braungart, M. (2002) *Cradle to cradle: remaking the way we do things*, North Point Press, New York.

McDowell, M. (2019) *Burberry's partnership with The RealReal signifies a real shift*, Vogue (online): https://www.voguebusiness.com/companies/burberrys-partnership-realreal-secondhand, 23/10/2021.

McGregor, K. (2019) *Bringing it home. Why retailers are taking pattern cutting in house*, Drapers (online): https://www.drapersonline.com/companies/bringing-it-home-why-retailers-are-taking-pattern-cutting-in-house, 17/10/2021.

Ministry of Supply (2020) *Zero waste production*, Ministry of Supply (online): https://www.ministryofsupply.com/about/zero-waste, 17/10/2021.

Miu Mlu (2019) *Upcycled by Miu Miu*, Miu Miu (online): https://www.miumiu.com/gr/en/miumiu-club/special-projects/upcycled.html, 23/10/2021.

MUD Jeans (2021) *Meet our new circular denim system*, MUD Jeans (online): https://mudjeans.eu, 26/09/2021.

Mukendi, A., and Henninger C.E. (2020) Exploring the spectrum of fashion rental, *Journal of Fashion Marketing & Management*, 24(3), 455–469.

Niinimäki, K. (2013) *Sustainable fashion: new approaches*, Aalto ARTS Books, Helsinki, Finland.

Niinimäki, K. (2017) Fashion in a circular economy, in Henninger, C.E., Alevizou, P.J., Goworek, H., and Ryding, D. (eds.), *Sustainable fashion a cradle to upcycle approach*, Springer, Heidelberg, Chapter 8, pp. 151–169.

Oceanness (2021) *From plastic bottles to soft tees*, Oceanness (online): https://oceanness.com/pages/how-we-do-it, 26/09/2021.

Park, H., and Armstrong, C.M.J. (2017) Collaborative apparel consumption in the digital sharing economy: an agenda for academic inquiry, *International Journal of Consumer Studies*, 41, 465–474.

Parish, P. (2020) *Pattern cutting: the architecture of fashion*, Bloomsbury, London, 2nd edition.

Revapparel (2012) *The Versalette by {r} evolution apparel*, YouTube (online): https://www.youtube.com/watch?v=tGu8lOogDgI, 17/10/2021.

RSA Action and Research Centre (2016) *Design for a circular economy: lessons from the great recovery*, RSA (online): https://www.thersa.org/globalassets/pdfs/reports/the-great-recovery---designing-for-a-circular-economy.pdf, 28/01/2017.

Rutter, C., Armstrong, K., and Blazquez, M. (2017) The epiphanic sustainable fast fashion epoch: a new fashion ethical mandate, in Henninger, C.E., Alevizou, P.J., Goworek, H., and Ryding, D. (eds.), *Sustainable fashion a cradle to upcycle approach*, Springer, Heidelberg, Chapter 2, pp. 11–30.

Schor, J.B. and Attwood-Charles, W. (2017) The 'sharing' economy: labor, inequality, and social connection on for-profit platforms, *Sociology Compass*, 11(8), e12493.

Sculpteo (2021) *3D leaning hub*, Sculpteo (online): https://www.sculpteo.com/en/3d-learning-hub/applications-of-3d-printing/3d-printed-clothes/, 17/10/2021.

Sharma, T.D., and Hall, C. (2010) *Green PLM for fashion & apparel, White Paper*, Infosys (online): http://www.infosys.com/industries/retail/white-papers/Documents/green-plm-fashion-apparel.pdf, 01/11/2018.

Shapeways (2018) *About us*, Shapeways (online): https://www.shapeways.com/about, 17/10/2021.

Statista (2021) *Leading exporters of denim fabric worldwide in 2020 (in million U.S. dollars)*, Statista (online): https://www.statista.com/statistics/1010223/leading-exporters-of-denim-worldwide/, 26/09/2021.

The RealReal (2021) *About The RealReal*, The RealReal (online): https://www.therealreal.com/about, 24/05/2021.

The True Cost (2015) *Directed by Andrew Morgan*, Production Companies: Untold Creative, Life is my movie entertainment.

ThreadUp (2021) *2021 resale report*, ThreadUp (online): https://www.thredup.com/resale/static/thredUP-Resale-and-Impact-Report-2021-980436a36adc4f84a26675c1fcf2c554.pdf, 17/10/2021.

Triple Pundit (2014) *Upcycling: the new wave of sustainable fashion*, Triple Pundit (online): https://www.triplepundit.com/story/2014 /upcycling-new-wave-sustainable-fashion /58691, 23/10/2021.

UN (n.d.) *Ensure sustainable consumption and production patterns*, UN (online): https://sdgs .un.org/goals/goal12, 20/09/2021.

UN (2021) *Ensure sustainbale production and consumption patterns*, UN (online): https:// sdgs.un.org/goals/goal12, 20/05/2022.

Vanderploeg, A., Lee, S.E., and Mamp, M. (2017) The application of 3D printing technology in the fashion industry, *International Journal of Fashion Design, Technology and Education*, 10(2), 170–179.

WCED (1986) *Our Common Future (The Brundtland Report)*, World Commission on Environment and Development, Oxford University Press, Oxford.

WRAP (2020) *Changing our clothes: why the clothing sector should adopt new business models*, WRAP (online): https://www.wrap .org.uk/content/changing-our-clothes -why-clothing-sector-should-adopt-new -business-models?_ga=2.182743332.30533189 .1593259255-1614214988.1593259255, 27/06/2020.

PART 2
Managing sustainable fashion through design

Part 2 extends the management focus into the design world and onto the designer's worktable. Managing the fashion system and its sustainability aspects through design is challenging. Designers seldom play a major decision-making role in the fashion system, which is driven more by industrial manufacturing realities, economic profit goals, and marketing strategy (see Section 1.1.1). Even in sustainability-minded companies, designers are limited in the decisions they can make and mainly focus on material choices and finding design attributes that offer functionality and can extend the lifetime of a garment. Therefore, designers mainly aim to provide users with satisfying wear experiences and longevity aspects and try to select sustainable materials for their fashion collections (Karell & Niinimäki, 2020).

Although it is possible to influence the environmental impacts of a product through material choices, very often the best sustainable material cannot be selected because of price or availability issues (see also **Part 4: Material Innovations in Sustainable Fashion**). Although the range of sustainable and ethically produced fabrics has increased, it is still difficult to find good-quality materials that suit their intended functions in a certain use context and meet the right ethical and ecological criteria. Moreover, other haberdashery that fulfils sustainability criteria might be even harder to find than fabric (Niinimäki & Aakko, 2014). One of the early barriers to creating a successful business in an emerging industry is access to raw materials. Often, more mature companies have already overcome this challenge (Porter, 2004). This is especially true for small and medium-sized enterprises (SMEs) and new business initiatives in the sustainable fashion field. There is currently great demand for sustainable fabrics and, for example, organic cotton or new regenerated cellulose-type recycled fibres, and this has created a tense, competitive situation. For small and new companies, this is not an easy situation. More mature companies have found their suppliers and established continuous collaboration with them to secure access to sustainable materials. Some big fashion brands also eagerly take part in different R&D projects to secure their involvement in new sustainable material developments.

The functionality of a product may also limit material choices (see Chapter 1.1). As the aim of the design process is to provide good, even the best, user experience through, for example, garment functionality, material choices are made accordingly. This aspect might prevent the selection of the most sustainable material with the lowest environmental impact if its attributes do not fulfil the functionality criteria, as in the sport clothing sector, for example. Another limiting factor in material choices might be the durability aspect (technical durability). Although designers want to secure a garment's

DOI: 10.4324/9781003097846-6

longevity, it is not worth selecting a fabric with low durability even if it is a more sustainable choice. The selected end-price category can also limit material selection. All these aspects create the frame within which designers work in industrial and commercial reality. Designers also claim that they do not have enough time to search for and find alternative materials and consider or test alternative strategies, as industrial design work is intensive and production seasons change rapidly. The collection requirements and schedules are so tight that you do not always have the energy to search for and think about sustainable alternatives (Karell & Niinimäki, 2020).

Product longevity is a controversial issue. A study in 2020 (Karell & Niinimäki, 2020) found that fashion designers working in a sustainability-minded company valued the longevity aspect in garments and tried to make design decisions that enhanced longevity. Material durability is essential, but so is sewing work quality and timeless design, and the repairability and reusability of a garment should also be a focus of design. Garment longevity can be understood as a higher category that includes design strategies such as physical durability through high quality, emotional durability, timeless design, slow fashion, trans-seasonality, co-creation with users, multifunctionality, adjustability, and modularity (Karell & Niinimäki, 2020). Yet we know that the current fashion system is based on the allure of rapidly changing trends and consumers' emotional need for newness. Furthermore, social acceptance, identity building through appearance, and symbolic elements are important drivers in fashion purchases (Kaiser, 1990). For some consumers, fashion has begun to be entertainment, and ease and cheap access to the newest trends, added to impulse online shopping, create a situation in which it is very hard for consumers to act in a sustainable way and reject the allure of fashion, even if designers are trying to support longer use time through design choices (Niinimäki,2018).

This part presents some fashion design views and strategies that are connected to sustainability. To manage sustainability, the large themes of transformation should focus on: system understanding, reducing and slowing, responsibility, and risk management. At the end of the part, all these aspects will be combined to construct a new paradigm for sustainable fashion design. All these approaches are needed when the goal is to find a new balance in fashion by reorganising the system and limiting environmental impacts. Safety issues are also important in design and manufacturing, and safety and control issues in the supply chain are also discussed in this part. The reputation of the brand is more important than ever to conscious consumers, therefore companies must do all they can to prevent the loss of consumers' trust.

The examples this part discusses and the industry/business cases it presents show that even if sustainability is a complex issue with no easy solutions, it is still possible to move forward and find some approaches to new sustainable design and system understanding. Although a wider system perspective of sustainability is needed, the reality remains that most companies are nevertheless trying to implement best practices on the basis of existing knowledge. To make sustainability a reality, it should be integrated throughout the system instead of being a mere add-on to a product design or based on too narrow a view (Goworek et al., 2013) (see also Chapter 1.2). Creative design thinking could guide, or at least support, the entire sustainability transformation process. This will be discussed in more detail in the following chapters.

2.1 New system understanding for design

Some good examples exist of companies, often more designer-driven ones, that are trying to provide alternative views and wider-ranging approaches to sustainability rather than focusing on only material selection. Very often, these companies are initiated and run by sustainability-minded designers and are SMEs, but exceptions exist (e.g., Stella McCartney). Many fashion designers launch their own brand so that they can build their own sustainable strategy into the business. In these designer-driven companies, the design and the strategies are often "crafted", meaning that the strategy, business, and design practices slowly evolve through practical experiments (Niinimäki & Aakko, 2014). As Mintzberg (1994) points out, strategy-building can be based on emerging processes, in which the practice and strategy work are intertwined and happen simultaneously. This requires constant feedback and reflection on success, but also time. It will therefore be a slower process than the traditional way of doing fashion business. As products communicate the company's strategy towards users, this "background work" – building a sustainable strategy – forms the foundations for sustainable fashion design. "Crafting" a sustainable fashion strategy therefore requires not only the newest scientific knowledge, but also creative, artful, and adaptive skills (Whittington et al., 2006). This kind of emerging approach to strategy construction can be applied in design-driven strategies – in other words, strategies based on design practice, design skills, and experienced design knowledge (Niinimäki & Aakko, 2014). This is easiest to implement in designer-driven companies, of which this chapter has some fine examples that will be discussed in more detail later (e.g., Anna Ruohonen, FRENN, Alabama Chanin).

The "crafting" strategy approach highlights not only the importance of practice-based knowledge in strategy-building, but also the emerging character of sustainable strategy. As new sustainable knowledge is emerging, it is important to form the attitude that sustainable design strategy needs to keep evolving, constantly; it has to be "a living document". This means that there should be a system for collecting new information and feedback, and for reflecting, evaluating, and setting new annual goals in the strategy. Design strategy needs to be a fundamental part of the sustainable strategy of a company. This work needs time and commitment, and very often a specific person nominated for the task.

We could also learn lessons from design management theories, which highlight that design management is a way of "thinking about and through design". It should include system-level and system-wide approaches, and not be limited to a single product approach (Cooper, et al., 2009). If this wider view was adapted into strategy-building, the company's actions and its standpoint in the whole fashion system could be clearer, and a strong sustainable identity could be communicated to all partners and consumers. A wider view in the strategy would mean a change in perspective, which in turn would affect design strategy, meaning that the focus on finding sustainable materials alone would not be enough. Thus, the focus should be on the sustainability transition

DOI: 10.4324/9781003097846-7

and even system-level changes in the industry. While traditional design management has focused on product design and incremental improvements, "design thinking represents a more radical shift in an overall way of doing business" (Cooper et al., 2009, p. 50.) The design-thinking approach should help us focus more on system-level issues, how to slow down the material throughput in the system, how to slow down manufacturing and make production more accurate (avoiding overproduction and disposing of or burning unsold products), and how to create a safer, more sustainable, and just fashion system. This approach also needs new design knowledge. We need to design products that enable the transition towards sustainability throughout the system: during manufacturing, use, disposal, and even in the way the fashion business is conducted. Expanding the design approach to system-level problem-solving would enhance the creative solutions in the system level. Sinha (2000, pp.37–40) points out that the fashion designers' skill set, knowledge, and creativity could already be integrated when the company's mission and business processes are being planned and strategy being built. In this way, the design strategy could also be part of the foundations of the business and be an integrated part of the way of doing fashion business.

> **Design management** – a way of "thinking about and through design". It should include system-level and system-wide approaches, and not be limited to a single product approach.

The current linear fashion economy is based on ever-changing trends, effective mass manufacturing in lower-cost countries, and short lead times. Consumers purchase on impulse, use garments for a very short time, and dispose of them easily. All these aspects create a system that has huge environmental impacts and constantly increases textile waste streams (Niinimäki et al., 2020). In the fast fashion system, design is not very accurate, resulting in second-rate quality in manufacturing, a great deal of overproduction, and stock surpluses (e.g., left-over fabrics when the collection being manufactured changes). It is estimated that up to 20–30 per cent of manufactured garments are of second-rate quality or remain unsold and end up in discount sales or incineration. McKinsey & Company estimated that only 60 per cent of garments are currently sold without a markdown (Berg, et al., 2020), and *Ecotextile News* reported in 2016 that only a third of all imported clothing in the European Union (EU) is sold at full retail price, a third is sold at a discounted price, and a third is not sold at all (Mathews, 2016). These figures show the imbalance in the fashion system and are a clear sign of inaccurate overproduction. Creating a more accurate system for designing and manufacturing could drastically slow down the system and create less overproduction and waste. This is where creative design thinking and braver business experimentation could support system-level transformation.

2.1.1 Redesigning industrial design processes

The linear system is based on fast material throughput: design–manufacture–use–disposal. The circular model, which is discussed in more detail in the next chapter, is an alternative to this: it attempts to keep the value of the product and the material as high as possible for as long as possible. But other ways to redesign the industrial manufacturing system also exist. Traditional industrial manufacturing wastes a great deal of resources, as all production is based on a simple model of mass-manufacturing, resulting in "sameness". To produce one fashion collection, all the fabrics needed for it are pre-ordered and placed in storage. More fabric is always ordered than is actually used in the garment collection, leading to a huge amount of deadstock of fabrics in storage when the manufacturing of a certain collection is over. Another source of textile material waste is offcut waste from garment production. These leftovers and off-cuts could still be used in garment manufacturing. Therefore, better resource control and an even more creative and flexible ways of producing garments could improve the efficiency of the fashion industry. Reverse Resources (Runnel et al. 2017) has created a design approach in which all leftover fabric and offcuts could be taken back into garment production, ending up by saving fabric. Leftover fabrics and offcut pieces could be used as invisible (e.g., lining) or visible parts in the garments (e.g., pockets, collars), and this way even create aesthetic diversity in mass-manufacturing (Niinimäki, 2018). This way of approaching industrial garment manufacturing challenges the current way of producing garments and aims for only similarity in the end-product. This could be a way to extend the designer's role from the design studio to industrial production, and make it not only more creative, but also more resource-efficient. This way of being more efficient in production has an impact. Reverse Resources (Runnel et al., 2017) has calculated that producing 10,000 hoodies using this design approach (visible remanu-facturing) can:

- Save 2,843 yards (17 per cent) of virgin fabrics.
- Avoid 0.88 tonnes of fabrics being disposed of.
- Save 7,827 kg in CO_2 emissions.

CASE: STELLA MCCARTNEY AND RESOURCE EFFICIENCY THROUGH CREATIVITY

The COVID-19 crisis led to a global temporal moment of pause for the fashion indus-try. Many companies tried to stop manufacturing collections that had already been ordered and started to manufacture new collections that had been left in storage partly unsold because the pandemic had reduced consumers' incomes and thus the volumes of fashion purchases. Some companies used this moment to re-evaluate their value base and methods of operating in the fashion business. Stella McCartney, a lead-ing sustainable fashion brand with a highly innovative and open-minded approach to fashion design, used this time to be creative, considering what to do with leftover stock. Stella McCartney created a design concept for using leftover textile stock from previous collections to be more resource-efficient in design and manufacturing. At the same time, she created strong, unique design aesthetics by combining different fabrics and fashion impressions taken from sportswear. This design approach is a lim-ited-edition type of manufacturing – overstocks are limited, so a limited amount of fabric results in a limited number of garments. This strategy also supports the aspect of zero waste. The approach suits this brand's design-driven DNA (Madsen. 8.2.2021).

> I have been thinking a lot about our wider impact. How can we reduce what we produce? How can we do more with less? How can we achieve truly zero waste?
>
> (Stella McCartney)

References

Berg, A., Granskog, A., Lee, L., and Magnus K. (2020) *Fashion on climate*, McKinsey & Company (online): https://www.mckinsey.com/industries/retail/our-insights/fashion-on-climate, 22/7/2021.

Cooper, R., Junginger, S., and Lockwood, T. (2009) Design thinking and design management: a research and practice perspective, *Design Management Review*, 1, 46–55.

Madsen, A.C. (2021, February 8) *Stella Mc Cartney Pre Fall 2021* (online): https://www.vogue.com/fashion-shows/pre-fall-2021/stella-mccartney, 1/6/2021.

Mathews, B. (2016) *One third of all clothing "Never Sold"*, Ecotextile News (online): https://www.ecotextile.com/2016042122078/fashion-retail-news/one-third-of-allclothing-never-sold.html, 1/1/2018.

Mintzberg, H. (1994) *The rise and fall of strategic planning*, Free Press, New York.

Niinimäki, K. (2018) Knowing better, but behaving emotionally: strong emotional undertones in fast fashion consumption, in Becker-Leifhold, C., and Heuer, M. (eds.), *Eco friendly and fair: fast fashion and consumer behavior*, Routledge, London, pp. 49–57.

Niinimäki, K., and Aakko, M. (2014) Creative control in sustainable fashion, in *19th ADMC, Academic Design Management Conference, Design Management in the Era of Disruption*, 2–4 September 2014, UAL, London, UK, pp. 583–600.

Niinimäki, K., Peters, G., Dahlbo, H., Perry, P., Rissanen, T., and Gwilt, A. (2020) The environmental price of fast fashion, *Nature Reviews; Earth and Environment*, 1, 189–200.

Runnel, A., Raihan, K., Castel, N., Oja, D., and Bhuiya, H. (2017) *Creating digitally enhanced circular economy*, Reverse Resources (online): http://www.reverseresources.net/about/white-paper, 1/1/2018.

Sinha, P. (2000) The role of designing through making across market levels in the UK fashion industry, *The Design Journal*, 3(3), 26–44.

Whittington, R., Molloy, E., Mayer, M., and Smith, A. (2006) Practices of strategising/organising: broadening strategy work and skills, *Long Range Planning*, 39(6), 615–629.

Design for a circular economy

Learning outcomes

1. To understand the importance of the closed-loop system in the textile/fashion sector.
2. To understand how product design should be tied to the business model to enhance system-level sustainability in the best way.

The circular economy (CE; see Chapter 1.4) needs a new kind of system understanding that is also included in design. This chapter provides the foundation for this new knowledge and for future design practices. It will provide principles for how to design for the CE, especially how to design for a specific lifetime and end of lifetime, taking into account current recycling technologies and their possibilities and limitations for garment design.

CE is a system that minimises waste and uses all resources wisely, aiming to make the most of them. Discussions on CE often only focus on the end-of-life strategies and textile waste recycling, yet CE also extends the use-time of garments, offers business strategies to support longer product lifetimes (e.g., product-service systems) and a new kind of manufacturing (e.g., reuse of components in manufacturing), and its final stage is reverse logistics and the recycling of textile waste back into industrial fibre production. In CE, the focus should be on the value aspect. The aim is to keep the value of the product and material as high as possible for as long as possible, which leads to slowing down the system. Therefore, the product should be:

1) Repairable (by the consumer him/herself or a company).
2) Reusable and redistributable (to another consumer).
3) Remanufactured (by a company).
4) Recycled (in the closed-loop material system).

All these levels require different, new kinds of design considerations, but also enable the construction of new kinds of business models. The reuse of a garment needs to focus on making high-quality (best quality) and durability aspects part of the design process so that use time is as long as possible. Garments are currently not designed in such a way that they allow easy repairability. Some companies provide repair services for their garments, and others offer additional services, such as kits so that consumers can repair garments themselves. For example, the childrenswear company Reima offers repair kits with its outfits: "Because accidents do happen,

DOI: 10.4324/9781003097846-8

we offer a Repair Kit to help you fix the most common damage, like tears, or worn foot loops. In some of our European stores, we also have a biannual pop-up repair service" (Reima 2019). Outdoor clothes made by Reima use very special fabrics (e.g., waterproof finishes) and have their own print design, so this service not only enables the extension of the use time of the garment, but also sustains the usability and aesthetic of the garment.

The Vaatelaastari company produces special textile patches that are easy to attach to a garment. The patches can be used not only for repairing, but also as a decoration. As the patches are self-adhesive, they do not require repairing skills: "The Vaatelaastari Patch attaches to clothes and gear anywhere, anytime, by anyone – just press on and rub for one minute. It makes it super easy to patch holes, cover stains and decorate clothing and accessories" (Vaatelaastari).

Remanufacturing means a process in which some part of the product is returned to the manufacturer and used to construct a new product. Finnish company Arela, which produces high-quality cashmere knits, offers a repair service for its garments, but also gathers back its old knits, from which it develops new products (Arela). The remanufacturing approach is not common in the garment sector yet, but has been used to, for example, collect pre-consumer waste (offcut textile waste from garment assembly processes) which is then used in mechanical or chemical recycling processes for new yarns. Aiming for resource-efficiency, the most important aspect in CE is to extend the use time of a garment, followed by textile waste recycling into new high-value fibres, textiles, and products after their use time is over.

2.2.1 Intentional design for recycling

Recently, larger companies have been actively collaborating with other stakeholders in the CE ecosystem to be able to construct new kinds of design strategies suitable for closing the material loop, and in this way enable a circular system. New knowledge regarding a product's end of life and regarding new ways to recycle textile materials are required so that completely new design guidelines for the original product can be designed and manufactured. This approach could be defined as *intentional design for recycling*, in which the goal is to create products that are suitable for recycling and enable easy disassembly, recycling, and recovery (Niinimäki & Karell, 2019). Fashion companies are collaborating with textile waste sorters to be able to obtain inside knowledge regarding what kind of textile waste can be identified, sorted, and recycled through mechanical, thermal, or chemical recycling processes (for more detail, see **Part 4**). It is important to include this new information from the end-of-life stage in the design process so that textile waste recycling becomes easier and more economically viable in the future.

Design for recycling strategies is constructed according to product lines, and includes instructions on which materials, colours, chemicals, sewing yarns, trims, finishes, construction, etc. can be used and which should not be used so that the product is suitable for a specific type of recycling process. The idea is to give designers design boundaries for what certain types of recycling systems can and cannot tolerate, and through this approach to begin to tailor product design to certain types of recycling processes.

As waste sorting and recycling technologies are constantly developing, these design strategies need to be living documents that can be constantly updated when new knowledge on recycling emerges. This new design knowledge (design for recycling) is especially important for chemical recycling. Chemical recycling of textile material is strongly emerging, and several new technologies for regenerative cellulose recycling are scaling up and becoming a commercial reality. Only certain kinds of fabrics (cotton, viscose, hemp, linen, man-made fibres such as cellulose) are suitable for chemical recycling, and the recycling process has limitations to tolerate other kinds of fabrics (e.g., polyester or Spandex; elastane, Lycra or elastic). It should also be remembered that in blended materials, one of the fibres is often lost in the chemical recycling process. But this new knowledge is only just growing, and while these new regeneration technologies are scaling up, new knowledge will emerge regarding design limitations in material mixing. In addition, colours, prints (e.g., floc printing types of techniques, laminates), or finishing chemicals can prevent the chemical recycling of textile waste.

Mechanical recycling is more tolerant of different kinds of materials and blended textile materials, but even in mechanical recycling, it is important to be able to separate different parts (e.g., zippers, buttons) so that the recycling process goes smoothly. In mechanical recycling, a great deal of virgin material needs to be added to keep the quality of the recycled yarn high enough (the required amount of virgin material can be as high as 30–50 per cent). Mechanical recycling often uses pre-consumer waste collected from the garment assembly phase (cutting waste, surplus materials). This makes it easier to identify the material content, and the material quality is higher than in post-consumer textile waste (length of fibres decreases after use and repeated laundering).

Many companies are currently releasing garments onto the market that are made using the mono-material strategy, which enables recycling (e.g., Halti, Reima a, Patagonia). In most cases, these garments are made from polyester, and the recycling process may not be simple. Thermal recycling (melt-spun) is used with thermoplastic synthetic materials in, for example, some workwear material (polyester), and these garments can be recycled up to eight times (Heikkilä et al., 2018, p.206). The chemical recycling process for synthetic materials, such as polyester (by Teijin) and polyamide) (by Econyl), offers options to effectively recycle synthetic materials and create several lifecycles for garments. Yet these technologies are quite challenging and easier to implement with mono-materials. It is worth noting that even with these technologies, textile-to-textile recycling is quite difficult, therefore most recycled polyester is actually made from recycled PET bottles, which are technically easier to recycle. Moreover, in these recycling processes the input material needs to have high purity. The recycling process does not tolerate dust, dirt, or surface treatments, elastane, or other blends. In melt spinning, the removal of pigment is not possible (Roos et al., 2019, p.31).

As textile waste recycling will increase in the near future, it may also be possible to consider recycling colours or other chemicals in the textile waste. Avoiding two processes – bleaching and overdyeing – would save water, chemicals, and energy. This strategy could create totally new ways of designing and mixing colours on the basis of their ability to, for example, retain colour or change colour during the chemical recycling process. This has been studied in the chemical regeneration process with cellulose-based fabrics (Määttänen et al., 2019; Smirnova et al., 2016; Smirnova, 2017).

As the use of textile waste is increasing, new automatic sorting processes are being developed, mainly for material identification, but also to identify certain textile structures. These processes use robotics and currently have many limitations in identifying different textile materials. Therefore, when the aim is to close the material loop through recycling, the limitations of automatic material identification need to be taken into account in the design process. In some woven structures, if one fibre hides others (e.g., double weave), this can lead to mistakes in automatic waste sorting. Textile structures should be designed with these limitations in mind so that recycling can take place at the end of the product's lifetime. Another option is to design the product to be suitable for a certain recycling path and to add a code to the garment (e.g., QR code), which is easy to read at the sorting stage and provides the required information on fibre content.

Focusing on only the mono-material approach in the design for recycling strategy might limit the functionality of the product, therefore it is important that when design strategies are updated, the newest knowledge on recycling options and recycling technologies is included in the design briefing so that not only is the best user experience designed into the garment through its properties, but also the end-of-life strategy. The recycling path should already be decided when the original product is being designed.

Table 2.2.1   Limitations and Possibilities in Intentional Design for Recycling

Intentional design for recycling	Limitations	Possibilities
Material	Only textile materials (and textile structures) suitable for recycling can be used Material blends limit textile recycling It should be possible to identify and separate materials before recycling	Substituting virgin cotton with regenerated fibres Recycling textile waste Resource efficiency
Colour	Some colours (especially prints) prevent textile waste recycling Colours should be selected according to the recycling strategy (Do we want the colour to fade or stay in the recycling system?)	Including new design strategies and design aesthetics based on colour variation
Design briefing	The selected recycling technology should be decided on and included in the design briefing Design understanding needs constant updating according to the newest scientific knowledge of recycling technologies	Several lifetimes can be designed into a garment, material, colours, chemicals
Information	The material, colour, and chemical content of textile waste must be known	Transparency enables textile recycling Information on the content of the waste increases its market value

CASE: ADIDAS AND FUTURECRAFT.LOOP

In 2019, Adidas launched a 100 per cent recyclable performance running shoe. The shoe design is based on the "closed loop" and circular manufacturing model. It is made from recycled material, and at the end of its life it can be disassembled. All its parts can be upcycled into a new shoe. Adidas calls this approach "made to be remade": Futurecraft.Loop is a transformative approach to designing performance shoes that are made to be remade from the outset, by using one material type and no glue" (Adidas., 17.4.2019). Avoiding glue in shoe manufacture enables easy disassembly of each part and upcycling them to obtain the best recycling value. When plastic parts cannot be separated, in most cases this means downcycling the material mix and taking the lower-value recycling path.

> Futurecraft.Loop is our first running shoe that is made to be remade. It is a statement or our intent to take responsibility for the entire life of our product.
>
> (Adidas, 17.4.2019)

Task

1. Discuss what kinds of product design and business approach are needed to create a closed-loop process.
2. Discuss how business models can enhance product and material circulation.

2.2.2 Design for alternative business models

Alternative business models in the sustainability context could be simplified to focus on the approaches of preventing product obsolescence and closing the material loop. Other business approaches are also focusing on reducing at the system level (efficiency or even sufficiency). Design strategies need to be modified according to the selected business model (see Table 2.2.2).

Product obsolescence includes aspects such as technical, economic (e.g., repairing the product is no longer economical), or psychological obsolescence. Burns (2010) points out that consumer products that are deeply connected to our own identity and appearance are evaluated on aesthetic and social grounds, therefore consumers may experience psychological obsolescence with fashion items quite easily, resulting in premature disposal of a product followed by the purchasing of new garments.

Den Hollander (2018) has summarised design principles in the context of product obsolescence, as shown in Table 2.2.3. In design, the focus should be on long use, extended use, and recovery. Long use resists product obsolescence through emotional or physical durability. Extended use aims to postpone obsolescence, and includes designing for maintenance, designing for repair, and designing for upgrading. The recovery approach aims to reverse obsolescence through designing for recontextualising, designing for refurbishment, and designing for remanufacturing.

Table 2.2.2 Business Strategy, Approach for Sustainability, and Design Principles

Sustainability strategy	Approach	Design principles
Reduce	Avoiding overproduction More accurate production Resource efficiency No waste Less environmental impact Less risks in the business	Smaller collections More focused design Made-to-measure Made-to-order Zero waste design No deadstock Local design and production Using recycled materials High design-quality warrantees
Rewear	Extending garment lifetime through multiple users	High quality Timeless design
Repair	Extending garment lifetime	Repairable product Easy construction Offering repair kits Offering repair services
Resell	Secondhand fashion	High garment quality High brand value Uniqueness through redesign Upcycling
Recycle	Closing the material loop	Design suitable for recycling Multiple lifecycles

Table 2.2.3 How to Handle Product Obsolescence through Design Approaches

Long use and resisting obsolescence	Extended use and postponing obsolescence	
Emotional durability Physical/technical durability	Maintenance Repair Upgrading	Recontextualising Refurbishment Remanufacturing

Source: Adapted from den Holland (2018, 31).

The linear business model is based on fast and cheap processes in the take–make–sell–dispose paradigm, in which garments lose their value and begin to be disposed of after a very short use time. The CE approach aims to keep the value of a product and materials as high as possible for as long possible. The newest approaches are even more radical, aiming to slow down the whole system (Bocken et al., 2018). This means that businesses cannot collect their profits from one-time selling only, but other actions need to be created on the basis of, for example, resource efficiency and sufficiency approaches in production, extended use time, customer emotional satisfaction, and reselling (secondhand fashion). Bocken et al. (2016) highlight that circular business includes strategies for slowing, closing, and narrowing. The change in the business model also requires changes in design strategies. When starting to construct a new business model, it is essential to collaborate with the designers so that product design and the outcome of production are in line with the business model actions. Some fore-running companies are leading the way and showing examples of how to do this in creative ways in practice. Very often, they combine different approaches and strategies, and conduct brave experimentations in their business. For example, a product-service system, including repair services, needs a durable product, a repairable design, repair materials, equipment, and a service concept (how the business works). Table 2.2.1 lists the sustainability strategies, their main approaches, and suitable design principles.

Task

1. Discuss how system-level understanding could be enhanced in the textile/fashion industry and business.
2. Discuss what kind of system-level changes are needed to make CE and textile circulation a functional practice in two years' time.

References

Adidas (2019) *Adidas unlocks a circular future for sports with FUTURECRAFT.LOOP* (online): https://www.adidas-group.com /en/media/news-archive/press-releases /2019/adidas-unlocks-circular-future-sports -futurecraftloop/, 22/7/2021.

Burns, B. (2010) Re-evaluating obsolescence and planning for it, in T. Cooper (ed.), *Longer lasting products: alternatives to the throwaway society*, Gower, Farnham, pp. 39–60.

Bocken, N., de Pauw, I., Bakker, C., and van den Grinten, B. (2016) Product design and business model strategies for a circular economy, *Industrial Product Engineering*, 5(33), 308–320.

Bocken, N., Miller, K., Weissbrod, K., Holdago, M., and Evans, S. (2018) Slowing resource loops in the clothing industry through circular business model experimentation, in Niinimäki, K. (ed.), *Sustainable fashion in a circular economy*, Aalto ARTS Books, Helsinki, pp. 152–167.

Den Hollander, M. (2018) *Design for managing obsolescence. A design methodology*, Doctoral dissertation, Delft University of Technology, Delft, Netherlands.

Heikkilä, P., Fontel, P., Määttänen, M., and Harlin, A. (2018) Review of textile recycling ecosystem, and a case of cotton, in Niinimäki, K. (ed.), *Sustainable fashion in a circular economy*, Aalto ARTS Books, Helsinki, pp. 192–217.

Määttänen, M., Asikainen, S., Kamppuri, T, Ilen, E., Niinimäki, K., Tanttu, M., and Harlin, A. (2019) Colour management in

CE; decolourization of cotton waste, *RJTA Research Journal of Textiles and Apparel*, 23(2), 134–152.

Niinimäki, K., and Karell, E. (2019) Closing the loop: intentional fashion design defined by recycling technologies, in Vignali, G., Reid, L.F., Ryding, D., and Henninger, C. (eds.), *Technology-driven sustainability; innovation in the fashion supply-chain*, Palgrave Macmillan, Cham, Switzerland, pp. 7–27.

Reima (2019) *Corporate responsibility report* (online): https://www.reima.com/medias/CSR -report-2019-final-web.pdf?context=bWF zdGVyfHJvb3R8NjQxNzQyNXxhcHBsaWNhdGl vbi9wZGZ8OTE4NDIwODMyMjU5MC5wZGZ 8MzlmODkxOGVjMGMxZjU1OGRkY2U0MGM zZDFiY2M2ZTc1YzU3MmQzYTdiYmExNjFjM2E 2MThhYzljZTE1YjcwNQ, 1/7/2021.

Roos, S., Sandin, G., Peters, G., Spak, B., Schawarz, L., Perzon, E., and Jönsson, C. (2019) *White paper on textile recycling*, Mistra Future Fashion report number: 2019: D4.3.3.1 (online): S.-Roos.-White-paper-on-t extile-recycling.-Mistra-Future-Fashion.pdf (mistrafuturefashion.com), 1/1/2020.

Smirnova, E. (2017) *Colours in a circular economy*, Master thesis, Aalto University, Helsinki. (online): https://aaltodoc.aalto.fi/ handle/123456789/24669, 1/1/2020.

Smirnova, E., Elina Ilén, E., Sixta, H., Hummel, M., and Niinimäki, K. (2016) Colours in a circular economy, in *Circular Transitions – Mistra Future Fashion Conference on Textile Design and the Circular Economy*, 23–24 November 2016, Chelsea College of Arts & Tate Britain, London.

Slowing down the fashion system through design

1. To understand the importance of speed in the fashion system.
2. To understand the opportunities for constructing new business understanding, taking into account the speed aspect (slowing down).

2.3.1 Slow fashion and garment lifetimes

Slow fashion has recently emerged as a possible solution to the environmental problems in the fashion sector. At present, fast fashion consumers have too many garments, most of which are quite meaningless for the user or meaningful for only a very short time and therefore easy to dispose of. Slowing might also provide an opportunity for more conscious consumption and a wardrobe that it is not only functional, but has content that users love and try to take good care of, extending the use time of these garments. But what does "slow" actually mean in this context? How can we manage time in the fashion system? Grosse-Hering et al. (2013, p.3439, cited in den Hollander 2018, p.45) have defined the principles of slow design and mindfulness (see Table 2.3.1).

Many of these principles can easily be applied and interpreted in the context of fashion. Slow design has potential for deeper consumer mindfulness and for strengthening the person–product attachment, but often the emerging attachment needs deep emotional bonding, and the reason for this bonding is very personal. One study in Finland (Niinimäki & Koskinen, 2011b) claimed that the elements behind person–product attachments to garments are: emotional values, quality aspects, functionality, design/style/beauty, material aspects, connection to self and one's own identity-building, personal value base, effort and achievements (e.g., DIY), and present or future experiences. Based on this, we can argue that person–product attachments to garments have physical, psychological, ethical, and social levels. The person–product attachment needs time to evolve, and when the attachment has developed to the stage that the garment has gained personal symbolic and sentimental value, it has reached the level of cherishability (Chapman, 2009) and products begin to be meaningful, even precious to the user/owner. Such special items will be taken good care of (Walker, 2006).

Yet in the context of fashion design, these attachment elements, often very personal ones (see Table 2.3.2), are not easy to include in design, so it is worth discussing the use experiences of the garments and how to deepen use satisfaction through design. In this context, quality, functionality, and aesthetics are important dimensions that foster use satisfaction from garments (Niinimäki, 2014). Quality in garments means

DOI: 10.4324/9781003097846-9

Table 2.3.1   Seven Principles of Slow Design

The principles of slow design	
Reveal	Creating awareness Uncovering the essence of a product
Expand	Offering a bigger picture Zooming in and out
Reflect	Providing time for the user to consider and reflect on what they do with the product Creating narratives
Engage	Person–product attachment e.g., do-it-yourself
Participate	Consumers' own activity e.g., personalisation, modifications
Evolve	Products that change over time
Ritual	Rituals for better use experiences Stimulating social interactions

Source: Grosse-Hering et al. (2013, pp.34–39).

good fit, durable materials, durability in use, durability while laundering, and high-quality sewing work. The functional aspects include suitability/functionality in a certain use context, use experiences, and easy maintenance. Aesthetic aspects include beauty, style, colour, fit, and tactile feeling (Niinimäki, 2014.) These are the elements the designer can work with to make design choices. Moreover, it is also important to understand consumers' personal value bases. For some consumers, local production and ethical and ecological aspects are very important elements in purchase decisions, and these more conscious consumers also value the long lifetime of garments (ibid.). Knowing the company's end-consumer is therefore important, especially if the aim is to build an alternative business model.

In the context of fashion, what else does slow design mean in addition to emotional attachments? As Aakko (2013, p.58) defines it:

> slow fashion stands in opposition to everything that fast fashion represents – it moves at a slower pace, disregards trends, is concentrated with a classic of "signature" look and stresses the importance of artisanal production and emotions attached to the clothes we own.

It not only focuses on speed and time management at the system level, but also considers scale and geographical issues, highlighting the importance of small-scale and local production, but also quality and skilful manufacturing (Fletcher, 2010). If the aim is more local and small-scale production, this approach also enables focusing on quality, and all design decisions can be made through better consideration. If the production is local and closer to the designer, it can be better followed and controlled, which will

Table 2.3.2   Elements Providing Attachments in Textiles and Garments

Attachment elements

Emotional values	Emotional values, memories (history/past, places, people, moments, childhood) Family ties Positive associations (e.g., safe and soft tactile feeling)
Quality	High quality in design, materials and realisation Technical durability
Functionality	Multifunctionality Fit Reparability
Design/style/beauty	Classical, timeless design Strong design, representing some unique period of design style Experience of beauty in multi-sensorial ways
Material	Ageing well, aesthetically, gracefully
Connection to "self"/personal values	Expression of "self" Uniqueness Made for me One's own ideology
Effort, achievement	Handmade Tailor-made Self-made Self-designed
Present/future experiences	Promise of experiences (e.g., modification possibility, party garments, opportunities for narratives to emerge) Family ties and continuity aspects, objects as heirlooms Suitability for gift-giving Satisfying experiences

Source: Niinimäki & Koskinen (2011, p.170).

result in fewer mistakes during assembly. Designers of large-scale brands have to make their design choices in a hurry (no time to find information on alternative materials, for example) and production often takes place on the other side of the globe (mass-production by another company), resulting in a lower level of quality in manufacturing (Karell & Niinimäki, 2020) (see also Section 1.1.3).

Yet even in slow fashion, management of product lifetimes is a challenging task. Product lifetimes can be divided into three different categories: technical lifetime, functional lifetime, and emotional lifetime (Raebuild & Hasling, 2018). *Technical lifetime* refers to the phase during which the product is in use before it breaks or wears out. With garments, this very often means the time before a zipper or a seam or the fabric breaks or wear is too visible, creating an inaesthetic look (e.g., material pilling). The garment's technical lifetime is very often determined by its weakest part if it is not repairable or the user has no skills to repair it (Niinimäki, 2011). *Functional lifetime* refers to user experience and the period when the user's functionality expectations of the product, especially its use, are fulfilled. *Emotional lifetime* is linked to person–product attachment and the emotional side of fashion (e.g., emotional experiences through beauty and social acceptance) (Niinimäki, 2011). The emotional side of fashion is often the most critical aspect affecting active use time: when the consumer no longer gains satisfaction from the garment or loses emotional attachment to it, the garment is put into storage as a memento, or is disposed of (Niinimäki & Armstrong, 2013).

The consumption of fast fashion has resulted in the early disposal of garments, meaning that even functional garments are disposed of, landfilled, or incinerated. The emotional need for newness and change is essential when purchasing fashion items (especially fast fashion items). Constantly seeking new, fun items leads to impulse buying and very short garment lifetimes (Niinimäki 2011). Consumers can easily and cheaply buy new items and change their appearance using fashion without any consequences for this unsustainable action (Gabrieli, Baghi & Codeluppi, 2013). Therefore, it is very hard to influence consumer behaviour and guide consumers towards more sustainable and conscious consumption practices. The following may be good ways in which to influence consumers: affecting their value base through education (ethical and environmental values), fostering their creativity through inspiration (educating skills), and affecting fashion emotions through offering new experiences of satisfaction (offering change in more sustainable ways, e.g. renting) (Niinimäki, 2018). Designers can also use certain elements to slow down consumption. Quality and functionality are the key design choices to ensure a long lifetime for a garment and to offer user satisfaction, but other aspects could also be included. Slow fashion not only means alternative ways of designing and producing fashion, it can also include new ways of offering sustainable satisfaction to consumers. Very often this is done by offering some service to the consumer: repair services, updating services, or even made-to-measure services build connections between a brand and a consumer. Moreover, mass-customisation offers consumers some options for selecting materials or colours (from a limited offering) to create a more personal look, and in this way make the garment more personal and perhaps meaningful to the consumer (e.g., Converse and customised shoes).

CASE: ANNA RUOHONEN AND SLOW, CONTEMPORARY FASHION

Some companies, such as Anna Ruohonen, have gone much further by building their design strategies on premium quality through technical and aesthetic quality, but also a collection design based on slower cycles in fashion, longer-lasting design language, and better service offerings. Services can differentiate a company from others, even if the product itself is not superior or very different to those of competitors (Porter 2004). For example, offering excellent customer service distinguishes the brand and creates product satisfaction and brand loyalty among customers. This results in lower price sensitivity – in other words, an opportunity to offer good quality at a premium price (Porter 2004). Anna Ruohonen relies strongly on made-to-order service and production on demand, good individual service, and slow fashion. It also invests in high-quality materials, local production, and high-quality technical skills in garment assembly. It has a fashion house in Paris where in-house production takes place, which enables constant quality control. The made-to-order strategy enables more accurate business operations and prevents surplus storage. Creating a good customer experience and constructing a loyal customer network enables stable business and avoids slavishly following fashion seasons. It is possible to create seasonless fashion and publish a new collection in slower cycles. Anna Ruohonen relies on slow design, and in its collection, designs stay in production for a long time, even years, and it only adds new designs to a continuing collection. These garments can be seen as consumers' investments in sustainability and high-level design. The price is affordable, and the garment is designed for long use. Even if managing garment lifetime is uncertain, Anna Ruohonen's example shows that providing high quality, design value, and a more individual service can result in more respect for garments, and in this way this strategy slows down the fashion system.

CASE: ALABAMA CHANIN AND LOCAL, SLOW, AND OPEN FASHION

Natalia Chanin from the USA runs a true slow fashion company called Alabama Chanin:

> Alabama Chanin aims to make "garments that last forever" and don't necessarily cater to seasonal trends, but flow from season to season. This means a sustainable wardrobe can be built over the course of time and pieces go together regardless of which collection they come from. She insists that figuring out how to build a sustainable wardrobe can replace the satisfaction of retail therapy.
> (Hansen 14.6.2016)

Chanin started her business by recycling old cotton T-shirts and jersey fabrics into new, beautiful garments using embroidery techniques. Today, the business has grown, and the recycled materials have been substituted with organic cotton made in the USA. However, the embroidery techniques are still used to create contemporary fashion pieces. This approach, using these hand-sewn decorations, gives the materials and garments an exclusive hand-crafted value. This slow way of producing garments results in unique aesthetics and a premium price. Chanin states that if you cannot buy these garments, you can make them yourself. She encourages a DIY approach, and many garment designs are published as open access so anyone can make them. Using these techniques on old materials (e.g., old T-shirts) is a way of aesthetically extending and redesigning the use time of garments and making something valuable from old or even waste materials. Chanin has also launched the School of Making, and runs workshops to teach consumers to use these old, slow embroidery techniques and to help them understand the supply chain of textiles and fashion.

She uses "botanical colours", plant-based colours of natural origin, to produce a "limited edition collection" which is pre-order only. She stresses that as the colour originates from nature (madder root) and all garments are hand-dyed, the colour shades of garments may differ. This merely adds special beauty and uniqueness to each garment.

2.3.2 Designing value for secondhand fashion

From the sustainability point of view, we should challenge the linear take–make–sell–dispose model that causes fast material throughput in the system. To slow down the system, we need to appreciate products more and to try to extend their use time. After the peak of the COVID-19 pandemic, secondhand fashion businesses are emerging. Many brands have begun to take back their old garments and resell them. For some companies, this has been a way to avoid producing new collections, but for most companies it has been an experiment alongside their normal business. As the global fashion business was in a loop caused by its environmental impacts (e.g., Niinimäki et al., 2020) and its societal reputation in 2020, secondhand fashion became an experiment to turn consumers' eyes towards something more positive and climate-neutral, a more resource-efficient way to do fashion business. Yet some brands have been selling secondhand fashion for a long time, even before COVID-19. For example, Filippa K in Sweden sells its own secondhand garments in the same shops in which it sells new clothes (secondhand sales are handled by an actor other than Filippa K itself). Filippa K has even set a goal to adopt a Wearability KPI in its garments, which would show the wearability assessment and in this way enable long use time to be measured and even priced. Making the lifetime of the garment visible could make running secondhand fashion businesses a profitable part of the normal fashion business.

CASE: FILIPPA K AND COST PER WEAR

During 2019, we conducted our first wearability study to gauge how many times a Filippa K garment is used by our consumers, which revealed an average use of 75 times in a garment's active lifetime. For 2021, we have an ambition to set up and implement an improved way of measuring usage of our garments among our consumers to be able to follow up on our wearability goal on a year-to-year basis. Measuring the usage of our garments will not only allow us to better understand the footprint of our garments and how we can improve it but will also enable us to calculate cost per wear of our garments to inspire our consumers to make long-term investments.

(Filippa K, 2020)

Finnish company Reima's childrenswear is of high quality and has a premium price, and the garments still have value in the secondhand business because of their well-known and highly respected brand. Consumers know this, and are ready to invest in the brand because they know they will get money back when they sell the garments later. Designing high-quality garments under a well-known brand promotes the secondhand fashion business.

CASE: NUDIE JEANS AND DESIGN VALUE IN PRELOVED FASHION

High-quality jeans made from sustainable materials, and supplementary repair services are the elements behind the Nudie Jeans company. Nudie Jeans also takes back its old jeans and places them in the loop as secondhand jeans or raw material for new products. The Re-use Jeans concept is part of its business, whereby preloved and well-worn denim is sold on. Jeans are collected, washed, and repaired before reselling them to consumers. From 2018, Nudie Jeans has also upcycled old jeans. The reuse approach involves design elements – design symbols are embroidered onto old jeans, inspired by a tattoo type of decoration. This rebirth strategy uses design value to give an extra boost to the life extension of these garments.

CASE: EMMY AND SECONDHAND VALUE THROUGH BRAND AND QUALITY

After the owner of a garment has tired of it, the best way to extend its use time is to ensure that another consumer will take it into use. Emmy provides a platform enabling consumers to sell its brand clothes to other consumers. It collects, checks, photographs, and places garments for sale online, then posts the garment to the new owner. It does not accept brands that have no secondhand value or are replicas. Emmy checks all garments and gives them a quality category, which is based on four levels. The first is "as new": these garments may even still have price tags. The second level is "good as new": no marks of wear are visible. The third level is "good": the garment has been used, but is in good condition, with no visible stains or pilling. The fourth level is "used condition": wear and tear are visible, and are listed in detail in the sales information for each garment. This is a good example of how products of high quality and well-known brands enable the creation of secondhand value to resell fashion items.

Task

1. Discuss how businesses must change and their values become more sustainability-based.
2. Discuss what alternative practices could lead businesses away from the linear way of doing business and emphasise cost savings in production and cheap end-prices.
3. Discuss how to define value in sustainable fashion.

References

Aakko, M. (2013) Artisanal and slow: the case of Anna Ruohonen, in Niinimäki, K. (ed.), *Sustainable fashion: new approaches*, Aalto ARTS Books, Helsinki, pp. 56–67.

Chapman, J. (2009) *Emotionally durable design; objects, experiences & empathy*, Earthscan Publication, London.

Den Hollander, M. (2018) *Design for managing obsolescence. A design methodology*, Doctoral dissertation, Delft University of Technology, Delft, Netherlands.

Filippa K, *Sustainability report 2020* (online): https://www.filippa-k.com/globalassets/home/reports/sustainability-reports/filippa-k-sustainability-report_2020-1.pdf?ref=F9185891B0, 22/7/2021.

Fletcher, K. (2010) Slow fashion: an invitation for systemic change, *Fashion Practice*, 2(2), 559–566.

Gabrieli, V., Baghi, I., and Codeluppi, V. (2013) Consumption practices of fast fashion products: a consumer-based approach, *Journal of Fashion Marketing and Management*, 17(2), 206–224.

Grosse-Hering, B., Mason, J., Aliakseyeu, D., Bakker, C., and Desmet, P. (2013, April) Slow design for meaningful interactions, in *Proceedings of the SIGGHI Conference of Human Factors in Computing Systems,* Paris, France.

Hansen, S. (2016) *The ultimate luxury is time: this 'Slow Fashion' brand is rooted in DIY*, Observer (online): https://observer.com/2016/06/the-ultimate-luxury-is-time-this-slow-fashion-brand-is-rooted-in-diy/, 1/7/2021.

Karell, E., and Niinimäki, K. (2020) A mixed-method study of design practices and designers' roles in sustainable-minded clothing companies, *Sustainability*, 12, 4680.

Niinimäki, K. (2011) *From disposable to sustainable. The complex interplay between design and consumption of textiles and clothing*, Doctoral dissertation, Aalto University, Helsinki. https://aaltodoc.aalto.fi/handle/123456789/13770.

Niinimäki, K. (2014) Sustainable consumer satisfaction in the context of clothing, in Vezzoli, C., Kohtala, C., Srinivasan, A., Diehl, J.C., Fusakul, S.M., Xin, L., and Sateesh, D. (eds.), *Product-service system design for sustainability*, Greenleaf, Sheffield, UK, pp. 218–237.

Niinimäki, K. (2018) Knowing better, but behaving emotionally: strong emotional undertones in fast fashion consumption, in Becker-Leifhold, C., and Heuer, M. (eds.), *Eco friendly and fair: fast fashion and consumer behavior*, Routledge, London, pp. 49–57.

Niinimäki, K., and Armstrong, C. (2013) From pleasure in use to preservation of meaningful memories: a closer look at the sustainability of clothing via longevity and attachment, *International Journal of Fashion Design, Technology and Education*, 6(3), 190–199.

Niinimäki, K., and Koskinen, I. (2011) I love this dress, it makes me feel beautiful: emotional knowledge in sustainable design, *Design Journal*, 14(2), 165–186.

Niinimäki, K., Peters, G., Dahlbo, H., Perry, P., Rissanen, T., and Gwilt, A. (2020) The environmental price of fast fashion, *Nature Reviews; Earth and Environment*, 1, 189–200.

Porter, M. (2004) *Competitive strategy. Techniques for analyzing industries and competitors*, Free Press, New York. (Original work published 1980).

Raebuild, U., and Hasling, K. (2018) Sustainable design cards: a learning tool for supporting sustainable design strategies, in Niinimäki, K. (ed.), *Sustainable fashion in a circular economy*, Aalto ARTS Books, Helsinki, pp. 128–151.

Walker, S. (2006) *Sustainable by design. Exploration in theory and practice*, Earthscan, London.

Designing carbon-neutral fashion

Learning outcomes

1. To understand why widening the perspective of sustainable fashion is important.
2. To understand the connection between the textile/fashion system and climate change.
3. To understand the importance of continuous sustainability work in companies.

Estimations have been made of the climate change caused by the current fashion industry. It is estimated that the textile and garment industry cause around 4–10 per cent of global CO_2 emissions (Quantis, 2018; United Nations Climate Change, 2018). Even if this figure is not accurate and varies according to what is included in or excluded from the estimation, we know that this sector causes huge amounts of greenhouse gases each year. It is estimated that textiles (including garments), together with aluminium, result in the highest amount of GHG emissions per unit of material (Kissinger et al., 2013). This fact is now well acknowledged in the fashion industry, and the sector is working hard to decrease its climate impacts. The carbon footprint measures the amount of GHGs that are produced through burning fossil fuels in electronic production, heating, transportation etc., and reports it as the equivalent of tonnes or kilograms or grams of CO_2. Other types of GHGs are: methane (CH_4), which comes from composting, for example, nitrous oxide (N_2O), hydrofluorocarbons (HFCs), per-fluorocarbons (PFCs), and sulphur hexafluoride (SF_6) (Rana et al., 2015).

Many companies are aiming to reduce their CO_2 footprint and have set clear goals to reach climate neutrality. For example, Adidas has set goals of a 15 per cent reduction of CO_2 emissions per product by 2025, to reduce 30 per cent of CO_2 emissions from its own operations by 2030, and furthermore to be totally climate-neutral by 2050 (Adidas, 2020a). Achieving these demanding goals requires critically evaluating, considering, and measuring all aspects: design, manufacturing, logistics, use, reverse logistics, and recycling. For example, Adidas states that "avoiding oil-based plastic helps reduce carbon emissions" and "thinner or lighter materials mean less waste and less embedded carbon" (ibid.). Developments in industrial processes such as dry-dyeing save water, chemicals, and energy (Adidas, 2020b). Development work is also underway to create material production processes that use recycled carbon. An example of this is polyester, whose manufacturing process uses 30 per cent recycled carbon emissions, originating from, for instance, steel production (ongoing development work is being carried out by Lululemon and LanzaTech; Anderson 26.7.2021). Overall, natural fibres have a lower carbon footprint than synthetic fibres, therefore the easiest way to currently lower CO_2 emissions when selecting garment materials would be to substitute the use of polyester with the use of natural fibres. Moreover, plant-based materials

DOI: 10.4324/9781003097846-10

are renewable, and they can act as a carbon sink by taking atmospheric carbon into the soil. To illustrate this: 1 tonne of dry jute is the equivalent to the absorption of 2.4 tonnes of carbon. Other kinds of fibres with low carbon emissions are linen and hemp (Niinimäki et al., 2020; Rana et al., 2015).

Most of the textile colours used in industry are petroleum-based, which has a CO_2 impact. But alternatives exist for colour from these origins. Plants that provide renewable bio-based dyes can be cultivated in a manner that creates carbon-neutral colours. Plant roots sequester carbon, and the action of sequestration can be maximised through different agricultural practices and cultivation technologies (e.g., crop rotation, selecting plants with deep roots, using ground cover plants). For example, the synthetic form of the well-known blue colour indigo is produced from petroleum, which is processed in high-energy conditions to break it down into its component molecules. After this, a substance called benzene is isolated and mixed with other chemicals (cyanide and formaldehyde), resulting in an indigo dye. But indigo can also be made in other ways. The tradition of using natural indigo (*Indigofera tinctoria*) in textile dyeing is still alive and strong in Asian countries. Furthermore, Japanese indigo (*Persicaria tinctoria*) is cultivated in the USA (by Stony Creek Colors), and woad (*Isatis tinctoria*) is cultivated in some European countries (e.g., France and Finland) on a larger scale (for further details, see **Part 4**).

A highly important aspect in efforts to decrease CO_2 emissions is to favour recycled materials over virgin materials in textile manufacturing. Constructing a circular system in fashion can also enhance the decarbonisation of fashion. Yet it is important to critically evaluate each industrial phase and its impact. Roos et al. (2019) have studied textile recycling and its environmental benefits. They highlight that if, for example, replacement rates are high (constant purchasing of new garments and disposing of them after a very short use time) and we have "efficient recycling technology powered by renewables, the climate benefit could be up to a few kg CO_2 equivalent per kg recycled material" (Roos et al. 2019, p.20, based on Östlund et al. 2015) – this means "roughly 10% of the climate impact of a typical garment life cycle". Patagonia has been collaborating with the Japanese company Teijin in polyester recycling, and argues that textile-to-textile recycling uses 76 per cent less energy and emits 42 per cent less CO_2 than making it from petroleum: "'This confirmed that closed-loop recycling considerably reduces environmental harm" (Patagonia).

A garment's use phase is also important, not only in terms of how we maintain the clothing (e.g., avoiding excessive laundry and favouring line drying), but also in terms of the use time of the garment. WRAP (2012) has estimated that in the UK, the average garment is used for 2.2 years. If we extended this figure by 10 per cent (three months), carbon savings would be 8 per cent, and if the extension was 33 per cent (nine months), CO_2 savings could amount to 27 per cent (ibid.). How much energy and what types of energy are used in production and during use phases are critical issues here. Moreover, substituting virgin cotton with recycled, regenerated cellulose material has a great influence on the water footprint, and can improve it by as much as 90 per cent (ibid.). So the decarbonisation of fashion can also have other environmental benefits.

The many logistics steps throughout the supply chain and how they increase the carbon footprint should also be considered. Online shopping and its speed increase this problem. Air cargo has a larger environmental impact than container boats. It is estimated that changing 1 per cent of garment transportation from Asian manufacturing locations to Western consumers from ship to air cargo would result in a 35 per cent increase in carbon emissions (Quantis, 2018). It is important to also reduce online shopping returns and reduce overproduction overall in the fashion system; this would also improve CO_2 emission figures and slow down the climate change caused by the fashion system.

As previous examples show, calculating CO_2 emissions is a complex process, and all actors throughout the supply chain need to contribute by driving the decarbonisation issue. This requires a new kind of transparency and a system to identify and collect these data throughout the supply chain. When evaluating the carbon footprint and aiming for carbon-neutral fashion, it is important to measure and identify the critical points not only in a company's operations, but also in the supply chain. Absolute energy consumption and CO_2 emissions need to be measured in a company's own operations as well as in the supply chain and in different tiers (see Table 2.4.1). This is often simplified as Scope 1, 2, and 3: Scope 1 emissions are "direct emissions from owned or controlled sources", Scope 2 emissions are "indirect emissions from the generation of purchased energy", and Scope 3 emissions are "all indirect emissions (not included in Scope 2) that occur in the value chain of the reporting company, including both upstream and downstream emissions" (Sadowski et al., 2019, p.3).

The transformation from fossil energy to clean energy, a decrease in the use of total energy, and exploring new energy-harvesting methods are key points on which to focus. As new knowledge on CO_2 emissions emerges, it is also easier to make design decisions that are really connected to decarbonisation. These design decisions are linked to material and colour choices, the use of chemicals, wet processes, manufacturing locations, garment construction, and decreasing all the logistic steps in the supply chain. Here we can say that slow fashion and more accurate and local production may create a competitive advantage when estimating the carbon emissions of garment manufacturing. Now, when climate policies are tightening, this competitive advantage may strongly benefit leading sustainable companies that are able to calculate and show their life cycle assessment, carbon and water footprints, and the total environmental impacts of their products.

CASE: FRENN AND CARBON FOOTPRINT

We have started profound work in calculating our carbon footprint annually. We have succeeded to reduce our carbon footprint about 26% from 2018 to 2019 including company own operation, business flying, material and transportation emissions. Work is done with a calculating tool launched by Finnish carbon footprint company Clonet.

COMPENSATION BASED ON CALCULATIONS

As a short term act we have compensated all our climate emissions calculated in 2019 by Finnish **CO2esto** who acquires emission allowances from The EU Emissions Trading System (EU ETS) to keep them off the market. This is actual and proven emission preventing guaranteed by EU legislation.

Compensated amount 29 kg CO_2e includes all company own operation and Scope 3 operation including business flying, material and transportation emissions. We will compensate our climate emissions, that we are not able to reduce, yearly according to financial year carbon footprint calculation report.

(FRENN a; b)

Table 2.4.1 Environmental Impact and CO_2 Analysis per Tier to Help Enhance System-level Thinking in Fashion

Tier 4 Raw material extraction	Tier 3 Raw material processing	Tier 2 Material production	Tier 1 Finished production assembly	Tier 0 Office, retail, distribution	Use phase Consumer care	End of life Reuse, recycle
Cultivation and extraction of raw materials from the earth, plants, or animals	Processing of raw materials into yarn and other intermediate products	Production and finishing of materials (e.g., fabric, trims) that go directly into finished product	Assembly and manufacturing of final products	Corporate real estate not involved in production process Logistical steps	Maintenance practices Short or long lifetime	Extending product lifetime Disposal Closing material loop through recycling

Examples from textile, clothing, and footwear sectors

Tier 4 Raw material extraction	Tier 3 Raw material processing	Tier 2 Material production	Tier 1 Finished production assembly	Tier 0 Office, retail, distribution	Use phase Consumer care	End of life Reuse, recycle
Bottle recycling (for recycled polyester) Conversion of oil/gas into polymers Cultivation of cotton, wood, and natural rubber products Cattle grazing	Yarn production (extrusion, spinning, etc.) Production of dyes, inks, adhesives, resin, etc. Conversion of wood products into pulp Leather preparation (including tanning)	Knitting and weaving textiles Fabric bleaching, dyeing, finishing, washing Production of footwear mid- and outsole components (extrusion, moulding, vulcanisation)	Cutting, sewing, stitching, embroidery Screen printing Product packaging	Corporate real estate not directly involved in production process Business travel and employee commuting	Laundering, drying, dry cleaning, repairing, etc.	Reuse as a product Repurposing Upcycling, updating, redesigning Landfilling Incineration Mechanical, thermal, or chemical recycling

Source: Adapted from Sadowski et al. (2019, 14).

CASE: SHEEP INC. AND THE CARBON-NEGATIVE HOODIE

Sheep Inc. is a company that produces woollen knits. It focuses on sustainability. For example, it produces hoodies that are not just carbon-neutral, but carbon-negative. The carbon footprint is evaluated throughout the supply chain (verified by Carbon Footprint Ltd). The total of emissions for each knit is -6.84kg CO_2e, not including carbon offsetting. To reach this figure, the strategy has been to source wool from regenerative farms in New Zealand that sequester more carbon than they emit, to use manufacturing sites powered by 100 per cent solar energy, and to partner with carbon-neutral logistics company Airbox (Sheep Inc. a; b).

2.4.1 Responsibility, safety, and risk management

Learning outcomes

1. To understand responsibility and brand value in the sustainability context.
2. To understand control and risk management as part of a company's sustainability work.

Sustainability does not only mean implementing the best practices in the industrial processes to decrease the environmental impact of production and products; it is also strongly connected to companies' responsibilities and reputations. The COVID-19 crisis exposed the backstage of fashion to a large audience, along with the power issues between big international fashion brands and manufacturers in the Global South: many big brands did not pay for manufactured garments when the global crisis hit in spring 2020 and caused fashion purchasing to drastically decrease. This situation in which international fashion brands did not carry their responsibility left factory workers without salaries for completed sewing work, and this caused societal restlessness in many developing countries. For example, in Bangladesh, the garment industry forms the main industrial sector and nearly half of the population earns a living in this industry. In Cambodia, around 85 per cent of industrial workplaces are in the garment industry (Anguelov, 2016.). The next section will discuss some of the aspects linked to company responsibility and risk management.

2.4.2 Transparency and code of conduct

The societal problems and ethical issues in garment manufacturing have been under discussion for several years, but the COVID-19 period has heated up this discussion, and consumers are more interested than ever in sustainability issues in the fashion sector, wanting more information on the practices of companies and their suppliers

(Granskog et al., 2020). Demand for transparency is growing in the fashion sector, and consumers are demanding more information on garment manufacturing. Consumers are "rating" companies in their minds, and *would like to follow why I am with them, which basically means that customers are looking for a reason to buy a certain brand instead of another"* (Piippo & Niinimäki, 2021). In a study by Claxton and Kent (2020), companies that were trying to reach more sustainable aims saw "future opportunities for competitive strategy based on product differentiation by engaging the consumer emotionally through the branding, identity and creative concept behind sustainable products". Consumers are increasingly appreciating brands that reveal their operations, are transparent and honest, and communicate their progress in sustainability work. Companies have to open up and inform consumers of their value base, sustainable measures, and industrial practices. Many companies publish their code of conduct principles and sustainability reports on their websites to build trust among their consumers. This type of communication with consumers is more important than ever. Consumers' trust is part of the brand's value, and can be the crucial factor in a consumer's purchase decision.

This constant work towards transparency is also a part of quality work. Companies themselves acknowledge that responsibility and sustainability are important parts of their quality work. Quality attributes in products and processes can be defined and measured, but quality work also includes more abstract levels, such as trust and reputation. It is important that things are done as agreed with different suppliers and manufacturers, so trust and transparency is also needed in these actions (Piippo & Niinimäki, 2021). When the company has a code of conduct, it can demand that all its suppliers comply with it. Companies should organise inspection visits to manufacturing plants. Some companies connect this code of conduct work to the quality of the end-product, and claim that they can achieve excellent quality by securing all the manufacturing phases. Product quality can be communicated to consumers by providing a guarantee for garments or a promise to repair them if something goes wrong. For example, FRENN provides a one-year repair service for FRENN clothes that have been in normal use and washed according to care instructions (FRENN a).

CASE: FRENN AND CODE OF CONDUCT

Frenn Helsinki Oy (later FRENN) is committed to respect the human rights and ensure sustainable working methods. This Code of Conduct aim is setting up the values and principles that the FRENN strive to implement in the supply chains. The Code of Conduct is based on international conventions such as the Universal Declaration of Human Rights, key UN conventions, UN Guiding Principles for Business and Human Rights and International Labour Organization (ILO) conventions and recommendations.

The principles set out in the Code of Conduct represent minimum expectations that FRENN have for their suppliers and other subcontractors. It is the responsibility of FRENN suppliers to inform their subcontractors about FRENN's Code of Conduct.

To monitor our business partners conformity with our requirements, we shall have the right to make unannounced visits to all units producing goods for

FRENN. FRENN also reserve the right to appoint an independent third party to conduct audits to evaluate compliance with this Code of Conduct. Unwillingness to cooperate or repeated violations of the Code of Conduct may lead to termination of the business relationship with FRENN.

LEGAL REQUIREMENTS

All FRENN business partners must follow the national laws in the countries in which they operate. Business partners are also committed to the requirements set out in this document. Business partners should note that these may go beyond the requirements set out in national law.

WORKERS' RIGHTS

All FRENN business partners shall have a written employment contracts with all employees. Employment contracts must be written in the local language and include the employment terms and conditions.

NO BONDED LABOUR

FRENN does not accept any form of forced, bonded or non-voluntary labour. Every employee shall be treated with respect and dignity. Business partners shall ensure that migrant workers have the same entitlements as local employees. All workers shall have right to leave work and freely terminate their employment without any punishment.

NO DISCRIMINATION

FRENN does not accept any discrimination. Business partners shall not discriminate employee because of gender, age, religion, race, caste, pregnancy, disability, social background, sexual orientation, political opinions, diseases or any other condition that could give rise to discrimination. Workers shall not be harassed or disciplined on any of the grounds listed above.

FREEDOM OF ASSOCIATION

All FRENN business partners shall respect the employees right to form or join associations of their own choosing and bargain collectively. Discrimination against workers because of trade union membership is not allowed.

When operating in countries where trade union activity is unlawful, business partners shall allow workers to freely elect their own representatives with whom the company can enter dialogue about workplace issues.

CHILD LABOUR

FRENN does not accept child labour. Business partners shall not employ children younger than 15 years. All business partners must ensure that they do not employ anyone below this age. In cases when business partners are removing children from the workplace, they should identify in a proactive manner, measures to ensure the protection of affected children. When appropriate, they shall pursue the possibility to provide decent work for adult household members of the affected children's family.

YOUNG WORKERS

All FRENN business partners must follow the legal limitations on the employment of persons below the age 18. Where young workers are employed, business partners should ensure that the kind of work is not harmful to their health and their working hours do not prejudice their attendance at school.

WAGES

All FRENN business partners shall respect the right of the workers to receive fair remuneration that is sufficient to provide them with a decent living for themselves and their families. Wages must be paid regularly on time, refer to regular working hours and shall reflect the skills, education and experience of the employee.

Business partners shall pay at least the statutory minimum wage, the prevailing industry wage or the wage negotiated in a collective agreement, whichever is higher.

WORKING HOURS

All FRENN business partners shall ensure that workers are not required to work more than 48 regular hours per week. Overtime work must be exceptional, always voluntary for employee and compensated in accordance with the law. Overtime hours should never exceed 12 hours per week. Furthermore, business partners shall grant their workers the right to resting breaks in every working day and the right to at least one day off in every seven days.

HEALTH AND SAFETY

All FRENN business partners shall ensure a safe and healthy work environment for all employees. The premises must be regularly maintained and cleaned and must provide a healthy working environment.

Business partners shall ensure that there are systems in place to detect, assess, avoid and respond to potential threats to the health and safety of workers. Hazardous equipment or unsafe buildings are not accepted. Relevant first aid equipment must be available. Emergency exits must be clearly marked and unblocked. Everyone must have right to exit the premises from imminent danger without seeking permission.

Business partners shall ensure access to drinking water, safe and clean eating and resting areas as well as clean and safe cooking and food storage areas.

ENVIRONMENT

All FRENN business partners must respect the environment and comply with all environmental laws in the countries in which they operate. Business partners must have the relevant environmental permits for their operations.

Water is a scare resource in many parts of the world and should be used as efficiently as possible. Business partners must ensure that all wastewater is treated and disposed according to the local legislation.

Business partners shall work to improve resource efficiency and reduce waste during their production. All waste must be taken care of in responsible manner and in accordance with local laws.

CHEMICALS

All FRENN business partners must follow the current European Chemical regulation REACH. There should be a material safety data sheet (MSDS) available on site where the chemicals are used.

ANIMAL WELFARE

FRENN does not accept any harm or cruelty to animals during production. Business partners shall ensure that materials derived from animals are from animals that are treated according to the animal welfare laws and international recommendations.

COMMITMENT TO THE CODE OF CONDUCT

Signing up for the Code of Conduct is mandatory for all business partners having a business relation with FRENN.

(FRENN c)

2.4.3 Clean chemistry and ethical fashion

The textile and fashion industry uses huge amounts of different types of chemicals that are often very hazardous for the environment, cotton farmers, factory workers, and even end-users. The majority of the chemicals found in textiles in the EU area are added to them outside the EU, where the industrial textile factories and garment assembly plants are located and where most of the textiles and garments for Western markets are produced (Niinimäki et al., 2020). Hazardous chemicals and microplastics from polyester garments are also released during garment laundry. A study conducted in Sweden (Kemi, 2014, cited by Niinimäki et al., 2020, p. 194) reported that:

2450 chemicals related to textile manufacturing were investigated for their hazardous properties. 10% of these chemicals were identified to be of high potential concern for human health, including fragrances of direct and acid-type azo dyes, as well as reproductive toxins such as brominated flame retardants, highly fluorinated water, stain repellents and phthalates.

Hazardous chemicals are used in the production of textiles mainly to enhance their functional properties, such as antibacterial agents (these increase antibiotic resistance risks) and chemically stable fluoropolymers to create a waterproof surface (bioaccumulation risks), causing unpredictable risks to the environment and all living organisms (Peters et al., 2014; Niinimäki et al., 2020). High quality of garments often increases the chemical content, as several aesthetic or functional finishes are added to the textiles: for example, dyeing, printing, softening, and mercerisation. Functional finishes are added to improve durability, antimicrobial properties, waterproofness, grease resistance, and antistatic properties. This shows that when trying to avoid chemical risks, some limitations on functionality, appearance, or comfort need to be considered at the designer's desk. Durability is another complicated aspect when trying to improve the sustainability of fashion. Extending a product's lifetime is one of the critical issues in the fashion sector, but durability should be increased without using harmful chemicals.

Ecolabels and eco-standards are important tools for managing certain risks in the fashion system and the supply chain (see Section 1.2.1). They also form a way in which to communicate sustainability issues and a company's risk management work to consumers. Oeko-Tex is an important tool based on standards according to a product type. It forms a certain "safety for user" level and is an important tool for communicating information to consumers, yet it does not include the environmental impacts of a product or its production. Other important tools, which differ in content, are the EU ecolabel (flower), the Nordic ecolabel (swan), Bluesign, and the Global Organic Textile Standard. Cradle-to-cradle certificates guide designers and manufacturers through improvement aspects of product quality; material health, material reutilisation, renewable energy and carbon management, water stewardship, and social fairness in production. In the chemical sector, REACH, regulated by European chemical legislation, is becoming a more important tool for producers to avoid hazardous chemicals (harmful or even toxic chemicals) (Fransson et al., 2013). Design companies can also use REACH to inform and instruct their suppliers about which chemicals must be avoided in the manufacturing process (see Reima and the Restricted Substances List, RSL: Reima 2019). Many of these chemicals are used in fibre, yarn, and textile processes, especially in wet processes, therefore it is important that this communication flows through the whole supply chain, not only to Tier 1 upstream or downstream. Designers and retail companies are generally located in the Global North, whereas manufacturers are generally in the Global South, where legislation and regulations are much weaker. This makes chemical risk management very challenging, and means that companies in the Global North need to take the lead in chemical control (Fransson et al., 2013). On the other hand, the current demand for more transparency in the supply chain and the need for information (e.g., the chemical content) which either enables or prevents textile waste being suitable for recycling might be the decisive factor. In the Design for Recycling strategy, fibre and chemical content need to be defined and limited in the design phase according to the selected recycling path's requirements. This information needs to be available when the garment has become waste and is entering a recycling path.

Another controversial issue is material origin from animals (see **Part** 4). In the mass-production of materials, the way in which animals are handled is often unethical. Therefore, many companies include statements on what kind of animal-origin materials can be used in their products in their codes of conduct. Real fur is often substituted by synthetic alternatives; mulesing-free wool is recommended, and when using down and feathers, the Responsible Down Standard (RDS) may be followed. The RDS ensures that down and feathers are only produced as a by-product of food production. Leather processes have an environmental impact (e.g., in the tanning process). Leather use is also linked to animal rights, yet it should be remembered that most leather is a by-product of food production (and would otherwise end up as waste). Currently, some companies are testing and piloting the use of fake leather, but depending on the use context, the durability of fake leather might be a risk for the technical lifetime of the product. Technical lifetime refers to the time the product remains in use before it breaks or wears out (Raebuild & Hasling, 2018).

CASE: REIMA AND PRODUCT SAFETY

SAFE AND SUSTAINABLE DESIGN PRINCIPLES

Chemical safety: Safety is the foremost priority for Reima products, so it is crucial to not only comply with regulations but to exceed them. Our Restricted Substances List (RSL) defines our chemical safety framework for material manufacturing.

- We do not use nanomaterials in our materials and products. They can be toxic and bio accumulative and their impact on human health and especially children is still underexamined and tested. E.g. nanosilver, the most common nanotech in textiles, can be toxic to aquatic life.
- Our clothing and accessories products are free from PFCs (perfluorinated carbons) since 2017 and our highlight and popular shoe styles will be PFC-free, too, starting in 2020. None of our products contain PFOA (Perfluorooctanoic acid).
- PVC was banned in Reima products over a decade ago due to phthalates. In textile industry, phthalates can be used in PVC materials, in printing and in manmade leather. Phthalates are known hormone-disruptors that can be absorbed through the skin.

(Reima, 2019)

2.4.4 Control, trust, and crisis management

The COVID-19 crisis hit the fashion industry hard, and at least for a while the global fashion business slowed down drastically. In Finland, a third of companies reported that their turnover had dropped to less than half the normal amount in 2020 (STJM, 2020). Yet history has taught us that crises can also offer opportunities to renew business, and in the case of COVID-19, special attention has been given to renewing business in terms of sustainability. The crisis showed that a smaller organisational structure might offer flexibility, which is a benefit if fast redirections are needed when business circumstances are changing in an unanticipated way. Higher price levels, local production and shorter supply chains are very often connected to sustainable SMEs, and their size might offer surprising benefits such as better relationships with suppliers (personal connection), places of manufacture, and customers. Trust in business operations leads to better control and an easier way to negotiate, for instance, production timetables during crises, but size might also be an advantage when building tighter relationships with customers. Smaller size also enables more precise production (avoiding overproduction), new business experimentation, and selling directly to consumers. Moreover, local manufacturing enables avoiding the ethical risk factors caused by manufacturing on the other side of the globe.

A smaller business not only provides the designer with the potential to strategically influence the whole product lifecycle (Delong et al., 2013; Lawless and Medvedev, 2016), it also offers opportunities to try out alternative design and business actions. During the COVID-19 pandemic, many companies began to produce face masks when other products did not sell, some designers created a "Covid fashion collection" from leftover materials from stock and garments, aimed at use in remote work (e.g., REMAKE 2021), and other companies organised home fittings for their customers when society was locked down (FRENN, 2020), and in this way they were able not only to continue business, but also to avoid returns (normal in online shopping). Also, made-to-measure companies offered gift cards so that consumers could support suffering companies and place the actual garment order after the crisis was over (Anna Ruohonen, 2020). The very popular event *Helsinki Design Market* was cancelled in autumn 2020 because meetings were restricted in Finland, but design companies organised the market as a network event in several small shops in Helsinki's city centre where customers could book a visiting slot (Design Market, 2020). Many designer-led fashion houses participated in this event. Thus, smaller company size offered flexibility and creativity to try out new actions that might lead to a competitive advantage and new supporting networks even after the crisis is over.

References

Adidas (2020a) *Strategy* (online): https://report.adidas-group.com/2020/en/group-management-report-our-company/strategy.html, 22/7/2021.

Adidas (2020b) *Sustainability innovation* (online): https://www.adidas-group.com/en/sustainability/products/sustainability-innovation/, 22/7/2021.

Anderson, D. (2021, July 26) *Lululemon, LanzaTech are reshaping carbon waste into fabric*, GreenBiz (online): https://www.greenbiz.com/article/lululemon-lanzatech-are-reshaping-carbon-waste-fabric, 22/7/2021.

Anguelov, N. (2016) *The dirty side of the fashion industry. Fast fashion and its negative impact to environment and society*, CRC Press, Boca Raton, FL.

Claxton, S., and Kent, A. (2020) The management of sustainable fashion design strategies: an analysis of the designer's role, *Journal of Cleaner Production*, https://doi.org/10.1016/j.jclepro.2020.122112.

DeLong, M., Goncu-Berk, G., Bye, E., and Wu, J. (2013) Apparel sustainability from a local perspective, *Research Journal of Textile and Apparel*, 17(1), 59–69.

Design Market (2020) *Design market online* (online): https://www.helsinkidesignweek .com/design-market-online/, 22/7/2021.

Fransson, K., Brunklaus, B., and Molander, S. (2013) Managing chemical risk information, in Gardetti, M.A., and Torres, A.L. (eds.), *Sustainability in textile and fashion*, Greenleaf, Sheffield, pp. 82–96.

FRENN (2020) Jarkko Kallio & Frenn: We can help each other, MyHelsinki (online): https:// www.myhelsinki.fi/en/see-and-do/shopping /jarkko-kallio-and-frenn-we-can-help-each -other.

Granskog, A., Lee, L., Magnus, K.-H., and Sawers, C. (2020) *Survey: consumer sentiment on sustainability in fashion.* McKinsey & Company (online): https://www.mckinsey .com/industries/retail/our-insights/survey -consumer-sentiment-on-sustainability-in -fashion, 5/8/2021.

KEMI Swedish Chemicals Agency (2014) *Chemicals in textiles – risks to human health and the environment. Report from a government assignment*, Report 6/14. (online): https://www.kemi.se/global/ rapporter/2014/rapport-6-14-chemicals-in -textiles.pdf, 1/10/2021.

Kissinger, M., Sussmann, C., Moore, J., William, E., and Rees, W.E. (2013) Accounting for greenhouse gas emissions of materials at the urban scale-relating existing process life cycle assessment studies to urban material and waste composition, *Low Carbon Econ*, 4, 36–44.

Lawless, E., and Medvedev, K. (2016) Assessment of sustainable design practices in the fashion industry, experiences of eight small sustainable design companies in the northeastern and southeastern United States, *Internationla Journal of Fashion Design, Technology and Education*, 9(1), 41–50.

Niinimäki, K., Peters, G., Dahlbo, H., Perry, P., Rissanen, T., and Gwilt, A. (2020) The environmental price of fast fashion, *Nature Reviews; Earth and Environment*, 1, 189–200.

Östlund, Å., Wedin, H., Bolin, L., Berlin, J., Jönsson, C., Posner, S., and Sandin, G. (2015) *Textilåtervinning, Tekniska möjligheter och utmaningar*, Naturvårdsverket, Bromma Sweden. (online): http://www.diva-portal.org

/smash/get/diva2:920405/FULLTEXT01.pdf, 1/8/2021.

Raebuild, U., and Hasling, K. (2018) Sustainable design cards: a learning tool for supporting sustainable design strategies, in Niinimäki, K. (ed.), *Sustainable fashion in a circular economy*, Aalto ARTS Books, Helsinki, pp. 128–151.

Reima (2019) *Corporate responsibility report* (online): https://www.reima.com/medias/CSR -report-2019-final-web.pdf?context=bWF zdGVyfHJvb3R8NjQxNzQyNXxhcHBsaWNhdGl vbi9wZGZ8OTE4NDIwODMyMjU5MC5wZGZ 8MzlmODkxOGVjMGMxZjU1OGRkY2U0MGM zZDFiY2M2ZTc1YzU3MmQzYTdiYmExNjFjM2E 2MThhYzljZTE1YjcwNQ, 1/7/2021.

REMAKE (2021) *CO*ID-collection* (online): https://www.remake.fi/coid-mallisto.html, 1/7/2021.

Ruohonen, A. (2020) *Mekko&Maski*, personal communication, 15/5/2020.

Peters, G., Granberg, H., and Sweet, S. (2014) The role of science and technology for sustainable fashion, in Fletcher, K., and Tham, M.(eds.), *Routledge handbook of sustainability and fashion*, Routledge, London, pp. 181–190.

Piippo, R., and Niinimäki, K. (2021) Garment quality and product lifetimes, in *PLATE product lifetimes and the environment 2021 - Conference proceedings*, The University of Limerick, 26–28 May (online): https://ulir.ul.ie/ handle/10344/10244.

Quantis (2018) *Measuring fashion: insights from the environmental impact of the global apparel and footwear industries. Full report and methodological considerations.* (online): https://quantis-intl.com/measuring-fashion -report, 1/1/2021.

Rana, S., Pichandi, S., Karunamoorthy, S., Bhattacharyya, A., Parveen, S., and Fangueiro, R. (2015) Carbon footprint of textile and clothing products, in Muthu, S.S. (ed.), *Handbook of sustainable apparel production*, CRC, London, pp. 141–165.

Roos, S., Sandin, G., Peters, G., Spak, B., Schawarz, L., Perzon, E., and Jönsson, C. (2019) *White paper on textile recycling*, Mistra Future Fashion report number: 2019: D4.3.3.1 (online): S.-Roos.-White-paper-on-t extile-recycling.-Mistra-Future-Fashion.pdf (mistrafuturefashion.com), 1/1/2020.

Sadowski, M., Yan, C., Cummis, C., and Aden, N. (2019) *Apparel and footwear sector: science-based targets guidance*, World Resources Institute,Washington, USA.

STJM (2020) *Tekstiili- ja Muotialan Yritysten Tilanne Eelleen Todella Vaikea, Osalle Helpotusta Suojavarustetuotannosta [Textile and fashion companies are still struggling - some search ease from protective clothing production for health care purposes]* (online): https://www.stjm.fi/tiedotteet-kannanotot -ja-lausunnot/tekstiili-ja-muotialan-yritysten -tilanne-edelleen-vaikea/, 4/10/2021.

United Nations Climate Change (2018) *UN helps fashion industry shift to low carbon.* (online): https://unfccc.int/news/un-helps -fashion-industry-shift-to-low-carbon, 1/8/2021.

WRAP (2012) *Valuing our clothes: the true cost of how we design, use and dispose of clothing in the UK*, Waste & Resources Action Programme, Oxon, UK.

2.5 Fashion design in a new paradigm

Learning outcomes

1. To understand the new fashion design paradigm.
2. To understand the multilevel approach towards sustainability.
3. To understand that all sustainability approaches are important, and to select the level at which a designer can work in a certain company.

As stated by Claxton and Kent (2020), "in their conventional role, designers tend to have an influence on the choice of materials, aesthetics, silhouette, trims, manufacturing quality and the level of fashionability". Moreover, especially in sustainability-minded companies, fashion designers are interested in focusing on quality issues and ways to secure the longevity of a garment, for which technical durability aspects, consumers' emotional satisfaction, and timeless design are essential (Karell & Niinimäki, 2020). The CE approach adds the aspect of multiple garment lifetimes to the designer's worktable as well as the emerging knowledge on the end-of-life processes and garment/textile recycling into valuable new materials (Corvelec & Stål, 2017; Niinimäki, 2018, Piippo & Niinimäki, 2021). At a time when the sustainable fashion paradigm is being renewed and becoming the new norm – i.e., no longer a niche – and system-level transformation is taking place, new demands on designer's roles are emerging. This moment can also be seen as an opportunity to extend the designer's work from implementing a tightly framed design brief towards a more strategic role. As described earlier in this part, the designer may contribute strongly to the strategy construction of a company, and through this, link product design work more tightly to new business models and sustainable value creation to ensure that the product is really implementing the company's sustainable strategy. The product should provide value in a transformable sustainable system.

The designer does not do this alone: in SMEs, and even more so in designer-driven companies, the designer plays a bigger role and has more influence over decision-making and strategy-building. In larger companies, the designer can work in close collaboration with the sourcing, technical, and production teams to create company-based sustainable guidelines for design, production, and manufacturing processes. In some companies (especially bigger ones), an R&D team takes the lead in this work, but designers should also contribute because they have creative skills, insight into design, manufacturing knowledge, and very often user-centred understanding (empathic design). In the best cases, the designer can even participate in the company's strategy-building, and here the design process and the product can really represent and communicate the selected value base of the company. In a study by Claxton

DOI: 10.4324/9781003097846-11

and Kent (2020, p.3), companies that were trying to reach more sustainable aims saw "future opportunities for competitive strategy based on product differentiation by engaging the consumer emotionally through the branding, identity and creative concept behind sustainable products". Here, the product itself and its differentiation through design are no longer enough; all the other aspects, such as manufacturing, garment lifetime, business models, and environmental impacts need to be in line so that consumers are convinced that this is a truly sustainable brand and a sustainable product. As Claxton and Kent (2020, p.3) describe: "Design direction has a strategic perspective that is implemented at tactical and operational levels" (based on Borja de Mozota, 2002; Cooper & Press, 1995).

Table 2.5.1 summarises the discussion in this chapter. Sustainable fashion design has a system-level impact, and should not be understood as aesthetic and material selection alone. Designers should not design only products, but also product life-times, products which support alternative business models, or even the sustainable systems around the products. Designers can take part in constructing a transformative system and the products that enable this transformation. Design-thinking and design-management approaches can enhance system-level transformation, including providing new business models and consumer insights. Fashion design can help in taking into account carbon, water, and environmental impacts of textiles and garments. Designers should avoid rapidly changing trends and place more trust in seasonless fashion. Ecolabels and audit systems should be used. Design choices can be linked to safeguarding brand reputation and building trust among consumers.

The table shows all the aspects through which design can be connected to different levels in sustainable transformation. The designer can work on either some of these aspects or several of them, and have a narrow or more holistic view of sustainability. The aim is to enable and encourage a new understanding of the fashion system and to create a better balance in it.

As John Thackara (2014, p.45) points out, political demand might not be the best driver of sustainability transformation, but transformation is "a condition that emerges as the effects of incremental change, at many different scales, accumulate (see also the discussion of the macro level in Section 1.1.1).

The chapters in this part have revealed different views of sustainable fashion design, from material selection and aesthetic creation to a more systemic understanding of design and manufacturing processes, the aspect of time in sustainability (slowing), and the importance of responsibility and trust. The aim of the part was to widen the understanding of creativity and design throughout the fashion system while building a new paradigm for sustainable fashion.

Task

1. Using one or more company cases, consider what kinds of approaches the designer can take, bearing in mind company strategy and company size.
2. Select one example company and study its sustainability report. What actions have been taken, and what approaches are included, or perhaps excluded, on the basis of the company's sustainability reporting.
3. Discuss with your peer students how fashion design practices should change so that the designer can play a more important role in the company's sustainability work.

Table 2.5.1 Design for System-level Transformation

Product design	Production	Garment lifetime	Use phase	End-of-life	Business	System-level
Selecting sustainable materials	Resource-efficiency	Technical lifetime	Easy to care for	Postponing the end-of-life stage in all possible ways	Design for product-service system	Time (slowing)
Choosing low-impact materials	Carbon-neutral approach	Functional lifetime	Repairing	Closing the material loop and enabling material recycling	Design suitable for alternative business models	Scale (decreasing)
Quality and structural considerations	Renewable energy	Emotional lifetime	Emotional satisfaction		Customer-to-customer business platforms	Volumes (more accurate)
Limiting chemical use and finishes	Water and chemical use		Avoiding fashion that is too trendy		Brand value in secondhand fashion	Taking into account system limitations (environmental impacts)
Avoiding rapidly changing trends	Environmental impacts		Learning from garment quality		Business for CE	Implementing a CE approach in the fashion system
Considering styles and fashion aesthetics	Waste-handling in manufacturing				Transformative business (for system-level change)	Using creativity and wide-ranging collaboration to solve problems in the system
Providing functionality	Manufacturing location(s)					
Including user-centred understanding	Workers' rights					
Preferring eco-labels and eco-standards	Eco-labels and standards					
Creating recyclable design and defining the recycling path	Transparency					

Goal: Design for system-level transformation

References

Aakko, M. (2013) Artisanal and slow: the case of Anna Ruohonen, in Niinimäki, K. (ed.), *Sustainable fashion: new approaches*, Aalto ARTS Books, Helsinki, pp. 56–67.

Anguelov, N. (2016) *The dirty side of the fashion industry. Fast fashion and its negative impact to environment and society*, CRC Press, Boca Raton, FL.

Berg, A., Granskog, A., Lee, L., and Magnus K. (2020) *Fashion on climate*, McKinsey & Company (online): https://www.mckinsey.com/industries/retail/our-insights/fashion-on-climate, 22/7/2021.

Bocken, N., de Pauw, I., Bakker, C., and van den Grinten, B. (2016) Product design and business model strategies for a circular economy, *Industrial Product Engineering*, 5(33), 308–320.

Bocken, N., Miller, K., Weissbrod, K., Holdago, M., and Evans, S. (2018) Slowing resource loops in the clothing industry through circular business model experimentation, in Niinimäki, K. (ed.), *Sustainable fashion in a circular economy*, Aalto ARTS Books, Helsinki, pp. 152–167.

Borja de Mozota, B. (2002) Design and competitive edge: a model for design management excellence in European SMEs, *Design Management Journal*, 1(2), 88–103.

Burns, B. (2010) Re-evaluating obsolescence and planning for it, in T. Cooper (ed.), *Longer lasting products: alternatives to the throwaway society*, Gower, Farnham, pp. 39–60.

Chapman, J. (2009) *Emotionally durable design; objects, experiences & empathy*, Earthscan Publication, London.

Claxton, S., and Kent, A. (2020) The management of sustainable fashion design strategies: an analysis of the designer's role, *Journal of Cleaner Production*, https://doi.org/10.1016/j.jclepro.2020.122112.

Cooper, R., Junginger, S., and Lockwood, T. (2009) Design thinking and design management: a research and practice perspective, *Design Management Review*, 1, 46–55.

Cooper, R., and Press, M. (1995) *The design agenda: a guide to successful design management*, John Wiley, Chichester, UK.

Corvellec, H., and Stål, H.I. (2017) Evidencing the waste effect of Product-Service Systems (PSSs), *Journal of Cleaner Production*, 145, 14–24.

DeLong, M., Goncu-Berk, G., Bye, E., and Wu, J. (2013) Apparel sustainability from a local perspective, *Research Journal of Textile and Apparel*, 17(1), 59–69.

Den Hollander, M. (2018) *Design for managing obsolescence. A design methodology*, Doctoral dissertation, Delft University of Technology, Delft, Netherlands.

Fletcher, K. (2010) Slow fashion: an invitation for systemic change, *Fashion Practice*, 2(2), 559–566.

Fransson, K., Brunklaus, B., and Molander, S. (2013) Managing chemical risk information, in Gardetti, M.A., and Torres, A.L. (eds.), *Sustainability in textile and fashion*, Greenleaf, Sheffield, pp. 82–96.

Gabrieli, V., Baghi, I., and Codeluppi, V. (2013) Consumption practices of fast fashion products: a consumer-based approach, *Journal of Fashion Marketing and Management*, 17(2), 206–224.

Goworek, H., Hiller, A., Fisher, T., Cooper, T., and Woodward, S. (2013) Consumers' attitudes towards sustainable fashion, in Gardetti, M. & Torres, A. (eds.), *Sustainability in Fashion and Textiles*, Greenleaf Publishing, Sheffield, pp. 377–392.

Granskog, A., Lee, L., Magnus, K.-H., and Sawers, C. (2020) *Survey: consumer sentiment on sustainability in fashion*. McKinsey & Company (online): https://www.mckinsey.com/industries/retail/our-insights/survey-consumer-sentiment-on-sustainability-in-fashion, 5/8/2021.

Grosse-Hering, B., Mason, J., Aliakseyeu, D., Bakker, C., and Desmet, P. (2013, April)

Slow design for meaningful interactions, in *Proceedings of the SIGGHI Conference of Human Factors in Computing Systems,* Paris, France.

Heikkilä, P., Fontel, P., Määttänen, M., and Harlin, A. (2018) Review of textile recycling ecosystem, and a case of cotton, in Niinimäki, K. (ed.), *Sustainable fashion in a circular economy,* Aalto ARTS Books, Helsinki, pp. 192–217.

Karell, E., and Niinimäki, K. (2020) A mixed-method study of design practices and designers' roles in sustainable-minded clothing companies, *Sustainability,* 12, 4680.

KEMI Swedish Chemicals Agency (2014) *Chemicals in textiles – risks to human health and the environment. Report from a government assignment,* Report 6/14. (online): https://www.kemi.se/global/rapporter/2014/rapport-6-14-chemicals-in-textiles.pdf, 1/10/2021.

Kissinger, M., Sussmann, C., Moore, J., and Rees, W.E. (2013) Accounting for greenhouse gas emissions of materials at the urban scale-relating existing process life cycle assessment studies to urban material and waste composition, *Low Carbon Econ,* 4, 36–44.

Lawless, E., and Medvedev, K. (2016) Assessment of sustainable design practices in the fashion industry, experiences of eight small sustainable design companies in the northeastern and southeastern United States, *Internationla Journal of Fashion Design, Technology and Education,* 9(1), 41–50.

Määttänen, M., Asikainen, S., Kamppuri, T, Ilen, E., Niinimäki, K., Tanttu, M., and Harlin, A. (2019) Colour management in CE; decolourization of cotton waste, *RJTA Research Journal of Textiles and Apparel,* 23(2), 134–152.

Mathews, B. (2016) *One third of all clothing "Never Sold",* Ecotextile News (online): https://www.ecotextile.com/2016042122078/fashion-retail-news/one-third-of-allclothing-never-sold.html, 1/1/2018.

Mintzberg, H. (1994) *The rise and fall of strategic planning,* Free Press, New York.

Niinimäki, K. (2011) *From disposable to sustainable. The complex interplay between design and consumption of textiles and clothing,* Doctoral dissertation, Aalto University, Helsinki. https://aaltodoc.aalto.fi/handle/123456789/13770.

Niinimäki, K. (2014) Sustainable consumer satisfaction in the context of clothing, in Vezzoli, C., Kohtala, C., Srinivasan, A., Diehl, J.C., Fusakul, S.M., Xin, L., and Sateesh, D. (eds.), *Product-service system design for sustainability,* Greenleaf, Sheffield, UK, pp. 218–237.

Niinimäki, K. (2018) Sustainable fashion in a circular economy, in Niinimäki, K. (ed.), *Sustainable fashion in a circular economy,* Aalto ARTS Books, Helsinki, pp. 12–41. https://aaltodoc.aalto.fi/handle/123456789/36608.

Niinimäki, K. (ed.) (2018) *Sustainable fashion in a circular economy,* Aalto ARTS Books, Helsinki. https://aaltodoc.aalto.fi/handle/123456789/36608.

Niinimäki, K., and Aakko, M. (2014) Creative control in sustainable fashion, in *19th ADMC, Academic Design Management Conference, Design Management in the Era of Disruption,* 2–4 September 2014, UAL, London, UK, pp. 583–600.

Niinimäki, K., and Armstrong, C. (2013) From pleasure in use to preservation of meaningful memories: a closer look at the sustainability of clothing via longevity and attachment, *International Journal of Fashion Design, Technology and Education,* 6(3), 190–199.

Niinimäki, K., and Karell, E. (2019) Closing the loop: intentional fashion design defined by recycling technologies, in Vignali, G., Reid, L.F., Ryding, D., and Henninger, C. (eds.), *Technology-driven sustainability; innovation in the fashion supply-chain,* Palgrave Macmillan, Cham, Switzerland, pp. 7–27.

Niinimäki, K., and Koskinen, I. (2011) I love this dress, it makes me feel beautiful: emotional knowledge in sustainable design, *Design Journal,* 14(2), 165–186.

Niinimäki, K., Peters, G., Dahlbo, H., Perry, P., Rissanen, T., and Gwilt, A. (2020) The environmental price of fast fashion,

Nature Reviews; Earth and Environment, 1, 189–200.

Östlund, Å., Wedin, H., Bolin, L., Berlin, J., Jönsson, C., Posner, S., and Sandin, G. (2015) *Textilåtervinning, Tekniska möjligheter och utmaningar*, Naturvårdsverket, Bromma Sweden. (online): http://www.diva-portal.org /smash/get/diva2:920405/FULLTEXT01.pdf, 1/8/2021.

Peters, G., Granberg, H., and Sweet, S. (2014) The role of science and technology for sustainable fashion, in Fletcher, K., and Tham, M.(eds.), *Routledge handbook of sustainability and fashion*, Routledge, London, pp. 181–190.

Piippo, R., and Niinimäki, K. (2021) Garment quality and product lifetimes, in *PLATE product lifetimes and the environment 2021 - Conference proceedings*, The University of Limerick, 26–28 May (online): https://ulir.ul.ie/ handle/10344/10244.

Porter, M. (2004) *Competitive strategy. Techniques for analyzing industries and competitors*, Free Press, New York. (Original work published 1980).

Quantis (2018) *Measuring fashion: insights from the environmental impact of the global apparel and footwear industries. Full report and methodological considerations.* (online): https://quantis-intl.com/measuring-fashion -report, 1/1/2021.

Raebuild, U., and Hasling, K. (2018) Sustainable design cards: a learning tool for supporting sustainable design strategies, in Niinimäki, K. (ed.), *Sustainable fashion in a circular economy*, Aalto ARTS Books, Helsinki, pp. 128–151.

Rana, S., Pichandi, S., Karunamoorthy, S., Bhattacharyya, A., Parveen, S., and Fangueiro, R. (2015) Carbon footprint of textile and clothing products, in Muthu, S.S. (ed.), *Handbook of sustainable apparel production*, CRC, London, pp. 141–165.

Roos, S., Sandin, G., Peters, G., Spak, B., Schawarz, L., Perzon, E., and Jönsson, C. (2019) *White paper on textile recycling*, Mistra Future Fashion report number: 2019: D4.3.3.1 (online): S.-Roos.-White-paper-on-t extile-recycling.-Mistra-Future-Fashion.pdf (mistrafuturefashion.com), 1/1/2020.

Runnel, A., Raihan, K., Castel, N., Oja, D., and Bhuiya, H. (2017) *Creating digitally enhanced circular economy*, Reverse Resources (online): http://www.reverseresources.net/about/ white-paper, 1/1/2018.

Ruohonen, A. (2020) *Mekko&Maski*, personal communication, 15/5/2020.

Sadowski, M., Yan, C., Cummis, C., and Aden, N. (2019) *Apparel and footwear sector: science-based targets guidance*, World Resources Institute,Washington, USA.

Sinha, P. (2000) The role of designing through making across market levels in the UK fashion industry, *The Design Journal*, 3(3), 26–44.

Smirnova, E. (2017) *Colours in a circular economy*, Master thesis, Aalto University, Helsinki. (online): https://aaltodoc.aalto.fi/ handle/123456789/24669, 1/1/2020.

Smirnova, E., Elina Ilén, E., Sixta, H., Hummel, M., and Niinimäki, K. (2016) Colours in a circular economy, in *Circular Transitions – Mistra Future Fashion Conference on Textile Design and the Circular Economy*, 23–24 November 2016, Chelsea College of Arts & Tate Britain, London.

STJM (2020) *Tekstiili- ja Muotialan Yritysten Tilanne Eelleen Todella Vaikea, Osalle Helpotusta Suojavarustetuotannosta* [*Textile and fashion companies are still struggling - some search ease from protective clothing production for health care purposes*] (online): https://www.stjm.fi/tiedotteet -kannanotot-ja-lausunnot/tekstiili-ja -muotialan-yritysten-tilanne-edelleen -vaikea/, 4/10/2021.

Thackara, J. (2014) A whole new cloth: politics and the fashion system, in Fletcher, K., and Tham, M. (eds.), *Routledge handbook of sustainability and fashion*, Routledge, London, pp. 43–51.

United Nations Climate Change (2018) *UN helps fashion industry shift to low carbon.* (online): https://unfccc.int/news/un-helps -fashion-industry-shift-to-low-carbon, 1/8/2021.

Walker, S. (2006) *Sustainable by design. Exploration in theory and practice*, Earthscan, London.

Whittington, R., Molloy, E., Mayer, M., and Smith, A. (2006) Practices of strategising/

organising: broadening strategy work and skills, *Long Range Planning*, 39(6), 615–629.

WRAP (2012) *Valuing our clothes: the true cost of how we design, use and dispose of clothing in the UK*, Waste & Resources Action Programme, Oxon, UK.

Websites

adidas (2019) *Adidas unlocks a circular future for sports with FUTURECRAFT.LOOP* (online): https://www.adidas-group.com/en/media/news-archive/press-releases/2019/adidas-unlocks-circular-future-sports-futurecraftloop/, 22/7/2021.

adidas (2020a) *Strategy* (online): https://report.adidas-group.com/2020/en/group-management-report-our-company/strategy.html, 22/7/2021.

adidas (2020b) *Sustainability innovation* (online): https://www.adidas-group.com/en/sustainability/products/sustainability-innovation/, 22/7/2021.

Alabama Chanin (online): https://alabamachanin.com/, 22/7/2021.

Anderson, D. (2021, July 26) *Lululemon, LanzaTech are reshaping carbon waste into fabric*, GreenBiz (online): https://www.greenbiz.com/article/lululemon-lanzatech-are-reshaping-carbon-waste-fabric, 22/7/2021.

Anna Ruohonen (online): https://annaruohonen.com/, 22/7/2021.

Arela (online): https://www.arelastudio.com/, 22/7/2021.

Clonet, *Clonet Oy – your partner in developing climate business* (online): http://www.clonet.fi/en/, 22/7/2021.

Converse, *Create your look for tomorrow* (online): https://www.converse.com/fi/en/landing-design-your-own?lang=en_FI&csid=PSH_PRF_CNV_WE_FI_EN_20191101_FPMX_Go-DSA-FIN-B+G_9657627288_PPC_X_X_G oogle_DSA-ALLPages-B+G_X_dsa-890136 200582_102852586281_537148103965_c &gclid=Cj0KCQjwu7OIBhCsARIsALxCUaMHO 3j0wE4iHTtIMSWObs2CHbqnGdzZ6itg9yUW 9Z2ci4zmJHPvUskaAgK_EALw_wcB&gclsrc =aw.ds, 1/1/2021.

Design Market (2020) *Design market online* (online): https://www.helsinkidesignweek.com/design-market-online/, 22/7/2021.

Emmy, *Emmy-Kuntoluokitus Myytäville Vaatteille [Emmy quality categorization for second hand garments]* (online): https://store.emmy.fi/pages/emmy-kuntoluokitus-myytaville-tuotteille, 22/7/2021.

Filippa K, *Sustainability report 2020* (online): https://www.filippa-k.com/globalassets/home/reports/sustainability-reports/filippa-k-sustainability-report_2020-1.pdf?ref=F9185891B0, 22/7/2021.

FRENN a, *Honest sustainability* (online): https://frennhelsinki.com/pages/sustainability, 22/7/2021.

FRENN b, *Waste, recycling and carbon footprint* (online): https://frennhelsinki.com/pages/waste-recycling-carbonfootprint, 22/7/2021.

FRENN c, *Code of conduct* (online): https://frennhelsinki.com/pages/code-of-conduct, 22/7/2021.

FRENN (2021) *Home delivery and fitting* (online): https://frennhelsinki.com/collections/home-fitting, 22/7/2021.

FRENN d, *FRENN story* (online): https://frennhelsinki.com/pages/story, 22/7/2021.

Halti. (2020) *Our most sustainable garment: the next generation jacket* (online): https://halti.com/blogs/news/our-most-sustainable-design-the-halti-next-generation-jacket, 1/1/2021.

Hansen, S. (2016) *The ultimate luxury is time: this 'Slow Fashion' brand is rooted in DIY*, Observer (online): https://observer.com/2016/06/the-ultimate-luxury-is-time-this-slow-fashion-brand-is-rooted-in-diy/, 1/7/2021.

Madsen, A.C. (2021, February 8) *Stella Mc Cartney Pre Fall 2021* (online): https://www.vogue.com/fashion-shows/pre-fall-2021/stella-mccartney, 1/6/2021.

Nudie Jeans, *Re-use* (online): https://www.nudiejeans.com/blog/re-use-news-this-just-in/, 1/7/2021.

Patagonia, *Closing the loop – a report on Patagonia's common threads garment recycling program* (online): https://www.patagonia.com/stories/closing-the-loop-a-report-on-patagonias-common-threads-garment-recycling-program/story-19961.html, 1/7/2021.

Reima (2019) *Corporate responsibility report* (online): https://www.reima.com/medias/CSR-report-2019-final-web.pdf?context=bWFzdGVyfHJvb3R8NjQxNzQyNXxhcHBsaWNhdGlvbi9wZGZ8OTE4NDIwODMyMjU5MC5wZGZ8MzlmODkxOGVjMGMxZjU1OGRkY2U0U0MGMzZDFiY2M2ZTc1YzU3MmQzYTdiYmExNjM4E2MThhYzljZTE1YjcwNQ, 1/7/2021.

Reima a. *Kids' winter mono-material fully recyclable Ski Jacket – Kulkija* (online): https://us.reima.com/products/kids-recyclable-winter-jacket-kulkija, 1/7/2021.

REMAKE (2021) *CO*ID-collection* (online): https://www.remake.fi/coid-mallisto.html, 1/7/2021.

Sheep Inc. a, *Welcome to Sheep Inc. A naturally carbon negative knitwear brand working extremely closely with sheep* (online): https://eu.sheepinc.com/, 1/7/2021.

Sheep Inc. b, *I005 the Hoobie* (online): https://eu.sheepinc.com/collections/sweater/products/005-hoodie?variant=40608677331093, 1/7/2021.

Stella McCartney, *Eco impact report 2018/2019* (online): https://www.stellamccartney.com/us/en/stellas-world/stella-mccartney-eco-impact-report-2018-19.html, 1/7/2021.

Stony creek colours (online): https://www.racked.com/2017/6/16/15792068/stony-creek-colors-natural-dye-indigo.

Vaatelaastari, pacth (online): https://vaatelaastari.fi/pages/in-english, 1/7/2021.

PART 3
Digital sustainable fashion

This part focuses on new trends in the industry that have been enabled by the development of new technology and technological processes. It highlights how aspects raised in Part 2 concerning sustainable fashion design can be transformed through a technological revolution by keeping sustainability as the key focus. Leading on from Part 1, it will demonstrate how the industry is dealing with consumer perceptions and acceptance of digital sustainable fashion.

DOI: 10.4324/9781003097846-12

3.1 Sustainability, fashion, and technology

Learning outcomes

1. To introduce the current retail scenario for fashion brands: multichannel versus omnichannel.
2. To review the current use of technology in this omnichannel scenario.
3. To look at digital convergence in physical fashion stores.
4. To realise how this technology can be used to promote more sustainable behaviours.
5. To review the importance and challenges of sustainability communication.
6. To consider the contribution of the physical store to conveying these sustainability messages.

The fashion retail scene has changed considerably in the last few years, which has had implications for sustainable fashion management. The growth of online channels and ongoing digitisation of the fashion industry has led to an increasing use of technologies as part of the omnichannel shopping experience. The external environment, often analysed through the PEST(EL) framework (see Chapter 1.1), can significantly impact these changes. For example, the COVID-19 pandemic has accelerated this process, creating further challenges in terms of sustainability in the fashion industry related to the increasing number of deliveries and returns. Within this context, physical stores faced key challenges as they had to close in accordance with government regulations, but having a physical presence is relevant and important for fashion consumers. It is a place for interaction, for socialization, and for experiencing the product. Physical stores cannot be seen in isolation as they are part of a larger experience that is more connected with other channels. The use of technology is one of the main points of connection with other touchpoints such as websites, mobile channels, or social media. These technologies have different applications and can be used to promote sustainability in many forms. One of them is to educate consumers through sustainability communication by increasing awareness about sustainability-related issues.

3.1.1 The current scenario for fashion retail: from multichannel to omnichannel

The retail scene has changed in the last few years due to the growth of online retail and ongoing digitalisation. Retailers have evolved from being single-channel to embrace omnichannel strategies, which represents a shift in the retail paradigm (Verhoef et al., 2015). Nowadays, consumers access the internet through an increasing range of digital

DOI: 10.4324/9781003097846-13

devices and expect consistent and seamless shopping experiences using a growing number of offline, online, and mobile channels and touchpoints. The physical and digital channels of distribution and communication have become more integrated (Grewal et al., 2017, Grewal and Roggeveen, 2020). This new omnichannel scenario is clearly applicable to the fashion sector, with some peculiarities that will be addressed later (Alexander and Blazquez Cano, 2019).

The concept of omnichannel focuses on the interplay of channels and brands and includes, but is not limited to retail channels such as mobile, social media, and any other touchpoints between the consumer and the brand (Alexander and Blazquez Cano, 2020). Thus, in the current retail scenario it is difficult to differentiate the role played by individual channels. Consumers consider their own shopping journey as a unique experience, and they interact with the brand more than with individual channels. They perceive the brand in a holistic manner that is the sum of technology, interaction, design of space, and multisensory experience in a physical place (Alexander and Blazquez Cano, 2019). As a consequence, they do not consider channels in isolation. This being said, this chapter will focus on the current role played by technology in physical retailing while considering the physical store as part of a wider and more connected experience (Blazquez, 2014).

> **Omnichannel** – the interplay of channels used to communicate between the consumer and the brand itself.

The process of integrating different channels has not always been straightforward in the fashion industry, and differences need to be established between different types of fashion formats as they will have differing impacts on sustainable fashion management. The case of department stores is particularly relevant. Luxury department stores have aligned staff, services, layout, and merchandise to create a strong offline presence, and have always provided a high level of interaction with their customers (Kent et al., 2016). The physical space aims to build an emotional connection with the brand, and it is perceived by customers more as points of experience than as points of sale. Consumers are immersed in the brand's values and heritage that build up the brand's symbolic universe, and the multiple channel touchpoints reinforce the relationship between the consumer and the retailer. However, the heritage and experiential elements of their brands are not easily transferable to other platforms and channels. There appears to be something special about the physical touchpoints of these stores that is not present in their other channels. Therefore, the transfer of the in-store experience into new media remains a major challenge, one that is only partially achieved through online content and use of visual media.

Kent et al. (2016) found that cross-channel integration in department stores has benefits for the long-term relationship with customers and also promotes further engagement with a wider audience, and consequently increases sales: the use of online and social media is more appealing for younger consumers and gives the department stores access to a new generation. In addition to the management of different touchpoints, department stores need to face the management of the brands they sell as well as their own brand. Luxury department stores such as Harrods or Selfridges have their own brand identities with strong values associated with them. Also, the brands they sell have their own brand values and identity, and in some cases there may be a clash between the identity of the retailer and the identity of the brands. This applies to sustainable fashion management. The decision of some department stores to have in their portfolios brands that do not follow sustainable practices may have consequences and damage their corporate brand images. A good example may be the demonstrations groups of activists stage in front of the main entrances of some department stores to raise awareness about the unsustainable practices of some of the brands sold. For example, activists have sought to raise awareness about the fact that some department stores sell different brands that still use real fur in their garments by encouraging pedestrians not to enter certain department stores as doing so would be supporting those practices against animal welfare. Consequently, department stores also face different challenges due to the socially visible nature of their physical buildings.

Department stores share many aspects with physical stores. In a context of increasingly competitive retailing, where physical stores compete not only with other physical stores, but also with online and mobile retailers, the differentiation of the point of sale is crucial to continue to attract consumers and sustainability could act as a relevant competitive factor. Retailers play a key role in the transmission of sustainability values because they are in close contact with the ultimate consumers (Kent et al., 2016).

The store is a place of transaction, but also a space for interaction and enjoyment. Many consumers visit physical fashion stores from hedonic motivations, and they may be more willing to engage with certain in-store communications. Technology acts as a medium to interact with certain messages. In the next section, we will consider the use of technology in the physical store.

3.1.1.1 The role of technology in omnichannel retailing

In spite of the growth of online shopping, the physical store still plays an important role in fashion retailing. The physical store is the place where consumers can experience the product (i.e., see, touch, and try on the garments) and the service (i.e., personal services, sales assistants). For retailers, it is crucial to interact with consumers and get feedback and information from them. However, as consumers become more experienced in the use of digital channels, they expect a similar or even superior experience in physical stores through the use of technology (Blazquez, 2014).

The store has become a place of convergence of different channels, and its design must be able to translate the brand identity from the product and services into customer experience. The physical space needs to be agile and responsive to format evolution, with an emphasis on flexibility, integration, and entertainment (Alexander and Blazquez Cano, 2019). The use of technologies contributes to the store environment in terms of design, experience, and functionality (Blazquez, 2014, Kent et al., 2015). New technologies enable human–computer interaction for consumers and retailers, and change the consumption experience in the physical space (Siregar and Kent, 2019).

Kent et al. (2015) identified different levels of presence of technology in fashion stores. Some stores may *not present technology at all*, even if this is quite rare nowadays. This may be a way to create an experience that is unique and completely separated from other channels. It could also be that the retailer is a single-channel brand and the store is looking for a way to differentiate itself from competitors. The second level refers to stores that present some form of technology that is relevant in terms of in-store *design*. It is very common to include screens showing videos of catwalks or related to the production of the garments. These may include static pictures or even light installations. The third level is the use of *technology as a facilitator*. This could include the provision of free Wi-Fi in fashion stores or the use of in-store self-checkouts, as they facilitate the shopping experience and also give access to other technologies. The last and more advanced level is related to the use of *technology to merge the physical and virtual channels*. In this group, we find retailers that use immersive and experiential technologies such as virtual reality or augmented reality. Next, we will review the main technologies used in fashion retail.

> **In-store technologies (ISTs)** – the different consumer-facing technologies that facilitate the shopping process in physical stores.

Although a wide range of technologies can be found in physical stores serving different purposes, this section will focus on consumer-facing technologies. In-store technologies (ISTs) refer to the different consumer-facing devices that facilitate the shopping process in the physical store and are distinct from in-store technologies with which consumers cannot interact (Mosquera et al., 2018). For the customer, cutting-edge tools can create an immersive experience and aid decision-making by means of interactive devices (Business of Fashion, 2020; see also Section 1.1.1). Pantano and Vannucci (2019) classify them as info/product display technologies, shopping experience technologies, information search technologies, and payment technologies. These technologies may include, but are not limited to, automatic checkouts, beacons, radio-frequency identification (RFID) technologies, interactive screen, signage, tablets, virtual reality, smart mirrors or augmented reality (Alexander and Blazquez Cano, 2019, 2020). Hoyer et al. (2020) argue that there are three technology clusters at the centre of the digital transformation: the Internet of Things (IoT), augmented reality (AR), virtual reality (VR), mixed reality (MR), and virtual assistants, chatbots, or robots which will result in an entirely new concept of customer experience.

However, despite the debate about the presence of technology in physical fashion stores, the truth is that there is a lack of standardisation in the presence of technology between different retailers. Alexander and Blazquez Cano (2019) summarised the key forms of technology currently present at fashion stores as discussed with fashion practitioners. These included contactless payment, iPads, kiosks, virtual mirrors, QR codes, iBeacons, virtual reality, and augmented reality. Additionally, mobile capabilities provide real-time access to product details and reviews via near-field technology (Business of Fashion, 2020). The "store of the future" could include technologies such as consumer-facing displays with enhanced augmented reality applications that layer personalised pricing for example, or thermal imaging technology that detects replenishment needs while determining patterns in customer movement through space (Business of Fashion, 2020). These in-store technologies provide new opportunities to influence consumers' attitudes, behaviours, and experiences, and this effect is suggested to be particularly strong in fashion retailing (Pantano and Vanucci, 2019). Alexander and Blazquez Cano (2019b) have identified four different roles of consumer-facing technologies in the physical space, including their use to provide better customer service, act as brand educators, enhance the senses, and heighten brand immersion. First, technology has an evident use to provide better *customer service*. Technologies like self-checkouts or mobile apps that indicate the availability of items in the store contribute to providing a better customer experience. This could include the use of RFID technologies for inventory purposes to offer updated information about the stock of items in the store. They substitute, in a way, the role of the sales associate and make the shopping experience more efficient. Second, technologies can act as *brand educators*. This includes the use of interactive screens or videos with varying purposes. They can show images of the current collection to inspire customers or broadcast different communication campaigns. They are useful media to communicate key messages to customers. The third and fourth role of technologies in fashion stores are related to the *creation of experiences*. In order to do that, retailers have introduced advanced technologies to create immersive retail experiences that connect with consumers at an emotional level. These retail experiences are generated through the use of immersive technologies that appeal to the senses and make consumers feel they are interacting with the brand and experiencing the product (Alexander and Blazquez Cano, 2019a). This is especially relevant in the fashion sector, where hedonic motivations such as adventure shopping (i.e., the feeling of being immersed in another world) or idea shopping (i.e., looking for inspiration) are important drivers for fashion consumption (Blazquez, 2014). In addition to this, the introduction of technology in retailing contributes to transforming traditional retail management to smart retailing management.

From the roles of consumer-facing technologies in fashion stores, it looks like the use of technology as brand educator could be relevant to communicate information related to sustainability. In fact, H&M has used in-store screens to communicate its compromise with sustainability and its sustainability initiatives such as the Conscious Collection. Other brands utilise the store space to increase awareness about their sustainability commitments (i.e., the percentage of sustainable materials used in their collections or the expected deadline to address sustainable goals). This is the case with Mango, which has declared that 79 per cent of its garments have sustainable properties and that by 2022 it will be 100 per cent. It seems clear that fashion brands want to be aligned to the UN Sustainable Development Goals, and more specifically with SDG 12, related to responsible consumption and production (UN, 2021). It would also be relevant to develop immersive experiences to educate consumers about the impact of their decisions on sustainability and to promote the consumption of sustainable garments rather than others from the same brand. However, for technology to be successful and engaging, it needs to provide value to consumers. Next, we will review consumers' approach to the use of technology by fashion retailers.

3.1.1.2 Consumers' approach to the use of technology

Overall, technology plays a critical role in the evolution of society. Consumers may be constantly connected to the internet, and this has changed the way they live, work, shop, and play. They are more informed, demanding, and impatient than previous generations. They are eager for experiences, and technology is key, as it often serves an underlying role in enabling consumers to experience more (Blazquez, 2014).

As mentioned at the beginning of this chapter, the digital revolution has added new touchpoints and channels to the customer shopping journey. The customer journey is iterative and dynamic (Hoyer et al., 2020), and it is important that technologies eliminate all friction points in the shopping journey while being innovative and engaging (Dugar et al., 2020). In any case, it is necessary to understand the benefits of technology before implementing it (Alexander and Blazquez Cano, 2019). For hedonic products such as fashion, AR, VR, or MR could be more advantageous due to their ability to facilitate the imagination and provide a richer experience (Hoyer et al., 2020). However, successful physical retail spaces should be both experiential and functional to meet high expectations of service, personalization, and convenience (Grewal et al., 2020, Mosquera et al., 2018).

In research carried out by Dugar et al. (2020), fashion consumers gave some indications about the technologies they would like to find in fashion stores and how they would like to use them. They mentioned *digital fitting rooms*, meaning that they would not need to carry clothes to the fitting rooms and they could order different clothes without stepping out. The second technology mentioned was *magic/smart mirrors*, and here it would be important that they work well and respond quickly and accurately due to the issues mentioned in the previous section. They felt that *beacon technology* would help them to search for information about products. With the same objective, they said they would like to use *smart shelves*, but they would also like to see style advice and outfit suggestions. Shop windows are still very important for consumers, both *traditional and interactive windows*. Last, they said that *augmented reality* should be used to increase convenience for customers. Even though there was not a specific mention of sustainability, the technologies used for utilitarian purposes could have an impact on making better shopping decisions, and thus reduce the impact of unwanted items and returns.

From an omnichannel retail perspective, Mosquera et al. (2018) found that consumers expect stores to offer them technological devices in the physical space, to facilitate the use of their own devices, and to equip their fitting rooms with additional technological services. They also found gender differences related to consumers' expectations of technology which are consistent with those found in previous research, meaning that male consumers tend to be more utilitarian (i.e., requesting information on item availability or the range of products) and women tend to be more hedonic (i.e., browsing products or requesting staff advice) in their use of technology (Blazquez, 2014).

The reality for the fashion industry is that the use of technology is polarised. While some consumers like to interact with technology during their visits in physical stores, others prefer to enjoy the hedonic experience and disconnect from everything else. Research results are not necessarily based on age, either. They will also depend on the nature of the technology. Stores packed with cameras, sensors, and data analytics may produce negative reactions due to privacy concerns (Business of Fashion, 2020). Considering that the investment in technology can be substantial, it is common for companies to test new technologies through small experiments or dedicated test spaces (Business of Fashion, 2020). In fact, many of the technologies mentioned earlier have recently been tested through "The Trending Store" in Westfield, London, which combines the smart trending of online shopping via artificial intelligence with a group of stylists who curated collections for the store (Drapers, 2020).

It is also important to consider that cultural differences or even geographical differences can lead to a higher or lower level of experience in shopping online, which will be translated into perceptions and expectations with regard to the use of technology. So when retailers decide to go global, they must take into consideration these cultural expectations and offer a relevant proposition to consumers (Blazquez, 2012). For the fashion sector, consumers with less experience of online shopping tend to avoid the use of technology in their shopping experiences, while consumers with high expertise in online shopping prefer to use technologies both in physical stores and online channels (Blazquez Cano, 2016).

The impact of COVID has accelerated the use of e-commerce as consumers have spent more time online out of necessity. As a result, they have discovered new channels and gained more confidence in online shopping (Drapers, 2020). On the other hand, some consumers may have a greater desire to socialise and they may react more favourably to technologies that facilitate the connection with other people (Hoyer et al., 2020). In addition to changing consumer behaviour, the retail landscape is evolving more rapidly than ever, and consumers are driving the need for retailers' wider transformation, dictating how and where they want to interact with them in each platform (Drapers, 2020). Today, connecting with customers at the right place at the right time is critical to success.

3.1.1.3 Digital channels

Online retailing has traditionally been considered utilitarian in nature while hedonic consumption has been strongly associated with physical settings (Blazquez, 2014). However, advances in digital technologies and website design have led to the development of digital environments combining ambient, interactive, and social factors, creating immersive and exciting online experiences (Blazquez, 2014, Blazquez Cano et al., 2017). The recent pandemic has forced many retailers to create experiences in the digital environment as physical stores remained closed. Restaurants like Wagamama and the Michelin-starred Gastro Gods (Massimo Bottura) have been getting involved with live-streamed cook-alongs to upsell their culinary connections. For the latter, 2020's hamstrung holiday season offered inspiration, while FAO Schwarz's *Academy of Wonder* website hosted virtual magic or science classes centred on its science, technology, engineering, and math, and magic toys, guided by a "professor" or "'magician", which exemplifies the rising power of the product + (remote) experience brand package (Baron, 2021).

Recent literature has focused on the role of digital technologies such as chatbots and service robots (Wirtz et al., 2018) as assistants or substitutes for sales personnel in stores. More well-established technologies include augmented reality (Watson et al., 2018) or image interactive technologies (IIT). The role of these technologies in the retail experience and their contribution to sustainable consumption will be considered in detail in the next chapter.

3.1.2 The use of technology to promote sustainable behaviours

This section will consider the specific application of technologies in fashion retail to promote sustainability. The technologies reviewed will be virtual fitting rooms, interactive screens (or other technologies that allow information search), and predictive technology.

Even when their presence is still marginal in physical stores, *virtual fitting rooms* contribute to increase customer satisfaction and increase conversion rates. They allow consumers to try on items without the need to take off their clothes by virtually positioning the fashion garment over their bodies. It is especially relevant for customers shopping with kids, for example, or in cases where there is a long queue for fitting rooms and customers prefer not to wait. They have been demonstrated to reduce returns, leading to a positive impact on the carbon footprint.

An important form of technology present in many fashion stores are devices that allow *information search* (i.e., tablets, QR codes). They increase convenience for consumers and make shopping decisions more conscious, with a positive impact on sustainability. This is also the case with *predictive technology*, which can help brands to find new ways for consumers to reuse, resale, and recycle, enabling a huge new ecosystem that combines sales with sustainability (Taylor, 2020). It also includes the use of free Wi-Fi. Although Wi-Fi is normally seen as a facilitator, one of the risks of using online connectivity in physical stores is that it makes the product so readily available for consumers that there is a risk of developing "showrooming" behaviours. "Showrooming" refers to the use of the physical store as a pure information channel, then using an online channel to make the actual purchase (Sit el al., 2018). Nevertheless, it will contribute to making more conscious shopping decisions.

> **Showrooming** – the use of the physical store as a pure information channel, then using an online channel to make the purchase.

Regarding the role of these specific technologies, *RFID technologies* make it possible to connect the full customer journey by means of RFID tags which allow the gathering of rich customer data (Business of Fashion, 2020), although more advanced near field communication (NFC) technology is necessary for establishing two-way communication with the consumer. As an example, consumers with an NFC-enabled smartphone can tap their phone on an NFC tag and access additional information about an item or suggestions related to it (EI, 2018). Burberry is currently using content-connected swing tags that are attached to the garments. When the customer scans one of these tags, it shows related content and how the item looks on a model (Baron, 2021). Other technologies are more utilitarian, like *self-checkout technologies* that allow payment to be made by the customer in a certain area, as currently deployed by retailers such as Zara and Benetton (Alexander and Kent, 2021).

In order to promote the use of technology for sustainability, it is interesting to review how consumers relate to innovations. According to Rogers (2017), innovation adopters can be classified as: (1) innovators, who are technology enthusiasts, believing that the new technology will lead to huge benefits; (2) early adopters, who tend to buy a new product in the belief that being the first to adopt the new technology will maximise their benefits; (3) the early majority, who adopt a certain new technology because it has already been largely adopted, believing that having the new technology has become standard); (4) the late majority, consisting of the more conservative part of the market, being quite uncomfortable towards an innovation and showing a risk-averse attitude (they adopt the technology mainly because they are influenced by social norms and reference groups); and (5) laggards, who display negative attitudes towards new technology in general, being very sceptical towards the benefits emerging from its adoption. Based on this classification, it looks like innovators and early adopters would be good targets for communicating sustainable messages through the use of technology, as we will review in the next section.

Last, and although it is not the focus of this chapter, it is worth mentioning that to guarantee the social sustainability of the points of sale and avoid burdening staff, an increasing number of stores are adopting digital technologies to offer efficient and continuous services. On the other hand, the increasing number of digital technologies can diminish the role and importance of store staff, impacting their perception of usefulness. This problem is reflected in the image of ethics and sustainability of the retailer itself (Wirtz et al., 2018).

3.1.3 The importance of sustainability communication

Sustainability communication aims to raise awareness about sustainable development, and to influence sustainable behaviours and people's lifestyle (Kruse, 2011). Godemann (2021) refers to it as a "process of mutual understanding dealing with the future development of society" (p. 23). Sustainability communication should include all corporate and marketing communications related to environmental, social, and economic issues, and thus is part of a broader sustainability strategy which applies a comprehensive and holistic approach (Siano et al., 2016; see also Section 1.2.1). The aim of this communication is to engage consumers and stakeholders who are committed to sustainable fashion, and also educate sceptics or non-consumers (Mukendi et al. 2020). Without adequate communication, messages around sustainability will not gain currency in society and people may not engage with it (Godemann, 2021).

> **Sustainability communication** – aims to raise awareness about sustainable development, to influence sustainable behaviours and people's lifestyle.

According to Blazquez et al. (2020), there is a need to educate consumers about what sustainability means. Although consumers seem to understand the term "sustainability", there is no common definition of what constitutes sustainability and the differences between the different approaches to it (i.e., environmental, ethical, social; see also Section 1.1.3). Also, they identified a need for clear communication in terms of messages broadcast by fast fashion retailers to consumers regarding their sustainability practices. Although various fast fashion retailers have sustainability policies on their websites and clearly indicate how they are tackling 21st-century challenges, this has not yet manifested itself within their communication practices.

Looking at sustainability communication involves considering the roles of channels or touchpoint journeys. A touchpoint has been defined as any point of interaction between consumers and retailers/brands. It must fulfil at least one of the following functions: (a) to raise awareness about a company's products and services; (b) to help consumers to evaluate a company's value proposition; (c) to allow consumers to buy products and services; and (d) to provide post-purchase support. Looking at these functions, although traditionally touchpoints were identified with media, nowadays it seems necessary to adopt a broader approach, including any encounter in the customer journey that may be related to a brand (Ieva and Ziliani, 2018). Consequently, these touchpoints can take different forms, such as online platforms, physical environments, or personal interactions. Revising touchpoint journeys has been identified as a key factor in facilitating long-term customer loyalty in the frame of customer experience management (Homburg et al., 2017, Ieva and Ziliani, 2018).

In terms of frequency of exposure, the *store* is one of the touchpoints with higher exposure between different types of consumers, so it is relevant to use it as a hub of corporate communications (Ieva and Ziliani, 2018). Stores have become experiential spaces where consumers enjoy spending time (Alexander and Blazquez Cano, 2019). For example, "third places" – which are defined as settings beyond work and home – have social, experiential, and restorative dimensions for consumers (Alexander, 2019,) and that makes them an important channel to articulate brand communications, and in this case, sustainability communications. Recent research shows that third places are relevant to developing educational experiences, as conceptualised by Pine and Gilmore (2011). The flagship store format shares similar characteristics and potential for communicating sustainability with third places. In this regard, it is interesting to consider that artistic expression within the physical store increases the perception of a retail store as environmentally friendly (Kim and Heo, 2021). In spite of this emphasis on the physical store, retailers are advised to pursue omnichannel strategies and ensure that all touchpoints are consistent (Ieva and Ziliani, 2018). Also, males tend to prefer online media more than females do, and younger consumers tend to be more exposed to any touchpoint (Ieva and Ziliani, 2018). Specific communication strategies in online channels will be reviewed in Chapter 3.2, and the role of influencers in digital fashion will be looked at Chapter 3.3.

Sustainability communication faces important challenges (Godemann, 2021). First, sustainability-related topics are mostly invisible, which makes it necessary to communicate them in a social environment. Second, the impact of sustainability issues is distant and not immediate, and the issues communicated are complex and uncertain. But more importantly, sustainability communication needs to deal with the different understandings and assumptions people hold about sustainability and their own interests and values. There is no single audience for sustainable communication, and specific societal contexts can make a significant difference (Godemann, 2021). The latter applies to how sustainability is communicated in specific fashion sectors such as fast fashion or luxury fashion. But cultural differences are also important, and need to be considered by international retailers (Blazquez Cano, 2016). Although fashion retailers tend to adopt a global strategy that uses standardised advertising and positioning to control brand image and maintain brand consistency (Liu et al. 2016), it is true that marketing communications in these complex markets require cultural congruity and a careful adaptation of the traditional values of local luxury consumption (Zhou et al., 2018).

Overall, the communication of sustainability for fashion brands is not always evident, and this applies to the luxury fashion sector to a wider extent. The concept of luxury is associated with exclusivity, prestige, and rarity (Kapferer and Michaut-Denizeau,

2020), which is opposed to the values embedded in sustainability, such as altruism, ethics, or frugality (Quach et al., 2022). When luxury embodies possessions as a pathway to get happiness and social recognition, sustainability appeals to abandoning the endless pursuit of material possessions in order to preserve limited global resources (Kapferer and Michaut-Denizeau, 2020). This is the reason why luxury fashion brands face a dilemma when communicating their sustainable initiatives, as consumers are likely to view luxury and sustainability as contradictory (Kang and Sung, 2021). However, the luxury fashion industry has navigated this sort of controversy before. Luxury fashion retailers were later than other fashion brands in developing a digital presence, as the exclusivity and value associated with luxury brands was better provided through face-to-face interaction in physical store settings (Kent at el., 2016). Thus, luxury brands have been slow to address boomerang effects, such as those arising from greenwashing (Kapferer and Michaut-Denizeau, 2020). However, there are potential avenues to link luxury fashion and sustainability. For example, consumers buy luxury items not just for the high quality of the products, but to present their social status and identity to others. That is why they may value the altruistic benefits of sustainable communication to compensate for their search for self-oriented benefits when buying luxury brands. If luxury brands communicate sustainability messages that incorporate environmental benefits, it could lead consumers to believe that the firms' environmental practices are for the social good, and that positively affects the evaluation of the company (Kang and Sung, 2022). Also, the idea of pro-environmental luxury may be more appealing to consumers who are more aware of the environmental and social impacts of fashion (Quach et al., 2022). Specific fashion sectors lead to specific preconceptions about sustainable practices. For luxury fashion, millennial consumers consider that the high price paid implies that luxury brands have irreproachable behaviour in every aspect, unlike fast fashion and mass products in general (Kapferer and Michaut-Denizeau, 2020). On the other hand, they tend to consider that fast fashion and value fashion brands are not committed to sustainable practices, whilst the reality may be quite different.

The message is really important when it comes to effective communication. Regarding luxury fashion brand communication, consumers are more likely to perceive luxuriousness from a product advertisement if it uses hedonic appeals, which further result in more favourable consumer attitudes (Amatulli et al., 2020). However, for sustainable communication (and the broader spectrum of CSR communication), it has been claimed it should be conveyed with objective messages to deliver accurate and explicit information. The fact that luxury brands appear to use vague and subjective messages when it comes to communicating their sustainability could lead to consumers being confused about those messages, leading to scepticism and low message credibility (Kang and Sung, 2022). To prevent that, sustainability communication should be built on clear, strong, and objective messages, as opposed to product or brand communication (Kang and Sung, 2022). Also, sustainability communication relies on scientific facts (i.e., the impact of consumption on the environment) and involves a complex set of ethical, technological, legal, and societal considerations which make it difficult to communicate certain messages in language that can be easily understood; the challenge is to bridge the gap between scientific discourse and the public (Godemann, 2021). Quach et al., (2022) have also found that using visual arts in sustainability communication can be a way to influence attitudes associated with pro-environmental luxury brands and contribute to overcoming preconceptions about the incompatibility between luxury and sustainability. It is important to resonate with different audiences, understanding their concerns and recognising their values, with a communication that is attractive, engaging, and provides relevant and accurate information (Godemann, 2021).

Task

- How will the store of the future contribute to sustainability?
- How can technology be used at the point of sale to promote sustainability?
- What are the roles of specific technologies to promote more sustainable behaviours?
- What are the complexities around sustainability communication?
- What are the main challenges of sustainability communication?
- What is the effect of different marketing mix instruments (i.e., promotions) used across touchpoints and channels on communication effectiveness?
- What is the impact of in-store communication on consumers' perceptions about sustainability?
- What types of message can be more powerful for sustainability communication?

References

Alexander, B. (2019) Commercial, social and experiential convergence: fashion's third places, *Journal of Services Marketing*, 33(3), 257–272.

Alexander, B., and Blazquez Cano, M. (2019) Futurising the physical store in the omnichannel retail environment, in W. Piotrowicz and R. Cuthbertson (eds.), *Exploring omnichannel retailing: common expectations and diverse realities*, pp.197–224. Springer Press. Oxford, UK

Alexander, B., and Blazquez Cano, M. (2020) Store of the future: towards a (re)invention and (re)imagination of physical store space in an omnichannel context, *Journal of Retailing and Consumer Services*, 55, 101913.

Alexander, B., and Kent, A. (2021) Tracking technology diffusion in-store: a fashion retail perspective, *International Journal of Retail and Distribution Management*, 49(10), 1369–1390.

Amatulli, C.M., Angelis, M. D., and Donato, C. (2020) An investigation on the effectiveness of hedonic versus utilitarian message appeals in luxury product communication, *Psychology & Marketing*, 37(4), 523–534.

Baron, K. (2021) *From silver bullets to strategic overhauls: 9 retail trends, tactics and innovations for success in 2021*, Forbes (online): https://www.forbes.com/sites/katiebaron/2021/01/04/from-silver-bullets-to-strategic-overhauls-9-retail-trends-tactics--innovations-for-success-in-2021-/?sh=64d4ab7bd3bd, 04/01/2021.

Blazquez, M. (2012) Fashion E-commerce: consumers' shopping experiences in the UK and Spain, *The Retail Digest*, 20, 10–13.

Blazquez, M. (2014) The fashion shopping experience in a multichannel retail environment: the role of technology in enhancing the customer experience, *The International Journal of Electronic Commerce*, 18(4) (Summer), 7–116.

Blazquez, M., Henninger, C.E., Alexander, B., and Franquesa, C. (2020) Consumers' knowledge and intentions towards sustainability: a Spanish fashion perspective, *Fashion Practice*, 12(1), 34–54.

Blazquez Cano, M. (2016) The role of cross-country differences in international fashion retailing: E-commerce development in Spain and the UK, in Vecchi, A. and Buckley, C.

(eds.), *Handbook of research on global fashion management and merchandising*, IGI Global, pp. 622–648.

Blazquez Cano, M., Perry, P., Ashman, R., and Waite, K. (2017). The influence of image interactivity upon user engagement when using mobile touch screens. *Computers in Human Behavior*, 77, 406–412.

Business of Fashion (2020) *The state of fashion, 2020*, Business of Fashion & McKinsey Company.

Drapers (2020) *How technology is enhancing sustainability, Editor's comment*, Drapers, 30th April, 2020.

Dugar, V., Blazquez, M., and Henninger, C.E. (2020) Does technology affect customer-brand relationships? A study of premium fashion consumers, in Vignali, G., Reid, L., Ryding, D., and Henninger, C. (eds.), *Technology-driven sustainability*. Palgrave Macmillan, Cham, pp. 195–217.

Godemann, J. (2021) Communicating sustainability. Some thoughts and recommendations for enhancing sustainability communication, in *The sustainability communication reader: a reflective compendium*, pp. 15–29.

Grewal, D., Noble, S.M., Roggeveen, A.L., and Nordf€alt, J. (2020) The future of in-store technology, *Journal of the Academy of Marketing Science*, 48, 96–113.

Grewal, D., and Roggeveen, A.L. (2020) Understanding retail experiences and customer journey management, *Journal of Retailing*, 96(1), 3–8.

Grewal, D., Roggeveen, A.L., and Nordfält, J. (2017) The future of retailing, *Journal of Retailing*, 93(1), 1–6.

Homburg, C., Jozić, D., and Kuehnl, C. (2017) Customer experience management: toward implementing an evolving marketing concept, *Journal of the Academy of Marketing Science*, 45(3), 377–401.

Hoyer, W.D., Kroschke, M., Schmitt, B., Kraume, K., and Shankar, V. (2020) Transforming the customer experience through new technologies, *Journal of Interactive Marketing*, 51, 57–71.

Ieva, M., and Ziliani, C. (2018) Mapping touchpoint exposure in retailing: Implications for developing an omnichannel customer experience, *International Journal of Retail and Distribution Management*, 46(3), 304–322.

Kang, E.Y., and Sung, Y.H. (2022) Luxury and sustainability: the role of message appeals and objectivity on luxury brands' green corporate social responsibility, *Journal of Marketing Communications*, 28(3), 291–312.

Kapferer, J.N., and Michaut-Denizeau, A. (2020) Are millennials really more sensitive to sustainable luxury? A cross-generational international comparison of sustainability consciousness when buying luxury, *Journal of Brand Management*, 27(1), 35–47.

Kent, A., Dennis, C., Cano, M.B., Schwarz, E., Brakus, J.J., and Alamanos, E. (2015) Branding, marketing and design: experiential experiential in-store digital environments environments, in Pantano, E. (ed.), *Successful technological integration for competitive advantage in retail settings*, Advances in Business Research Book Series, IGI Global.

Kent, A., Vianello, M., Cano, M.B., and Helberger, E. (2016) Omnichannel fashion retail and channel integration: the case of department stores, in Vecchi, A. and Buckley, C. (eds.), *Handbook of research on global fashion management and merchandising*, IGI Global, pp. 398–419.

Kim, J., and Heo, W. (2021) Interior design with consumers' perception about art, brand image, and sustainability, *Sustainability*, 13(8), 4557.

Kruse, L. (2011) Psychological aspects of sustainability communication, in *Sustainability communication*, Springer, Dordrecht, pp. 69–77

Liu, S., Perry, P., Moore, C., and Warnaby, G. (2016) The standardization- localization dilemma of brand communications for luxury fashion retailers' internationalization into China, *Journal of Business Research*, 69(1), 357–364.

Mosquera, A., Olarte-Pascual, C., Ayensa, E.J., and Murillo, Y.S. (2018) The role of technology in an omnichannel physical store: assessing the moderating effect of gender, *Spanish Journal of Marketing-ESIC*, 22(1), 63–82.

Mukendi, A., Davies, I., Glozer, S., and McDonagh, P. (2020) Sustainable fashion: current and future research directions, *European Journal of Marketing*, 54(11), 2873–2909.

Pantano, E., and Vannucci, V. (2019) Who is innovating? An exploratory research of digital technologies diffusion in retail industry, *Journal of Retailing and Consumer Services*, 49, 297–304.

Pine, B.J., and Gilmore, J.H. (2011) *The experience economy*. Harvard Business Press.

Quach, S., Septianto, F., Thaichon, P., and Nasution, R.A. (2022) The role of art infusion in enhancing pro-environmental luxury brand advertising, *Journal of Retailing and Consumer Services*, 64, 102780.

Rogers, E.M. (2017) *Diffusion of innovations*, 4th ed, The Free Press, New York.

Siano, A., Conte, F., Amabile, S., Vollero, A., and Piciocchi, P. (2016) Communicating sustainability: an operational model for evaluating corporate websites, *Sustainability*, 8(9), 950.

Siregar, Y., and Kent, A. (2019) Consumer experience of interactive technology in fashion stores. *International Journal of Retail & Distribution Management*, 47(12), 1318–1335.

Sit, J.K., Hoang, A., and Inversini, A. (2018) Showrooming and retail opportunities: a qualitative investigation via a consumer-experience lens, *Journal of Retailing and Consumer Services*, 40, 163–174.

UN (2021) Sustainable development goals. Goal 12: ensure sustainable consumption and production patterns, United Nations (online): https://www.un.org/sustainabledevelopment/sustainable-consumption-production/.

Verhoef, P.C., Kannan, P.K., and Inman, J.J. (2015) From multi-channel retailing to omni-channel retailing: introduction to the special issue on multi-channel retailing, *Journal of Retailing*, 91(2), 174–181.

Watson, A., Alexander, B., and Salavati, L. (2018) The impact of experiential augmented reality applications on fashion purchase intention, *International Journal of Retail & Distribution Management*, 48(5), 433–451.

Wirtz, J., Patterson, P.G., Kunz, W.H., Gruber, T., Lu, V.N., Paluch, S., and Martins, A. (2018) Brave new world: service robots in the frontline. *Journal of Service Management*, 29(5), 907–931.

Zhou, S., McCormick, H., Blazquez, M., and Barnes, L. (2019) eWOM: the rise of the opinion leaders, in Boardman, R., Blazquez, M., Henninger, C., and Ryding, D. (eds.), *Social commerce*, Palgrave Macmillan, Cham, pp. 189–212.

3.2 Digital sustainability

Learning outcomes

1. To develop the concept of digital sustainability.
2. To review the impact of online shopping and returns on sustainability.
3. To consider the importance of vision and touch in the online shopping experience.
4. To review the role of technologies on the digital shopping experience and their impact on fashion sustainability.
5. To look at sustainability communication in different digital channels.
6. To analyse the importance of brand narratives in social media communication.
7. To explore key developments and industry practices.

The physical store represents important challenges for fashion retailers. In terms of sustainable management, it is necessary to look at the role of specific technologies, but also at sustainability communication in the physical space. However, the store acts in conjunction with digital channels (i.e., websites, social media, mobile applications) that have their own challenges. First, the growth of online shopping is aligned with the increasing number of deliveries and returns, which represents an added threat in terms of sustainability for the fashion industry. Second, online channels have their own barriers in terms of the lack of visual and tactile sensation of fashion garments, which also impacts the number of returns due to a product perhaps not being as expected. That is why technology plays a major role in overcoming some of these barriers and providing an experience with the product which is closer to the real experience. But also, digital channels and digital media have become a key point in the customer shopping journey. Their influence on consumers is more relevant compared to traditional media, therefore they are a key channel to communicate sustainability. Both technologies applied in the digital scenario and communication on digital media can have a great impact on sustainability in the fashion industry. Thus, the concept of digital sustainability is developed and considered in this chapter.

3.2.1 Introduction

There is no unified academic or practice-based definition of digital sustainability However, there are some indicators about the impact of online shopping on sustainability and how the use of technology may contribute to reducing this impact. Also, as seen in Chapter 3.1, there is a need to educate consumers about sustainability, and digital channels can play a key role in that. We have been immersed in a fragmentation

DOI: 10.4324/9781003097846-14

in the use of media, with more media available (mainly digital media) to consumers, and less attention paid to them. It is common for consumers to look at different screens and devices at the same time with shorter attention spans due to the increasing number of stimuli received. Traditional media are less relevant for these consumers, and this is why digital technology can be a powerful tool, both for the diffusion of sustainability values and the valorisation of sustainable retail business models.

In the context of this research, *digital sustainability will be considered as the use of digital tools to promote sustainable behaviours.* Within digital tools, we include both consumer-facing technologies and communication tools to diffuse and promote sustainability.

> **Digital sustainability** – the use of digital tools to promote sustainable behaviours.

Changes in the macro environment can have impacts on digital sustainability: for example, events such as the COVID-19 pandemic that saw lockdown restrictions have emphasised the power of digital media and also conscious or sustainable consumption. Fashion designers have had to rethink every aspect of their creative process – from concept and creation to production and output, thereby thinking beyond the physical to create new levels of interest using digital methods. Even the idea of window shopping has changed as a result of COVID-19. Now, many consumers intending to visit a shop are more likely to research products on digital channels first. Consumers have become more adventurous, and this presents a great opportunity for brands to experiment with different approaches through digital channels. Digital adoption has soared during the pandemic, with many brands embracing digital innovations like livestreaming, video chat, or social shopping (Business of Fashion, 2021). The same applies to augmented reality's importance as a bridge between the physical and the digital. Worldwide spending on augmented reality and virtual reality is forecast to accelerate because of the pandemic, growing from just over $12 billion in 2021 to $72.8 billion dollars in 2024 (Deloitte Digital, 2021).

By embracing technology, fashion brands can better evolve to create sustainable alternatives to fast fashion. Among other things, retailers are leveraging data to improve purchasing and stocking processes to reduce wastage of new items in store (Taylor, 2020).

3.2.2 The impact of online shopping: returns

Online shopping represents a challenge for the sustainability of the fashion industry. The growth of e-commerce in the fashion industry (including mobile commerce and social commerce) has increased the impact of environmental pollution through two main aspects: first, the emissions associated with deliveries (although it has been pointed out that online shopping reduces the use of fuel to travel to shopping areas), and second, which is more crucial, the role of returns. Fashion business models have evolved to adapt to an increasing consumer demand for free returns. However, the cost for the environment is unaffordable. In the early days of e-commerce, some companies like Amazon offered free shipping and returns to overcome the risk perception associated with online shopping at that time. These standards have been adopted by many fashion retailers, to the extent that e-commerce return rates have increased 95 per cent in the last five years, with a forecast value of returned goods of $550 billion in 2020 in the US (Schiffer, 2019). The return rates for goods bought online are three times higher than those bought in stores, with the consequent negative impact on carbon emissions, packaging, plastic waste, and landfill contributions (Silberstein, 2021). However, it is also necessary to educate retailers so they can understand the reasons for returns and may try to minimise them (Silberstein, 2021).

In the view of experts, the environmental and financial impacts of returns are linked, and any reduction may address both problems simultaneously. They have estimated that the 11.2 per cent average annual US retail return rate could be reduced to 7.7 per cent with proactive retail interventions, which could represent $125 billion avoided returns (Silberstein, 2021). Digital technologies provide consumers with the tools to make more conscious shopping decisions, and consequently reduce the number of returns. Also, through the increasing use of digital channels, consumers have got used to using technologies as part of their shopping experience (Blazquez, 2014). If these technologies can provide information enabling them to make more informed decisions, the impact of returns may be minimised.

However, for these technologies to be successful, it is necessary to understand the main reasons for returning fashion items. According to recent research, the main reasons are issues related to expected quality, products not matching their descriptions, problems with fit, the wrong item being sent, and products arriving damaged (Silberstein, 2021). In the same way as it is important to educate retailers, consumers also need to be made aware of the impact their shopping habits have. It has become a common practice to order the same item in different sizes to replicate as much as possible the shopping experience in physical stores, so that the consumer can try on different sizes and decide which one to keep, if any. This puts a lot of pressure not just on the environment, but also on smaller fashion brands that cannot compete with big fashion groups. Social media platforms and fashion influencers could be good channels to increase awareness about this issue. We will consider it later in the chapter, but first we will look at the specifics of the fashion industry and how they can have an impact on returns.

3.2.3 The nature of online shopping: the importance of touch and vision

Fashion shopping is multisensory, with a specific focus on vision and touch (Workman, 2010). Vision is preferred to gather geometric information, such as shape properties, while touch is preferred to gather information on materials. Both visual and tactile information facilitate product identification and guide product perceptions (Schifferstein and Cleiren, 2005).

Furthermore, certain object characteristics are difficult to translate from the physical to the digital domain: for example, flow (weight, thickness, drape) and movement (stretchiness, comfort) (see also Part 4). Object interactivity allows direct manipulation of objects in the virtual space, thus reducing the perceptual gap between online and offline shopping (Schlosser, 2003).

Information components on apparel websites can be classified into low- and high-involvement categories. Background icons or patterns are low-involvement elements, while the site-map or pictures of the merchandise are high-involvement elements that help consumers evaluate a product. Blazquez et al. (2015) demonstrated that consumers focus their overt attention primarily on the high-involvement elements when looking at fashion websites. They also stated that it was important to show the clothes in the closest representation of end use possible.

Visual product presentation is also highly relevant to internet shopping (Klatzky and Peck, 2012). It can lead to inferences about other sensory attributes, such as tactile characteristics (Workman and Caldwell, 2007,) so visual depictions of products along with written descriptions of haptic qualities can help to compensate for the lack of physical touch in online environments (Blazquez et al., 2015). The combination of direct visual experiences and simulated tactile experiences produces affective, cognitive, and conative responses (Park et al., 2005).

Consumers will be more likely to purchase a product with primarily material properties after they have touched it, so they will prefer to buy it in environments that permit or recreate physical inspection of the product (Peck and Childers, 2006). Schifferstein and Cleiren (2005) tested the importance of the sensory modalities across different products, finding that touch was rated most important for the evaluation of fashion. The tactile input influences the evaluation of these products, increasing consumer confidence (Grohmann et al., 2007). With regard to the translation of tactile input to online settings, the product features can be described in terms of their touch properties more than their visual properties. In some cases, online shopping has led to the use of synaesthetic correspondence to evoke tactile sensations via visual modalities (Spence and Gallace, 2011). Also, virtual technologies can improve visual product presentation and other tactile experiences, as well as developing more informative virtual product experiences (Yu et al., 2012). A good example is image interactivity technology (IIT), which assists consumers in evaluating apparel online. It will be considered in the next epigraph.

3.2.4 The role of specific technologies

In the omnichannel scenario mentioned in the previous chapter, the brands relate to their customers through multiple touchpoints or channels. Social media has been and is a key channel for both communication and transaction purposes. The nature and role of social media platforms are in constant evolution, and the impact of COVID-19 has also changed the way consumers interact with them. Many social media platforms have been incorporating their own commercial functions. Pinterest has a catalogue, and Instagram has evolved its checkout and augmented reality functions, enabling customers to try on some items. Also, some messenger apps use chatbots to generate direct sales rather than being a sole customer service channel.

3.2.4.1 Image interactive technology

Advances in digital technology allow retailers to develop web atmospherics in the form of image interactivity technology. IIT stimulates the tactile, visual and aural senses excited when shopping in a physical store. The online shopping experience is a combination of functionality and stimulation, and in an increasingly competitive marketplace, online retailers may gain a differential advantage by providing a unique and appealing web experience for their customers.

By enabling the creation and manipulation of product images on a retailer's website, IIT provides enriched product information for the viewer (Merle et al., 2012), thus reducing the sensory deprivation typically associated with online shopping. Compared with static images, object interactivity enables users to form more vivid mental images of products, resulting in heightened tactile sensations and more realistic judgements, and therefore higher purchase intentions (Schlosser, 2003). There are different levels of interactivity, from image enlargement to more advanced IIT technologies such as 3D virtual models (Lee et al., 2010). Examples include close-up pictures, zoom facilities, 2D or 3D rotation, mix-and-match functions which simulate how items would look together, 3D virtual try-on facilities using personalised or non-personalised models in virtual dressing rooms, and augmented reality apps, all of which provide online shoppers with an enhanced ability to evaluate the properties of the item online. These different levels of interactivity have varying effects on consumer responses: for example, a high level of interactivity positively influences affective aspects of the consumer experience (Lee et al., 2010)

Gestural interactivity is a form of IIT that enables the artificial recreation of tactile and visual sources of product information for more intuitive and interactive websites, which allow the consumer to digitally interact with products using their fingertips in a more natural manner than using a keyboard and mouse, and therefore closer to the way they would interact with the item in a physical context (Padilla et al., 2012). Chung's (2015) experimental study found use of touchscreens to browse items of clothing led to greater shopper engagement, which subsequently led to higher satisfaction with shopping, higher purchase intentions, and more positive product evaluations. Touchscreen devices allow consumers to interact with images and videos using their fingertips, and thus mimic the physical store experience to a greater degree than a desktop PC and mouse. Blazquez Cano et al (2017) found that visual rotation and tactile simulation features on a touch screen, specifically an iPad, contribute to an increase in user engagement when compared to a static image.

Gestural interactivity – enables the artificial recreation of tactile and visual sources of product information, which allows consumers to interact digitally with products using their fingertips

---

Next, we will review different forms of IIT and discuss them in the context of sustainable management.

Augmented reality describes the visual alignment of virtual content with real-world contexts (Scholz and Duffy, 2018). AR blends the virtual and real worlds through a virtual layer that can add images, text, videos, and other virtual elements (Bonetti et al., 2018). It is defined as a real-time direct or indirect view of a physical environment that has been augmented by adding virtual computer-generated information to it (Carmigniani and Furht, 2011). Currently, it is applied in a variety of contexts and scenarios, such as in-store settings (i.e., virtual fitting rooms), online settings, and mobile devices. The latter allow the use of this technology in public and private spaces, and are becoming the most prevalent devices to access AR technology (Scholz and Duffy, 2018).

Augmented reality has been applied in the fashion industry in the form of *virtual try-on* technology. Used in the context of social commerce and e-commerce, virtual try-on has become a key technology to overcome the limitation of not being able to try on items in digital settings. Previous research found that both hedonic and utilitarian values were important when using virtual try-on apps with mobile devices, but utilitarian considerations were more dominant for consumers (Scholz and Duffy, 2018). They relate to the ability to make purchase decisions more confidently and efficiently, helping to decrease the perceived cognitive risk arising from the uncertainty of not seeing the products in real life (Bonetti et al., 2018). Thus, AR could reshape the mobile shopping experience and shopping cycle (Shankar et al., 2016). Consequently, this could have an important impact on sustainability, as consumers would be able to make more informed shopping decisions. In the specific case of fashion e-shopping, Kang (2014) found that consumers' utilitarian performance (i.e., convenience, monetary, and social values) expectations were positively related to usage intentions. AR apps improve the sensory richness of the experience, and thus should be considered as a tool to create effective interactions with consumers (Watson et al., 2018).

Application of AR includes the use of personalised and non-personalised models to virtually try on clothes and suggest product combinations. One of the most recent innovations in virtual try-on technology has been developed by Snapchat. Snapchat users are now able to try on clothing and accessories virtually with technology that detects and responds to body movements and facial dimensions (McDowel, 2021). Farfetch is one of the brands that is testing this technology with some garments (jackets). It uses technologies such as 3D Body Mesh, which maps the body and joints, cloth simulation, which helps clothes respond as if affected by gravity, and voice-enabled controls. For example, a user can say, "Show me a windbreaker jacket with a pattern," and the mobile screen will show a suggested item over the person's body.

Also, Gucci enables instant virtual try-ones for sneakers. Its software detects a user's feet, generating a 3D overlay simulating how the sneakers will look on their feet (Baron, 2021). In this way, 3D can be used to bring flat images on an e-commerce website to life by enhancing the illusion of depth perception. 3D is also being used to help consumers find the perfect fit for everything from footwear to glasses – both online and in-store. In the footwear example, a retailer with 3D technology could take a scan of a consumer's foot in order to capture all the necessary measurements in a matter of seconds, and from there offer the consumer a selection of footwear that would fit best (Euromonitor International, 2018).

Unlike augmented reality, *virtual reality* does not offer real-world content. It can be seen as a new type of experience where subjects perceive a simulated real world and the illusion that what is happening virtually is really happening (Slater, 2009). It offers real-time interaction with products, and the ability to view them in a realistic way and to request personalised information that could influence purchase decisions. VR uses devices which block out real-world sensory experiences by immersing users in a virtual world (Bonetti et al, 2018). These VR devices can include high-resolution screens, smartphones connected to VR headsets, or immersive cubes (Martinez-Navarro et al., 2019). The content can also be displayed by realistic images or video in 360 degrees or

3D digital representations. VR technology has been claimed to enhance the shopping experience, but it is not widely available for most retail brands.

Artificial intelligence, which refers to technologies capable of performing tasks normally requiring human intelligence, has arrived centre stage for commerce. At its lowest common denominator, AI enables brands to better synthesise mounds of data and incorporate those learnings to improve the consumer experience. Artificial intelligence is being used by a number of merchants and brands to improve recommendations, as well as to enable more powerful e-commerce search results (Euromonitor International, 2018).

The application of artificial intelligence to messenger **chatbots** or conversational agents for commercial purposes is referred to as *conversational commerce*. Conversational commerce has been described as using chat, texting, and other natural-language frameworks to communicate with individuals, brands, or services. Chatbots are a form of AI that simulates conversations with human users, improving interactions over time by implementing continuous learning algorithms (Moriuchi et al., 2021). They have the ability to conduct complex interactions with consumers, offering 24/7 customer service and greater customer engagement across technological platforms. Chatbots use natural-language processing, which means that they are designed to interact with customers as if the chatbot were a real person. They serve several functions, including site guides, virtual support, and even visual search, and they have become an important communication tool for fashion brands (Moriuchi et al., 2021). Overall, they offer high-quality support by ensuring that personalised service is available to meet customer needs at any time and anywhere (Chung et al., 2018). Further improvements in natural-language processing combined with the shift towards messaging as a primary channel for communication have contributed to increasing the popularity of chatbots in the retail industry (DeCicco et al., 2020). The main reasons for using chatbots are productivity, entertainment, and the social-relational benefits they provide.

> **Conversational commerce** – the application of artificial intelligence to messenger chatbots or conversational agents for commercial purposes.

Chatbots could be a relevant tool to engage consumers, considering that millennials predominantly use instant text messaging, for example (DeCicco et al., 2020). The authors suggest that chatbots need to be fun to attract young customers through more enjoyable experiences resulting from social interactions. These social interactions could include small talk, exclamatory feedback, emoticons, and moving images to increase the level of social presence, and as a consequence, trust and positive attitudes towards the chatbot (DeCicco et al., 2020).

Many fashion brands, including luxury brands, have engaged in the use of chatbots. For example, Louis Vuitton offers a chatbot service that provides access to personal service agents regarding product care, and conversational interfaces that show the craftsmanship behind the products (Forbes, 2020). Previous research has demonstrated the impact of this tool on customer satisfaction, linked to the fact that they receive high-quality communications, and the chatbots are time-saving, credible, accurate, and efficient (Chung et al., 2018). In view of this, chatbots could be an important tool to broadcast sustainability messages and to educate consumers on sustainability.

The Internet of Things allows previously separate objects to communicate with other devices. This can be applicable to the fashion industry through identifiers attached to clothing items. Kestenbaum (2021) mentions two interesting examples that can be applied to the field of fashion and sustainability. For example, if a consumer buys a vintage product and does not know whether it is genuine or not, this technology could be used to communicate directly with the manufacturer by entering the product's unique identifier into a website/app and gain an insight into the authenticity of the product and its history. This could be a way to reassure secondhand shoppers (more specifically, luxury shoppers investing in secondhand/vintage clothing), and consequently to promote the secondhand market. Also, by scanning the identifiers of their favourite clothing items, consumers can share that information with brands and retailers so that they can make more personalised recommendations, leading to more secure shopping decisions. Partnerships with logistics platforms such as *ZigZag Global*, which analyse data from returned items, can help to optimise production and future campaign planning.

3.2.5 Sustainability communication and digital channels

Digital channels play a relevant role in the diffusion of sustainability communication, and especially in the wake of COVID-19, digital platforms have become the main points of communication between consumers and fashion companies (Luo et al., 2021). When brands use digital channels, it is important to communicate in a transparent manner what is meant by sustainability (Luo et al., 2021).

In the digital communication environment, one of the most important communication channels for companies is their *corporate websites*, which are often used to communicate their sustainability initiatives (Wong and Dhanesh 2017; Mukendi et al. 2020). Unlike other media, companies have full control over what is published on their websites and can update and customise information for their different targets (Da Giau et al. 2016). Corporate websites provide constructive platforms for companies to directly convey sustainability information to customers (Da Giau et al. 2016) and all their stakeholders because they have the ability to transmit corporate statements and sustainability initiatives in a more direct and visual way (SanMiguel et at., 2021). Content marketing has impacted the communication of sustainability on corporate websites with the use of testimonials, success stories, editorial content on sustainable collections, and even content created by users. All of these tools can be employed to create a two-way communication approach focused on stakeholders in general, or focused solely on the consumer (SanMiguel et at., 2021). However, it needs to be done in a certain way. Luo et al. (2021) found that luxury fashion companies that are communicating their sustainability initiatives on their corporate websites need to do it carefully and in a manner that is appealing to their audience.

Social media is another key channel for the diffusion of sustainability communication. Datareportal (2021) reports that there are 4.48 billion social media users around the world, which equates to almost 57 per cent of the total global population. The typical user actively uses or visits an average of 6.6 different social media platforms each month and spends an average of close to 2½ hours using social media each day. The use of social media has increased recently, with 520 million new users to July 2021. Social media facilitate consumer engagement through a multidirectional communication pattern and multidimensional transmission of information, shaping and affecting consumer attitudes and purchase behaviours, and encouraging consumers to be web-fortified decision-makers (Dwivedi et al., 2020, Zhou et al., 2021). Unlike corporate websites, where brands have full control over the sustainability messages, social networks allow conversations to be generated between companies and other companies, companies and organisations, companies and users, organisations and users, and users and users, which presents obvious risks for the companies (San Miguel et al., 2021). Also, the way social media platforms work is totally different. Although there are six social media platforms that claim to have more than 1 billion monthly active users, Facebook remains the world's most widely used social media platform, with 2.853 billion active users, and potential advertisers could reach 1.386 billion users on Instagram (Datareportal, 2021). These figures, along with the relevance of visual content for the fashion industry in the case of Instagram, make them two relevant social media to consider for sustainable communication management. However, there is a need to keep updated on new functionalities and new social networks, as social media evolve quite quickly (Mondalek, 2021). For example, two networks to consider are Twitch and Reddit. Twitch is an Amazon-owned livestreaming gaming and entertainment platform with 30 million daily users, which, according to research, are three times more likely than the average consumer to wear something they saw their favourite influencer promote. On the other hand, in Discord there are no brand profiles, but there are servers that brands can use to create digital spaces (Mondalek, 2021).

Fashion brands can communicate their own messages in their own social media profiles. However, they do not have control over the potential reactions of different targets, so they cannot influence their messages. It is different when the messages are posted by influencers or creators of content who have been paid by the brand or who act as advocates for it. In other cases, there may be "haters" who post negative messages about the brand or its publications. The specific role of fashion influencers will be considered in the next chapter, whereas we will now review the importance of narrative strategies in social media communication.

Social networks are important, but there are other media that should be considered to communicate sustainable messages. *Blogs*, and more specifically fashion blogs, are important media to spread information about secondhand fashion and to reach consumers in innovative ways (Blazquez Cano et al., 2018). This is relevant because the UK's secondhand clothing market is set to become 1.5 times bigger than the fast fashion sector by 2028 (ThredUp, 2019).

3.2.5.1 The importance of narrative strategies in social media communication

As defined by Zhou et al. (2019, p. 198), opinion leaders' narrative strategies are "the language, tone, practices, signs, symbols, and substance to introduce brands and products in creating eWOM [electronic word-of-mouth] messages, with the association of their physical identities, inner thoughts and feelings, ideas, cultural backgrounds, economic and social positions, and social roles".

> **Narrative strategies** – the language, tone, practices, signs, and symbols to introduce brands and products in creating eWOM messages.

Zhou et al. (2020) identified six narrative strategies used by social media influencers (SMIs) to create eWOM, and the rhetorical tactics used to implement them. These narrative strategies included advising, enthusing, educating, appraising, amusing, and assembling. *Advising* refers to giving advice/suggestions on the use of brands or products to solve the issues faced by consumers or potential issues that might occur in the future. SMIs' messages constructed with an advising strategy often contain a detailed description of the context and problem along with solution suggestions. The rhetorical tactics used to implement them range from claiming expertise to attention-attracting. In the case of sustainable communication, advising can be used to raise awareness among consumers about the environmental impact of their fashion consumption choices as their attention is expected to be attracted by these logical arguments.

Enthusing refers to expressing worship of a brand to motivate consumers to adopt its norms and values and cultivate a strong desire for ownership of the brand. Although attracting attention is a rhetorical tactic also used with this narrative strategy, mood-affecting can be more relevant. An example could be promoting sustainable fashion brands and their values. *Educating* means improving consumers' knowledge and understanding of brands and products, and influencers do it by claiming expertise, and mood-affecting. It seems to be one of the main narratives that should be adopted by brands/influencers in digital settings to increase consumers' awareness about sustainability. As mentioned earlier, it is necessary to educate consumers about the real meaning of sustainability and the potential consequences of their shopping behaviour (Blazquez et al., 2020). *Appraising* refers to judgement of the performance, value, or contributions of a brand or product from different perspectives, and can be done by claiming expertise, and collaboration. Again, it could be used by fashion brands to communicate messages related to their sustainable practices. *Amusing* is related to creating eWOM in a creative and dramatic way to satisfy the consumers who are entertainment seekers. For an experiential category like fashion, this is a relevant narrative strategy to consider as it will allow you to connect with customers looking for hedonic gratification. It will also be useful in communicating strong messages such as sustainability in a powerful way. Last, *assembling* highlights the value of a brand or a product for identifying construction and self-defining behaviour through meaningfulness (Zhou et al., 2020). The latter is relevant as there is a more conscious approach to sustainability and environmentally responsible behaviour from different perspectives, so sustainability is expected to become a relevant value used by brands, social media influencers, and consumers to build their identity.

With all these narrative strategies in mind, it is important to bear in mind that people construct their own realities based on their perceptions and experiences, and social media can be a powerful tool to educate about sustainability because they are media consumers have chosen. Successful sustainability communication will depend on its ability to create information that resonates within society and develop communication strategies that make sustainable actions more likely (Godemann, 2021).

3.2.6 Key developments and industry practices

Next, we will review some specific examples of industry practices related to the use of technology with sustainable purposes along with sustainable communication examples.

- Research has found that consumers just use part of their wardrobes, and one of the main reasons seems to be that they are simply not aware of the items they own. With this insight in mind, the digital wardrobe management app *Save Your Wardrobe* taps into consumer behaviours and data to drive further innovations in the space. The app encourages users to document everything stored in their wardrobes so they can view all the clothes they own and be aware of the number of items they are not using. It also recommends specific looks thanks to the use of artificial intelligence technology (Taylor, 2020).
- *Fitch* has realised the high demand for sustainable innovation in retail, and is developing new experience design models which weave mixed realities, digital activations, and equipment in-store for consumers to interact with and enjoy (Taylor, 2020).
- The rise of fashion's personalised and on-demand models is also turning a new page for production and textiles. Robotics and apparel company *Unspun* creates customised jeans for each customer using 3D body scanning and weaving technology. As a result, it holds zero inventory as it only produces items that have previously been bought (and as they are personalised, cannot be returned). Digitally native companies such as *Queen of Raw* operate to connect brands with deadstock for new creations (Taylor, 2020).
- One interesting app that may offer a view into the future is *Douyin*, TikTok's counterpart in China. Douyin, which is extremely popular with young people, has just launched a game-changing in-video search function through which users can zoom in on clothing or other items in the video, and link through to related content and even directly purchase products – all from within the app. These are not videos that are actively selling or promoting products, but rather regular user-generated content – any post from anyone could become a potential sale. Douyin users' home pages feature AI-powered curation of content, and users become co-creators of content as well as consumers (Business of Fashion, 2020).
- The infrastructure put in place through high-performance apps such as *Depop* has incentivised the development of exchange platforms, including *Swish*. Other fashion secondhand apps such as *Vinted* are becoming more prevalent, and social media marketplaces have enabled the take-off of this trend (ThredUp's, 2019).
- In terms of digital sustainability campaigns, *H&M* is well known for the launch of its Conscious Collection campaigns every year. They use a combination of media and channels, with special emphasis on social media. Many other fast fashion retailers communicate sustainable messages though digital channels, such as *Mango* and *Primark*. For luxury brands, communication about sustainability tends to be less obvious, for the reasons mentioned earlier.

Task

- How can the environmental impact of online shopping be reduced?
- What role can technology play in reducing this impact?
- What technologies can contribute most to this? How should they be used?
- Why are digital media important in delivering sustainability messages?
- What are the best social media to deliver sustainability messages to different age groups?
- Which tone/language should be used in different social media?
- What brand narratives are best suited to communicating sustainability messages?

References

Baron, K. (2021) From silver bullets to strategic overhauls: 9 retail trends, tactics and innovations for success in 2021, *Forbes*, 4th January, 2021, (online): https://www.forbes.com/sites/katiebaron/2021/01/04/from-silver-bullets-to-strategic-overhauls-9-retail-trends-tactics--innovations-for-success-in-2021-/?sh=64d4ab7bd3bd.

Binkley (2020) *How the fashion industry will change after Covid-19*, (online): https://www.voguebusiness.com/fashion/the-fashion-show-as-we-know-it-is-over-covid-19.

Blazquez, M. (2014) The fashion shopping experience in a multichannel retail environment: the role of technology in enhancing the customer experience, *The International Journal of Electronic Commerce*, 18(4) (Summer), 7–116.

Blazquez, M., Henninger, C.E., Alexander, B., and Franquesa, C. (2020) Consumers' knowledge and intentions towards sustainability: a Spanish fashion perspective, *Fashion Practice*, 12(1), 34–54.

Blazquez, M., Velasco, C., Salgado-Montejo, A., and Spence, C. (2015) How do people look at online fashion? An exploratory study of attention to design elements in fashion websites, in *Global Fashion Management Conference at Florence Proceedings* (pp. 1–14) (June 2015), https://doi.org/10.15444/GFMC2015.01.01.01.

Blazquez Cano, M., Perry, P., Ashman, R., and Waite, K. (2017) The influence of image interactivity upon user engagement when using mobile touch screens, *Computers in Human Behavior*, 77, 406–412.

Bonetti, F., Warnaby, G., and Quinn, L. (2018) Augmented reality and virtual reality in physical and online retailing: a review, synthesis and research agenda, *Augmented Reality and Virtual Reality*, 119–132.

Bradley, K. (2007) Defining digital sustainability, *Library Trends*, 56(1), 148–163.

Business of Fashion (2021) *The state of fashion, 2021*, Business of Fashion and McKinsey & Company.

Cano, M.B., Doyle, S., and Zhang, Y. (2018) Do fashion blogs influence vintage fashion consumption? An analysis from the perspective of the Chinese market, in Ryding, D., Henninger, C., and Blazquez Cano, M. (eds.), *Vintage luxury fashion*, Palgrave Macmillan, Cham, pp. 167–183.

Carmigniani, J., and Furht, B. (2011) Augmented reality: an overview, in *Handbook of augmented reality*, Springer, New York, pp. 3–46.

Chitakorn, K. (2021) Are branded virtual worlds the new marketing terrain?, *Vogue Business*, May, 2021 (online): https://www.voguebusiness.com/technology/are-branded-virtual-worlds-the-new-marketing-terrain.

Chung, M., Ko, E., Joung, H., and Kim, S.J. (2018) Chatbot e-service and customer satisfaction regarding luxury brands, *Journal of Business Research*, https://doi.org/10.1016/j.jbusres.2018.10.004.

Chung, S. (2015) Do touch screen users feel more engaged? The impact of touch interfaces on online shopping, in K. Diehl and C. Yoon (eds.), *Proceedings of NA-advances in consumer research*, 43, ACR, Duluth, pp. 488–486.

Da Giau, A., Macchion, L., Caniato, F., Caridi, M., Danese, P., Rinaldi, R., and Vinelli, A. (2016) Sustainability practices and web-based communication: an analysis of the Italian fashion industry, *Journal of Fashion Marketing and Management*, 20(1), 72–88.

Datareportal (2021) *Global social media stats*, Datareportal (online): https://datareportal.com/social-media-users.

De Cicco, R., Silva, S.C., and Alparone, F.R. (2020) Millennials' attitude toward chatbots: an experimental study in a social relationship perspective, *International Journal of Retail & Distribution Management*, 48(11), 1213–1233.

Dwivedi, Y.K., Ismagilova, E., Hughes, D.L., Carlson, J., Filieri, R., Jacobson, J., and Wang, Y. (2020) Setting the future of digital and social media marketing research: perspectives and research propositions, *International Journal of Information Management*, https://doi.org/10.1016/j.ijinfomgt.2020.102168.

Gentsch, P. (2019) Conversational AI: how (chat) bots will reshape the digital experience, in *AI in Marketing, Sales and Service*, Palgrave Macmillan, Cham, pp. 81–125.

Godemann, J. (2021) Communicating sustainability. Some thoughts and recommendations for enhancing sustainability communication, in *The sustainability communication reader: a reflective compendium*, pp. 15–29.

Grohmann, B., Spangenberg, E.R., and Sprott, D.E. (2007) The influence of tactile input on the evaluation of retail product offerings, *Journal of Retailing*, 83(2), 237–245.

Kang, M.J.-Y. (2014) Augmented reality and motion capture apparel e-shopping values and usage intention, *International Journal of Clothing Science and Technology*, 26(6), 486–499.

Kestenbaum, R. (2021) This technology will have a profound effect on the fashion industry, *Forbes*, 3rd August 2021 (online): https://www.forbes.com/sites/richardkestenbaum/2021/08/03/this-technology-will-have-a-profound-effect-on-the-fashion-industry/?sh=34bb4c4223e9.

Klatzky, R.L., and Peck, J. (2012) Please touch: object properties that invite touch, *IEEE Transactions on Haptics*, 5(2), 139–147.

Kruse, L. (2011) Psychological aspects of sustainability communication, in *Sustainability communication*, Springer, Dordrecht, pp. 69–77.

Lee, H.H., Kim, J., and Fiore, A.M. (2010) Affective and cognitive online shopping experience effects of image interactivity technology and experimenting with appearance, *Clothing and Textiles Research Journal*, 28(2), 140–154.

Luo, S., Henninger, C.E., Le Normand, A., and Blazquez, M. (2021) Sustainable what…? The role of corporate websites in communicating material innovations in the luxury fashion industry, *Journal of Design, Business & Society*, 7(1), 83–103.

Martínez-Navarro, J., Bigné, E., Guixeres, J., Alcañiz, M., and Torrecilla, C. (2019) The influence of virtual reality in e-commerce, *Journal of Business Research*, 100, 475–482.

McDowell, M. (2021) Snapchat boosts AR try-on tools: Farfetch, Prada dive in, *Vogue Buiness*, 21st May 2021 (online): https://www.voguebusiness.com/technology/snapchat-boosts-ar-try-on-tools-farfetch-prada-dive-in.

Merle, A., Senecal, S., and St-Onge, A. (2012) Whether and how virtual try-on influences consumer responses to an apparel web site, *International Journal of Electronic Commerce*, 16(3), 41–64.

Mondalek, A. (2021) Finding fashion consumers beyond Instagram, *Business of Fashion*, 2nd November 2021 (online): https://www.businessoffashion.com/articles/marketing-pr/finding-fashion-consumers-beyond-instagram/?utm_source=newsletter_dailydigest&utm_medium=email&utm_campaign=Daily_Digest_021121&utm_term=VKODSKTEIBFW7MCDWPVJZ4OINY&utm_content=top_story_2_cta.

Moriuchi, E., Landers, V.M., Colton, D., and Hair, N. (2021) Engagement with chatbots versus augmented reality interactive technology in e-commerce, *Journal of Strategic Marketing*, 29(5), 375–389.

Mukendi, A., Davies, I., Glozer, S., and McDonagh, P. (2020) Sustainable fashion: current and future research directions, *European Journal of Marketing*, 54(11), 2873–909.

Padilla, S., Orzechowski, P., and Chantler, M.J. (2012) Digital tools for the creative industries, *Digital Futures*, October 23–25, Aberdeen, UK.

Park, J., Lennon, S.J., and Stoel, L. (2005) Online product presentation: effects on mood, perceived risk, and purchase intention, *Psychology and Marketing*, 22(9), 695–719.

Peck, J., and Childers, T.L. (2006) If I touch it I have to have it: Individual and environmental influences on impulse purchasing, *Journal of Business Research*, 59(6), 765–769.

SanMiguel, P., Pérez-Bou, S., Sádaba, T., and Mir-Bernal, P. (2021) How to communicate sustainability: from the corporate web to E-commerce. The case of the fashion industry, *Sustainability*, 13(20), 11363.

Schiffer, J. (2019) The Unsustainable cost of free returns. Vogue Business, July, 2019. https://www.voguebusiness.com/consumers/returns-rising-costs-retail-environmental.

Schifferstein, H.N., and Cleiren, M. (2005) Capturing product experiences: a split-modality approach, *Acta Psychologica*, 118(3), 293–318.

Schlosser, A.E. (2003) Experiencing products in the virtual world: the role of goal and imagery in influencing attitudes versus purchase intentions, *Journal of Consumer Research*, 30(2), 184–198.

Scholz, J., and Duffy, K. (2018) We ARe at home: how augmented reality reshapes mobile marketing and consumer-brand relationships, *Journal of Retailing and Consumer Services*, 44, 11–23.

Siano, A., Conte, F., Amabile, S., Vollero, A., and Piciocchi, P. (2016) Communicating sustainability: An operational model for evaluating corporate websites, *Sustainability*, 8(9), 950–966.

Silberstein, N. (2021) How returns drag down sustainability efforts (and what retailers can do about it), *Retail Touchpoints*, 11th May 2021, (online): https://retailtouchpoints.com/topics/digital-commerce/how-returns-drag-down-sustainability-efforts-and-what-retailers-can-do-about-it.

Slater, M. (2009) Place illusion and plausibility can lead to realistic behaviour in immersive virtual environments, *Philosophical Transactions of the Royal Society B: Biological Sciences*, 364(1535), 3549–3557.

Spence, C., and Gallace, A. (2011) Multisensory design: reaching out to touch the consumer, *Psychology & Marketing*, 28, 267–308.

Taylor, T. (2020) How technology is enhancing sustainability, *Drapers*, 30th April 2021. https://www.drapersonline.com/news/comment-how-technology-is-enhancing-sustainability.

ThredUp's (2019) Resale report 2019, *ThredUp*, March 2019 (online): https://www.thredup.com/resale/2019?tswc_redir=true.

Watson, A., Alexander, B., and Salavati, L. (2018) The impact of experiential augmented reality applications on fashion purchase intention, *International Journal of Retail & Distribution Management*, 48(5), 433–451.

Williams, G. (2021) Luxury's battle for the metaverse, *Jing Daily*, June 2021, https://jingdaily.com/metaverse-luxury-brands-china/.

Workman, J.E. (2010) Fashion consumer groups, gender, and need for touch, *Clothing and Textiles Research Journal*, 28(2), 126–139.

Workman, J.E., and Caldwell, L.F. (2007) Centrality of visual product aesthetics, tactile and uniqueness needs of fashion consumers, *International Journal of Consumer Studies*, 31(6), 589–596.

Yu, U.J., Lee, H.H., and Damhorst, M.L. (2012) Exploring multidimensions of product performance risk in the online apparel shopping context visual, tactile, and trial risks, *Clothing and Textiles Research Journal*, 30(4), 251–266.

Zhou, S., Barnes, L., McCormick, H., and Blazquez Cano, M. (2020) Social media influencers' narrative strategies to create eWOM: a theoretical contribution, *International Journal of Information Management*, 59, 102293.

Zhou, S., Blazquez, M., McCormick, H., and Barnes, L. (2021) How social media influencers' narrative strategies benefit cultivating influencer marketing: tackling issues of cultural barriers, commercialised content, and sponsorship disclosure, *Journal of Business Research*, 134, 122–142.

Zhou, S., McCormick, H., Blazquez, M., and Barnes, L. (2019) eWOM: the rise of the opinion leaders, in Boardman, R., Blazquez, M., Henninger, C., and Ryding, D. (eds.), *Social commerce*, Palgrave Macmillan, Cham, pp. 189–212.

3.3 Digital fashion

Learning outcomes

1. To define what digital fashion is and everything that it embeds.
2. To determine the role of virtual garments for sustainable consumption.
3. To introduce the metaverse and its potential for the fashion industry.
4. To review the most relevant industry practices.
5. To explore two case studies: HOT·SECOND and The Dematerialised.

Within the fashion industry, the concept of digital fashion has become a hot topic. From a broad perspective, digital fashion refers to everything from digital representation of fashion (i.e., technologies used in e-commerce) to digital fashion shows and digital garments. However, "digital fashion" is commonly used to refer to virtual clothes, non-fungible tokens (NFTs), and the metaverse. After reviewing in the previous chapter the impact of digital channels and digital media on sustainability, this chapter will focus on the new world of the metaverse, NFTs, and virtual clothing from the perspective of sustainable fashion management.

3.3.1 What is digital fashion?

Although there is no agreed upon definition of digital fashion, it has been widely acknowledged that it relates to information and communication technologies (ICTs), and more specifically, to the use of the internet (Noris et al., 2021), and it may also include the use of digital tools both for the fashion business itself and to improve consumers' experience. A systematic literature review carried on by Noris et al. (2021) found that digital fashion mostly relates to the communication and marketing domains, including aspects like omnichannel experiences and the use of digital channels (i.e., social networks, blogs) to engage consumers, and other technological advances, including consumers' acceptance of new technologies like 3D fashion products.

> **Digital fashion** – a relatively new term used to describe garments and accessories which are computer-generated and therefore are only virtual.

DOI: 10.4324/9781003097846-15

Digital fashion has gained significant media attention recently, with an increasing number of terms related to the digital fashion universe: virtual fashion, digital garments, virtual clothes or digital-only clothes, among others. Digital fashion may refer to digitally rendered garments presented in digitally rendered surroundings, and also physical clothes showcased digitally via livestreams and films (Benson, 2021). The reality behind all of them is that fashion is becoming increasingly digital, and some garments may not exist in the real world.

The increasing pressure on the fashion industry to become more sustainable is creating a transition from analog to digital (Roberts-Islam, 2020). The impact of the COVID pandemic has made digital fashion more relevant in a variety of ways. The examples mentioned earlier are clear examples of the impact of sustainability (Benson, 2021). Digitally rendered garments are clothes without physical production costs, pollution, and waste, and showcasing physical clothes digitally means having fashion shows without the need for international flights.

3.3.1.1 Digital fashion

Digital fashion is a relatively new term used to describe garments and accessories which are computer-generated and therefore are virtual only. The creation of 3D clothes saves time, making it possible to consume less materials, prevent overproduction, and avoid the need to transport items all over the world (Benson, 2021). DRESSX, a digital-only retailer, measured the impact of creating a digital garment, and found that the production of a digital garment emits 97 per cent less CO_2 and saves 3,300 litres of water per garment on average. This contributes to complying with UN SDG 12 and sustainable management through promoting the efficient use of natural resources. Digital fashion also relates to the promotion of more sustainable consumption (UN, 2021).

The reasoning behind digital clothing is that we are facing a generation of consumers whose digital personas require constant newness. Digital lives and digital selves may be completely different from the real world, so fashion displays need to portray a specific image. Also, digital-only luxury garments are reimagining how fashionistas consume clothing (Daswani, 2020). Influencers used to buy one-off outfits solely for Instagram (Semic, 2019), whereas now they can buy digital garments instead.

However, high-fashion garments that exist in physical form may have obvious elements of craftsmanship that the keen luxury eye has come to know (Daswani, 2020). From a luxury standpoint, the concepts and details that go into a digital garment may require similar skills, but the language and ways of creating are where innovation and agility come in. And despite looking deceptively real, the most exclusive thing about digital fashion is the capability to create what is not possible in the physical space (Daswani, 2020). Also, it would be interesting for new designers to debut with virtual collections, where the designers can see what did and did not work before samples go into production. Buyers and consumers could try the items on virtually (Benson, 2021). As there is no material wastage, there is more room for creativity, as designers can create anything they wish (Semic, 2019). In fact, not all elements of digital fashion mimic the physical world, and many of them capitalise on this aspect.

From a consumer perspective, digital clothing can be an answer to the culture of disposable fashion. However, some critical voices warn that it may pose the same dangers, as consumers may relegate digital garments to the back of their virtual wardrobe and not use them again (Semic, 2019). Also, being more affordable and not taking up physical space may even be a motivation to consume more. It will mean creating a completely new relationship with clothes. Fashion has been considered a highly hedonic category that needs to be touched and worn to be fully enjoyed (Blazquez, 2014). The tactile experience has been considered very important, and that is why the transition to e-commerce was difficult at the beginning. However, it is still considered that so much of the joy of fashion is dressing up, and reducing fashion consumers to social media users would be too restrictive, as not everyone is on Instagram, so consumers will still need to dress for real life.

However, it is unclear whether consumers are ready for digital fashion. Karina Nobbs, founder of HOT:SECOND, a concept store trading physical products for digital experiences (see the case study later in this chapter) based this innovation on her research into the perceptions of consumers and key stakeholders about digital fashion. She found that consumers were confused and sceptical about what digital fashion means and how it works. Sixty per cent of the sample were curious about digital fashion, and 27 per cent said they thought interaction with digital garments would help them decide whether to buy a physical garment. In relation to sustainability, 22 per cent of the sample thought that digital fashion could offer a way to enjoy fashion in a more sustainable way.

3.3.1.2 Non-fungible tokens

In March 2020, a studio called RTFKT made £3.1 million selling digital sneakers. The underlying technology is NFTs – non-fungible tokens – which is still a novel concept for the fashion industry (Nanda and Bain, 2021). In October 2021, Dolce & Gabbana generated £6.1 million in sales in an auction of an NFT collection paired with physical objects and access to different experiences. What is interesting is that among the buyers were crypto collectors and collectives trying to boost their own profile in the space (Nanda and Bain, 2021). NFT prices overall have been volatile, but experts observe that NFTs are a low-cost way to generate hype and reach new customers. So many brands are considering NFTs more from a marketing perspective rather than a business perspective, because the impact on public relations mentions is huge. Collecting fashion items such as bags or garments can be seen as an extension of ourselves, linked to how we form and communicate our identity. The more we extend our lives and our selves in digital contexts, the more the concept of collecting and displaying objects changes (Kansara, 2021).

A variety of strategies have been followed by different brands. Rebeca Minkoff released 15 NFTs on a digital marketplace, The Dematerialized, that sold out quickly. The marketplace connected consumers with a designer and produced and minted the collection on blockchain. Other brands have decided to create their NFTs in-house, but others have needed to rely on outside firms and designers to craft the pieces into covetable digital assets (Nada and Bain, 2021). In some cases, NFTs can be related to creative assets such as a designer's sketch or a memorable runway moment that will drive a variety of marketing outcomes and will increase brand loyalty (Kansara, 2021). Probably the most strategic way to engage the space is for NFTs to be linked to physical products (like the example of Dolce & Gabbana) that also act as proof of authenticity. This could also impact the resale market, as with NFTs, the blockchain that authenticates them can create a contract that controls their future use. For example, the artist Beeple makes

10 per cent in royalties every time one of his NFTs is sold on the secondary market (Kansara, 2021). What is still being defined is what buyers can do with these NFTs. In the example of Dolce & Gabbana, the brand has given buyers two years to decide how they want their NFT to be rendered – in a Snapchat filter or for a metaverse.

The target market for these NFTs is not necessarily fashionistas. In many cases, buyers of virtual garments are investors interested in their fashion value, although it seems too early to evaluate their full potential. In March 2020, prices fell by 70 per cent, therefore many platforms adjusted their pricing strategies and limited their numbers of drops to avoid oversaturation (Nanda and Bain, 2021). Overall, well-recognized brands, like Dolce & Gabbana, can charge higher prices

3.3.1.3 Digital fashion marketplaces

Digital-only fashion is becoming an important category for digital marketplaces, bolstered by the COVID pandemic. One of the pioneers was Drest, selling digital-only but also physical garments. After that, others, such as Dress-X or The Dematerialised, launched places for designers to sell and for customers to buy digital clothing (McDowell, 2021). Experts warn that these digital fashion marketplaces will disrupt the fashion industry, for many reasons: first, because they can offer additional revenue for designers and brands and cannot be ignored from a business perspective; second, because they will create new "visceral experiences" for consumers and, today more than ever, it is really important to connect to consumers in emotional ways; and third, because digital fashion will become more relevant as related technology (e.g., augmented reality) matures and consumers get used to it.

These digital marketplaces have the peculiarity that they do not carry any inventory, but some brands offer limited availability to promote the exclusivity of their digital garments (McDowell, 2021). For example, in the case of Dress-X, their items come from purely digital fashion houses and traditional fashion brands that have created digital versions of their designs, while just 30 per cent are from in-house designers. In the case of The Dematerialised, brands and individual creators can sell their own work, and the stores are designed as an immersive virtual world, providing a superior customer experience that makes them unique.

The way they work is slightly different to traditional marketplaces. The browsing experience is quite similar, but once the customer buys a 3D digital design, they need to submit a photo that will be dressed by a digital tailor. The item "arrives" via email and is ready to be "worn". Some marketplaces also sell static and moving versions of items. In some cases, digital fashion tries to be as unique and different to traditional fashion as possible, and many fashion brands try to create digital garments that could not exist in real life. An example is a sneaker created by Buffalo London and The Fabricant that was adorned with moving flames.

Apart from marketplaces, other fashion outlets are trying to prepare for a digital future where they will meet their customers within video games and other virtual environments. However, many of them still need to attend to physical customers in physical stores. This is the case with department stores, some of which are taking their first steps into digital fashion. One good example is Selfridges, which has opened a pop-up virtual city in its London flagship store in an attempt to evolve in bridging the gap between the physical and virtual worlds (Kent et al., 2016, Bain, 2021). The pop-up has been named Electric City, and can be accessed using a variety of technologies, such as QR codes, AR, or VR chats. It is designed like a video game, and aims to give visitors the feeling that they are travelling through the city and interacting with it. The shopping experience is very important, and Selfridges' customers are being offered the possibility of buying physical or digital versions of garments (Bain, 2021).

3.3.1.4 The metaverse

Related to digital fashion, the concept of the metaverse has emerged, and it is considered the largest revolution the fashion industry has seen so far (BOF, 2021b). The metaverse is an online world that fulfils real-world desires and activities. Williams (2021) states that the COVID lockdown has accelerated digital efforts and that luxury brands have been consistent in creating metaverse realities through narratives and immersive storytelling. These communities mimic real-life activities, including the purchase of products. In fact, they are evolving from being marketing-only playscapes to transaction-capable brand territories (Baron, 2021).

> **The metaverse** – an online world that fulfils real world desires and activities.

Games like *Animal Crossing* have prepared consumers for the creation of digital identities in virtual hangouts. In fact, fashion gaming has been a long time in the making, with brands dressing avatars, spinning up virtual clothes, or promoting their real-world collections in-game (Lee, 2021). Gucci partnered with *The Sims* on a digital version of its campaign, while Marc Jacobs and Valentino both dropped looks on *Animal Crossing*. The lockdown game of choice for millions of people globally, it spawned a culture of digital designer recreations, helped along massively by creator Kara Chung, who held the first *Animal Crossing* fashion show (Benson, 2021). This has proven to be a good strategy to reach Generation Z consumers (Lee, 2021). Also, Balenciaga and *Fortnite* have launched a collaboration that includes real and digital clothes and 3D billboards that appear in key real-life cities and within *Fortnite*. It featured the same assets in both, creating continuity between the game and real life (Bain, 2021). The truth is that in the gaming world, the avatar is part of the user's personality. The more fashion consumers transition to the virtual world, the more they will consume digital sneakers, digital clothing, digital jewelry, and so on (BOF, 2021b).

Experts feel that games have to offer more to the fashion industry than just brand awareness or sales, starting with the tools used to create these worlds and the culture of innovation (Lee, 2021). Some brands are responding by creating their own virtual worlds (Chitakorn, 2021). Fashion examples include the creation of Valentino's 3D Villa, inspired by the home of creative director Pierpaolo Piccioli, or the launch of a replica of Burberry flagship store in Tokyo. The Fabric of Reality VR experience allows avatars of users to talk with one another while they explore designers' worlds across diverse club/room settings and try on virtual garments (Baron, 2021).

The benefits of these virtual worlds include the enhancement of brand values, the provision of customer feedback, and the flexibility resulting from the fact that they are easily changeable and can be tailored to customer preferences (Chitakorn, 2021). They are a combination of convenience, personalization, and fun. And the use of different technologies contributes to providing enjoyment in the browsing experience – an example would be the use of a VR headset for full immersion versus a browser-based experience, to avoid alienating those with access issues (Baron, 2021). But thinking about more specific benefits, the metaverse is especially relevant for younger generations that spend a lot of time on online gaming, that hang out with friends online through social media and instant messaging applications, and that are even attending classes through Zoom. For this new generation of fashion consumers, having a digital fashion collection that everyone can see makes more sense than having a physical collection that no one is going to see (BOF, 2021b). For them, differentiating between virtual and digital worlds is a misconception and makes no sense (BOF, 2021b).

3.3.1.5 Digital fashion shows

Zero to Market (2020) measured the carbon emissions from the travel of buyers and designers to attend the four major fashion weeks (Paris, London, New York, and Milan). They found that the total emissions amounted to 241,000 tonnes of CO_2, the equivalent to lighting the Eiffel Tower for 3,060 years. However, according to Fashion United, there are more than 100 fashion weeks across the globe, which will multiply the emissions. The strategies to address this have varied in different countries. London Fashion Week offered flexible solutions that integrated technology, visual and audio storytelling, and physical products, while Helsinki Fashion Week (HFW) went a step further with a completely digital fashion week on *Digital Village*, a social metaverse. Buyers and editors could attend as avatars, shows could be accessed at any time, and attendees could even try clothes on *Digital Village* and pre-order them to wear them in real life.

However, digital does not automatically mean sustainable. HFW tracked the impact of its most recent fashion week, and found that the carbon footprint per visitor dropped from 137 kg to 0.66 kg CO_2e after holding it purely digitally. The reduction is significant, but it must not be forgotten that data centres used to power digital services contributed approximately 2 per cent of GHG emissions in 2016, according to the UN (Benson, 2021).

> ## 3.3.2 Will digital fashion become mainstream?
> ## The importance of communication

Earlier, we reviewed the importance of communication to educate consumers and promote sustainability. We looked at different channels, different messages, and different communication strategies. In this section, we will review the importance of social media and influencers in creating awareness about digital fashion through eWOM.

What are fashion opinion leaders? The term "opinion leader" has been defined in many ways, but its description is consistently linked with information-sharing behaviour and influence on opinion followers (Zhou et al., 2019).

> **Opinion leaders** – defined in many ways, but consistently linked with information-sharing behaviour and influence on opinion followers.

They are perceived by their followers as knowledgeable experts in specific fields and appropriate sources for information and recommendations. They can alert their social networks to significant matters around their environments, including new product launches (Nisbet and Kotcher, 2009). Fashion opinion leaders are classified according to the level of fashion innovativeness and opinion leadership involved in the diffusion and adoption process, and fashion consumers can be categorised as fashion leaders or fashion followers. They can be fashion innovators, who adopt a new fashion trend earliest in the fashion life cycle; fashion opinion leaders, who accelerate the speed and scope of fashion diffusion process, legitimising the adoption of new trends and acting as sources of information and advice; and innovative communicators, who combine the roles of fashion innovators and fashion opinion leaders (Workman and Johnson 1993). Fashion opinion leaders play a crucial role in the fashion diffusion and adoption process. They seem to have different sets of values and psychological characteristics, as they appear to have unique self-images and may perceive themselves as more excitable, indulgent, and contemporary than others (Goldsmith et al. 1996). The activities fashion opinion leaders conduct online include providing product descriptions and outfit advice to help consumers make purchase decisions (Kwahk and Kim 2016). They may also hold livestreams via videos, which is becoming more popular due to platforms such as Instagram, where opinion leaders can discuss products in real time, with positive effects at the cognitive and affective levels (Hu et al. 2017). In terms of social interaction, this can enhance shopping entertainment and increase purchase intentions (Kim et al. 2011). With the empowerment and use of digital wear now present in the metaverse, modern technological developments can create a new route of sustainability, and this is why it looks like a sensible channel to promote digital fashion (Hackernoon, 2021).

Cyberspace allows people to present themselves and form multiple identities by using digitally presented products and brands rather than the physically presented forms in the real world. Opinion leaders portraying their leadership roles in relation to goods consumption on social media require strategies for manipulating the languages, signs, and symbols that stand for products and brands (Zhou et al., 2019). Capitalising on digital fashion is a way to portray themselves as fashion innovators and work on their self-image, which is a win–win strategy with fashion brands investing in digital fashion.

Social media influencers infuse eWOM with their expertise, reputation, and reliability, creating sophisticated content in the forms of stories, videos, and visuals (Audrezet et al., 2020). Digital fashion brands can use SMIs to target foreign markets, but they need to be careful about cultural differences. They need to interpret local consumers' preferred brand meanings, deliver local consumers' desired values of brands, portray an international brand identity, and position and maintain consistency in brand images (Zhou et al., 2021). With reference to the narrative strategies reviewed in the previous chapter, self-identity construction can be used by influencers for different purposes, including breaking cultural barriers and interpreting consumer-preferred luxury brand meanings, but also to portray luxury brands' identities and positions, and to maintain consistency in luxury brands' images (Zhou et al., 2021). This can be especially relevant in promoting digital fashion and generating eWOM so that digital fashion becomes a way to create a specific self-identity and communicate it through social media. It also means that promoting digital fashion will not be exclusive to fashion leaders. Experts maintain that letting users layer digital garments on themselves creates a "wow" moment, and it is highly likely that they will decide to share their experience on social media and advocate in favour of digital fashion. In this way, every user can become an influencer. Immersive experiences have the power to make shoppers feel more connected to a product or brand if the experience feels authentic. The process of dressing virtually links back to academic literature about experiential retailing and the importance of developing strong narratives. But digital fashion also relates to self-image and personal ego, which makes it more relevant to consumers.

From the brand perspective, there are interesting aspects to consider in relation to influencers and digital fashion (McDowell, 2021b). Digital garments make the process of giving samples to influencers easier than with physical ones. In September 2021, Fartfetch became one of the first big retailers to test the practice of digital sampling to dress influencers. The way it works is quite similar to the process reviewed earlier: Farfetch collaborated with 3D designers to digitise the garments, then they were sent to influencers to choose their favourite looks. Influencers also sent different images of themselves to have the garments digitally tailored to their bodies. Although there are some challenges, like reproducing the movement of the garment or tactile sensations, the results were quite accurate. The impact of this strategy on sustainability can be considered from different perspectives. First, it reduces the environmental footprint of sending physical garments to influencers. Second, testing products that consumers may buy through influencers avoids producing a large stock that may not be bought. And finally, promoting digital fashion will be a way to increase the customer base and hopefully reduce the consumption of physical garments, and consequently, reduce the impact on the environment.

3.3.3 Key developments and industry practices

- **The Fabricant**, a digital fashion house, made its name in Hong Kong after creating a solely digital collection for luxury fashion retailer I.T as part of the concept store's 30th anniversary celebrations (Daswani, 2020). The Amsterdam-based fashion label auctioned the first digital couture dress for $9,500 in New York: "Iridescence", a silver bodysuit and transparent coat that only exists digitally. It is limited to one owner thanks to blockchain, and the design is made to fit the buyer via "digital tailoring", which justifies the price paid for it (Daswani, 2020). After receiving a photo of the owner, a digital double is created as a 3D fitting model, on which the garment is draped and fit before it is rendered out as a photorealistic image without the double, and composited onto the owner's photo. The Fabricant's digital fashion collections can be bought in its e-commerce store in the form of an image of the user wearing the item that can be shared online. The brand also releases a digital outfit monthly which is free to download, in size XS, but there is no easy method to adapt and wear it. This sort of approach can be an interesting tactic to get publicity.
- **Carlings** launched its first digital-only collection in November 2020, titled "Neo-Ex". The collection was inspired by the aesthetic of videogames and was composed of 19 items priced at £9–30 each. Once bought, Carling's 3D designers fitted the look onto a photo of the buyer ready to post on social media. The company stated that they had democratised the economy of the fashion industry while

opening up the world of taking chances with styling without leaving a negative environmental footprint (Semic, 2019).

- **More Dash** is a wholesale showroom founded by Daria Shapovalova and Natalia Modenova in Paris in 2014. In 2019, they launched their first business-to customer fashion venture through pop-up shops in the US to test their hypothesis that there was a significant demand for fashion consumption for the sole purpose of digital content creation. Recognising the power of this "purchase, Instagram, return" trend, they used the pop-ups as content creation studios with stock from their wholesale showrooms. Users paid $10 to dress up, take pictures, and create videos. Sometimes they came back to buy the items after getting validation of the outfit from their "followers". As a result, they launched the start-up Dress-X. They design 3D garments that have a structure and form that could work in the physical world. For them, digital fashion is the new fast fashion, because if we want things fast, they should be digital. The impact on sustainability is evident: "At Dress-X, the total carbon footprint of producing one digital item is 95 per cent less than the average production for a physical garment."
- Digital clothing is not exclusive of more technological brands, but luxury houses have started to launch digital collections or individual pieces of clothing. This is the case with **Moschino**, which launched a *Sims*-inspired capsule complete with green diamond-printed swimsuits. It also launched a virtual version of the Freezer Bunny hoodie for all *Sims* titles (Semic, 2019). Some experts have predicted that it will not be long before we see a luxury brand produce a completely digital collection.

3.3.4 Case studies

HOT:SECOND

What is it?

HOT:SECOND has been defined as the world's first circular economy concept store trading physical products for digital experiences. It opened from Tuesday 19 to Thursday 21 November 2019 in Shoreditch, London. It was developed by fashion educator and futurist Karinna Nobbs in collaboration with innovation studio Holition and 3D artist Emily Switzer. The pop-up store encouraged consumers to experience in an immersive way digital fashion garments from well-known brands such as The Fabricant and Carlings.

How did it work?

At HOT:SECOND, visitors could trade physical products for these digital experiences. They could donate an item of unwanted clothing to the charity Love Not Landfill, and in exchange they were given a token which granted entry to one of the futuristic pods where the journey started. Inside the pods, a human digital tailor showed the mixed-reality magic mirror developed by Holition. Then, for three to five minutes, the visitor tried on a variety of digital garments ranging from couture to streetwear. At the end,

Figure 3.3.1   Metallic Tracksuit by CARLINGS_VIRTUE and DEEP by The Fabricant © HOT:SECOND

visitors were able to take away both a digital and a physical memory of their experience whereby the company hoped "a transformation of feelings and attitudes towards digital fashion garments will have taken place'".

What made it unique?

This retail prototype aimed to induce a new type of retail experience where the physical and the digital combine, co-creating a distinct and individualised experience for potential consumers.

> We asked consumers to exchange physical garments they no longer wanted for the ability to try on four digital garments in a magic mirror type of experience," Nobbs said. "It was really successful. The notion of intellectual property and fashion is a new area. Authentication will be what make digital fashion go from niche to mainstream.

(Baron, 2021)

Figure 3.3.2   Store Illustration © HOT:SECOND

The Dematerialised

What is it?

The Dematerialised is a blockchain-backed platform allowing fans to acquire digital garments they can carry into numerous other digital spaces (Baron, 2021). The company claims that its purpose is "to converge and nurture the emerging digital fashion ecosystem providing viable new revenue streams and visceral experiences with a Web3 marketplace for authenticated virtual goods". It develops an "experimental yet empathic" approach to digital fashion assets that aims to challenge traditional fashion business models of production, consumption, and ownership.

When was it created?

On 12 December 2020, Karinna Nobbs and Marjorie Hernandez, the co-founders of The Dematerialised, launched a groundbreaking new online platform to a tight community of highly innovative fashionistas, gamers, and cryptoheads. The Dematerialised is a Web3 digital fashion marketplace where consumers and creators can buy, sell, and experience authenticated virtual goods.

What makes it unique?

What makes The Dematerialised unique is that its virtual items are released as NFTs which are generated and authenticated on the LUKSO blockchain. This means that each virtual item which is bought or sold on the platform has a unique identifier, enabling a fully transparent product journey to be visible for all invited users. On entering a code, invited users are dropped into a 3D space where they can interact with the digital garments for sale in a new and visceral manner. When they click through to get more information on the product, they can see the designer's face and learn about the creative process. Not only that, but users can bring the garment into their own environment, using augmented reality to zoom in to the detail and look inside at the craft behind the design.

Another aspect that makes The Dematerialised unique is the fact that it accepts both fiat and crypto currencies. This is an important enabler in making digital fashion assets such as NFTs accessible to the non-crypto audience. After payment is processed, the invited user is directed to an exclusive area where they can experience their digital asset in four ways: WEAR (get digitally dressed ready for social media), PORT (direct to avatar in a game), TRADE (peer-to-peer marketplace), and DISPLAY (showcase the assets you have collected). Each of these post-purchase pathways offer new ways to be able to use digital garments. And this helps to fight against one of the main barriers for digital fashion, as items can be owned and used not just in static images, but in video games, virtual reality, and to collect and sell as digital art. One of the main criticisms of digital fashion is that it will not exist outside Instagram. However The Dematerialised and its authenticating system have demonstrated that digital fashion has many more applications than showing an outfit on social media (McDowell, 2021). This is something that crypto enthusiasts have been embracing for a long time. The blockchain can certify the artist, the owner, and the edition, which will allow the item to be retained even if The Dematerialised were to disappear (McDowell, 2021).

What pieces has it launched?

The first iconic piece launched by The Dematerialised was a futuristic, gender-fluid metallic sweatshirt named HEXJERZO. The piece was designed by Berlin based designer Schirin Negahbani. Only 1,212 pieces were released, and the price of the asset was €121.21. Other pieces include a drop (icon) of Karl Lagerfeld (Karl by Karl) that was sold out in 2 minutes and 57 seconds.

What are its future prospects?

The Dematerialised will bridge the gap between the physical and digital worlds, challenging the notion of clothing ownership and exploring a potentially more sustainable and conscious cycles of production and consumption, while introducing as many people as possible to digital fashion garments for the first time.

Figure 3.3.3   Drop Karl Lagerfeld © The Dematerialised

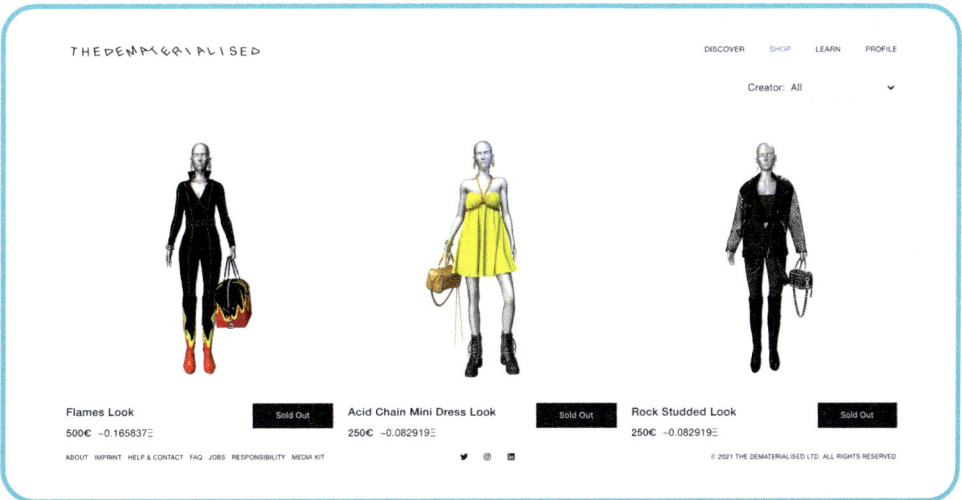

Figure 3.3.4   Drop Rebecca Minkoff © The Dematerialised

Task

- What is the future of digital fashion in the context of the flexible/remote working philosophy? Will people invest in new garments that can be worn online for meetings?
- What are the main benefits and drawbacks of digital fashion?
- What is the real impact on sustainability of digital fashion?
- Can digital fashion make consumers more aware about their fashion consumption? Or is it going to promote the disposable culture and the need to wear a different outfit every day?
- What will be the role of social media influencers in digital fashion? Will they contribute to popularising the use of digital garments?

References

Audrezet, A., De Kerviler, G., and Moulard, J.G. (2020) Authenticity under threat: when social media influencers need to go beyond self-presentation, *Journal of Business Research*, 117, 557–569.

Bain, M. (2021) How selfridges is bringing virtual fashion to stores, *The Business of Fashion*, 4th October 2021 (online): https://www.businessoffashion.com/articles/technology/how-selfridges-is-bringing-virtual-fashion-to-physical-stores.

Baron, K. (2021) From silver bullets to strategic overhauls: 9 retail trends, tactics & inovations for success in 2021, *Forbes*, 4th January 2021 (online): https://www.forbes.com/sites/sharonedelson/2020/11/02/blockchain-startup-lukso-explains-the-digital-wardrobe-and-why-youll-want-one/?sh=6b0c3641f390.

Benson, S. (2021) Is digital fashion really the industry's eco-friendly saviour?, *Dazed*, 25th August 2021 (online): https://www.dazeddigital.com/fashion/article/53877/1/digital-fashion-clothing-industry-saviour-climate-sustainability-the-sims-avatar.

Blazquez, M. (2014) The fashion shopping experience in a multichannel retail environment: the role of technology in enhancing the customer experience, *The International Journal of Electronic Commerce*, 18(4) (Summer), 7–116.

Business of Fashion (BOF) (2021a) *The state of fashion, 2021*, Business of Fashion and McKinsey & Company.

Business of Fashion (BOF) (2021b) *Dematerialisation: why the metaverse is fashion's next goldmine*, Business of Fashion, 12th November 2021 (online): https://www.businessoffashion.com/videos/technology/the-bof-show-with-imran-amed-episode4-dematerialisation/.

Chitakorn, K. (2021) Are branded virtual worlds the new marketing terrain?, *Vogue Business*, May 2021 (online): https://www.voguebusiness.com/technology/are-branded-virtual-worlds-the-new-marketing-terrain.

Daswani, S. (2020) 5G meets high fashion: why luxury designers are rethinking their creative process – with skins augmented for the digital space, *South China Morning Post*, 25th May 2020 (online): https://www.scmp.com/magazines/style/luxury/article/3085685/5g-meets-high-fashion-why-luxury-designers-are-rethinking?fbclid=IwAR17Lm0m2rJ3mkyokPnM7mhjphWA2sVwG13mbC4FV6rZ6GnkoqAYv7wJMw.

Goldsmith, R.E., Flynn, L.R., and Moore, M.A. (1996) The self-concept of fashion leaders, *Clothing and Textiles Research Journal*, 14(4), 242–248.

Hackernoon (2021) The rise of digital fashion and sustainability in the metaverse,

Hackernoon, 26th November 2021 (online): https://hackernoon.com/the-rise-of-digital -fashion-and-sustainability-in-the-metaverse.

Hu, M., Zhang, M.L., and Wang, Y. (2017) Why do audiences choose to keep watching on live video streaming platforms? An explanation of dual identification framework, *Computers in Human Behavior*, 75, 594–606.

Kansara, V.A. (2021) NFTs for fashion: fad or opportunity?, *Business of Fashion*, 19th March 2021 (online): https://www.businessoffashion .com/briefings/technology/nfts-for-fashion -fad-or-opportunity/.

Kent, A., Vianello, M., Cano, M.B., and Helberger, E. (2016) Omnichannel fashion retail and channel integration: the case of department stores, in Vecchi, A. and Buckley, C. (eds.) *Handbook of research on global fashion management and merchandising*, IGI Global, pp. 398–419.

Kim, Y.H., Lee, M.Y., and Kim, Y.K. (2011) A new shopper typology: utilitarian and hedonic perspectives, *Journal of Global Academy of Marketing*, 21(2), 102–113.

Kwahk, K.Y., and Kim, B. (2016) Effects of social media on consumers' purchase decisions: evidence from Taobao, *Service Business*, 11(4), 803–829.

Lee, A. (2021) What gaming, virtual fashion can teach real-life fashion about tech. How gaming technologies and digital goods are disrupting the fashion business from back end to front, *WWD*, 27th April 2021 (online): https://wwd.com/business-news/technology/ what-gaming-virtual-fashion-can-teach-real -life-fashion-about-tech-1234808400/.

McDowell, M. (2021a) These platforms want to be the Farfetch of digital fashion, *Vogue Business*, 25th January 2021.

McDowell, M. (2021b) Influencers are wearing digital versions of physical clothes now, *Vogue Business*, 21st September 2021 (online): https://www.voguebusiness.com/technology /influencers-are-wearing-digital-versions-of -physical-clothes-now.

Nanda, M.C., and Bain, M. (2021) Unpacking fashion latest wave of NFT sales. What's selling and who'sbuying as fashion brands from Dolce & Gabbana to Rebeca Minkoff jump into the surging NFT market, *The*

Business of Fashion, 20th October 2021 (online): https://www.businessoffashion.com/ articles/technology/unpacking-fashions-latest -wave-of-nft-sales.

Nisbet, M.C., and Kotcher, J.E. (2009) A two-step flow of influence? Opinion- leader campaigns on climate change, *Science Communication*, 30(3), 328–354.

Noris, A., Nobile, T.H., Kalbaska, N., and Cantoni, L. (2021) Digital fashion: a systematic literature review. A perspective on marketing and communication, *Journal of Global Fashion Marketing*, 12(1), 32–46.

Roberts-Islam, B. (2020) How digital fashion could replace fast-fashion, and the startup paving the way, 21st August 2020 (online): https://www.forbes.com/sites/ brookerobertsislam/2020/08/21/how digital -fashion-could-replace-fast-fashion-and-the -startup-paving-the-way/?sh=4f5f055f70d8.

Semic, S. (2019) Virtual fashion: the digitally generated clothes appearing on your IG influencer feeds, *Elle*, 2nd July 2019 (online): https://www.elle.com/uk/fashion/a28166986/ digital-fashion-dressing-virtually/.

UN (2021) *Sustainable development goals. Goal 12: ensure sustainable consumption and production patterns*, United Nations, 2021 (online): https://www.un.org/sustain abledevelopment/sustainable-consumption -production/.

Williams, G. (2021) Luxury's battle for the metaverse, *Jing Daily*, June 2021 (online): https://jingdaily.com/metaverse-luxury -brands-china/.

Workman, J.E., and Johnson, K.K. (1993) Fashion opinion leadership, fashion innovativeness, and need for variety, *Clothing and Textiles Research Journal*, 11(3), 60–64.

Zhou, S., Blazquez, M., McCormick, H., and Barnes, L. (2021) How social media influencers' narrative strategies benefit cultivating influencer marketing: tackling issues of cultural barriers, commercialised content, and sponsorship disclosure, *Journal of Business Research*, 134, 122–142.

Zhou, S., McCormick, H., Blazquez, M., and Barnes, L. (2019) eWOM: the rise of the opinion leaders, in *Social commerce*, Palgrave Macmillan, Cham, pp. 189–212.

PART 4
Material innovations in sustainable fashion

As highlighted previously, all parts of this book are interconnected, in that we have signposted you, the reader, to various chapters and sections where you gain a more in-depth understanding of certain issues. Part 4 of this book is dedicated to raw materials, which, as explored in Chapter 1.1, play a vital role in a manager's decision-making process. In simple terms, these raw materials ensure that the production and consumption of fashion items is possible.

This part covers technical aspects in the early stages of the apparel pipeline, which is essential to understand the topical issues surrounding sustainability in the fashion industry and to comprehend current practices and solutions. The apparel pipeline is defined as "a series of interrelated activities, which originates with the manufacture of fibre and culminates with the delivery of a product into the hands of the consumer" (Jones, 2006, p.1). Within this part, the apparel pipeline or the soft goods chain is seen to be formed out of three segments: textile, apparel, and retail. The textile segment is the focal point of this part of the book, as it looks at the raw materials and focuses its attention predominantly on fibre and yarn production, the manufacturing of fabric, and the finishings of these fabrics (see Boardman et al. 2020).

DOI: 10.4324/9781003097846-16

Learning outcomes

1. To critically examine key technical terminology surrounding textile fibre origin, sourcing, cultivation, production and properties.
2. To understand the significant role these fibres play in the material footprint of fashion garments, reflecting on current and future origins, sourcing, cultivation and production processes.
3. To critically investigate the significance of sustainable challenges associated with material innovations in the 21st century.

4.1.1 20th-century production

In **Part 1,** we discussed the decision-making process and alluded to the fact that this process has five key steps: (1) recognition of a problem, (2) information search, (3) evaluating alternatives, (4) making a purchase decision, and (5) evaluating the purchase decision. We further illustrated that making these decisions is not an easy task, but rather complex. Some of these complex decisions relate to the selection of (sustainable) raw materials, which is a vital aspect of this chapter. If we are thinking about producing a product, one of the first aspects we need to consider is what our product will be made of.

We usually have various choices: on the one hand we can produce our fashion item from natural materials, on the other hand we can use man-made materials, or we may decide on a combination of the two. What choice we make depends not only on the performance properties that are essential for our products (e.g., waterproof coating, stretchiness), but also what implications our choice may have on aspects of sustainability. The raw materials we source to produce our fashion items are part of the apparel pipeline and linked to, often, long fashion supply chains. Depending on the raw material, we may need to consider what the impacts of these are on agriculture, mining, and forestry, all of which will be impacted by climate change.

Historically, garments were produced from raw materials that were readily available to us, such as those from animals and plants. Although it is beyond the scope of this book, it needs to be highlighted here that a complex decision-making process is involved in terms of which raw material to choose, as all of them can have ethical (social) and environmental implications. Sometimes decisions may be made according to trends and what is perceived to be a "must have", whilst at other times decisions may be made based on the organisation's values. For example, we have seen various

DOI: 10.4324/9781003097846-17

fashion brands taking a stance against using animal skins in their collections, thereby promoting plant-based leather replacements. On the other hand, companies have also reported using more environmentally friendly plant-based resources, which may be certified (e.g., Fair Trade, GOTS) (see Section 1.2.1). It is important to note that whilst we continue to use these natural fibres today, we have developed man-made fibres in the hope of tailoring materials to meet our ever-changing needs.

In this chapter, we will begin by briefly exploring the historical timeline of natural fibres through to the development of man-made materials, highlighting the challenges we face in terms of sustainability.

4.1.2 Natural fibres

When reflecting on the timeline of when and how fibres have been created and utilised, it is important to link this to supply chain management. Supply chain management includes aspects "from end-user through original suppliers, that provides products, services, and information that add value for customers and other stakeholders" (Lambert et al., 2006: 2). In earlier times, garments were produced locally, meaning not only assembling products, but also using resources that were commonly available within the local environment. After the Industrial Revolution, which started in the 18th century in the UK, this changed, with companies developing global supply chains and resources being acquired on the global market. Companies are no longer reliant on what they can produce in their own countries, but rather can gain any resource they want, as globalisation has made trading raw materials relatively cheap.

> **Supply chain management** – managing the flow of goods, services, and informa-tion along the entirety of the production process, thereby involving a variety of stakeholders.

Let's focus on natural fibres first. Humans have been using natural fibres for clothing for around 30,000 years. The use of wild flax fibres is one of the earliest to be docu-mented (Kvavadze et al., 2009). Natural fibres originate from plants and animals, and thus derive from nature. A key implication here for supply chain management is con-sidering where different plants, for example, find their natural habitat and can flour-ish, as this has an impact on lead time and transportation. At this point, you may also want to think back to Chapter 1.1, where we discussed the macro environment and PEST(EL), as there are various implications you can consider which may impact on sourcing our raw materials and especially the quantity we may need, which has impli-cations for our micro environmental analysis.

To explore the last point further, the quantity of a raw material required may be quite high, considering that we do not commonly use all parts of a plant for each fibre, but rather different parts of the plant are suitable for textile fibre use. For example, cotton fibres derive from the fruit of the cotton plant, which appear like soft cotton wool balls, whereas flax fibres derive from the bast (stem) of the plant, which could be described as straw-like. Understanding where raw materials come from and what parts of the plant are made into fibres and fabrics is vital, as this links to social aspects that need to be considered. For example, whilst some plants might be mechanically harvested, others may need to be handpicked, which is labour-intensive. We have already alluded to the fact that the latter aspect can have implications not only for economic sustainability due to the cost associated with it, but also social sustainability, in terms of working conditions.

As mentioned, not only do we gain natural fibres from plants, we can also derive these from animals, for example from fleeces and cocoons. Wool fibres can be obtained from the fleeces of sheep, alpacas, rabbits, and goats, whereas silk fibres are made from the cocoons of the mulberry silk moth.

Within this book, we do not take a stance on whether some methods of obtaining fibres are more ethical than others, nor do we position ourselves to promote one over the other. What we do try to communicate here is that historically, for a significant period of time, natural fibres have been obtained from either plant or animal sources. The process of how these fibres are made into fabrics has been optimised since the beginning of the Industrial Revolution, either through the use of machinery or chemicals. Globalisation and the introduction of technology have enabled fashion companies to operate in a world that seems almost local. What we mean by this is the fact that we now no longer rely on raw materials to be produced within our vicinity, but can access these from other geographic regions, no matter the distance. This has both advantages and disadvantages. An advantage may be that raw materials that are grown in a climate that is favourable may produce a stronger crop and ultimately stronger fibres, whilst a disadvantage may be depletion of resources, as crops such as cotton use a lot of water. It may be no surprise that each of the natural fibres mentioned are associated with different sustainability implications. We will come back to this later by further considering the United Nations SDGs.

Linking back to the beginning of this chapter, let's consider how the decision-making process, the choice of raw materials, and sustainability are linked. Let's consider a plain white T-shirt. If we use our T-shirt for sports, it may need to be breathable and have high absorption, thus we may want to use 100 per cent cotton fibres. However, if we want this T-shirt to also have easy care properties, be less prone to creases, and be quick drying, a percentage of polyester fibres may be included. And this is where a lot of complexities arise: are we wanting to design a T-shirt that can be easily recycled, in which case blending fibres may present challenges, or are we focusing more on the performance properties? Are we wanting to use plant-based materials that may use a lot of water, or plastics that are made from fossil fuels? In order to fully understand the implications the raw material choices may pose (not only for the product, but also aspects surrounding sustainability), we need to understand a bit more about the fibres themselves.

4.1.2.1 Plant fibres

As mentioned earlier, plant fibres fit within the category of natural fibres. Examples that can be listed here are cotton and flax. These fibres are often used in garments to provide breathability due to their high absorption and wicking properties. The term "wicking" is used to describe the transport of moisture or liquid from the wearer through a fibre or fabric. As plant fibres are hydrophilic (water-loving), they have this property. You may not be surprised that both cotton and flax are thus used for sportswear or as undergarments because of these performance properties.

Garments containing flax fibres feel cool, which is why linen fabrics are typically used in summer clothing. Yet you may be aware that linen often crinkles, and thus can lose its shape after one wear.

Cotton can be spun into yarns for a variety of products. It can be used in woven fabrics, such as denim used in the production of jeans, through to knitted jersey used to create staple T-shirts. Cotton made up 23 per cent of global fibre production in 2019, the second largest after polyester ("Preferred Fiber & Materials Market Report 2020," n.d.).

Although consideration of performance properties is vital within the decision-making process, especially when it comes to choosing the raw material, there may be other aspects that need to be considered, namely issues associated with the production process of these fibres. Plants grown for textiles require soil (land), water, and certain weather conditions. Thus, certain fibres are more commonly grown in different geographic regions. For example, 70–80 per cent of world flax production is in Europe, in countries such as France, where the humid conditions and nutrient-rich soil are ideal for cultivation ("European Linen – Le lin et le chanvre européen," n.d.; Gomez-Campos et al., 2021), whilst cotton plantations are found in warmer climates. From an environmental sustainability perspective, growing raw materials in Europe and producing garments in Europe would imply less transportation costs and greenhouse gas emissions compared to, for example, importing cotton from countries such as Pakistan or India, which are geographically further afield.

Since the Industrial Revolution, economic sustainability has increasingly become a prominent factor. To be more profitable, the ways raw materials are cultivated have changed. For example, historically carried out by hand, and today by machine, when it is time to harvest the flax plants, they are pulled from the soil and laid out to dry, in a process called retting. Scutching and combing of the retted plant release the flax fibres from the bast of the plant, and they can then be transformed into yarns and fabrics. However, as already mentioned, flax needs humid conditions and nutrient-rich soil, which implies that aspects related to climate change, such as drought periods or flooding, could harm the harvest and fibre quality. This in turn can have impacts on other stages along the apparel pipeline and the supply chain in more general terms.

Although cotton dominates the natural fibre market, making a conscious decision to switch to another fibre could have various advantages. Since flax production is "close to home" in parts of Europe, lead times associated with raw material delivery could be cut, and similarly, the environmental footprint could be reduced as the raw material has less of a journey to undertake compared to, for example, cotton ("European Linen – Le lin et le chanvre européen," n.d.). In order to promote sustainability, the European Confederation of Flax and Hemp (CELC) provides two certifications, EUROPEAN FLAX® and MASTERS OF LINEN®, which aim to ensure traceability and ethical production, thus providing additional value for consumers, who are increasingly environmentally conscious and actively look for more "sustainable fashion" products (see also Section 1.1.3) ("I love linen | in celebration of linen in partners retailers (e) shop," n.d.). The two certifications are third-party-accredited and independently audited, thereby allowing for transparency in the process.

By sourcing raw materials that are grown in close proximity, managers not only consciously or unconsciously align themselves with sustainability aspects, but also with UN SDG 12 (responsible consumption and production) (Table 4.1.1). Upon closer examination of SDG 12, you may have noticed that one of the suggested indicators is the recording of material footprint and publishing sustainability reports. Certifications such as EUROPEAN FLAX® and MASTERS OF LINEN® enable retailers to trace raw materials in their fashion products, and may provide a way of recording and tracing sustainability information.

We have discussed flax fibres a lot, yet, as indicated, cotton is dominating the natural fibre market, so it is important to take a closer look at its production. In contrast to flax fibres, cotton fibres are picked from the plant, much like picking fruit. The seeds and "trash" are removed through a process called ginning before the fibres are blended, combed, and carded into slivers (or tops) ready for yarn spinning. You may already understand that this is quite labour-intensive. But cotton not only needs a lot of resources in terms of human and machine power, but also requires high use of pesticides, which can be environmentally challenging. Moreover, there may be ethical issues associated with hand-picking cotton, as working outdoors in hot conditions can be unpleasant and unhealthy.

Fashion companies do not simply buy cotton, but rather they have a choice of what type of cotton fibres they want or may need. For example, cotton fibres with extra-long staple (ELS) fibre length, such as "Pima", "Sea Island" and "Egyptian", which represent about 8 per cent of world cotton production (Gordon 2007), are considered the most luxurious cotton varieties in the fashion industry. Longer, finer cotton fibre lengths ensure less processing waste, efficient yarn spinning, greater yarn strength, and quality (Gordon 2007), which in turn is beneficial when looking at aspects of sustainability. These fibres can be used to create yarns suitable for automated knitted and woven fabrics, but also for hand knitting (see Chapter 4.2). These varieties are cultivated in warm, sunny conditions, and are grown in countries such as India, the USA, and the Caribbean islands. Whilst some of the ELS varieties are hand-picked, the majority of world cotton production, such as "Upland" cotton, is mechanically harvested across Asia, North America, and Western Africa (Zhang et al, 2020).

Although it might be assumed that as a natural fibre cotton is environmentally friendly, its production may not necessarily be. To explain, water plays a vital role in growing plant fibres, with cotton receiving particular interest. This is partly due to cotton cultivation in these warm climates requiring supplemental irrigation systems to ensure successful growth during the growing season when there may not be enough rainfall. A variety of irrigation systems are used, the choice of which is dependent on location, and one of the main environmental challenges is the efficiency of these systems (Gordon and Hsieh, 2007). Here we can link again to a key challenge that needs to be addressed, which links to SDG 6 regarding clean water and sanitation, highlighting the need to increase water-use efficiency.

Yet water efficiency is not the only challenge; crop production is also impacted by pests and pathogens. This can range from fungi and bacteria growing on fruit, leaves, stems, and roots through to plant-feeding pests such as bollworm and boll weevil (Tarazi et al., 2019). To overcome these losses, approaches include, but are not limited to, genetically modifying cotton varieties and pesticide use during cultivation. In order to overcome these challenges, attention has turned to the use of biopesticides, which intend to be more pest-specific (Malinga and Laing, 2021), and the use of "natural"

Table 4.1.1 United Nations Sustainable Development Goals Relating to Fibre Selection

SDG	Targets	Indicators	Examples of Implications/challenges for fibre sourcing, production, and selection
12 - Responsible Consumption and Production	12.2 – By 2030, achieve the sustainable management and efficient use of natural resources	• Material footprint • Domestic material consumption	Footprint may need to include where raw materials are sourced from for production. Researchers have noted challenges with retailers obtaining this information from their suppliers (de Brito et al., 2008)
	12.5 – By 2030, substantially reduce waste generation through prevention, reduction, recycling and reuse	• National recycling rate, tons of material recycled	Considering the end-of-life of textile materials, the use of virgin materials versus recycled, and the circular economy
	12.6 – Encourage companies, especially large and transnational companies, to adopt sustainable practices and to integrate sustainability information into their reporting cycle	• Number of companies publishing sustainability reports	Traceability and provenance, choice of certification and auditing.
6 Clean Water and Sanitation	6.3 – By 2030, improve water quality by reducing pollution, eliminating dumping, and minimising release of hazardous chemicals and materials, halving the proportion of untreated wastewater, and substantially increasing recycling and safe reuse globally	• Proportion of wastewater safely treated • Proportion of bodies of water with good ambient water quality	The agriculture and cultivation processes used to grow natural fibres involve in some cases the use of harmful pesticides and insecticides, some of which are released into rivers and streams.

(Continued)

Table 4.1.1   Continued

SDG	Targets	Indicators	Examples of Implications/ challenges for fibre sourcing, production, and selection
	6.4 – By 2030, substantially increase water-use efficiency across all sectors and ensure sustainable withdrawals and supply of freshwater to address water scarcity and substantially reduce the number of people suffering from water scarcity	• Change in water-use efficiency over time • Level of water stress: freshwater withdrawal as a proportion of available freshwater resources	• Some plants are more water-intensive than others and require irrigation systems, having a devastating impact on the environment, which is showcased through the degradation of the Aral Sea, for example
	6.6 - By 2020, protect and restore water-related ecosystems, including mountains, forests, wetlands, rivers, aquifers and lakes	• Change in the extent of water-related ecosystems over time	Forests used for wood pulp in the production of man-made regenerated cellulosic fibres
7 Affordable and Clean Energy	7.3 – By 2030, double the global rate of improvement in energy efficiency	• Energy intensity measured in terms of primary energy and GDP	Energy used not just in the production of man-made fibres but textile production processes along the supply chain.
14 Life below Water	14.1 – By 2025, prevent and significantly reduce marine pollution of all kinds, in particular from land-based activities, including marine debris and nutrient pollution	• Index of coastal eutrophication and floating plastic debris density	• Microfibre pollution is currently seen as a key issue that needs further industry attention (Yan et al., 2020) • More fish are digesting microfibres

(Continued)

Table 4.1.1   Continued

SDG	Targets	Indicators	Examples of Implications/ challenges for fibre sourcing, production, and selection
15 Life on Land	15.2 – By 2020, promote the implementation of sustainable management of all types of forests, halt deforestation, restore degraded forests and substantially increase afforestation and reforestation globally	• Progress towards sustainable forest management	• Forests used for wood pulp in the production of man-made regenerated cellulosic fibres
	15.3 – By 2030, combat desertification, restore degraded land and soil, including land affected by desertification, drought and floods, and strive to achieve a land degradation-neutral world	• Proportion of land that is degraded over total land area	• Land for pastures for wool production • Impact of cotton cultivation on the soil and land
	15.9 – By 2020, integrate ecosystem and biodiversity values into national and local planning, development processes, poverty reduction strategies, and accounts	• Progress towards national targets established in accordance with Aichi Biodiversity Target 2 of the Strategic Plan for Biodiversity 2011–2020	

Source: "THE 17 GOALS|Sustainable Development," n.d.

chemicals as opposed to synthetic fertilisers and pesticides through "organic" cultivation methods (Gordon and Hsieh, 2007).

As media attention has focused on these environmental challenges associated with cotton, brands are looking to source cotton fibres with provenance and traceability. This has led to the development of the Better Cotton Initiative (BCI), Fairtrade Cotton and OEKO-TEX® labelling (see Chapter 1.2). As highlighted in UN SDG 12 (see Table 4.1.1), these may help integrate sustainability information into reporting cycles. Researchers have challenged the sustainability and efficiency of such schemes, specifically the benefits of Fairtrade cotton to producers in developing countries (Balineau, 2013). Balineau (2013) concluded that Fairtrade had a significant impact on the quality of cotton produced by certified Malian growers, in part by reducing scepticism from growers towards new agricultural and pest control methods. This links further to UN SDG 15 (Life on Land) and Aichi Biodiversity Target 2 of the Strategic Plan for Biodiversity 2011–2020 (Unit, 2020).

In summary, although natural fibres derive from nature, there are still various challenges associated with growing and transforming them into yarns and textiles. The choice of what raw material to use is not only dependent on the performance properties of the material, but may also be influenced by where the raw material can be sourced from and what challenges may be faced in terms of economic, social, and economic sustainability.

4.1.2.2 Animal fibres

Whilst once animal fibres may have played a major role within fashion production, they now make up less than 1 per cent of the global fibre market, with wool fibre production obtained from the fleeces of sheep dominating this sector ("Preferred Fiber & Materials Market Report 2020," n.d.). Australia and New Zealand combined account for 92 per cent of world wool exports (Champion and Fearne, 2001). Wool fibres are typically associated with winter clothing, used in knitwear and outerwear such as jumpers, coats, and jackets. However, finer wool fibres can be used in base layer clothing and summer clothing, promoted through the Cool Wool campaign by the Woolmark Company ("Cool Wool (Knitwear) | The Woolmark Company," n.d.).

Once the fleece is removed from the sheep, the wool fibres go through a process known as carding. The type of carding process depends on the type of fibre obtained from the fleece and the end use of the product. Again, we have multiple choices here: for example, *woollen yarns* can be used in carpets and upholstery, whereas *worsted yarns* can be used for apparel. Different breeds of sheep produce different fibres; for example, fibres obtained from the fleeces of Merino sheep are considered the finest. These finer yarns from the Merino sheep are used in garments associated with the Cool Wool campaign. To promote these lightweight Merino wool fabrics as ideal for transitional seasons, the campaign has collaborated with various fashion designers for use in their spring and summer collections ("Cool Wool (Knitwear) | The Woolmark Company," n.d.). In 2012, Jonathan Saunders, Mark Fast, and Richard Nicoll all showcased Cool Wool in their SS2013 collections ("Top designers showcase Cool Wool at London Fashion Week," n.d.).

The processes of rearing the sheep, through to obtaining fleece and then through to yarn production, are all labour-intensive, and thus have similar social implications to those discussed in the previous section on natural fibres. Once removed from the sheep, due to impurities such as grease and dirt, the fleece requires scouring, washing, and bleaching. These processes all require large volumes of water and various toxic chemicals, leading to the desire to find alternative methods to reduce the environmental impact of these production processes (Allafi et al., 2021a, b).

Yet these social and environmental aspects are not all we need to think of, as these, technically speaking, occur later on in the supply chain. Before we can think of fleeces, we need to think of the sheep. Sheep require pastures to graze on across Australia and New Zealand, therefore research has been carried out to assess the impact of climate change on pasture growth and production and their impact on wool production in future (Harle et al., 2007). This links to the UN SDG 15 (Life on Land, shown in Table 4.1.1) and the targets of combating desertification, restoring degraded land and soil, including land affected by desertification, drought, and floods, and striving to achieve a land degradation-neutral world.

One key advantage wool has as a fibre, which is also shown in its performance properties, is that the fibre has evolved to protect the animal from being exposed to various weather conditions. Due to their natural crimp which gives wool fibres a zig-zag appearance, air is trapped between the skin of the wearer and the fibre, providing insulation and thus keeping us cosy and warm. Wool fibres also have natural elasticity, which means that wool fabrics are more crease-resistant than other animal fibres, such as silk. Thus, when producing garments and deciding on the raw materials, it may be essential to think about the purpose of the end-product. For example, if we design winterwear, wool might be a perfect fibre, as it is not only insulating, but also does not crease, and thus can be worn more than once between washes.

A further example of animal fibre is silk. Silk fibres are associated with lustrous fabrics such as satin, used in garments such as wedding dresses and occasion wear, or luxury blouses. Silk fibres are obtained from the cocoons of the mulberry silk moth (*Bombyx mori*), with China being the world's single biggest silk producer (Yang et al., 2020). To produce these cocoons, the caterpillars eat large quantities of mulberry leaves and then search for a rough surface to start producing their cocoon when they are ready to transform into a moth. The caterpillar wraps the silk threads around its body, which harden to form the cocoon. In the process of sericulture, the long filaments are preserved by preventing the moth hatching by placing the cocoons in hot water. The threads are unravelled and reeled onto a winch ready for yarn spinning. In the wild, the moth would chew through its cocoon to escape, producing shorter fibres for textile production.

Researchers have found that the cost, availability, and resources required to rear the silkworms and process the silk fibres poses future constraints (Reddy et al., 2021). Similarly to climate change potentially impacting on the wool industry with sheep requiring pastures to graze, it has been suggested by researchers that silk fibre production in India will face challenges. India is the next biggest producer after China, with plans to increase mulberry tree harvesting to meet consumer demands (Ricciardi et al., 2021). However, according to Ricciardi et al. (2021), the expansion is constrained by availability of land and freshwater, and those areas that have already expanded are experiencing water scarcity and food insecurity compared with pre-expansion times. Again, this links back to UN Sustainable Development Goal 6 (shown in Table 4.1.1,) highlighting the importance of addressing, and the need to substantially reduce, the number of people suffering from water scarcity. It also highlights the potential challenges faced in the future in deciding whether to use land in these areas to grow food or for raw materials for fashion.

4.1.2.3 Man-made (manufactured) fibres

Man-made fibres are the last category we will explore, and are artificially created by humankind. The development of these fibres began in the pursuit of "artificial silk", with viscose rayon being the first man-made fibre commercially produced in 1905.

These manufactured fibres are relatively "new" in the context of the historical time-line. Man-made (manufactured) fibres can derive from natural polymers, such as cellulose derived from wood pulp in the production of viscose rayon and lyocell fibre, and bamboo and cotton linters (short fibres). These fibres are referred to as regenerated cellulosic fibres. It is predicted that in a growing bio-economy, cellulose chemical derivatives from wood pulp for textile fibres will gain economic importance (Schier et al., 2021). Seventy-nine per cent of man-made cellulosic fibres on the global market are viscose fibres ("Preferred Fiber & Materials Market Report 2020," n.d.), and man-made fibres are often used in fashion garments as alternatives to cotton in fast fashion and high-end products.

It will be interesting to see how the fashion industry may develop and what fibres will become "trendy" in future. With plant and animal fibres both having different sustainability challenges associated with their production, developing man-made fibres further to overcome some of these challenges could foster a more sustainable industry. Moreover, using more man-made fibres could potentially have implications for supply chain management. If wood pulp can be processed in any country, yarn and textile production could in some circumstances move even closer to "home" and thus reduce lead times and cost.

Although there are some advantages in producing these man-made viscose fibres, there are also some challenges, which can be again linked back to social and environmental concerns. Focusing on the entire process of the viscose dope production from wood pulp, we will become aware that this requires a variety of chemicals. A number of authors (Iavicoli et al., 2020; Sieja et al., 2018; Tan et al., 2001) have noted that workers have been negatively, impacted in that the production process releases various toxins (such as carbon disulphide) which can negatively impact human health. Moreover, a lack of sound environmental practices could lead to continued air emissions and water pollution (Adu et al., 2021). Furthermore, the energy-intensive production of viscose emits higher amounts of greenhouse gases when compared with cotton production (Muthu, 2020a). Some of these issues have been addressed, in that it is possible today to create regenerated cellulosic fibres using alternative chemicals and feedstocks, thus, overall, potentially being less harmful compared to producing virgin raw materials.

The sourcing of wood feedstock for viscose production has also been regarded as problematic. According to a recent report by Canopy (2020), 3.3 million tonnes of viscose pulp production originates from wood obtained from Ancient and Endangered Forests ("2020 SURVIVAL A Plan for Saving Forests and Climate A Pulp Thriller," n.d.). As a result, the industry has highlighted the need to explore alternative feedstocks, better management of forest practices, substitution of chemicals, and internal control and monitoring ("Preferred Fiber & Materials Market Report 2020," n.d.). UN SDG 15 (Life on Land; shown in Table 4.1.1) set the goal that by 2020 the UN would promote the implementation of sustainable management of all types of forests, halt deforestation, restore degraded forests, and substantially increase afforestation and reforestation globally through sustainable forest management. We can also link back here to Chapter 1.1, which focused on stakeholders. Fibre production processes are a great example that illustrate that the fashion industry is not operating in a vacuum, but rather is connected to a variety of other industries, such as agriculture, and can thus have a major impact on them, not only in monetary terms, but also in environmental terms.

One alternative that overcomes the challenge of using feedstock from ancient and endangered forests is the use of bamboo. Not only is bamboo as a plant fast-growing (Afrin et al., 2014) and sequesters carbon (Xu et al., 2020), but bamboo viscose also has performance properties such as breathability and comfort. Bamboo is often used within athleisure wear and yoga clothing, thereby competing with cotton. Yet in order to obtain bamboo fibres that can be spun into a yarn, the industry is currently relying on the viscose production process, which is reliant on toxic chemicals.

An alternative to the viscose process is the lyocell production process, as it not only addresses the need for alternative feedstocks, but also the environmental issues surrounding toxic chemical use in the viscose fibre spinning process. Lyocell fibres are produced from the wood pulp of eucalyptus trees (White et al., 2005). A closed-loop production process with a non-toxic solvent is used, and this again links to what you read in Chapter 1.4 about the circular economy. Going into a bit of detail, in the lyocell process, the cellulose is directly dissolved in N-methylmorpholine-N-oxide, which is recovered and reused (Yang et al., 2021), and thus part of a circular process. Unlike the viscose method, all effluent from the lyocell process is non-hazardous, thus also reducing the social and environmental impacts that have previously been outlined. Similarly to cotton, lyocell can be used in denim fabrics for jeans and is noted for a softer, silky touch due to the fibre's ability to fibrillate and produce a peach skin effect – this may also be a key selling point when adverting the fibre to consumers. What becomes apparent here is that as managers, it is not only important to understand that decisions can be complex, but also why certain raw materials may be used (or not), depending on their production processes. Having this background knowledge can help inform decisions by choosing materials that align with a company's ethos.

We have previously focused on man-made fibres derived from plant-based materials. Yet man-made fibres can also be derived from synthetic polymers using petrochemicals such as polyethylene terephthalate in the production of polyester fibres. Other synthetic polymers are used in the production of nylon, elastane, and acrylic.

If you were to check your garments right now, you might see that an item of clothing contains polyester. This would not be surprising as polyester fibres dominate global fibre production, in 2019 accounting for 52 per cent of production ("Preferred Fiber & Materials Market Report 2020," n.d.). As the production process enables a variety of cross-sections to be produced, polyester fibres can be utilised for a variety of products and applications, and this may be one of many reasons why it accounts for the greatest proportion of global fibre production. Other reasons may be cost, the easy-care properties it provides, and some argue, good marketing. However, recently, microfibre pollution and a desire to move away from plastic-based products have shone the spotlight on the high use of polyester fibres in fashion products.

In the production of polyester fibres, polymer chips are melted and extruded into textile filaments which can be kept continuous or cut into short staple fibre lengths. The cross-section of these fibres can be altered depending on the desired properties and end use of the fibre. This fibre spinning process, melt spinning, can also be used in the production of nylon (polyamide) fibres. Polyester and nylon fibres can be co-extruded to produce bi-component fibres with different cross-section arrangements. The ability to co-extrude polymers with different properties offers designers and textile manufacturers the opportunity to produce innovative materials. One example is the Morphotex® fibre by Teijin Fibres. Inspired by the structural coloration achieved by the male Morpho butterfly, the core of the fibre is composed of 61 alternate layers of Nylon 6 and PET, covered in a polyester sheath. The multi-layer interference core of the fibre is responsible for the iridescent appearance achieved, mimicking that of the male Morpho butterfly. The appeal of producing such fibres that exploit structural colour as an alternative to traditional textile colourants is highlighted in Chapter 4.3 (Jones et al., 2020).

Polyester is also typically blended with cotton, in products that are typically referred to as polycotton. These products have the breathability of natural garments along with the easy-care properties (less ironing and quick drying) of synthetics. Elastane is also combined with other fibres to provide stretch and comfort. However, it cannot be used on its own and has to be blended with other fibres, which raises sustainability issues surrounding blended textiles, highlighting concerns for those considering end-of-life and recycling issues, discussed further in Chapter 4.2.

In summary, man-made fibres can overcome some of the challenges described in the previous section, yet they come with their own set of challenges. What you should take away from this section is that as managers, we need to carefully weigh all of our options and make an informed decision as to what type of raw material we want to use in our garments. Because this book focuses on sustainability, highlighting challenges with current fibre production is essential, as this may not only influence our choice, but also impact on us as an organisation.

4.1.3 21st-century developments

This section highlights how 20th-century production processes are used for 21st-century fibres and looks forward to new approaches in the industry. In particular, we will begin by looking at how manufacturing processes used in the production of man-made fibres can be harnessed to mechanically and chemically recycle waste. If you remember, in Part 1 we indicated that waste is a key issue, with only 1 per cent of materials currently being recycled (Close the Loop, 2020). By 2030, the target set by UN SDG 12 (shown in Table 4.1.1) is to substantially reduce waste generation through prevention, reduction, recycling, and reuse. Some of these aspects have been introduced in Parts 1 and 2. This highlights the need to consider the end of life of textile materials, and the use of virgin materials versus recycled in fashion products. It is also important to note that this links to the circular economy, which can be defined as "an approach to promote sustainable use of resources and address environmental challenges" (Navare et al., 2021), and the technical and biological cycle ("Cradle to Cradle – Rethinking Products – EPEA," n.d.).

Mechanical and chemical recycling

The polymer chip feedstock used in the production of polyester fibres can be substituted with PET waste. Using post-consumer flakes manufactured from PET bottles is one approach to recycling this waste. It can also be used to recycle other forms of plastic waste. Adidas recently launched a collection collaborating with Parely to create products made from fabrics containing recycled polyester created from marine plastic waste

("CREATIVITY VERSUS PLASTIC," n.d.). This global campaign and marketing strategy to raise awareness of plastic pollution in the oceans was not only used in advertising on social media platforms, but also as part of a global event: Run for the Oceans ("Ads We Like: Adidas knits together campaign promoting Parley for the Oceans collaboration | The Drum," n.d.).

In recent years, as polyester production has increased, the lifespan of polyester garments has decreased, leading to an increase in polyester textile waste (Guo et al., 2021a), which is often linked to the fast fashion movement. Expanding on recycling PET bottles through the polyester fibre spinning process, bottle manufacturing companies are working together with fashion brands to develop a system where a T-shirt can become a plastic bottle. This would make fashion brands a raw material provider, but would require collaboration throughout the supply chain. This stresses the need for industries to collaborate and work together to rethink and reuse these resources and raw materials. The chemical recycling process described has been created by Gr3n technology, aiming to make the linear supply chain more cyclical (Cornago et al., 2021). It has also been widely documented that chemically recycling polyester is preferable in terms of retaining mechanical properties and performance, (Häußler et al., 2021; Tournier et al., 2020). According to the research outputs from this project, bottle and garment producers need to work together in order for the quality of the new material to resemble that of virgin material.

As highlighted previously, waste is a major issue within the fashion industry, so how do we dispose of or reuse these garments? We have discussed a way of mechanically breaking down and reusing these materials, but we can also chemically recycle textile scraps. An example of this is the commercially available Refibra® fibre developed by Lenzing. It is produced using the lyocell production process, but a percentage of the feedstock is pre-consumer cotton waste combined with wood pulp.

To summarise this chapter, you should now be able to understand technical terms surrounding textile fibre origin, sourcing, cultivation, production, and properties. You should also be able to comprehend how the choice of fibre content in fashion items will contribute to the material footprint, and the response for this. Furthermore, you should be able to reflect in terms of sustainability on current and future origins, sourcing, cultivation, and production processes.

> ## 4.1.4 Case study task: alternative fibres for textile production – Bananatex®

Abstract

In the pursuit of exploring alternative textile fibre feedstocks, designers and researchers have found potential in plant-based substitutes. One such fibre is called Bananatex®, deriving from the abacá plant. This fibre is currently used in accessories such as shoes and handbags. This task will involve evaluating how plant-based alternatives, such as Bananatex, can be more suitable alternatives to synthetic fibres in an upcoming fashion collection.

Learning outcomes

After working through the case study, students will be able to:

- Categorise, define, and explain "traditional" textile fibre feedstocks.
- Evaluate plant-based alternatives to synthetic fibres for specific product categories.
- Reflect upon business perspectives of alternative textile fibre production processes based on the Bananatex® case study.
- Examine whether there is potential for further applications of the Bananatex® fibre in the fashion industry.

Introduction

The fibre content of our clothing and accessories can derive from a variety of resources, from the fruit and leaves of plants to minerals and fossil fuels. The cultivation, processing, and production of these raw materials require large amounts of resources, such as water and energy.

When examining global world fibre production, cotton and polyester make up the largest proportion, with PET fibres dominating the market (Guo et al., 2021b). The latter is partly attributed to the cost, properties, and variety of applications PET fibres have in the fashion industry. Due to their strength, weight, dyeability, easy-care, and performance properties (McIntyre, 2005), the applications of this man-made fibre range from leisurewear to sportswear, knitwear, and accessories.

There are plant-based man-made, manufactured fibres which do not derive from fossil fuels, but instead from natural polymers such as cellulose. We refer to these as regenerated cellulosic fibres. Examples of these fibres are viscose rayon and lyocell, the feedstock of which is wood pulp. Further examples are bamboo viscose, derived from the bamboo plant (Prakash, 2020), and cupro from cotton linters (Wojciechowska, 2021). Many designers and brands are always seeking new sustainable and more environmentally friendly alternatives because of the increasing interest from consumers to purchase natural, petroleum free products.

Whilst cotton dominates global natural fibre production, at around 81 per cent (Natural Fibres and the World Economy, July 2019), there are a small percentage of specialist natural fibres on the market, with abacá, sisal, and henequen accounting for 2.7 per cent. Abacá is typically used in the creation of ropes, pulp in paper production, and in the automotive industry (Townsend, 2020). This is attributed to the fibre's high cellulose content (Simbaña et al., 2020).

Bananatex® is a durable, waterproof fabric made purely from banana plants ("BANANATEX®," n.d.). Used in a variety of accessories from shoes to bags, one particular collection, "The New Minimal Collection", was developed in collaboration with "Swiss bag brand QWSTION, a Taiwanese yarn specialist and QWSTION's weaving partner based in Taipei, Taiwan" ("BANANATEX®," n.d.).

Cultivated in the Philippines, the process of obtaining the fibres from the abacá plant (shown in Figure 4.1.2) involves topping (cutting of the leaves), then tumbling the stalks, then leaving the leaves to decompose to release the fibres ("BANANATEX®," n.d.).

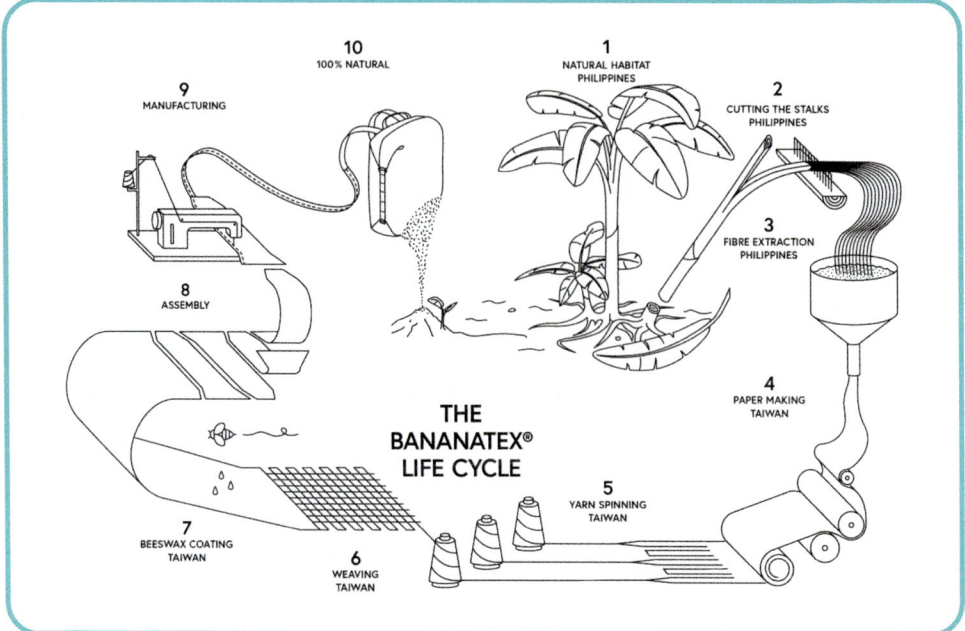

Figure 4.1.1   Bananatex® lifecycle

Figure 4.1.2   Bananatex® logo

These fibres then go through a "stripping" stage where they are combed to begin separating the fibres from one another, as shown in Figure 4.1.3. After this stage, they are bundled and stored at the warehouse of the farmer's cooperative, as shown in Figure 4.1.4 ("BANANATEX®," n.d.).

> Once the Abacá fibres have been transformed into yarn in a Taiwanese paper mill, the yarn – in the case of the All Black colourway – is coloured using the yarn dying method. This process is certified to the highest standard (Oeko-Tex® Standard 100) with the company also producing "The Natural White" which is accordingly not dyed ....
>
> ("BANANATEX®," n.d.)

Figures 4.1.5 and Figure 4.1.6 illustrates the fibre lifecycle process.

Figure 4.1.3   Fibres in storage

Figure 4.1.4   Bananatex® plant

Figure 4.1.5   Bananatex® stripping process 1

Figure 4.1.6   Bananatex® stripping Process 2 (© LAUSCHSICHT)

Questions

1. According to origin, compare and contrast the advantages and drawbacks of using synthetic and plant-based fibres in the fashion industry.
2. In your opinion, how could Bananatex® be used in further fashion applications?

Bibliography

Adu, C., Zhu, C., Jolly, M., Richardson, R.M., and Eichhorn, S.J. (2021) Continuous and sustainable cellulose filaments from ionic liquid dissolved paper sludge nanofibres, *Journal of Cleaner Production*, 280, 124503.

Afrin, T., Kanwar, R.K., Wang, X., and Tsuzuki, T. (2014) Properties of bamboo fibres produced using an environmentally benign method, *The Journal of The Textile Institute*, 105, 1293–1299.

Amutha, K. (2017) Sustainable chemical management and zero discharges, in Muthu, S.S. (ed) *Sustainable fibres and textiles*, Elsevier, Cambridge pp. 347–366.

An, Y., Miao, J., Fan, J., Li, M., Hu, M., Shao, M., and Shao, J. (2021) High-efficiency dispersant-free polyester dyeing using D5 non-aqueous medium, *Dyes and Pigments*, 190, 109303.

Anand, S.C., Brunnschweiler, D., Swarbrick, G., and Russell, S.J. (2007) *Handbook of nonwovens*, 201–297.

Annapoorani, S.G. (2017) Introduction to denim, in Muthu, S.S. *Sustainability in denim*, Elsevier, Cambridge, pp. 1–26.

Balineau, G. (2013) Disentangling the effects of fair trade on the quality of Malian cotton, *World Development*, 44, 241–255.

BANANATEX® (n.d.) (online): https://www.bananatex.info/, 10/6/2021.

Buljan, J., and Kral, I. (2019) *The framework for sustainable leather manufacture*. UNIDO (online): https://open.unido.org/api/documents/4670793/download/UNIDO-Publication-2015-4670793.

Campbell, J.R. (2008) Digital printing of textiles for improved apparel production, in Fairhurst, C. *Advances in apparel production*, Woodhead Publishing, Sawston, pp. 222–249.

Cao, X.L., Yan, Y.N., Zhou, F.Y., and Sun, S.P. (2020) Tailoring nanofiltration membranes for effective removing dye intermediates in complex dye-wastewater, *Journal of Membrane Science*, 595, 117476.

Champion, S.C., and Fearne, A.P. (2001) Alternative marketing systems for the apparel wool textile supply chain: filling the communication vacuum, *The International Food and Agribusiness Management Review*, 4, 237–256.

Close the lopp (2020) about this guide, CLose the loop (online): https://www.close-the-loop.be/en.

Colombi, B.L., de Cássia Siqueira Curto Valle, R., Borges Valle, J.A., and Andreaus, J. (2021) Advances in sustainable enzymatic scouring of cotton textiles: Evaluation of different post-treatments to improve fabric wettability, *Cleaner Engineering and Technology*, 4, 100160.

Cool wool (Knitwear) (n.d.a) The Woolmark Company (online): https://www.woolmark.com/industry/use-wool/product-innovations/cool-wool/, 13/7/2021.

Cool wool (Knitwear) (n.d.b) The Woolmark Company (online): https://www.woolmark.com/industry/use-wool/product-innovations/cool-wool/, 25/8/2021.

Cornago, S., Rovelli, D., Brondi, C., Crippa, M., Morico, B., Ballarino, A., and Dotelli, G. (2021) Stochastic consequential life cycle assessment of technology substitution in the case of a novel PET chemical recycling technology, *Journal of Cleaner Production*, 311, 127406.

Covington, T. (Anthony D.) (2009) *Tanning chemistry: the science of leather*, Royal Society of Chemistry, Cambridge, UK.

Cradle to cradle - rethinking products (n.d.). EPEA (online). https://epea.com/en/about-us/cradle-to-cradle, 25/8/2021.

CREATIVITY VERSUS PLASTIC (n.d.) adidas (online): https://www.adidas.co.uk/blog/361041-creativity-versus-plastic, 14/7/2021.

de Brito, M.P., Carbone, V., and Blanquart, C.M. (2008) Towards a sustainable fashion retail supply chain in Europe: organisation and performance, *International Journal of Production Economics*, 114, 534–553.

de Ferri, L., Tripodi, R., Martignon, A., Ferrari, E.S., Lagrutta-Diaz, A.C., Vallotto, D., and Pojana, G. (2018) Non-invasive study of natural dyes on historical textiles from the collection of Michelangelo Guggenheim, *Spectrochimica Acta Part A: Molecular and Biomolecular Spectroscopy*, 204, 548–567.

Dutta, P., Mahjebin, S., Sufian, M.A., Razaya Rabbi, Md., Chowdhury, S., and Imran, I.H. (2021) Study of auxetic beams under bending: A finite element approach, *Materials Today: Proceedings*, 9782–9787.

Eid, B.M., and Ibrahim, N.A. (2021) Recent developments in sustainable finishing of cellulosic textiles employing biotechnology, *Journal of Cleaner Production*, 284, 124701.

Elmogahzy, Y. (2019) *Structure and mechanics of textile fibre assemblies*, pp. 1–25.

El-Nagar, K., Sanad, S.H., Mohamed, A.S., and Ramadan, A. (2005) Mechanical

Properties and Stability to Light Exposure for Dyed Egyptian Cotton Fabrics with Natural and Synthetic Dyes. *Polymer-Plastics Technology and Engineering*, 44(7): 1269–1279.

Enes, E., and Kipöz, Ş. (2020) The role of fabric usage for minimization of cut-and-sew waste within the apparel production line: case of a summer dress, *Journal of Cleaner Production*, 248, 119221.

Engineered leather material for buses, trains & aircrafts (n.d.) ELeather (online): https://www.eleathergroup.com/, 22/7/2021.

Esteve-Turrillas, F.A., and de la Guardia, M. (2017) Environmental impact of recover cotton in textile industry, *Resources, Conservation and Recycling*, 116, 107–115.

European Linen - Le lin et le chanvre européen (n.d.) (online): http://news.europeanflax.com/lin/, 25/8/2021.

Fabrican spray-on fabric sprayable non-woven aerosol technology (n.d.) (online): https://www.fabricanltd.com/, 22/7/2021.

Flexible opals (n.d.) University of Cambridge (online): https://www.cam.ac.uk/research/news/flexible-opals, 17/9/2021.

Gomez-Campos, A., Vialle, C., Rouilly, A., Sablayrolles, C., and Hamelin, L. (2021) Flax fiber for technical textile: a life cycle inventory, *Journal of Cleaner Production*, 281, 125177.

Gordon, S., and Hsieh, Y. (2007) *Cotton: science and technology*, Woodhead Publishing in Textiles, Woodhead, Cambridge.

Goyal, A., and Nayak, R. (2020) *Sustainable technologies for fashion and textiles*, pp. 33–55.

GRS - Global Recycle Standard - Certifications (n.d.) (online): https://certifications.controlunion.com/en/certification-programs/certification-programs/grs-global-recycle-standard, 3/9/2021.

Guo, Z., Eriksson, M., Motte, H. de la, and Adolfsson, E. (2021) Circular recycling of polyester textile waste using a sustainable catalyst, *Journal of Cleaner Production*, 283, 124579.

Haight, J.M. (n.d.) Important terms, in *Safety professionals handbook - technical applications*, Volume II (2nd ed.), American Society of Safety Professionals., Park Ridge, IL.

Haji, A., and Naebe, M. (2020) Cleaner dyeing of textiles using plasma treatment and natural dyes: a review, *Journal of Cleaner Production*, 265, 121866.

Halimi, M.T., Hassen, M. ben, and Sakli, F. (2008) Cotton waste recycling: quantitative and qualitative assessment, *Resources, Conservation and Recycling*, 52, 785–791.

Harle, K.J., Howden, S.M., Hunt, L.P., and Dunlop, M. (2007) The potential impact of climate change on the Australian wool industry by 2030, *Agricultural Systems*, 93, 61–89.

Häußler, M., Eck, M., Rothauer, D., and Mecking, S. (2021) Closed-loop recycling of polyethylene-like materials, *Nature*, 590, 423.

Hildebrandt, J., Thrän, D., and Bezama, A. (2021) The circularity of potential bio-textile production routes: comparing life cycle impacts of bio-based materials used within the manufacturing of selected leather substitutes, *Journal of Cleaner Production*, 287, 125470.

How blue genes could green the cotton industry (n.d.) New Scientist (online): https://www.newscientist.com/article/mg13918841-000-how-blue-genes-could-green-the-cotton-industry/, 23/7/2021.

Iavicoli, S., Valenti, A., Barillari, C., Fortuna, G., Boccuni, V., Carnevale, F., Riva, M.A., Kang, S.K., and Tomassini, L. (2020) Making the difference in occupational health: three original and significant cases presented at ICOH Congresses in the 20th century, *Safety and Health at Work*, 11, 215–221.

I love linen | In celebration of linen in partners retailers (e) shop (n.d.) I love linen (online): https://ilovelinen.uk/, 25/8/2021.

Jones, C., Wortmann, F.J., Gleeson, H.F., and Yeates, S.G. (2020) Textile materials inspired by structural colour in nature, *RSC Advances*, 10, 24362–24367.

Jones, M., Gandia, A., John, S., and Bismarck, A. (2021) Leather-like material biofabrication using fungi, *Nature Sustainability*, 4, 9–16.

Kalia, S., Bhattacharya, A., Prajapati, S.K., and Malik, A. (2021) Utilization of starch effluent from a textile industry as a fungal growth supplement for enhanced α-amylase production for industrial application, *Chemosphere*, 279, 130554.

Khude, P. (2017) A review on energy management in textile industry, *Innovative Energy & Research*, 6: 169, https://doi.org/10.4172/2576-1463.1000169.

Kvavadze, E., Bar-Yosef, O., Belfer-Cohen, A., Boaretto, E., Jakeli, N., Matskevich, Z., and Meshvetiani, T. (2009) 30,000-year-old wild flax fibers, *Science* (American Association for the Advancement of Science), 325, 1359–1359.

Lambert, D.M., Croxton, K.L., Garcia-Dastugue, S.J., Knemeyer, M., and Rogers, D.S. (2006) *Supply chain management processes, partnerships, performance* (2nd ed.), Hartley Press Inc., Jacksonville, FL.

Langley, K.D., and Kim, Y.K. (2006) *Recycling in textiles: a volume in Woodhead Publishing Series in textiles*, pp. 137–164.

Long, D. (2018) Ads we like: adidas knits together campaign promoting Parley for the oceans collaboration, *The Drum* (online): https://www.thedrum.com/news/2018/07/09/ads-we-adidas-knits-together-campaign-promoting-parley-the-oceans-collaboration, 25/8/2021.

Malinga, L.N., and Laing, M.D. (2021) Efficacy of three biopesticides against cotton pests under field conditions in South Africa, *Crop Protection*, 145, 105578.

Materials - Organic cotton (n.d.) MUD Jeans (online): https://mudjeans.eu/pages/sustainability-materials, 3/9/2021.

McIntyre, J.E. (2005) *Synthetic fibres: nylon, polyester, acrylic, polyolefin*, Woodhead Publishing Limited series on fibres, CRC Press, Boca Raton.

Muthu, S.S. (2020) *Assessing the environmental impact of textiles and the clothing supply chain*, pp. 1–32.

Navare, K., Muys, B., Vrancken, K.C., and van Acker, K. (2021) Circular economy monitoring – How to make it apt for biological cycles?, *Resources, Conservation and Recycling*, 170, 105563.

Ozturk, E., Cinperi, N.C., and Kitis, M. (2020) Improving energy efficiency using the most appropriate techniques in an integrated woolen textile facility, *Journal of Cleaner Production*, 254, 120145.

Pattanayak, A.K. (2020) *Sustainable technologies for fashion and textiles*, pp. 57–72.

Picture this: fashion show uses spray-on clothing developed at Imperial (n.d.) Imperial College London (online): https://www.imperial.ac.uk/news/122898/picture-this-fashion-show-uses-spray-on/, 22/7/2021.

Prakash, C. (2020) Bamboo fibre, in Kozlowski, R., & Mackiewicz,-Talarczyk, M. (eds) *Handbook of natural fibres*, 2nd ed. Elsevier, Cambridge, pp. 219–229.

Ray, S.C. (2012a) *Fundamentals and advances in knitting technology*, Science Direct, Cambridge, pp. 293–315.

Ray, S.C. (2012b) *Fundamentals and advances in knitting technology*, pp. 44–55.

Reddy, R., Jiang, Q., Aramwit, P., and Reddy, N. (2021) Litter to leaf: the unexplored potential of silk byproducts, *Trends in Biotechnology*, 39, 706–718.

Redmore, N.A. (2020) *Woven textiles: principles, technologies and applications*, pp. 423–440.

Ricciardi, L., Chiarelli, D.D., Karatas, S., and Rulli, M.C. (2021) Water resources constraints in achieving silk production self-sufficiency in India, *Advances in Water Resources*, 154, 103962.

Rosenau, J.A. (2006) *Apparel merchandising: the line starts here*, 2nd ed., Fairchild, New York.

Salem Allafi, F.A., Hossain, M.S., Ab Kadir, M.O., Hakim Shaah, M.A., Lalung, J., and Ahmad, M.I. (2021) Waterless processing of sheep wool fiber in textile industry with supercritical CO_2: potential and challenges, *Journal of Cleaner Production*, 285, 124819.

Schier, F., Morland, C., Dieter, M., and Weimar, H. (2021) Estimating supply and demand elasticities of dissolving pulp, lignocellulose-based chemical derivatives and textile fibres in an emerging forest-based bioeconomy, *Forest Policy and Economics*, 126, 102422.

Schindler, W.D. (2004) *Chemical finishing of textiles*, Woodhead publishing in textiles, CRC, Boca Raton.

Shi, J., Huang, W., Han, H., and Xu, C. (2020) Review on treatment technology of salt wastewater in coal chemical industry of China, *Desalination*, 493, 114640.

Sieja, K., von Mach-Szczypiński, J., and von Mach-Szczypiński, J. (2018) Health effect of chronic exposure to carbon disulfide (CS2) on women employed in viscose industry, *Medycyna Pracy*, 69, 329–335.

Simbaña, E.A., Ordóñez, P.E., Ordóñez, Y.F., Guerrero, V.H., Mera, M.C., and Carvajal, E.A. (2020) Abaca: cultivation, obtaining fibre and potential uses, in Kozlowski, R., & Mackiewicz,-Talarczyk, M. (eds) *Handbook of natural fibres*, 2nd ed., Elsevier Inc., pp. 197–218.

Sinclair, R. (2015) *Textiles and fashion: materials, design and technology*, Woodhead Publishing series in textiles, Woodhead Publishing Limited in association with the Textile Institute, Cambridge, UK.

Sun, J., Sun, Y., and Zhu, Q.H. (2021) Breeding next-generation naturally colored cotton, *Trends in Plant Science*, 26, 539–542.

Sustainable Vegan Mycelium leather (n.d.) Mylo Unleather (online): https://www.mylo-unleather.com/, 22/7/2021.

Svensson, S.E., Ferreira, J.A., Hakkarainen, M., Adolfsson, K.H., and Zamani, A. (2021) Fungal textiles: wet spinning of fungal microfibers to produce monofilament yarns, *Sustainable Materials and Technologies*, 28, e00256.

Tan, X., Wang, F., Bi, Y., Su, Y., Li, Y., He, J., Yi, P., Yan, J., Bacquer, D. de, Braeckman, L., and Vanhoorne, M. (2001) The cross-sectional study of the health effects of occupational exposure to carbon disulfide in a Chinese viscose plant, *Environmental Toxicology*, 16, 377–382.

Tarazi, R., Jimenez, J.L.S., and Vaslin, M.F.S. (2019) Biotechnological solutions for major cotton (*Gossypium hirsutum*) pathogens and pests, *Biotechnology Research and Innovation*, 3, 19–26.

Tavangar, T., Karimi, M., Rezakazemi, M., Reddy, K.R., and Aminabhavi, T.M. (2020) Textile waste, dyes/inorganic salts separation of cerium oxide-loaded loose nanofiltration polyethersulfone membranes, *Chemical Engineering Journal*, 385, 123787.

THE 17 GOALS | Sustainable Development (n.d.) (online): https://sdgs.un.org/goals, 25/8/2021.

The Home of Harris Tweed® (n.d.) Harris Tweed Authority (online): https://www.harristweed.org/, 3/9/2021.

Top designers showcase Cool Wool at London Fashion Week (n.d.) (online): https://www.knittingindustry.com/top-designers-showcase-cool-wool-at-london-fashion-week/, 25/8/2021.

Tournier, V., Topham, C.M., Gilles, A., David, B., Folgoas, C., Moya-Leclair, E., Kamionka, E., Desrousseaux, M., Texier, H., Gavalda, S., Cot, M., Guémard, E., Dalibey, M., Nomme, J., Cioci, G., Barbe, S., Chateau, M., André, I., Duquesne, S., and Marty, A. (2020) An engineered PET depolymerase to break down and recycle plastic bottles, *Nature*, 580, 216–219.

Townsend, T. (2020) World natural fibre production and employment, in Kozlowski, R., & Mackiewicz,-Talarczyk, M. (eds) *Handbook of natural fibres*, 2nd ed., Elsevier Inc., pp. 15–36.

Ul-Islam, S., and Butola, B.S. (2019) *The impact and prospects of green chemistry for textile technology*, The Textile Institute book series, Woodhead Publishing, Duxford.

Unit, B. (2020) Aichi Biodiversity Targets, CBD (online): https://www.cbd.int/sp/targets/, 20/05/2022.

Vidaurre-Arbizu, M., Pérez-Bou, S., Zuazua-Ros, A., and Martín-Gómez, C. (2021) From the leather industry to building sector: exploration of potential applications of discarded solid wastes, *Journal of Cleaner Production*, 291, 125960.

White, P., Hayhurst, M., Taylor, J., and Slater, A. (2005) *Biodegradable and sustainable fibres* (A Volume in Woodhead Publishing Series in Textiles), pp. 157–190.

Wilson, J. (2012) *Woven textiles: principles, technologies and applications*, pp. 163–204.

Wojciechowska, P. (2021) Fibres and textiles in the circular economy, in Mondal, I.H. (ed.), *Fundamentals of natural fibres and textiles*, Woodhead Publishing, Swaston, UK, pp. 691–717.

Xu, L., Fang, H., Deng, X., Ying, J., Lv, W., Shi, Y., Zhou, G., and Zhou, Y. (2020) Biochar application increased ecosystem carbon sequestration capacity in a Moso bamboo forest, *Forest Ecology and Management*, 475, 118447.

Yan, S., Jones, C., Henninger, C.E., and McCormick, H. (2020) Textile industry insights towards impact of regenerated cellulosic and synthetic fibres on microfibre pollution, in Muthu, S.S., & Gardetti, M.A. (eds.) *Sustainability in the textile and apparel industry*, Springer, Chams, pp. 157–172.

Yang, G., Yang, Y., Zhang, H., and Shao, H. (2021) Influences of stabilizers on lyocell spinning dope and fiber properties, *Polymer Testing*, 99, 107228.

Yang, Y., He, W., Chen, F., and Wang, L. (2020) Water footprint assessment of silk apparel

in China, *Journal of Cleaner Production*, 260, 121050.

Zaw, A.K., Myat, A.M., Thandar, M., Htun, Y.M., Aung, T.H., Tun, K.M., and Han, Z.M. (2020) Assessment of noise exposure and hearing loss among workers in textile mill (Thamine), Myanmar: a cross-sectional study, *Safety and Health at Work*, 11, 199–206.

Zhang, X., Kong, X., Zhou, R., Zhang, J., Wang, L., and Wang, Q. (2020) Harnessing perennial and indeterminant growth habits for ratoon cotton (Gossypium spp.) cropping, *Ecosystem Health & Sustainability*, 6(1).

Zhang, X., Du, X., Ke, Y., Zhang, Y.-G., and Xu, Z.-K. (2021) Loose nanofiltration membranes with assembled antifouling surfaces of organophosphonic acid/Fe(III) for managing textile dyeing effluent, *Journal of Membrane Science*, 640, 119821.

Zhao, M., Zhou, Y., Meng, J., Zheng, H., Cai, Y., Shan, Y., Guan, D., and Yang, Z. (2021) Virtual carbon and water flows embodied in global fashion trade - a case study of denim products, *Journal of Cleaner Production*, 303, 127080.

ZOA :Modern Meadow (n.d.) (online): https://www.modernmeadow.com/zoa, 22/7/2021.

4.2 Fabric creation

Learning outcomes

1. To critically examine and understand key technical terminology surrounding woven, knitted, nonwoven, and leather production and properties.
2. To understand the significant role these fabrics play in the material footprint of fashion garments, reflecting on current and future creation and production.
3. To critically investigate the significance of sustainable challenges associated with material innovations in the 21st century.

In Chapter 4.1, we referred to a plain white T-shirt as an example of how we need to consider the raw materials used, how they are obtained, and considerations in terms of sustainability. This chapter focuses on creating fabrics and what considerations need to be taken into account when creating them.

Our fashion items are cut and sewn, or fully fashioned, from fabrics that are woven, knitted, nonwoven, or leather. The creation of these materials requires a wealth of machinery, expertise, and resources across the global supply chain. Just as a reminder, in Chapter 1.1, we looked at a simplified version of the supply chain (see Figure 4.2.1). In this part of the book, we will now move from the first stage (raw materials) to explore the second (spinning) and third stage (weaving/knitting).

By now, you should be aware that the manufacturing process of garments is resource-heavy and time-consuming, and involves multiple stages that all need to be monitored closely with the help of different departments and teams. For example, buyers and merchandisers may monitor the progress through the critical path, which outlines where in the process the product is and whether all the deadlines are being adhered to (Boardman et al., 2020). Buyers and merchandisers have to surrender full control of their product range at this stage, which brings with it many risks, as they have to trust their suppliers to conduct the mass-production of garments in a timely and ethical manner. Here again, we can think back to Chapter 1.1, where we discussed stakeholders, which includes suppliers. Building strong relationships with stakeholders is important, as trust, reliability, and transparency are vital within the manufacturing process.

> **Stakeholder** – an entity that has a vested interest (stake) in an organisation and forms a mutually dependent relationship with this organisation.

DOI: 10.4324/9781003097846-18

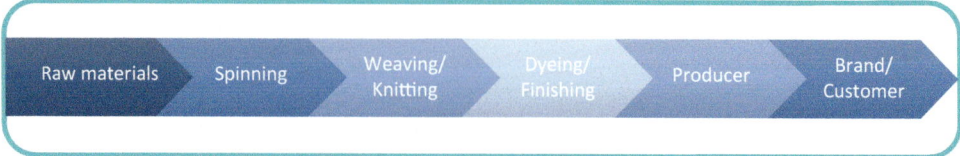

Figure 4.2.1   Simplified version of a linear supply chain

The demand for lower-cost production led traditional spinning and weaving industries in Europe to relocate to the Far East. One of the reasons for this is cost, in that countries outside Europe usually have lower labour costs, thus companies seek to either off-shore or near-shore. Yet moving outside a country and relocating to another one has implications. For example, within Europe, we have seen a decline in employment in traditional spinning and weaving industries, which has social implications for workers across the apparel pipeline (de Brito et al., 2008). But not only that, it also means that the geographical distance between manufacturers and retailers increases, which can have implications for lead times, and may impact on the speed from designing a product to getting it on the shop floor.

> **Nearshoring** – producing products in neighbouring countries that may have lower wages compared to the home country.
> **Offshoring** – producing products in countries that are geographically more distant.

Complexities on the supply chain may also have implications for the actual price consumers need to pay, because companies need to gain a financial profit, as otherwise they may not be able to stay in business. If you think back to factors in the external environment that can be analysed through the PEST(EL) framework, you may notice that, for example, having to pay import tax may increase the price of garments. Thus, managers need to carefully review decisions on a regular basis to ensure they are still getting the best deal.

Pricing is a very interesting aspect, as managers need to ensure that what we charge for, for example, a T-shirt, covers all the costs involved, from designing the product to gaining the raw materials, transportation costs, potential taxes, salaries, or running costs (e.g., rent, electricity), to name but a few. Yet how we come up with different pricing strategies may not be as obvious for consumers, as they are often unaware of the complexities of the manufacturing process. There is a difference between the actual cost of a product versus how much it costs to manufacture a product versus how much it is worth. What we mean here is that the manufacturing cost entails how much we as a company need to pay to make a product, whilst the actual cost also incorporates any expenses that need be paid in conducting the business. Worth, on the other hand, is a trickier aspect, as it can be quite subjective.

To provide a concrete example, Figure 4.2.2 illustrates the costs of a T-shirt (Purnaa, 2017). The key takeaway message from this infographic is the fact that 65 per cent of the costs of the T-shirt are incurred at the materials and finishing stage. This highlights how important it is to understand the resources that are being utilised in the garment production process, and also how time-consuming the actual garment manufacturing

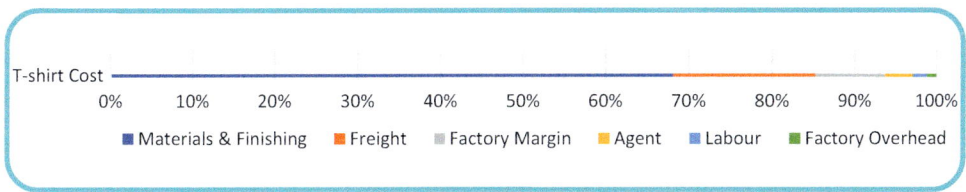

Figure 4.2.2   Percentages of cost for a T-shirt (adapted from Purnaa, 2017)

process is. This becomes even more complex when further considering the sustainability impacts of raw materials, as well as textile manufacturing.

Because materials and finishing account for approximately 65 per cent of the total cost of creating a T-shirt, this chapter starts by providing a brief introduction to how fabrics are created in the fashion industry. We then highlight potential challenges with textile manufacturing, such as pre- and post-consumer waste, which have various implications for sustainability (Enes and Kipöz, 2020). You may remember from Chapter 1.4 that "less than 1% of materials used to make clothing is currently recycled to make new clothing" (Fields, 2021). As such, waste becomes a new resource that can be quite lucrative. According to the Ellen MacArthur foundation (EMF, 2017), 70 per cent of our clothing (post-consumer) either ends up in landfill or is incinerated, with some garments being donated, and thus entering a different type of "waste stream". Furthermore, this is only one type of waste, and does not consider pre-consumer waste and how this is dealt with.

Various companies have started to invest more in recycling practices by using more recycled content in their collections. This brings a new opportunity, namely the use of certifications such as the GRS (Global Recycle Standard), which can increase trust in sourcing recycled content from suppliers and "to verify responsible social, environmental, and chemical practices in their production" (ControlUnion, 2021). The chapter will conclude by exploring how fabric waste is being re-purposed back into fabric creations and other innovative materials focusing on sustainability.

4.2.1 Preparation of raw materials

In Chapter 4.1, we introduced a variety of fibres (natural or man-made) which can be either used to create nonwoven fabrics, or can be spun (twisted) into yarns, which are then woven or knitted into fabrics. In some circumstances, especially when we think about natural materials that are animal-based, we can subject raw materials to various treatments to transform them into a material suitable for textile use. An example of this is leather.

Focusing on spinning first, both natural and man-made fibres can be spun into yarns by using machinery appropriate to the fibre length and type, and the desired properties of the yarn. Here we need to think about what we are using the yarn for: what are the performance properties we want from the yarn? Does it need to be able to stretch, or does it need to tolerate a lot of tension? Depending on what it is we want to do with the yarn and the subsequent fabric, we may need to spin it in a different manner. This leads us nicely to the next point: there are a variety of ways to spin these yarns, including ring, rotor, and air-jet spinning (Goyal and Nayak, 2020). The majority of these production processes ensure that homogenous yarns are produced in terms of colour or appearance, with a suitable level of twist for either knitting or weaving. "Twist" here refers to how fibres/yarns are bound together to form a continuous strand (thread), which can be achieved through spinning. Yet it must be highlighted that homogeneity may not always be a desirable outcome. Thus, it may not be surprising that there are production processes that also deliberately create uneven finishes, curls, and varieties of textures and colours. These are often referred to as fancy yarns.

> **Twist** – how fibres/yarns are bound together to form a continuous strand (thread), which can be achieved through spinning.

An interesting fact is that ring spinning is one of the oldest methods to create yarn, and to date produces the finest yarn that can be used for knitted and woven fabrics (Cotton Incorporate, 2021). Although it produces one-of-a-kind, soft yarn, one of the key drawbacks of this method is the fact that it needs an additional winding step, which can increase cost. On the other hand, rotor spinning can produce "up to 10 times the production per spindle" when compared to ring spinning (Cotton Incorporate, 2021), and thus is more cost-efficient as it does not require the winding step. Rotor-spun yarn has found its niche within denim fabric production (Elmogahzy, 2019).

Linking back to sustainability and an earlier point that has been made about waste and recycling, among the key questions are where do we currently see the majority of waste being generated, and how can be integrate recycling into the process? One area where we see a lot of waste happening is in blowrooms. Blowrooms are a key part in textile manufacturing, as they contain machinery to:

- Open the bales of natural fibre, which are made into smaller pieces.
- Cleanse fibres of any impurities and remove dust.
- Blend fibres, where required.
- Feed carding machines.
- Recycle waste (Texcoms, 2019).

Because raw materials are manipulated, it is not surprising that small fibres and particles may stay behind, which can be collected and made into yarns (Halimi et al., 2008). Research has started to investigate how yarn production processes could be reverse-engineered to be used to recycle fibres from pre- and post-consumer waste.

Although textile recycling may not yet be commonplace, it is increasingly gaining centre-stage, with supranational organisations highlighting its importance, such as through UN SDG 12 (see Table 4.2.1)

In the past, cotton waste has been used to produce fibres through mechanical shredding (Esteve-Turrillas and de la Guardia, 2017). A key advantage here is that it makes use of already-existing resources, which has a key benefit for the environment. Current challenges with reusing raw materials are linked to the quality and performance of these recycled yarns, which are dependent on the fabric structure of the cotton waste (e.g., woven or knitted) and the finishing processes applied to the textile. A company

Table 4.2.1   Textile Recycling and SDG 12

UN SDG	Title	Targets	Indicators	Implications/ challenges for fashion industry
12	Responsible Consumption and Production	12.5 – By 2030, substantially reduce waste generation through prevention, reduction, recycling and reuse	• National recycling rate, tons of material recycled	• Pressure to consider end-of-life of garments and to design cyclically, rather than linear production and consumption processes • Required to consider or include recycled materials and reduction of waste

that has successfully implemented a closed-loop recycling process is MUD Jeans, which uses 40 per cent GRS-certified, post-consumer, recycled cotton content in its jeans. It highlights its preference for using recycled post-consumer denim in its products, which is sourced from its own garments (MUD Jeans, 2021). Reusing predominantly its own denim jeans to make its post-consumer waste denim yarn brings advantages, as it can be sure that its material is "made from environmentally friendly materials; namely recycled and organic cotton" (MUD Jeans, 2021). This links back to Chapter 1.4, where we discussed circular design approaches.

In summary, we can see that sustainability issues emerge not only when looking at the raw materials, but are also relevant in the processes of creating yarns which are used to create textiles. Linking back to the core message of this book, sustainability plays a key role throughout the entirety of the production and manufacturing process. This implies that if waste cannot be avoided in any of the steps along the supply chain, processes should be in place to avoid these and make use of any waste as a new resource. Understanding where waste can be created and how is vital for any manager, as it can support the decision-making process and encourage thinking about solutions for waste prevention.

4.2.2 Woven fabrics

Whilst we may be familiar with certain woven fabrics used extensively in a variety of fashion products, we may not understand how these fabrics are constructed and the production processes involved. It can therefore be difficult to understand issues surrounding sustainable production.

Denim, for example, is a woven fabric used in the production of jeans. When denim jeans were first introduced, they were predominantly marketed as workwear for males (Levi Strauss, 2019). One of the key characteristics of denim fabric is that it not only has a particular method of construction, which produces a fabric with a hardwearing properties and appearance; but also has a particular method of colouration to achieve the "indigo" blue mentioned in the next section of this chapter. This particular method of dyeing enables a distressed look to be achieved in denim fabric.

Further examples of woven fabrics that we may be more familiar with are tartan and tweed. Tartan and tweed are created through the interlacing of coloured or fancy yarns combined with specific woven structures. From the previous section, you may remember that not all yarns are created to be homogenous, but rather some are "fancy", which creates a distinctive look and feel, as seen in tartan and tweed garments. A commonality between denim, tartan, and tweed is the fact that they are all typically heavyweight fabrics used for trousers, suiting, and jackets. Tweed and tartan are also fabrics associated with a specific global location, Scotland, as they are a traditional textile still produced in their country of origin and used by various fashion houses, such as Chanel and Vivienne Westwood.

Batch-produced fabrics containing the trademarked Harris Tweed® certification have been produced in mills and homes of islanders in the Scottish Outer Hebrides (Redmore, 2020; Harris Tweed Authority, 2021); by contrast, 50 per cent of the world's denim is mass-produced in China, India, Pakistan, Turkey, and Bangladesh (Annapoorani, 2017; Zhao et al., 2021). Linking back to a point made earlier in this chapter, production process and location not only play a role in the cost of the overall garment, but also the environmental cost, which we will now expand on. When considering the apparel pipeline, it is considered essential to determine how readily available the materials are in terms of quality and quantity in order to ensure the creation of the garment is successful (Rosenau, 2006).

All woven fabrics are created using a piece of machinery called a loom (see Figure 4.2.3). This machine is used to interlace the yarns in the construction of a variety

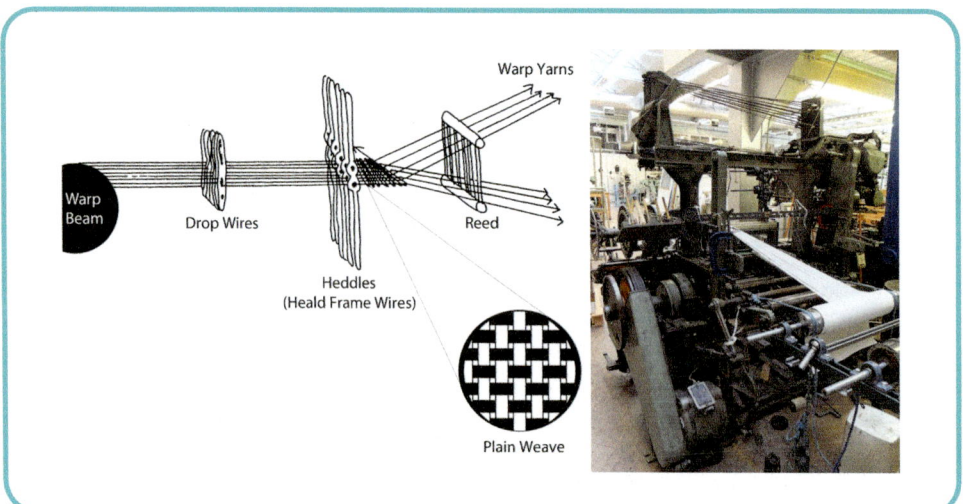

Figure 4.2.3   A loom, showing woven structure (Jones, 2016)

of woven textiles. The yarns running vertically direction in loom are warp yarns, and those running horizontally are weft yarns. Shafts can be used in the loom to raise and lower specific warp threads, and are selected manually or using an electronic shedding mechanism. The type of shedding mechanism used is dependent on how many shafts are required to create the design of the fabric. In this way, a variety of woven fabrics can be created with different patterns, aesthetics, and performance properties, which can be lightweight through to heavyweight. Some typical examples include, but are by no means limited to, plain, twill, and satin fabrics, which we will discuss later in this chapter in the context of sustainability.

The rapid mechanical process of raising and lowering the heddle frames within the loom and the insertion of the weft generate a high level of noise. As a result, workers in textile mills in developing countries are recorded to have suffered occupational hearing loss, which is of great concern in terms of social sustainability and highlighted in UN SDG 3, aiming to ensure healthy lives and promote well-being for people of all ages (Zaw et al., 2020). To withstand the mechanical process of weaving, warp yarns are treated with size to provide strength. The type of size used is dependent on the fibre type. For cotton, for example, we can use starch. To avoid interfering with finishing processes later in the production line, the size is removed after weaving. The environmental implications of the wet processes (fabric pre-treatments, dyeing, etc.) involved in the weaving process are discussed in Chapter 4.3. Here, it is important to note that research has been carried out to reduce the amount of energy (usually electricity) consumed in this part of the production process. Automated looms require energy to operate the shafts as well as for weft insertion. Weft insertion can be carried out using compressed air or water jets, for example. In a recent study, whilst electricity consumption takes place at all parts of the textile production process, it is at its highest at the weaving and spinning stage, as it is used to operate compressors, motors, and other parts of the looms (Khude, 2017; Ozturk et al., 2020).

One of the reasons why we are providing a lot of technical detail here is to convey the complexity of the manufacturing process. If we think of the cost of a T-shirt, we may no longer be surprised that the materials and finishing stages are among the most cost-intensive. If we think of actual woven structures, such as denim jeans, tartan, or tweed fabrics, we may now understand that not only is the creation process of these fabrics time-consuming, but different techniques will provide us with different fabrics, whether lightweight or heavyweight.

Plain woven fabrics have the simplest construction, with the highest amount of interlacing points of all woven structures. Poplin, which is typically used in the creation of shirts, is an example of a plain weave fabric. By introducing coloured yarns in the warp and weft, decorative effects can be achieved, such as checks and stripes, (Wilson, 2012). Gingham is another example of a plain woven fabric, but with the appearance of checks due to the use of coloured warp and weft threads.

Twill woven fabrics have a continuous diagonal line appearance due to the warp yarns being raised in relation to the weft. These fabrics are hard-wearing, the most commonly known example being denim. In the creation of denim fabrics, blue warp threads are interlaced with white weft threads. The process of dyeing these blue warp threads is discussed in a case study in Chapter 4.3.

Satin or sateen woven fabrics can be described as having warp (satin) or weft (sateen) facing, and are commonly associated with a lustrous sheen appearance. Synthetic and natural fibres can be used in these fabrics to produce silky, shiny fabrics for fashion products.

With certain shedding mechanisms, such as dobby and jacquard, a greater number of threads can be raised and lowered, therefore a variety of woven structures can be created using a punchcard mechanism or digitally using CAD software.

Chapter 4.1 highlighted that we tend to no longer source raw materials locally, but rather globally. Thus, it may not be surprising that this leads to environmental sustainability challenges in transportation. With raw materials being produced quite literally anywhere in the world, transportation costs may be quite high, depending on the geographic distance between the supplier and the weaving shed (Muthu, 2020b). If we use the PEST(EL) framework to consider this first segment of *the soft goods chain* (the textile segment), we can begin to see issues beyond environmental aspects that could be associated with the global nature of the apparel pipeline (see Boardman et al., 2020):

1. Political issues, which can impact quotas and tariffs, or working relationships between countries.
2. Economic issues, such as a financial crisis, which may act as a barrier to people making purchases.
3. Sociocultural issues, such as ageing populations.
4. Technological issues, which may emerge as technology evolves.
5. Environmental issues, such as droughts or floods, which may be linked to climate change and may affect growth of crops.
6. Legal aspects, such as labour law regulations and general working conditions.

It is important to note that these issues are not limited to woven structures: they relate to all the materials discussed in this part of the book.

Task

1. Using the PEST(EL) framework, consider what current challenges fashion organisations might face based on their macro environment when focusing on the textile element of the apparel pipeline.

4.2.3 Knitted fabrics

When we think of woven fabrics, we may think of silky, satin fabrics for luxury garments, or we may think of hard-wearing, heavyweight fabrics such as denim. With knitted fabrics and garments, we perhaps associate these more with stretch in garments such as leggings and T-shirts like the one mentioned earlier in this chapter. We may also think of warm, chunky winter knitwear for jumpers and cardigans. But how are these properties achieved, and do we use the same machinery as with woven fabrics?

In contrast to woven fabrics, knitted fabrics are be created by the *interlooping* of yarn. Multiple yarns can be used to provide various aesthetic effects or performance properties. Each loop is referred to as a stitch. Similarly to woven fabrics, there are technical terms used to describe the different directions of the knitted fabric, with horizontal stitches referred to as a course, and vertical ones as wales.

The construction of these fabrics involves the use of knitting needles, for both hand and machine knitting. Mass-production of knitted garments and fabrics involves the use of electronic knitting machines, with the use of computer-aided design (CAD) and computer-aided manufacturing (CAM) to aid the designing process. Both types of machines use latch knitting needles, and the size of these needles and the gauges of the machines depend on how fine the yarns being used are. Unlike woven fabrics, it is possible to knit parts of garments and carry out shaping on the knitting machine, which minimises waste in comparison to the traditional cutting and then sewing of fabric into a garment. You may remember that we previously discussed zero waste fashion, and complete garment knitting (also referred to as seamless knitting) is part of zero waste fashion, minimising garment make-up times, and eliminating fabric lay planning, cutting, and sewing (Ray, 2012a). As a result, knitting technology is regarded as more eco-friendly, as the yarns do not require the application and removal of size and other wet processes, so less energy and water are consumed than in the production of woven fabrics (Pattanayak, 2020).

> **Just-in-time manufacturing** – the process of carefully calculating when products are needed, only producing what is demanded by customers, reducing waste in terms of overproduction, for example, but also monetary waste from holding stock inventory.

In terms of the managerial implications of using complete garment knitting, we may think of just-in-time manufacturing. Just-in-time manufacturing combined with complete garment knitting potentially offer an opportunity for manufacturers to reduce waste. As these knitting machines use CAD/CAM software, they could also be combined with sizing and shaping systems through computer software and online platforms. Unmade, previously known as Knyttan, "is building a 'curated customisation' platform to reinvent knitwear" (Kansara, 2015). Customers can "choose between colours, patterns, and cuts – and then, they can take things a step further by inverting prints, adjusting the pattern, and altering the line weights" (Darwin, 2015). This just-in-time approach of mass-customising knitwear that can be made on demand is revolutionary in the way that it actively designs out waste in the manufacturing process. Only garments that are actually wanted are produced, which addresses the challenge of overproduction. At the same time, it avoids the issue of storage costs, as products are only produced when they are needed. Companies such as Unmade can also react more rapidly to customer demand by simply changing the patterns and colours they are offering, thereby moving with trends.

Similarly to woven fabrics, a variety of structures can be created on knitting machines. They can be separated into two categories: warp and weft knitted fabrics. As weft knitted fabrics are predominantly used in the mass production of apparel, they are the examples focused on in this book. Basic weft knitted structures for apparel include, but are not limited to, plain, rib, interlock, and purl (Ray, 2012b). When observing knitted garments, rib structures, for example, can be located at the cuffs and necks of garments to provide stretch. Heavy, chunky yarns can be used to create winter knitwear, as can fine cotton yarns for jerseys and T-shirts and fine synthetic nylon yarns for stockings.

4.2.4 Nonwoven fabrics

As previously mentioned, not all fibres are spun into yarns and then used to construct woven and knitted fabrics or garments. Nonwoven fabrics are converted straight from fibres into a web, and do not involve the creation of yarns or previously discussed construction methods. They are produced in a two-step process: web formation and web bonding. Fibres can be bonded through the use of hydroentanglement and needle felting. Furthermore, with man-made fibres such as thermoplastic synthetic fibres, they can be heat set.

It may not be apparent where these materials are used in fashion garments. This is because they are typically "hidden". Interlinings are nonwoven fabrics used to reinforce parts of fashion garments, sometimes with the aid of an adhesive. For example, they can be placed between the lining of a jacket and the outer fabric to reinforce areas and provide additional strength. For this reason, the consumer may not be aware that these materials have been used, but they play important roles in the performance and quality of the product.

There are other examples of nonwoven materials used in the fashion industry. The natural felting properties of wool can be harnessed in the creation of "boiled wool" fabrics for coats and other winter garments using processes such as needle punching. In this process, needles are used to interlock fibres to create the nonwoven web. This is achieved with thousands of barbed felting needles repeatedly passing into and out of the web (Anand et al., 2007). This process has gained interest from researchers adopting this technology to recycle textile fibres into new textile materials (Langley and Kim, 2006).

There are other processes to produce nonwoven fabrics, through the use of hydroentanglement, for example, where water is fired from jets, causing the fibres to intermingle, and the water is then recycled (Anand et al., 2007). From an environmental perspective, the appeal from researchers to adopt textile production processes that eliminate garment make-up times has expanded into nonwovens. Featured in London Fashion Week in 2010, Professor Paul Luckham and Spanish designer Dr Manel Torres showcased Fabrican©. The collection featured nonwoven white fabrics which had been sprayed straight from the bottle on to the wearer ("Fabrican Spray-on fabric sprayable non-woven aerosol technology," n.d.; "Picture This: Fashion show uses spray-on clothing developed at Imperial|Imperial News|Imperial College London," n.d.). When considering the plain white T-shirt mentioned at the beginning of this chapter, Fabrican© is an example of a garment being created without all the textile manufacturing processes mentioned previously, and further garment production processes such as cutting and sewing.

Whether this will be mainstream in the future is unclear, but what is apparent is that we can see a lot of innovation happening in the fashion industry to address both the environmental and social aspects of sustainability. Understanding different process and how they work is vital, as it can provide an insight into how things are costed, as well as how much we as organisations may need to invest to operationalise these ideas.

4.2.4.1 Leather

Chapter 4.1 discussed how natural fibres can be obtained from the fleeces and cocoons of animals, and these fibres can then be spun into yarns which are used to construct woven or knitted fabrics. There are other textile materials that are obtained from animals. Leather is made from the hides of large animals such as cattle, and skins of animals such as sheep (Covington, 2009). The rearing, processing, and use of leather in the fashion industry raises ethical, environmental, and social issues – most notably because the raw material is obtained from animals and is a by-product of the meat industry. As mentioned in Chapter 4.1, the use of raw materials associated with agriculture will not only be impacted by climate change, but may play a contributary role to CO_2 emissions. Environmental concerns are also raised by the process of converting the putrescible organic material into a stable textile through a process called tanning, which involves the use of chromium(III) salts (Covington, 2009). The need to prevent or reduce polluting emissions throughout the entire leather-making process is highlighted in the publication of the Framework for Sustainable Leather Manufacture by the United Nations Industrial Development Organisation (UNIDO) (Buljan and Kral, 2019). Along with presenting cleaner methods and alternatives, the authors of the report note that strict process monitoring, control, and minor modifications to traditional and conventional practices can achieve a decrease in pollutants (Buljan and Kral, 2019)

Along with improvements in the production process, researchers and brands are exploring ways of reusing leather and how it can be used or produced. Researchers have explored the reuse of solid production waste. Examples include the use of leather shavings for acoustic panels (Vidaurre-Arbizu et al., 2021) and leather scraps repurposed into a technical nonwoven material called ELeather, used in buses, trains, and aircraft ("Engineered Leather Material for Buses, Trains & Aircrafts | Eleather," n.d.).

Other researchers are exploring alleviating the agricultural concerns raised at the beginning of this chapter by growing leather-like materials in laboratories. These include, but are not limited to, fungi-derived and collagen alternatives. In the case of fungi-derived alternatives, researchers have found ways to upcycle agricultural and forestry by-products through a natural and carbon-neutral fungal growth process to produce leather-like materials (Jones et al., 2021). The wet spinning process, a production process associated with traditional textile fibres such as viscose and lyocell, is being used to create monofilaments from fungi-based hydrogels (Svensson et al., 2021). These monofilaments can then be used to create leather-like materials.

Brands such as Modern Meadow are aiming to produce commercially viable leather-like alternatives using proteins and bio-based polymers in bio-fabrication methods ("ZOA : Modern Meadow," n.d.). Another brand, Bolt Threads, has produced a leather-like alternative called Mylo produced from mycelium ("Mylo Unleather | Sustainable Vegan Mycelium Leather," n.d.).

However, researchers have pointed out that these materials can cause negative environmental impacts related to land-use change and intensification, to water use, and to energy use in polymer manufacturing (Hildebrandt et al., 2021). Thus, whilst trying to present a solution, these researchers are highlighting other potential problems to be considered.

To summarise this chapter, you should now be able to understand how fabrics are created in the fashion industry, specifically woven, knitted, nonwoven, and leather textile materials. You should also be able to comprehend how the choice of fabric, use, and waste are important considerations in terms of sustainability. You also should have an understanding of new approaches to how fabric waste is being re-purposed back into fabric creations and other innovative materials focusing on sustainability.

4.2.4.2 Case study task: the knitted jumper that used to be a pair of woven jeans – innovations in fabric construction by We Are Knitters

Abstract

With only 10 per cent of clothing waste in Europe recycled and 8 per cent reused (Ütebay et al., 2020), there have been calls for dramatic changes in the industry (WRAP, 2020). This case study utilises the **3R framework** (reuse, recycle, reduce) to illustrate how pre-consumer waste (e.g., in cotton jersey T-shirt fabrics) and post-consumer waste (in woven denim fabrics) could be eliminated through:

A. The **reuse** of pre-consumer waste (knitted T-shirt jersey).
B. The **recycling** of post-consumer waste (woven denim fabric) into skeins.
C. How using these yarns to knit their own clothes encourages consumers to **reduce** consumption.

The task therefore involves evaluating the 3R framework to reduce, reuse, and recycle against the (a), (b), and (c) examples provided in the We Are Knitters (WAK) case study.

Learning outcomes

After working through the case study, you will be able to:

- Define and explain different approaches to addressing textile waste through **reuse** and **recycling**.
- Understand the impact of using these reused and recycled materials to **reduce** consumption and promote engaging in slow fashion.
- Reflect upon a specific business model, such as the 3R framework, in context against the WAK case study.

Introduction

Waste associated with the textile and fashion industry can be categorised as pre- and post-consumer waste (see also Section 1.4.4.1, "Zero Waste Fashion"). This waste can be **recycled** chemically or mechanically. Chemical recycling involves the use of chemicals to dissolve and break down polymer chains into their monomers for recycling. On the other hand, mechanical recycling requires the use of machinery to physically separate, shred, and break down the textile fibres. For this case study, we will focus on the mechanical recycling process, which can be used to recycle woven fabrics used in jeans, often referred to as denim. Mechanical denim recycling can be used in both the pre- and post-consumer waste stages, where the fabric is shredded (Luiken and Bouwhuis, 2015). Once the mechanical recycling process is complete, we are left with shorter fibres, which is one of the reasons why virgin materials are added to impart strength. According to Luiken and Bouwhuis (2015), it is easier to construct knitted garments than woven fabrics from recycled denim yarns, especially when the yarn is plied with further yarns.

Pre- and post-consumer waste can also be addressed through **reuse**. In the context of this case study, we will focus on T-shirt yarn. In the pre-consumer waste phase, fabric knitted on a circular knitting machine for T-shirts can be reused and cut into yarns that are suitable for knitting items for interiors (rugs, baskets, etc.); similarly, we, as consumers, can also cut down our own T-shirts that may have reached their end-of-life and create our own yarns.

We Are Knitters

This Spain-based company provides consumers with knitting kits which include all the items needed to produce the garments they have chosen online, (knitting instructions, yarns, knitting materials, etc.). It also provides consumers with online video tutorials and guides to help support them while creating their knitted item. Consumers can choose from a range of yarns according to colour, count, and fibre content.

(c) Recycle

Within the collection of yarns available to the consumer, We Are Knitters offers "recycled yarn made from 95% cotton and 5 % other fibres. This idea started from wanting to give a second life to used jeans. Thanks to the recycling process, the fibres are treated and spun into a single strand which gives a great rustic appearance" (WAK, 2021a) (Figure 4.2.4).

(b) Reuse

Along with recycled yarn, We Are Knitters also offers consumers tape yarn, which derives from "the recycling of T-shirts, it will be perfect for your decorative knitted or crochet pieces. Its sturdiness and consistency will ensure that your projects are very durable" (WAK, 2021b).

I Reduce

The WAK website also outlines its ethos around sustainability, highlighting that "Knitting your own clothes makes you feel good and improves self-esteem. Also, we tend to take better care of our handmade pieces, so they last longer than the one we buy" (WAK, 2021b). Thus, WAK is actively trying to encourage younger and older generations to revisit skill sets that may have previously been thought to be lost. Creating garments themselves and understanding the investment of time that goes into making a garment can help consumers to reflect on current industry practices (Figire 4.2.5).

Questions

1. Thinking about recycling mechanical recycling processes of fabrics, either from pre- or post-consumer waste:
   a. What challenges and opportunities may companies face?
   b. What may be potential perceived risks from the consumer's perspective?
2. Utilising the 3R framework, identify opportunities and challenges WAK may face.
3. Can you identify any further Rs that may enable you to expand the framework and foster the promotion of sustainability? (Tip: think about the supply chain and entirety of the product-creation process.)

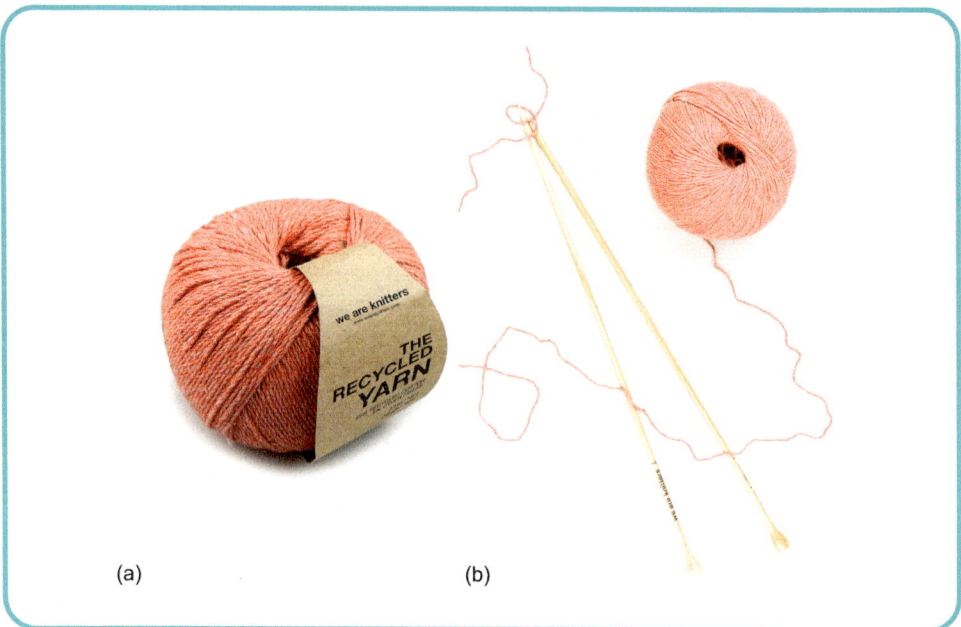

(a)   (b)

Figure 4.2.4   We Are Knitters© Recycled Yarn Spotted Pink

Figure 4.2.5   We Are Knitters© The Tape Yarn Beige

Bibliography

Adu, C., Zhu, C., Jolly, M., Richardson, R.M., and Eichhorn, S.J. (2021) Continuous and sustainable cellulose filaments from ionic liquid dissolved paper sludge nanofibres, *Journal of Cleaner Production*, 280, 124503.

Afrin, T., Kanwar, R.K., Wang, X., and Tsuzuki, T. (2014) Properties of bamboo fibres produced using an environmentally benign method, *The Journal of The Textile Institute*, 105, 1293–1299.

Amutha, K. (2017) Sustainable chemical management and zero discharges, in Muthu, S.S. (ed) Sustainable fibres and textiles, Elsevier, Cambridge pp. 347–366.

An, Y., Miao, J., Fan, J., Li, M., Hu, M., Shao, M., and Shao, J. (2021) High-efficiency dispersant-free polyester dyeing using D5 non-aqueous medium, *Dyes and Pigments*, 190, 109303.

Anand, S.C., Brunnschweiler, D., Swarbrick, G., and Russell, S.J. (2007) *Handbook of nonwovens*, 201–297.

Annapoorani, S.G. (2017) Introduction to denim, in Muthu, S.S. *Sustainability in denim*, Elsevier, Cambridge, pp. 1–26.

Balineau, G. (2013) Disentangling the effects of fair trade on the quality of Malian cotton, *World Development*, 44, 241–255.

BANANATEX® (n.d.) (online): https://www.bananatex.info/, 10/6/2021.

Boardman, R., Parker Strak, R., and Henninger, C.E. (2020) *Fashion buying & merchandising in the 21st century*, Routledge, Abingdon, UK.

Buljan, J., and Kral, I. (2019) *The framework for sustainable leather manufacture.* UNIDO (online): https://open.unido.org/api/documents/4670793/download/UNIDO-Publication-2015-4670793.

Campbell, J.R. (2008) Digital printing of textiles for improved apparel production, in Fairhurst, C. *Advances in apparel production*, Woodhead Publishing, Sawston, pp. 222–249.

Cao, X.L., Yan, Y.N., Zhou, F.Y., and Sun, S.P. (2020) Tailoring nanofiltration membranes for effective removing dye intermediates in complex dye-wastewater, *Journal of Membrane Science*, 595, 117476.

Champion, S.C., and Fearne, A.P. (2001) Alternative marketing systems for the apparel wool textile supply chain: filling the communication vacuum, *The International Food and Agribusiness Management Review*, 4, 237–256.

Colombi, B.L., de Cássia Siqueira Curto Valle, R., Borges Valle, J.A., and Andreaus, J. (2021) Advances in sustainable enzymatic scouring of cotton textiles: Evaluation of different post-treatments to improve fabric wettability, *Cleaner Engineering and Technology*, 4, 100160.

Cool wool (Knitwear) (n.d.a) The Woolmark Company (online): https://www.woolmark.com/industry/use-wool/product-innovations/cool-wool/, 13/7/2021.

Cool wool (Knitwear) (n.d.b) The Woolmark Company (online): https://www.woolmark.com/industry/use-wool/product-innovations/cool-wool/, 25/8/2021.

Cornago, S., Rovelli, D., Brondi, C., Crippa, M., Morico, B., Ballarino, A., and Dotelli, G. (2021) Stochastic consequential life cycle assessment of technology substitution in the case of a novel PET chemical recycling technology, *Journal of Cleaner Production*, 311, 127406.

Cotton Incorporate (2021) Yarn spinning processes, Cotton incorpriate (online): https://www.cottonworks.com/en/topics/sourcing-manufacturing/yarn-manufacturing/spinning-processes/.

Covington, T. (Anthony D.) (2009) *Tanning chemistry: the science of leather*, Royal Society of Chemistry, Cambridge, UK.

Cradle to cradle - rethinking products (n.d.). EPEA (online): https://epea.com/en/about-us/cradle-to-cradle, 25/8/2021.

CREATIVITY VERSUS PLASTIC (n.d.) adidas (online): https://www.adidas.co.uk/blog/361041-creativity-versus-plastic, 14/7/2021.

Darwin, L. (2015) This brand lets you design your own clothes, down to the label, Refinery29 (online): https://www.refinery29

.com/en-us/2015/06/88855/knyttan-clothing -brand.

de Brito, M.P., Carbone, V., and Blanquart, C.M. (2008) Towards a sustainable fashion retail supply chain in Europe: organisation and performance, *International Journal of Production Economics*, 114, 534–553.

de Ferri, L., Tripodi, R., Martignon, A., Ferrari, E.S., Lagrutta-Diaz, A.C., Vallotto, D., and Pojana, G. (2018) Non-invasive study of natural dyes on historical textiles from the collection of Michelangelo Guggenheim, *Spectrochimica Acta Part A: Molecular and Biomolecular Spectroscopy*, 204, 548–567.

Dutta, P., Mahjebin, S., Sufian, M.A., Razaya Rabbi, Md., Chowdhury, S., and Imran, I.H. (2021) Study of auxetic beams under bending: A finite element approach. Materials Today: Proceedings.

Eid, B.M., and Ibrahim, N.A. (2021) Recent developments in sustainable finishing of cellulosic textiles employing biotechnology, *Journal of Cleaner Production*, 284, 124701.

Elmogahzy, Y. (2019) *Structure and mechanics of textile fibre assemblies*, pp. 1–25.

El-Nagar, K., Sanad, S.H., Mohamed, A.S., and Ramadan, A. (2005) Mechanical Properties and Stability to Light Exposure for Dyed Egyptian Cotton Fabrics with Natural and Synthetic Dyes. *Polymer-Plastics Technology and Engineering*, 44(7), 1269–1279

EMF (Ellen MacArthur Foundation) (2017) *A new textile economy*, EMF (online): https:// www.ellenmacarthurfoundation.org/assets /downloads/publications/A-New-Textiles -Economy_Full-Report.pdf, 13/03/2021.

Enes, E., and Kipöz, Ş. (2020) The role of fabric usage for minimization of cut-and-sew waste within the apparel production line: case of a summer dress, *Journal of Cleaner Production*, 248, 119221.

Engineered leather material for buses, trains & aircrafts (n.d.) ELeather (online): https:// www.eleathergroup.com/, 22/7/2021.

Esteve-Turrillas, F.A., and de la Guardia, M. (2017) Environmental impact of recover cotton in textile industry, *Resources, Conservation and Recycling*, 116, 107–115.

European Linen - Le lin et le chanvre européen (n.d.) (online): http://news .europeanflax.com/lin/, 25/8/2021.

Fabrican spray-on fabric sprayable non-woven aerosol technology (n.d.) (online): https:// www.fabricanltd.com/, 22/7/2021.

Fields, D (2021) Secondhand cloothing recyclers growing into IPO digs, Forbes (online): https://www.forbes.com/sites/ mergermarket/2021/09/14/secondhand -clothing-recyclers-growing-into-ipo-digs/?sh =18b298d14ff0.

Flexible opals (n.d.) University of Cambridge (online): https://www.cam.ac.uk/research/ news/flexible-opals, 17/9/2021.

Gomez-Campos, A., Vialle, C., Rouilly, A., Sablayrolles, C., and Hamelin, L. (2021) Flax fiber for technical textile: a life cycle inventory, *Journal of Cleaner Production*, 281, 125177.

Gordon, S., and Hsieh, Y. (2007) *Cotton: science and technology*, Woodhead Publishing in Textiles, Woodhead, Cambridge.

Goyal, A., and Nayak, R. (2020) *Sustainable technologies for fashion and textiles*, pp. 33–55.

GRS - Global Recycle Standard - Certifications (n.d.) (online): https://certifications .controlunion.com/en/certification-programs /certification-programs/grs-global-recycle -standard, 3/9/2021.

Guo, Z., Eriksson, M., Motte, H. de la, and Adolfsson, E. (2021) Circular recycling of polyester textile waste using a sustainable catalyst, *Journal of Cleaner Production*, 283, 124579.

Haight, J.M. (n.d.) Important terms, in *Safety professionals handbook - technical applications*, Volume II (2nd ed.), American Society of Safety Professionals, Park Ridge, IL.

Haji, A., and Naebe, M. (2020) Cleaner dyeing of textiles using plasma treatment and natural dyes: a review, *Journal of Cleaner Production*, 265, 121866.

Halimi, M.T., Hassen, M. ben, and Sakli, F. (2008) Cotton waste recycling: quantitative and qualitative assessment, *Resources, Conservation and Recycling*, 52, 785–791.

Harle, K.J., Howden, S.M., Hunt, L.P., and Dunlop, M. (2007) The potential impact of climate change on the Australian wool industry by 2030, *Agricultural Systems*, 93, 61–89.

Häußler, M., Eck, M., Rothauer, D., and Mecking, S. (2021) Closed-loop recycling of polyethylene-like materials, *Nature*, 590, 423.

Hildebrandt, J., Thrän, D., and Bezama, A. (2021) The circularity of potential bio-textile production routes: comparing life cycle impacts of bio-based materials used within the manufacturing of selected leather substitutes, *Journal of Cleaner Production*, 287, 125470.

How blue genes could green the cotton industry (n.d.) New Scientist (online): https://www.newscientist.com/article/mg13918841-000-how-blue-genes-could-green-the-cotton-industry/, 23/7/2021.

Iavicoli, S., Valenti, A., Barillari, C., Fortuna, G., Boccuni, V., Carnevale, F., Riva, M.A., Kang, S.K., and Tomassini, L. (2020) Making the difference in occupational health: three original and significant cases presented at ICOH Congresses in the 20th century, *Safety and Health at Work*, 11, 215–221.

I love linen | In celebration of linen in partners retailers (e) shop (n.d.) I love linen (online): https://ilovelinen.uk/, 25/8/2021.

Jones, C., Wortmann, F.J., Gleeson, H.F., and Yeates, S.G. (2020) Textile materials inspired by structural colour in nature, *RSC Advances*, 10, 24362–24367.

Jones, M., Gandia, A., John, S., and Bismarck, A. (2021) Leather-like material biofabrication using fungi, *Nature Sustainability*, 4, 9–16.

Kalia, S., Bhattacharya, A., Prajapati, S.K., and Malik, A. (2021) Utilization of starch effluent from a textile industry as a fungal growth supplement for enhanced α-amylase production for industrial application, *Chemosphere*, 279, 130554.

Kansara, V.K. (2015) Knyttan aims to disrupt $200 billion knitwear market, BoF (online): https://www.businessoffashion.com/articles/technology/knyttan-raises-seed-round-aims-to-disrupt-200-billion-knitwear-market/.

Khude, P. (2017) A review on energy management in textile industry, *Innovative Energy & Research*, 6: 169, https://doi.org/10.4172/2576-1463.1000169.

Kvavadze, E., Bar-Yosef, O., Belfer-Cohen, A., Boaretto, E., Jakeli, N., Matskevich, Z., and Meshvetiani, T. (2009) 30,000-year-old wild flax fibers, *Science* (American Association for the Advancement of Science), 325, 1359–1359.

Langley, K.D., and Kim, Y.K. (2006) *Recycling in textiles: a volume in Woodhead Publishing Series in textiles*, pp. 137–164.

Levi Strauss (2019) The history of denim, Levi Strauss (online): https://www.levistrauss.com/2019/07/04/the-history-of-denim/.

Long, D. (2018) Ads we like: adidas knits together campaign promoting Parley for the oceans collaboration, *The Drum* (online): https://www.thedrum.com/news/2018/07/09/ads-we-adidas-knits-together-campaign-promoting-parley-the-oceans-collaboration, 25/8/2021.

Luiken, A., and Bouwhuis, G. (2015) Recovery and recycling of denim waste, in Paul, R. (ed) Denim, woodhead publishing, Cambridge pp. 527–540.

Malinga, L.N., and Laing, M.D. (2021) Efficacy of three biopesticides against cotton pests under field conditions in South Africa, *Crop Protection*, 145, 105578.

Materials - Organic cotton (n.d.) MUD Jeans (online): https://mudjeans.eu/pages/sustainability-materials, 3/9/2021.

McIntyre, J.E. (2005) *Synthetic fibres: nylon, polyester, acrylic, polyolefin*, Woodhead Publishing Limited series on fibres, CRC Press, Boca Raton.

Muthu, S.S. (2020) *Assessing the environmental impact of textiles and the clothing supply chain*, pp. 1–32.

Navare, K., Muys, B., Vrancken, K.C., and van Acker, K. (2021) Circular economy monitoring – How to make it apt for biological cycles?, *Resources, Conservation and Recycling*, 170, 105563.

Ozturk, E., Cinperi, N.C., and Kitis, M. (2020) Improving energy efficiency using the most appropriate techniques in an integrated woolen textile facility, *Journal of Cleaner Production*, 254, 120145.

Pattanayak, A.K. (2020) *Sustainable technologies for fashion and textiles*, pp. 57–72.

Picture this: fashion show uses spray-on clothing developed at Imperial (n.d.) Imperial College London (online): https://www .imperial.ac.uk/news/122898/picture-this -fashion-show-uses-spray-on/, 22/7/2021.

Prakash, C. (2020) Bamboo fibre, in Kozlowski, R., & Mackiewicz,-Talarczyk, M. (eds) *Handbook of natural fibres*, 2nd ed. Elsevier, Cambridge, pp. 219–229.

Purnaa (2017) What is the true cost of a Tshirt, Purnaa (online): https://www.purnaa .com/post/what-is-the-true-cost-of-a-t-shirt.

Ray, S.C. (2012a) *Fundamentals and advances in knitting technology*, Science Direct, Cambridge, pp. 293–315.

Ray, S.C. (2012b) *Fundamentals and advances in knitting technology*, pp. 44–55.

Reddy, R., Jiang, Q., Aramwit, P., and Reddy, N. (2021) Litter to leaf: the unexplored potential of silk byproducts, *Trends in Biotechnology*, 39, 706–718.

Redmore, N.A. (2020) *Woven textiles: principles, technologies and applications*, pp. 423–440.

Ricciardi, L., Chiarelli, D.D., Karatas, S., and Rulli, M.C. (2021) Water resources constraints in achieving silk production self-sufficiency in India, *Advances in Water Resources*, 154, 103962.

Rosenau, J.A. (2006) *Apparel merchandising: the line starts here*, 2nd ed., Fairchild, New York.

Salem Allafi, F.A., Hossain, M.S., Ab Kadir, M.O., Hakim Shaah, M.A., Lalung, J., and Ahmad, M.I. (2021) Waterless processing of sheep wool fiber in textile industry with supercritical CO2: potential and challenges, *Journal of Cleaner Production*, 285, 124819.

Schier, F., Morland, C., Dieter, M., and Weimar, H. (2021) Estimating supply and demand elasticities of dissolving pulp, lignocellulose-based chemical derivatives and textile fibres in an emerging forest-based

bioeconomy, *Forest Policy and Economics*, 126, 102422.

Schindler, W.D. (2004) *Chemical finishing of textiles*, Woodhead publishing in textiles, CRC, Boca Raton.

Shi, J., Huang, W., Han, H., and Xu, C. (2020) Review on treatment technology of salt wastewater in coal chemical industry of China, *Desalination*, 493, 114640.

Sieja, K., von Mach-Szczypiński, J., and von Mach-Szczypiński, J. (2018) Health effect of chronic exposure to carbon disulfide (CS2) on women employed in viscose industry, *Medycyna Pracy*, 69, 329–335.

Simbaña, E.A., Ordóñez, P.E., Ordóñez, Y.F., Guerrero, V.H., Mera, M.C., and Carvajal, E.A. (2020) Abaca: cultivation, obtaining fibre and potential uses, in Kozlowski, R., & Mackiewicz,-Talarczyk, M. (eds) *Handbook of natural fibres*, 2nd ed., Elsevier Inc., pp. 197–218.

Sinclair, R. (2015) *Textiles and fashion: materials, design and technology*, Woodhead Publishing series in textiles, Woodhead Publishing Limited in association with the Textile Institute, Cambridge, UK.

Sun, J., Sun, Y., and Zhu, Q.H. (2021) Breeding next-generation naturally colored cotton, *Trends in Plant Science*, 26, 539–542.

Sustainable Vegan Mycelium leather (n.d.) Mylo Unleather (online): https://www.mylo -unleather.com/, 22/7/2021.

Svensson, S.E., Ferreira, J.A., Hakkarainen, M., Adolfsson, K.H., and Zamani, A. (2021) Fungal textiles: wet spinning of fungal microfibers to produce monofilament yarns, *Sustainable Materials and Technologies*, 28, e00256.

Tan, X., Wang, F., Bi, Y., Su, Y., Li, Y., He, J., Yi, P., Yan, J., Bacquer, D. de, Braeckman, L., and Vanhoorne, M. (2001) The cross-sectional study of the health effects of occupational exposure to carbon disulfide in a Chinese viscose plant, *Environmental Toxicology*, 16, 377–382.

Tarazi, R., Jimenez, J.L.S., and Vaslin, M.F.S. (2019) Biotechnological solutions for major cotton (*Gossypium hirsutum*) pathogens and pests, *Biotechnology Research and Innovation*, 3, 19–26.

Tavangar, T., Karimi, M., Rezakazemi, M., Reddy, K.R., and Aminabhavi, T.M. (2020) Textile waste, dyes/inorganic salts separation of cerium oxide-loaded loose nanofiltration polyethersulfone membranes, *Chemical Engineering Journal*, 385, 123787.

Texcoms (2019) Blowroom processes, Texcoms (online): https://www.texcoms.com/blowroom-processes-and-variety-of-machines-used-in-blowroom.

THE 17 GOALS | Sustainable Development (n.d.) (online): https://sdgs.un.org/goals, 25/8/2021.

The Home of Harris Tweed® (n.d.) Harris Tweed Authority (online): https://www.harristweed.org/, 3/9/2021.

Top designers showcase Cool Wool at London Fashion Week (n.d.) (online): https://www.knittingindustry.com/top-designers-showcase-cool-wool-at-london-fashion-week/, 25/8/2021.

Tournier, V., Topham, C.M., Gilles, A., David, B., Folgoas, C., Moya-Leclair, E., Kamionka, E., Desrousseaux, M., Texier, H., Gavalda, S., Cot, M., Guémard, E., Dalibey, M., Nomme, J., Cioci, G., Barbe, S., Chateau, M., André, I., Duquesne, S., and Marty, A. (2020) An engineered PET depolymerase to break down and recycle plastic bottles, *Nature*, 580, 216–219.

Townsend, T. (2020) World natural fibre production and employment, in Kozlowski, R., & Mackiewicz,-Talarczyk, M. (eds) *Handbook of natural fibres*, 2nd ed., Elsevier Inc., pp. 15–36.

Ul-Islam, S., and Butola, B.S. (2019) *The impact and prospects of green chemistry for textile technology*, The Textile Institute book series, Woodhead Publishing, Duxford.

Unit, B. (2020) Aichi Biodiversity Targets, CBD (online): https://www.cbd.int/sp/targets/, 20/05/2022.

Ütebay, B., Çelik, P., and Çay, A. (2020) 'Textile wastes: status and perspectives, in A. Körlü (ed) *Waste in textile and leather sectors*, IntechOpen, London. 10.5772/intechopen.92234.

Vidaurre-Arbizu, M., Pérez-Bou, S., Zuazua-Ros, A., and Martín-Gómez, C. (2021) From the leather industry to building sector:

exploration of potential applications of discarded solid wastes, *Journal of Cleaner Production*, 291, 125960.

WAK (We Are Knitters) (2021a) *We're all about knitting*, WAK (online): https://www.weareknitters.co.uk/about-us, 10/06/2021.

WAK (We Are Knitters) (2021b) *Slow fashion*, WAK (online): https://www.weareknitters.co.uk/sustainability, 10/06/2021.

White, P., Hayhurst, M., Taylor, J., and Slater, A. (2005) *Biodegradable and sustainable fibres* (A Volume in Woodhead Publishing Series in Textiles), pp. 157–190.

Wilson, J. (2012) *Woven textiles: principles, technologies and applications*, pp. 163–204.

Wojciechowska, P. (2021) Fibres and textiles in the circular economy, in Mondal, I.H. (ed.), *Fundamentals of natural fibres and textiles*, Woodhead Publishing, Swaston, UK, pp. 691–717.

WRAP (2020) *Changing our clothes: Why the clothing sector should adopt new business models*, WRAP: https://www.wrap.org.uk/content/changing-our-clothes-why-clothing-sector-should-adopt-new-business-models?_ga=2.182743332.30533189.1593259255-1614214988.1593259255, 27/06/2020.

Xu, L., Fang, H., Deng, X., Ying, J., Lv, W., Shi, Y., Zhou, G., and Zhou, Y. (2020) Biochar application increased ecosystem carbon sequestration capacity in a Moso bamboo forest, *Forest Ecology and Management*, 475, 118447.

Yang, G., Yang, Y., Zhang, H., and Shao, H. (2021) Influences of stabilizers on lyocell spinning dope and fiber properties, *Polymer Testing*, 99, 107228.

Yang, Y., He, W., Chen, F., and Wang, L. (2020) Water footprint assessment of silk apparel in China, *Journal of Cleaner Production*, 260, 121050.

Zaw, A.K., Myat, A.M., Thandar, M., Htun, Y.M., Aung, T.H., Tun, K.M., and Han, Z.M. (2020) Assessment of noise exposure and hearing loss among workers in textile mill (Thamine), Myanmar: a cross-sectional study, *Safety and Health at Work*, 11, 199–206.

Zhang, X., Du, X., Ke, Y., Zhang, Y.-G., and Xu, Z.-K. (2021) Loose nanofiltration membranes with assembled antifouling surfaces of organophosphonic acid/Fe(III) for managing textile dyeing effluent, *Journal of Membrane Science*, 640, 119821.

Zhao, M., Zhou, Y., Meng, J., Zheng, H., Cai, Y., Shan, Y., Guan, D., and Yang, Z. (2021) Virtual carbon and water flows embodied in global fashion trade - a case study of denim products, *Journal of Cleaner Production*, 303, 127080.

ZOA :Modern Meadow (n.d.) (online): https://www.modernmeadow.com/zoa, 22/7/2021.

4.3 Fabric finishes and surface design

Learning outcomes

1. To critically examine and understand key technical terminology surrounding examples of textile finishing.
2. To understand the significant role these finishing processes play when considering issues surrounding sustainability of fashion garments, reflecting on current and future production processes.
3. To critically investigate the significance of sustainability challenges in the 21st century.

In Chapter 4.1, we referred to a plain white T-shirt as an example of how we need to consider the raw materials used, how they are obtained, and issues of sustainability. Chapter 4.2 looked at how we take those raw materials and create fabrics with them, such as jersey fabric to produce the T-shirt. However, if we wanted to apply colour to the plain white T-shirt, how is this achieved? What materials do we use? What machinery is involved? What do we need to consider in terms of sustainability?

To begin, we must firstly understand what, in the context of this book, is meant by the term "finish". It is used to describe the processes applied to a textile after the construction process, for example weaving and knitting. At this stage in the production process, we often refer to the unfinished textile as "greige" fabric. These steps are referred to as the wet processing of textiles. They include, but are not limited to, colouration using materials such as pigments and dyes, and chemical finishes such as desizing, bleaching, and mercerisation. It is important to note that colouration can be applied to fibres and yarns too, but its application to fabrics will be the main focus of this chapter.

These production processes can consume large quantities of energy (electricity and thermal), water, and chemicals, all of which have environmental implications (Haji and Naebe, 2020). Textile wet processing is considered one of the commonest sources of industrial environmental pollution (Schindler, 2004; Ul-Islam and Butola, 2019; "Gürses et al.," 2021). Thus, if we want to have a brand that is more sustainable, we need to understand what our options are and how we can overcome any potential challenges.

4.3.1 Fabric colouration – overview

Colour can be applied to textiles, such as knitted and woven fabrics, through the use of dyes and pigments. Historically, colourants were obtained from plants and animals,

DOI: 10.4324/9781003097846-19

such as woad, madder, and cochineal, (de Ferri et al., 2018), but today, synthetic dye-stuffs are used commercially. This is in part due to the improved fastness properties and range of colours that can be achieved (El-Nagar et al., n.d.). This is also one of the reasons why we see increasingly colourful garments in shops, whether they be neon, pastels, or earth tones – just about anything can be achieved – often led by the newest trends in the industry.

Recently, environmental concerns surrounding the use and application of synthetic dyestuffs have sparked renewed interest in using natural dyes to colour textiles. One influencing factor is the reduction in harmful effluent (Haji and Naebe, 2020), which, as Table 4.3.2 shows, is part of the UN SDG, specifically SDG 12 relating to responsible consumption and production. One of the targets identified was to reduce the release of waste and chemicals to water by 2020. But there are always two sides to a story, so whilst surface modification techniques, such as plasma treatment have been presented as processes that could help overcome the poor affinity of natural dyes to textile fibres (Haji and Naebe, 2020), natural dyes require the use of metallic mordants, which present further environmental concerns (Dutta et al., 2021).

It is important to note that for natural fibres such as cotton, brands and designers are looking to naturally coloured varieties to eliminate the colouration process. Currently, varieties of cotton that naturally grow brown, green, and pink are used, but these varieties typically have poorer fibre quality (Sun et al., 2021). In the early 1990s, scientists attempted to genetically modify cotton with genetic material from the indigo plant in the hope of growing blue cotton in the fields; this approach continues to generate interest, and may offer a new way of producing coloured cotton ("How blue genes could green the cotton industry | New Scientist," n.d.).

A key message to take away from this section is that colouring processes can have environmental implications, as dyes, even if natural, may need additional substances in order to adhere to fabrics and fibres. Although possibilities do exist to, for example, grow cotton in different colours, the resulting fibres may not be as strong, which has implications for garment production.

4.3.2 Fabric preparation

In preparation for colouration and other surface design techniques, fabrics may require the application of other chemical finishes or finishing processes. For example, the size used to coat yarns to enable them to withstand the weaving process needs to be removed. This is because the size can act as a resist and prevent colourants adhering to the textile material. In the case of fabrics containing cotton fibres, starch is the most common size used, and it can be removed via oxidation, reduction, or by enzymatic treatment (Eid and Ibrahim, 2021). According to Eid and Ibrahim (2021), the use of starch size increases the biological oxygen in textile effluents, which, with better resource recovery, could be used in the production of industrially useful enzymes (Kalia et al., 2021).

Other hydrophobic impurities from cotton and wool fibres (fats, waxes, and grease) can be removed by the scouring process. For cotton fibres, they are removed by alkali scouring with hot aqueous sodium hydroxide (Colombi et al., 2021), and for wool fibres an alkali or soap can be used (Salem Allafi et al., 2021b). It is important to remove these impurities as they could interfere with the application of colourants to the textile material: for example, wax could act like a resist and cause uneven colouration. For certain techniques, such as batik, we may deliberately use wax as a resist to create designs in our fabrics. However, in this instance, where we want to apply a colourant in a homogenous way throughout the fabric, the wax must be removed.

Another wet process used is bleaching, to ensure a homogenous ground shade, typically used with fabrics containing cotton fibres. This will ensure that subsequent dyeing and printing produce a uniform- colour or print. Singeing can be a further step for cotton fibres, which ensures that any surface fibres are removed and the fabric is smooth in preparation for printing and dyeing. Mercerisation causes cotton fibres to swell, and not only alters the cross section of the fibre for improved interaction with light and better fabric lustre, but also increases the fibre's affinity to dyestuffs. The high pH of the strong alkali used in the mercerisation process affects the pH of effluent from the wet process (Eid and Ibrahim, 2021). It is important to note that all of these processes involve a large amount of water and chemicals *prior* to applying any aesthetic or performance finishes. This obviously raises environmental concerns if, for example, a piece of cotton greige fabric is subjected to all these wet processes such as desizing, bleaching, mercerisation, and singeing before any dyeing or printing takes place. There are a variety of colourants that can be applied to textiles, and we will focus on the application of a few examples of synthetic dyestuffs and pigments.

4.3.3 Application of colourants

Once we have our greige fabric, there are a variety of colourants to choose from. The choice of dyes and pigments is partly dependent on the fibre content of the fabric, and the application process in part reflects the appropriate conditions required to apply the colourant. For example, if we choose to apply reactive dyes, alkaline conditions are preferable when applying them to cellulosic or protein fibres. Table 4.3.1 gives some examples of dyes that can be used for each fibre type.

Certain hazardous and carcinogenic dyes and chemicals have been abandoned (Amutha, 2017; "Environmentally sound textile wet processing," 2021) as a step towards sustainable production.

As mentioned earlier, to achieve the appropriate conditions for these dyes to be applied to the textile, vast quantities of water and energy (electricity and thermal) are

Table 4.3.1 Summary of Dyes That Can Be Used on Different Fabric Types

Cotton/flax/cellulosics	Protein fibres (wool and silk) and nylon	Synthetics such as polyester
Reactive	Reactive	Disperse
Vat	Acid	
Direct	Metal-complex	
Sulphur		

used. Certain dyeing processes require high temperatures, steam, and cooling, along with the rotation and agitation of fabrics within the dyeing equipment. When dyeing yarns, for example, we can use a hank dyeing machine, whereas for fabrics, we use a piece of equipment called a jig. Whilst they will each naturally differ in size, and therefore occupy a different amount of factory space, the jigs will rotate and agitate the textile material in and out of the dye bath solution.

The effluents from these production processes are of great concern, as according to researchers, they contain large amounts of residual dye, for example, which are difficult to degrade ("Environmentally sound textile wet processing," 2021). These concerns are further highlighted in Table 4.3.2, showing the UN SDG 6, referring to clean water and sanitation, and the dumping or release of hazardous chemicals. Furthermore, UN SDG 3 regarding good health and well-being targets deaths and illness from hazardous chemicals in water, with one of the indicators, mortality rate, attributed to unintentional poisoning. Researchers have highlighted the negative environmental impact of high-saline waste from textile effluent resulting from the use of salts in the process of applying reactive dyes, for example, and the impact on human health (Cao et al., 2020; Shi et al., 2020; Tavangar et al., 2020; Zhang et al., 2021). The Oeko-Tex Standard 100 can apply to dyed products, which provides manufacturers with the opportunity to highlight how they are reaching the targets set by the UN and tackling this issue (Sinclair, 2015). In the case of synthetic fibres such as polyester, large amounts of dispersant are used to ensure uniform dispersion in the dyebath, which is discharged in the wastewater from the production process (An et al., 2021). As a result, there have been many attempts to try to treat this effluent to resolve this issue and remove any harmful materials before they enter the local environment. UN SDG 6 highlights the need to increase recycling and reuse of chemicals in these production processes. Therefore, along with treatments, there is increasing interest in producing filters to capture, reuse, or recycle these chemicals (Cao et al., 2020; Tavangar et al., 2020; Zhang et al., 2021).

Dyes and pigments are not only applied through the use of a dyebath, they can also be applied to specific parts of a textile by means of a dye printing paste and digital printing inks. It is important to note that these two processes can be combined, as prints can be applied to dyed fabrics too. Traditionally, this could have been accomplished through the use of wooden blocks and stencils by hand, which are still used today.

Printing pastes and print designs can be applied to the textiles through the use of screens, by flat, or table, screen printing or rotary screen printing. Historically, screen printing was referred to as silk screen printing, as a piece of silk mesh fabric was stretched over a wooden frame to enable the designer to transfer the design to the fabric. Today, a synthetic mesh is stretched over a metal frame. The screen can be coated in an ultraviolet-sensitive film, onto which the desired print can be transferred using a transparent film. Repetitive strain injuries resulting from this printing process among workers loading and unloading the screens in large-scale production have been documented (Haight, n.d.). This is of great concern in terms of social sustainability, and is highlighted in UN SDG 3, aiming to ensure healthy lives and promote well-being for people of all ages. Whilst automated screen printing processes have been suggested as a way of reducing this type of injury, these systems do not necessarily perform as efficiently (Haight, n.d.).

Table 4.3.2 Textile Finishing and SDG 12

SDG	Title	Targets	Indicators	Implications/challenges for fashion industry
12	Responsible Consumption and Production	12.4 – By 2020, achieve the environmentally sound management of chemicals and all wastes throughout their lifecycle, in accordance with agreed international frameworks, and significantly reduce their release to air, water, and soil in order to minimise their adverse impacts on human health and the environment	• Number of parties to international multilateral environmental agreements on hazardous waste, and other chemicals that meet their commitments and obligations in transmitting information as required by each relevant agreement • Hazardous waste generated per capita and proportion of hazardous waste treated, by type of treatment	• Exploring alternative methods of application, production processes, and use of colourants to apply colour to textile materials
6	Clean Water and Sanitation	6.3 – By 2030, improve water quality by reducing pollution, eliminating dumping and minimizing release of hazardous chemicals and materials, halving the proportion of untreated wastewater and substantially increasing recycling and safe reuse globally	• Proportion of wastewater safely treated • Proportion of bodies of water with good ambient water quality	• The fashion industry uses a variety of chemicals throughout production processes, including finishing processes, some of which are released into rivers • Careful selection of colourants to minimize impact and use of treatments before discharged into local environment.
		6.4 – By 2030, substantially increase water-use efficiency across all sectors and ensure sustainable withdrawals and supply of freshwater to address water scarcity and substantially reduce the number of people suffering from water scarcity	• Change in water-use efficiency over time • Level of water stress: freshwater withdrawal as a proportion of available freshwater resources	• Textile finishing processes use vast quantities of water for pre-treatment processes, dyeing processes, steam, and post-treatment washing, for example

These printing processes and digital printing all require post-printing processes. In some cases, this involves curing the print on the textiles, and can involve steam (for digital printing) or an oven (stenter). All these processes require energy (electricity and thermal heat), as well as water for washing and for producing steam.

When comparing printing processes, it has been argued that digital printing cannot match screen printing in terms of cost and production time (Campbell, 2008). When considering our plain white T-shirt and applying a design or logo to the front of the garment, these are all points to bear in mind.

CAD software can be used to transfer and create a design in these printing processes. It can be used in digital printing to transfer photo-like images which would require significant colour separation and a number of screens to achieve with screen printing. These are also all points to consider in terms of production space and workforce.

It is important to note that pigments can also be applied through screen, rotary screen, and inkjet printing. This printing process is relatively straightforward. It merely involves printing, drying, and curing, which makes it cheap and simple. This pigment printing process can be applied to fabrics containing natural and synthetic fibres. Pigment printing is often used when applying logos and designs to T-shirts. It can be recognised on vintage T-shirts by its cracked and faded appearance. This is because the print sits on the surface of the fabric rather than being absorbed by it. This is an important consideration when printing onto T-shirt jersey which has stretch, since it can affect the ability of the material to stretch and can affect drape, and the stretching of the fabric can cause the print to crack. This is sometimes desired if the fashion garment needs to appear distressed, but if undesired, it would need be borne in mind when selecting appropriate finishes. Pigments can also be applied to man-made manufactured fibres using polymer chips in the melt spinning process. In contrast to pigment printing, where the print sits on the surface of the fabric, the pigment is applied to the whole fibre.

We have provided a few examples of printing processes that could be used to apply colourants to textile materials, but there are of course many further examples. We could, for example, use a digital printing process to apply disperse dyes in the sublimation (transfer) printing process onto polyester fabrics. This could be described as a "waterless process", as these dyes sublimate, turning straight from a solid to a gas in the presence of high temperatures and pressure.

This section of the chapter has focused on the application of colourants, but there are also tactile finishes we could apply to our plain white T-shirt using these printing processes. For example, the adhesive used to foil or flock a textile print requires a screen and an adhesive. These finishes could be used to give our T-shirt logo a 3D relief of reflective effect. As well as adding adhesives and coatings to textiles, fibres can be removed to produce surface designs, such as the in the devore process. This involves the removal of cellulosic fibres.

Lastly, it is important to note that finishing is not limited to colourants and removing impurities in our fabrics. There are also chemical finishes which we can apply to textiles to improve their appearance and performance properties. Examples could be, but are not limited to, flame-retardant finishes waterproofing, and stain-repellent finishes. Further examples include fabrics containing protein fibres such as wool, which require a moth-repellent finish to extend product life.

What is important to note here is that the way our fabrics are treated impacts on the colours we achieve. Thus, there are various considerations during this process that need to be carefully reviewed in order to not only provide consumers with garments in colours they want, but also to use techniques that are suitable and ideally less harmful to the environment.

4.3.4 Innovative approach to colouration

As highlighted at the beginning of this chapter, these finishing processes can consume large quantities of energy (electricity and thermal), water, and chemicals, all of which have environmental implications (Haji and Naebe, 2020). Textile wet processing is considered to be one of the commonest sources of industrial environmental pollution. As such, researchers have looked at ways of addressing this issue, and we have started to highlight these approaches in this section of the book. For example, the use of disperse dyes in the sublimation process avoids the use of water in the production process.

However, what if we were to completely remove the dye kitchen from the production process (Jones, and Henninger, 2020)? What if colour could be created without the use of colourants?

Researchers have looked to nature for inspiration in achieving this, and have attempted to mimic the structural colour naturally exhibited on the exoskeletons of beetles and the wings of butterflies. In the methods considered so far in this chapter, colour has been achieved by the interactions of light with the dyes or pigments applied to our textile materials. With structural colour, it originates from the physical interaction of light with nanoscale structures.

Chapter 4.1 mentioned the creation of the Morphotex® fibre, but it is important to note that researchers have also explored the use of structural colour in textile prints. This has been through the use of inkjet printing to apply cholesteric liquid crystal films to polyester fabrics (Jones et al., 2020). Structural colour, specifically "polymer opals", has also been successfully applied to stretch fabrics, enabling the fabric to change colour when stretched ("Flexible opals | University of Cambridge," n.d.).

To summarise this chapter, you should now have an understanding of different types of fabric finishes and the reasons for their uses. You should also be able to comprehend some of the issues surrounding the applications and the impact on workers, the local environment, and resources. You also should have an understanding of new approaches to tackling these issues, looking to the past with renewed interest, exploring improvements to current production process as well as innovative future approaches.

4.3.5 Case study: Sustaina-jeans Innovation Capsule

Abstract

Linked to the heritage of the brand, Sustaina-jeans has always used the traditional indigo dyeing process to create the signature blue of its denim jeans. This case study utilises the lean manufacturing model to help the company address the waste generated through this process. You should use the knowledge gained from this chapter to help Sustaina-jeans assess its current issues, future challenges, and potential alternatives.

Learning outcomes

After working through the case study, you will be able to:

- Define and explain "traditional" methods of preparing and dyeing cotton yarn via the indigo method prior to weaving into denim fabric.
- Understand the impact of this textile production process in terms of the water and energy required and the waste generated.
- Reflect upon this production process through the lean manufacturing model.

Introduction

Sustaina-jeans continues to manufacture its "Original 1970" jeans, which incorporate some of the traditional practices used in its first pair of jeans. In particular, this range uses synthetic dyestuffs to obtain the signature blue colour in the jeans. However, as part of Sustaina-jeans' new *Innovation Capsule*, which focuses on sustainable production and manufacturing, it would like to re-evaluate the "Original 1970" by showcasing an "Innovation 1970" pair of jeans, reducing waste at this particular stage of the production process. In order to do so, the company is using the lean manufacturing model to assess the amount of waste in its suppliers' production processes and wishes to research alternative dyeing techniques to the current method. To begin, Sustaina-jeans has asked an independent auditor to provide a brief overview of the dyeing process used by its supplier and to highlight some of the environmental concerns.

Report from DyCo© Limited, independent auditor visiting supplier of "Original 1970" denim fabric

Your woven "Original 1970" denim fabric contains 100 per cent pima cotton bleached, mercerised, warp yarns which have been dyed blue using synthetic indigo vat dye in the dyeing process. In order to make the dye soluble in water and enable it to adhere to the cellulose fibres, we observed that your supplier uses a process of vatting in order to create its leuco indigo. We believe your supplier is combining this with an alkali and reducing agent to successfully apply the dye to the yarns. We observed a variety of processes to oxidise the yarns to achieve the blue shade, which included air drying, submerging in water, and using oxidising agents. The final step of the process we believe involved the use of soap and water at boiling point to remove any loose pigment.

Lean manufacturing

Sustaina-jeans is interested in adopting lean production, as it seeks to reduce waste, thereby enhancing efficiency, effectiveness, and profitability of the overall manufacturing process, whilst at the same time ensuring that there is no impact on the overall quality (Womack & Jones, 1994). "Waste" here can refer to a number of different things at different stages of the textile production process, but in this context, we are focusing on the pre-treatment, dyeing, and post-treatment processes. The Six Sigma concept is often discussed in conjunction with lean manufacturing, which consists of the DMAIC (define, measure, analyse, improve, and control) guiding principles that can help an organisation to make its processes leaner:

1. Define: what is the source of waste within the manufacturing process?
2. Measure: how much of this waste is being produced, and how much does it cost the company?
3. Analyse: what measures could be taken in order to avoid this waste being created?
4. Improve: implement changes based on the analysis.
5. Control: ensure that these changes have the effect that was anticipated by the company – waste reduction.

Questions

1. Referring to the DMAIC guidelines in the Six Sigma concept, *define* what could be the source of waste within the pre-treatment, dyeing, and post-treatment processes of the vat- dyed 100 per cent cotton yarns in this case study.
2. Referring to the DMAIC guidelines in the Six Sigma concept, *analyse* what measures, if any, could be taken in order to avoid this waste being created.
3. Reflecting on the information provided in this chapter, and looking to expand the guidelines further, can you identify any suitable alternatives (i.e., in terms of raw materials, machinery, and colourants) to those used in the "Original 1970" jeans for the new "Innovation 1970" jeans which could help reduce waste?

Bibliography

Adu, C., Zhu, C., Jolly, M., Richardson, R.M., and Eichhorn, S.J. (2021) Continuous and sustainable cellulose filaments from ionic liquid dissolved paper sludge nanofibres, *Journal of Cleaner Production*, 280, 124503.

Afrin, T., Kanwar, R.K., Wang, X., and Tsuzuki, T. (2014) Properties of bamboo fibres produced using an environmentally benign method, *The Journal of The Textile Institute*, 105, 1293–1299.

Amutha, K. (2017) Sustainable chemical management and zero discharges, in Muthu, S.S.(ed) *Sustainable fibres and textiles*, Elsevier, Cambridge pp. 347–366.

An, Y., Miao, J., Fan, J., Li, M., Hu, M., Shao, M., and Shao, J. (2021) High-efficiency dispersant-free polyester dyeing using D5 non-aqueous medium, *Dyes and Pigments*, 190, 109303.

Anand, S.C., Brunnschweiler, D., Swarbrick, G., and Russell, S.J. (2007) *Handbook of nonwovens*, 201–297.

Annapoorani, S.G. (2017) Introduction to denim, in Muthu, S.S. (ed) *Sustainability in denim*, Elsevier, Cambridge, pp. 1–26.

Balineau, G. (2013) Disentangling the effects of fair trade on the quality of Malian cotton, *World Development*, 44, 241–255.

BANANATEX® (n.d.) (online): https://www.bananatex.info/, 10/6/2021.

Buljan, J., and Kral, I. (2019) *The framework for sustainable leather manufacture*. UNIDO (online): https://open.unido.org/api/documents/4670793/download/UNIDO-Publication-2015-4670793,

Campbell, J.R. (2008) Digital printing of textiles for improved apparel production, in Fairhurst, C. (ed) *Advances in apparel production*, Woodhead Publishing, Sawston, pp. 222–249.

Cao, X.L., Yan, Y.N., Zhou, F.Y., and Sun, S.P. (2020) Tailoring nanofiltration membranes for effective removing dye intermediates in complex dye-wastewater, *Journal of Membrane Science*, 595, 117476.

Champion, S.C., and Fearne, A.P. (2001) Alternative marketing systems for the apparel wool textile supply chain: filling the communication vacuum, *The International Food and Agribusiness Management Review*, 4, 237–256.

Colombi, B.L., de Cássia Siqueira Curto Valle, R., Borges Valle, J.A., and Andreaus, J. (2021) Advances in sustainable enzymatic scouring of cotton textiles: Evaluation of different post-treatments to improve fabric wettability, *Cleaner Engineering and Technology*, 4, 100160.

Cool wool (Knitwear) (n.d.a) The Woolmark Company (online): https://www.woolmark .com/industry/use-wool/product-innovations/ cool-wool/, 13/7/2021.

Cool wool (Knitwear) (n.d.b) The Woolmark Company (online): https://www.woolmark .com/industry/use-wool/product-innovations/ cool-wool/, 25/8/2021.

Cornago, S., Rovelli, D., Brondi, C., Crippa, M., Morico, B., Ballarino, A., and Dotelli, G. (2021) Stochastic consequential life cycle assessment of technology substitution in the case of a novel PET chemical recycling technology, *Journal of Cleaner Production*, 311, 127406.

Covington, T. (Anthony D.) (2009) *Tanning chemistry: the science of leather*, Royal Society of Chemistry, Cambridge, UK.

Cradle to cradle - rethinking products (n.d.). EPEA (online): https://epea.com/en/about-us/ cradle-to-cradle, 25/8/2021.

CREATIVITY VERSUS PLASTIC (n.d.) adidas (online): https://www.adidas.co.uk/blog /361041-creativity-versus-plastic, 14/7/2021.

de Brito, M.P., Carbone, V., and Blanquart, C.M. (2008) Towards a sustainable fashion retail supply chain in Europe: organisation and performance, *International Journal of Production Economics*, 114, 534–553.

de Ferri, L., Tripodi, R., Martignon, A., Ferrari, E.S., Lagrutta-Diaz, A.C., Vallotto, D., and Pojana, G. (2018) Non-invasive study of natural dyes on historical textiles from the collection of Michelangelo Guggenheim, *Spectrochimica Acta Part A: Molecular and Biomolecular Spectroscopy*, 204, 548–567.

Dutta, P., Mahjebin, S., Sufian, M.A., Razaya Rabbi, Md., Chowdhury, S., and Imran, I.H. (2021) Study of auxetic beams under bending: A finite element approach, *Materials Today: Proceedings*, 9782–9787.

Eid, B.M., and Ibrahim, N.A. (2021) Recent developments in sustainable finishing of cellulosic textiles employing biotechnology, *Journal of Cleaner Production*, 284, 124701.

Elmogahzy, Y. (2019) *Structure and mechanics of textile fibre assemblies*, pp. 1–25.

El-Nagar, K., Sanad, S.H., Mohamed, A.S., and Ramadan, A. (2005) Mechanical Properties and Stability to Light Exposure for Dyed Egyptian Cotton Fabrics with Natural and Synthetic Dyes, *Polymer-Plastics Technology and Engineering*, 44(7), 1269–1279

Enes, E., and Kipöz, Ş. (2020) The role of fabric usage for minimization of cut-and-sew waste within the apparel production line: case of a summer dress, *Journal of Cleaner Production*, 248, 119221.

Engineered leather material for buses, trains & aircrafts (n.d.) ELeather (online): https:// www.eleathergroup.com/, 22/7/2021.

Esteve-Turrillas, F.A., and de la Guardia, M. (2017) Environmental impact of recover cotton in textile industry, *Resources, Conservation and Recycling*, 116, 107–115.

European Linen - Le lin et le chanvre européen (n.d.) (online): http://news .europeanflax.com/lin/, 25/8/2021.

Fabrican spray-on fabric sprayable non-woven aerosol technology (n.d.) (online): https:// www.fabricanltd.com/, 22/7/2021.

Flexible opals (n.d.) University of Cambridge (online): https://www.cam.ac.uk/research/ news/flexible-opals, 17/9/2021.

Gomez-Campos, A., Vialle, C., Rouilly, A., Sablayrolles, C., and Hamelin, L. (2021) Flax fiber for technical textile: a life cycle inventory, *Journal of Cleaner Production*, 281, 125177.

Gordon, S., and Hsieh, Y. (2007) *Cotton: science and technology*, Woodhead Publishing in Textiles, Woodhead, Cambridge.

Goyal, A., and Nayak, R. (2020) *Sustainable technologies for fashion and textiles*, pp. 33–55.

GRS - Global Recycle Standard - Certifications (n.d.) (online): https://certifications .controlunion.com/en/certification-programs /certification-programs/grs-global-recycle -standard, 3/9/2021.

Guo, Z., Eriksson, M., Motte, H. de la, and Adolfsson, E. (2021) Circular recycling of polyester textile waste using a sustainable catalyst, *Journal of Cleaner Production*, 283, 124579.

Gürses, A., Günes, K., and Sahin, E. (2021) Environmentally sound textile wet processing, in Ibrahim, N., & Hussain, C.M. (eds) *Green Chemistry for sustainable textiles*, Elsevier, Cambridge Chapter 6, pp. 77–91.

Haight, J.M. (n.d.) Important terms, in *Safety professionals handbook - technical applications*, Volume II (2nd ed.), American Society of Safety Professionals, Park Ridge, IL.

Haji, A., and Naebe, M. (2020) Cleaner dyeing of textiles using plasma treatment and natural dyes: a review, *Journal of Cleaner Production*, 265, 121866.

Halimi, M.T., Hassen, M. ben, and Sakli, F. (2008) Cotton waste recycling: quantitative and qualitative assessment, *Resources, Conservation and Recycling*, 52, 785–791.

Harle, K.J., Howden, S.M., Hunt, L.P., and Dunlop, M. (2007) The potential impact of climate change on the Australian wool industry by 2030, *Agricultural Systems*, 93, 61–89.

Häußler, M., Eck, M., Rothauer, D., and Mecking, S. (2021) Closed-loop recycling of polyethylene-like materials, *Nature*, 590, 423.

Hildebrandt, J., Thrän, D., and Bezama, A. (2021) The circularity of potential bio-textile production routes: comparing life cycle impacts of bio-based materials used within the manufacturing of selected leather substitutes, *Journal of Cleaner Production*, 287, 125470.

How blue genes could green the cotton industry (n.d.) New Scientist (online): https://www.newscientist.com/article/mg13918841-000-how-blue-genes-could-green-the-cotton-industry/, 23/7/2021.

Iavicoli, S., Valenti, A., Barillari, C., Fortuna, G., Boccuni, V., Carnevale, F., Riva, M.A., Kang, S.K., and Tomassini, L. (2020) Making the difference in occupational health: three original and significant cases presented at ICOH Congresses in the 20th century, *Safety and Health at Work*, 11, 215–221.

I love linen | In celebration of linen in partners retailers (e) shop (n.d.) I love linen (online): https://ilovelinen.uk/, 25/8/2021.

Jones, C., and Henninger, C.E. (2020) Removing the dye kitchen from the textile supply chain, in Vignali, G., Reid, L., Ryding, D., and Henninger, C.E. (eds.), *Technology-driven sustainability*, Palgrave Macmillan, Cham, pp. 81–92.

Jones, C., Wortmann, F.J., Gleeson, H.F., and Yeates, S.G. (2020) Textile materials inspired by structural colour in nature, *RSC Advances*, 10, 24362–24367.

Jones, M., Gandia, A., John, S., and Bismarck, A. (2021) Leather-like material biofabrication using fungi, *Nature Sustainability*, 4, 9–16.

Kalia, S., Bhattacharya, A., Prajapati, S.K., and Malik, A. (2021) Utilization of starch effluent from a textile industry as a fungal growth supplement for enhanced α-amylase production for industrial application, *Chemosphere*, 279, 130554.

Khude, P. (2017) A review on energy management in textile industry, *Innovative Energy & Research*, 6: 169, https://doi.org/10.4172/2576-1463.1000169.

Kvavadze, E., Bar-Yosef, O., Belfer-Cohen, A., Boaretto, E., Jakeli, N., Matskevich, Z., and Meshvetiani, T. (2009) 30,000-year-old wild flax fibers, *Science* (American Association for the Advancement of Science), 325, 1359–1359.

Langley, K.D., and Kim, Y.K. (2006) *Recycling in textiles: a volume in Woodhead Publishing Series in textiles*, pp. 137–164.

Long, D. (2018) Ads we like: adidas knits together campaign promoting Parley for the oceans collaboration, *The Drum* (online): https://www.thedrum.com/news/2018/07/09/ads-we-adidas-knits-together-campaign-promoting-parley-the-oceans-collaboration, 25/8/2021.

Malinga, L.N., and Laing, M.D. (2021) Efficacy of three biopesticides against cotton pests under field conditions in South Africa, *Crop Protection*, 145, 105578.

Materials - Organic cotton (n.d.) MUD Jeans (online): https://mudjeans.eu/pages/sustainability-materials, 3/9/2021.

McIntyre, J.E. (2005) *Synthetic fibres: nylon, polyester, acrylic, polyolefin*, Woodhead

Publishing Limited series on fibres, CRC Press, Boca Raton.

Muthu, S.S. (2020) *Assessing the environmental impact of textiles and the clothing supply chain*, pp. 1–32.

Navare, K., Muys, B., Vrancken, K.C., and van Acker, K. (2021) Circular economy monitoring – How to make it apt for biological cycles?, *Resources, Conservation and Recycling*, 170, 105563.

Ozturk, E., Cinperi, N.C., and Kitis, M. (2020) Improving energy efficiency using the most appropriate techniques in an integrated woolen textile facility, *Journal of Cleaner Production*, 254, 120145.

Pattanayak, A.K. (2020) *Sustainable technologies for fashion and textiles*, pp. 57–72.

Picture this: fashion show uses spray-on clothing developed at Imperial (n.d.) Imperial College London (online): https://www.imperial.ac.uk/news/122898/picture-this-fashion-show-uses-spray-on/, 22/7/2021.

Prakash, C. (2020) Bamboo fibre, in Kozlowski, R., & Mackiewicz,-Talarczyk, M. (eds) *Handbook of natural fibres*, 2nd ed. Elsevier, Cambridge, pp. 219–229.

Ray, S.C. (2012a) *Fundamentals and advances in knitting technology*, Science Direct, Cambridge, pp. 293–315.

Ray, S.C. (2012b) *Fundamentals and advances in knitting technology*, pp. 44–55.

Reddy, R., Jiang, Q., Aramwit, P., and Reddy, N. (2021) Litter to leaf: the unexplored potential of silk byproducts, *Trends in Biotechnology*, 39, 706–718.

Redmore, N.A. (2020) *Woven textiles: principles, technologies and applications*, pp. 423–440.

Ricciardi, L., Chiarelli, D.D., Karatas, S., and Rulli, M.C. (2021) Water resources constraints in achieving silk production self-sufficiency in India, *Advances in Water Resources*, 154, 103962.

Rosenau, J.A. (2006) *Apparel merchandising: the line starts here*, 2nd ed., Fairchild, New York.

Salem Allafi, F.A., Hossain, M.S., Ab Kadir, M.O., Hakim Shaah, M.A., Lalung, J., and Ahmad, M.I. (2021) Waterless processing of sheep wool fiber in textile industry with supercritical CO2: potential and challenges, *Journal of Cleaner Production*, 285, 124819.

Schier, F., Morland, C., Dieter, M., and Weimar, H. (2021) Estimating supply and demand elasticities of dissolving pulp, lignocellulose-based chemical derivatives and textile fibres in an emerging forest-based bioeconomy, *Forest Policy and Economics*, 126, 102422.

Schindler, W.D. (2004) *Chemical finishing of textiles*, Woodhead publishing in textiles, CRC, Boca Raton.

Shi, J., Huang, W., Han, H., and Xu, C. (2020) Review on treatment technology of salt wastewater in coal chemical industry of China, *Desalination*, 493, 114640.

Sieja, K., von Mach-Szczypiński, J., and von Mach-Szczypiński, J. (2018) Health effect of chronic exposure to carbon disulfide (CS2) on women employed in viscose industry, *Medycyna Pracy*, 69, 329–335.

Simbaña, E.A., Ordóñez, P.E., Ordóñez, Y.F., Guerrero, V.H., Mera, M.C., and Carvajal, E.A. (2020) Abaca: cultivation, obtaining fibre and potential uses, in Kozlowski, R., & Mackiewicz,-Talarczyk, M. (eds) *Handbook of natural fibres*, 2nd ed., Woodhead Publishing, Swaston, UK, pp. 197–218.

Sinclair, R. (2015) *Textiles and fashion: materials, design and technology*, Woodhead Publishing series in textiles, Woodhead Publishing Limited in association with the Textile Institute, Cambridge, UK.

Sun, J., Sun, Y., and Zhu, Q.H. (2021) Breeding next-generation naturally colored cotton, *Trends in Plant Science*, 26, 539–542.

Sustainable Vegan Mycelium leather (n.d.) Mylo Unleather (online): https://www.mylo-unleather.com/, 22/7/2021.

Svensson, S.E., Ferreira, J.A., Hakkarainen, M., Adolfsson, K.H., and Zamani, A. (2021) Fungal textiles: wet spinning of fungal microfibers to produce monofilament yarns, *Sustainable Materials and Technologies*, 28, e00256.

Tan, X., Wang, F., Bi, Y., Su, Y., Li, Y., He, J., Yi, P., Yan, J., Bacquer, D. de, Braeckman, L., and Vanhoorne, M. (2001) The cross-sectional study of the health effects of occupational exposure to carbon disulfide in a Chinese viscose plant, *Environmental Toxicology*, 16, 377–382.

Tarazi, R., Jimenez, J.L.S., and Vaslin, M.F.S. (2019) Biotechnological solutions for major cotton (*Gossypium hirsutum*) pathogens and pests, *Biotechnology Research and Innovation*, 3, 19–26.

Tavangar, T., Karimi, M., Rezakazemi, M., Reddy, K.R., and Aminabhavi, T.M. (2020) Textile waste, dyes/inorganic salts separation of cerium oxide-loaded loose nanofiltration polyethersulfone membranes, *Chemical Engineering Journal*, 385, 123787.

THE 17 GOALS | Sustainable Development (n.d.) (online): https://sdgs.un.org/goals, 25/8/2021.

The Home of Harris Tweed® (n.d.) Harris Tweed Authority (online): https://www .harristweed.org/, 3/9/2021.

Top designers showcase Cool Wool at London Fashion Week (n.d.) (online): https:// www.knittingindustry.com/top-designers -showcase-cool-wool-at-london-fashion -week/, 25/8/2021.

Tournier, V., Topham, C.M., Gilles, A., David, B., Folgoas, C., Moya-Leclair, E., Kamionka, E., Desrousseaux, M., Texier, H., Gavalda, S., Cot, M., Guémard, E., Dalibey, M., Nomme, J., Cioci, G., Barbe, S., Chateau, M., André, I., Duquesne, S., and Marty, A. (2020) An engineered PET depolymerase to break down and recycle plastic bottles, *Nature*, 580, 216–219.

Townsend, T. (2020) World natural fibre production and employment, in Kozlowski, R., & Mackiewicz,-Talarczyk, M. (eds) *Handbook of natural fibres*, 2nd ed., Elsevier Inc., pp. 15–36.

Ul-Islam, S., and Butola, B.S. (2019) *The impact and prospects of green chemistry for textile technology*, The Textile Institute book series, Woodhead Publishing, Duxford.

Unit, B. (2020) Aichi Biodiversity Targets, CBD (online): https://www.cbd.int/sp/targets/, 20/05/2022.

Vidaurre-Arbizu, M., Pérez-Bou, S., Zuazua-Ros, A., and Martín-Gómez, C. (2021) From the leather industry to building sector: exploration of potential applications of discarded solid wastes, *Journal of Cleaner Production*, 291, 125960.

White, P., Hayhurst, M., Taylor, J., and Slater, A. (2005) *Biodegradable and sustainable fibres* (A Volume in Woodhead Publishing Series in Textiles), pp. 157–190.

Wilson, J. (2012) *Woven textiles: principles, technologies and applications*, pp. 163–204.

Wojciechowska, P. (2021) Fibres and textiles in the circular economy, in Mondal, I.H. (ed.), *Fundamentals of natural fibres and textiles*, Woodhead Publishing, Swaston, UK, pp. 691–717.

Womack, J.P., and Jones, D.T. (1994) From lean production to the lean enterprise, HBR (online): https://hbr.org/1994/03/from-lean -production-to-the-lean-enterprise.

Xu, L., Fang, H., Deng, X., Ying, J., Lv, W., Shi, Y., Zhou, G., and Zhou, Y. (2020) Biochar application increased ecosystem carbon sequestration capacity in a Moso bamboo forest, *Forest Ecology and Management*, 475, 118447.

Yang, G., Yang, Y., Zhang, H., and Shao, H. (2021) Influences of stabilizers on lyocell spinning dope and fiber properties, *Polymer Testing*, 99, 107228.

Yang, Y., He, W., Chen, F., and Wang, L. (2020) Water footprint assessment of silk apparel in China, *Journal of Cleaner Production*, 260, 121050.

Zaw, A.K., Myat, A.M., Thandar, M., Htun, Y.M., Aung, T.H., Tun, K.M., and Han, Z.M. (2020) Assessment of noise exposure and hearing loss among workers in textile mill (Thamine), Myanmar: a cross-sectional study, *Safety and Health at Work*, 11, 199–206.

Zhang, X., Du, X., Ke, Y., Zhang, Y.-G., and Xu, Z.-K. (2021) Loose nanofiltration membranes with assembled antifouling surfaces of organophosphonic acid/Fe(III) for managing textile dyeing effluent, *Journal of Membrane Science*, 640, 119821.

Zhao, M., Zhou, Y., Meng, J., Zheng, H., Cai, Y., Shan, Y., Guan, D., and Yang, Z. (2021) Virtual carbon and water flows embodied in global fashion trade - a case study of denim products, *Journal of Cleaner Production*, 303, 127080.

ZOA :Modern Meadow (n.d.) (online): https:// www.modernmeadow.com/zoa, 22/7/2021.

Index

Adidas 39, 44, 84, 97, 99, 109, 120, 129, 193
air cargo 110
Alabama Chanin 89, 105, 129
animal(s) 6, 8, 9, 15, 18, 37, 112, 117, 119, 135, 167, 181–183, 189–191, 207, 214–215, 225
Anna Ruohonen 89, 104–105, 108, 120, 126, 128, 129
Arela 94, 129
artificial intelligence 138, 153, 157; chatbots 136, 139, 150, 153–154
attachment 101–104, 108, 127
attitude-behaviour gap 49, 51–52, 58
augmented reality 136, 138–139, 148, 151–152; virtual try-on technology 152

Bananatex® 194–198
Bangladesh 113, 210
bioaccumulation 118
biological cycle 62–64, 193
boycott 53, 56
Brundtland Commission *see* sustainability
business model innovation 19, 59, 68–69, 77, 79
Buyer Power *see* Porter's 5 forces

certification 28–30, 33, 42, 184–186, 207, 210
chatbots *see* artificial intelligence
circular design thinking 6, 19, 64–68, 73
circular economy 1, 4, 31, 55, 59, 61–64, 68–73, 76–79, 82, 93, 171, 186, 192–193
circular fashion *see* sustainable fashion
climate change 21, 109, 111, 181, 184, 190, 215
climate neutral 106, 109
collaboration 26–27, 33, 77–78, 87, 123, 125, 156, 167, 171, 194–195
colourant 62–62, 193, 225–227, 229–231
communication 18, 20, 114, 118, 133–135, 137, 140–144, 147–148, 150, 153–157, 163, 168

conscious consumer 77, 88, 102
consumer perceptions 49–50, 52, 131, 144
corporate social responsibility 38, 42; CSR 25–26, 37–38, 143
COVID-19 21, 34, 36, 70–71, 76, 91, 106, 113, 119–120, 133, 148, 150, 154
cradle-to-cradle 61–62, 118
cradle-to-grave 59–61
creative design 72–73, 79, 90
CSR *see* corporate social responsibility
customisation 33, 104, 213

decision-making process 3–5, 7, 9, 11, 25, 34, 39, 43, 63–64, 69–70, 77, 179, 181, 209
dependency *see* stakeholder(s)
design-driven 92, 123
design management 89–90, 124
design strategy 89–90
design thinking 6, 19, 64–66, 68, 73, 88–90, 124
digital fashion 163–171; communication 168–170; fashion shows 168; marketplaces 167; NFTs 165
Digital Sustainability 147–148
DIY *see* do-it-yourself
do-it-yourself 32, 41, 53, 56, 102; DIY 32, 42, 56, 101, 105
downcycling *see* recycle
durability 87–88, 93, 97, 102, 118–119, 123

eco fashion *see* sustainable fashion
eco-label 16, 27, 33, 42, 52, 125; fair trade 15–16, 27–29, 42, 182, 188–189; gots 16, 27–29, 45, 182
economic aspects *see* sustainability
efficiency 30, 91, 94, 96–99, 117, 125, 185, 188, 229, 232
Emmy 107
EMS *see* environmental management systems
entertainment 56, 88, 135, 153, 169

environmental aspects *see* sustainability
environmental consciousness *see*
    environmental aspects
environmental issues *see* sustainability
environmental management systems 33;
    ems 33
ethical fashion *see* sustainable fashion
external environment 5, 12, 20, 34, 53, 72,
    133, 206
Extinction Rebellion 20; XR 20

fabric construction 210, 213, 216
Fair Trade *see* eco-label
Fashion Detox 21
fast fashion 12–13, 27–28, 30, 34, 38, 52, 54,
    60–61, 63, 74, 90, 101, 104, 143, 148, 155,
    157, 171, 194; fashion rental 27, 33; take-
    make-waste 62; throw away culture 12, 72
fibre 4, 6, 27, 29, 31–32, 38–39, 41, 63, 80,
    87, 93–96, 109–110, 118, 179, 181–195,
    207–208, 215–217, 225–228, 230–233
Filippa K 33, 106
FoMO 53–54
Freitag 64–68
Frenn 89, 111, 114–117, 120
functionality 74, 87–88, 96, 101–104, 118,
    125, 135, 151

gestural interactivity *see* image interactive
    technolgy
goal oriented *see* management
GOTS *see* eco-label
green fashion *see* sustainable fashion
greenwashing 20, 30, 52, 78, 143

Hetty Rose 79–82
HOT: SECOND 171–172

image interactive technology 150; gestural
    interactivity 151
impulse shopping 88, 104, 118
incremental improvements 90, 124
Industrial Revolution 11, 37, 182–184
Internet of Things 154

just-in-time manufacturing 213

knitwear 74, 130, 189, 195, 199, 212,
    219, 221

leather 80, 112, 119, 182, 205, 207, 214, 215
leftover 19, 75, 91, 120
life cycle 5, 33, 77, 110–112, 120, 169,
    196, 229
linear economy 59, 61–62, 64, 70, 90,
    99, 106
linear supply chain *see* supply chain

living document 89, 94
logistic 33–34, 69, 78, 93, 109–111
longevity 66, 68, 71, 87–88, 123
loom 210–211

macro environment 9–12, 148, 212;
    PEST(EL) 10–11, 49, 133, 182, 206, 212
made-to-measure 98, 104
made-to-order 6, 74, 98, 104–105
management 1, 3, 5, 9, 11, 14, 17, 25, 30–31,
    33, 59, 87, 89, 102, 118, 133–137, 142,
    151, 163, 186, 188; as art 3, 9, 11, 25; goal
    oriented 9; as science 3, 9, 11, 25
man-made fibre 6, 38, 63, 95, 181–182, 187,
    190–195, 207, 214
metaverse 167–168
micro environment 9–12; *see also* Porter's
    5 sources
microfibre 12, 14, 38–39, 53, 187, 192;
    pollution 12, 14, 38–39, 53, 187, 192
microfibre pollution *see* microfibre
mindfulness 101
minimalism 54–56
mono-material 95
multifunctionality 88, 103

narrative strategies *see* social media
nearshoring 37, 60, 206
nesting 32, 73
NFTs *see* digital fashion
Nudie jeans 107, 129

obsolescence 97–98
offshoring 37, 206
omnichannel 133–137
opinion leaders 168–169
organic fashion *see* sustainable fashion
Our Common Future see sustainability
overconsumption 52, 76–77
overproduction 60, 90, 98, 111, 120, 164, 213

Patagonia 26, 29, 33, 95, 111
pattern cutting 32, 72–73, 79, 85, 213
performance indicators 39–40, 64; cost
    39–40; dependability 39–40; flexibility
    39–40; quality 39–40; speed 39–40
performance properties 4, 6, 39, 62, 68, 76,
    181, 183–184, 190, 192, 194–195, 207,
    211, 230
PESTEL *see* macro environment
Porter's 5 forces 11; buyer power 11; rivalry
    among firms 11; supplier power 11; threat
    of new entrants 11; threat of substitutes
    11; *see also* micro environment
post-consumer waste *see* waste
pre-consumer waste *see* waste
product lifetime 103–104, 124

quality 88, 101, 107, 114, 118, 123

raw material 4–7, 10, 12, 17–18, 20, 26, 30, 32–33, 36, 39, 59–60, 62–64, 66, 69, 71, 79, 107, 112, 179–180, 183–185, 189, 192–195, 205–207, 212, 215, 225
REACH 117, 118
re-claim 31, 34
re-configure 31, 34–35
recycle 18, 31, 78; downcycling 32, 97; recycling 7, 31–32, 41, 62, 64, 69, 75–76, 78, 93–96, 110, 118, 123, 193–194, 207–209, 216–217, 229; up-cycling 32, 53, 56, 69, 75–76, 78, 80, 82, 97–98, 112
recycled fibre 27, 87
recycled material 27, 42–43, 51–52, 76, 97–98, 105, 110, 209
recycling *see* recycle
re-design 32, 91, 105
reduce 31–34, 109–111
Reima 93–95, 107, 119
re-imagine 33–35
re-loop 62–64, 68–69, 79
repair 7, 93–94, 107, 114
resale 33, 61, 77–78, 140, 165
re-style 31–34
returns 110, 120, 133, 138, 140, 147–149
reuse 31–32, 61–63, 69, 88
re-wear 31–32
risk management 88, 113, 118
rivalry among firms *see* Porter's 5 forces
R Model: 3R model 31; 9R model 31, 34

scale 78, 102, 110
SDG *see* Sustainable Development Goal
seasonless 105, 124
secondhand 7, 33–34, 54, 60–61, 69, 77–79, 98, 99, 106–107, 125, 154–155, 157
services 7, 30, 32, 69, 93, 104–105, 134–135, 138, 141–143, 153, 168, 182
sharing economy 69–71, 77–78
Sheep Inc. 113
showrooming 140
slow fashion *see* sustainable fashion
social aspects *see* sustainability
social issues *see* sustainability
social media 154–157
stakeholder engagement *see* stakeholder
stakeholder(s) 3, 5, 7–9, 11, 20–21, 29–30, 33–34, 37–38, 51, 94, 141, 165, 182, 191, 205; dependency 7; engagement 21, 33
standards 29, 30, 118, 125, 149
Stella McCartney 9, 77, 89, 91–92
Stony Creek 110
strategy 25–28, 36, 64, 79, 89, 105, 107, 114, 118, 123, 141–142, 156, 167, 169, 170, 194
sufficiency 97, 99

supplier power *see* Porter's 5 forces
supply chain 3–5, 16, 20, 25–25, 28–31, 33, 36–38, 42, 59, 69, 71, 77–78, 84, 88, 106, 110–111, 113–114, 118, 181–182, 184, 187, 189, 205–206, 209, 217; linear supply chain 3–4, 69, 194, 206; management 25, 30–31, 182, 191; sustainable supply chain management 30–31
supply chain management *see* supply chain
supply-demand curve 49–50
supranational organisation(s) 15–16, 25, 37, 77, 208
surface design 225–228
sustainability 1, 3–8, 11–12, 14–15, 17, 21, 25–28, 30, 33–34, 36, 41–43, 49, 51, 64, 66, 69, 75, 77, 78, 83, 87–90, 93, 97, 105–107, 109, 113–114, 118, 123–124, 131, 133, 135, 137, 141–144, 147–148, 152, 154, 156–159, 168–170, 179, 183–186, 188, 193–194, 205, 207–211, 214, 215, 217, 225, 228; Brundtland Commission 11, 17; communication 141–144, 154–156; economic aspects 10, 12, 15, 39–41, 64, 97, 189, 212; environmental aspects 6, 10, 12, 15, 18, 25–26, 28, 30, 38–40, 64, 69, 87–88, 90, 124, 148, 189, 212, 214; environmental consciousness 15; environmental issues 15, 18, 25–26, 28, 30, 38–40, 64, 69, 87–88, 90, 124, 148, 189, 214; *Our Common Future* 12; social aspects 6, 12, 15, 18, 30, 38, 88, 104, 183, 214; social issues 37–38, 215; tbl 12, 39, 41; triple bottom line 12, 15, 18, 36
sustainability strategy 25, 27, 28, 36, 89, 98, 141, 170; as an add-on strategy 27; as anti-capitalism 27; bare minimum approach 25; as a means to an end 27
Sustainable Development Goal 7, 12–13, 15, 70, 137, 186, 190; SDG 12–15, 20–21, 34–35, 41, 61, 68, 71, 75, 78, 137, 164, 183, 185–193, 208–209, 211, 226, 228
sustainable fashion 1, 3–7, 12, 15–18, 20, 25, 28, 31, 36, 49, 51–60, 87–89, 109, 123–124, 131, 141; circular fashion 16, 19, 73; eco fashion 15, 18; ethical fashion 18; green fashion 15, 20; organic fashion 14, 18; slow fashion 19, 42, 88, 101, 104, 111, 216
sustainable supply chain management *see* supply chain
system thinking 18–19, 62

take-make-waste *see* fast fashion
TBL *see* sustainability
technical cycle 62–63, 65
technology 135–141; consumer-facing technologies 137; in-store technologies 136

threat of new entrants *see* Porter's 5 forces
threat of substitutes *see* Porter's 5 forces
3D printing 72, 74, 84
Throw away culture *see* fast fashion
transformation 88, 90, 111, 123–124,
    136, 172
transition 89–90, 164–165; *see*
    transformation
transparency 25, 96, 111, 114, 118, 125,
    184, 205
trends 4–5, 9, 32, 52–53, 62, 88, 90, 124,
    131, 169, 181, 213, 226
triple bottom line *see* sustainability
twist 76, 207–208

up-cycling *see* recycle
user experience 87, 96, 104

Vaatelaastari 94
value base 102, 104, 114, 123
virtual reality 136, 148, 152, 174

virtual try-on technology *see* augmented
    reality

WAK *see* We Are Knitters
waste 14, 17, 19, 26, 28, 32–35, 38–39, 41,
    46, 51, 60–63, 68–70, 74–80, 82, 90–95,
    105, 109, 118–119, 164, 185, 193, 216,
    219, 226, 231; post-consumer 17, 72,
    75–76, 79, 80, 95, 192, 207, 209, 216,
    217; pre-consumer 17, 26, 34, 72, 75, 79,
    94–95, 207, 216–217
We Are Knitters 33–34, 44; WAK 42–44,
    154, 216–217

XR *see* Extinction Rebellion

yarn 43, 56, 76, 94, 112, 118, 179, 184,
    189–192, 195, 202, 209–212

zero waste fashion 51, 59, 69–70, 72, 75, 92,
    98, 216